# This Day in Maine

# Other Maine Books by Islandport Press

*Downeast Genius*
By Earl H. Smith

*Wild! Weird! Wonderful! Maine.*
By Earl Brechlin

*Evergreens*
By John Holyoke

*Hauling By Hand*
Dean L. Lunt

*Nine Mile Bridge*
By Helen Hamlin

*Whatever It Takes*
By May Davidson

*Shoutin' Into the Fog*
By Thomas Hanna

*In Maine*
By John N. Cole

These and other Maine books are available at
www.islandportpress.com.

# This Day in Maine

## By Joseph Owen

ISLANDPORT PRESS

ISLANDPORT PRESS

Islandport Press
P.O. Box 10
Yarmouth, Maine 04096
www.islandportpress.com
info@islandportpress.com

Revised printing, 2021

Published in the United States by Islandport Press, Inc.
Portions of this book have also appeared in the *Portland Press Herald, Maine Sunday Telegram, Sun Journal, Kennebec Journal, Morning Sentinel,* or *The Times Record.*

ISBN: 978-1-952143-16-8
Library of Congress Card Number: 2020932345
Printed in USA.

Dean L. Lunt, Publisher
Teresa Lagrange, Book designer

*This Day in Maine* was published in cooperation with the newspapers of Masthead Maine.

*This book is dedicated to my wife, Mary, who has supplied the several decades of cajoling, counsel, cooperation, and camaraderie that helped the inspiration for this book to take root; and who, although a tidy person, tolerated a ramshackle arrangement of books and papers cluttering our home office for months while the book was in progress.*

# TABLE OF CONTENTS

Cover images (clockwise from the top): USS *Maine* explodes in Cuba; Samantha Smith (collections of the Maine State Museum); *Double Eagle II* (courtesy of Presque Isle Historical Society); Joshua Lawrence Chamberlain; and HMS *Margaretta* being captured by the sloop *Unity* off Machais in 1775, illustration by Robert Lambdin (courtesy of US Navy).

# FOREWORD

As this book's first version was in preparation in early 2020, I looked forward to basking in the glow of a minor professional accomplishment upon seeing stacks of copies of *This Day in Maine* on display in my local bookstore and at book-signing events. I also expected to be doing some retirement travel that year with my wife, attending two weddings and a high school class reunion, catching some of the Kennebec Historical Society's live monthly lectures in the Augusta area, and spending more time with our friends.

Here's how many of those things happened after the book was published in May of that year—zero.

Basically, the worldwide coronavirus pandemic came along and threw a large bucket of sand into the gears of my agenda.

The reunion was canceled. The weddings were postponed. The lectures migrated to an online format, with the audience watching entirely from home. All group discussions of the book occurred via Zoom conferences. Friends gradually became strangers, or just voices on the phone or faces in a video chat. My wife and I remained in good health and managed to avoid driving each other crazy, but I started to get an inkling of what the English philosopher Thomas Hobbes was talking about when he described life outside of society as being "solitary, poor, nasty, brutish, and short."

As for the book, I saw one lonely copy, merely by chance, in the gift shop at the Maine Turnpike's West Gardiner rest area, but that was it. Trapped in their houses and desperate for something to do (or for an excuse to ignore other people in these houses), readers around the state apparently gobbled up almost the entire inventory within a matter of months. Maybe they were trying to limber up mentally in order to compete on the TV show "Jeopardy!" Or perhaps they were hoarding them in order to make a killing on the black market during the Great Book Shortage of 2027.

Whatever the reason, the housebound, book-devouring public cornered me psychologically like baying hounds at a fox hunt and forced me to get back to work. As a result, you now have in your hands an updated, improved, enlivened, factory-fresh compendium of anecdotes with which to revive any wilting conversation at your next soirée in Kennebunkport or Bar Harbor or Wytopitlock, assuming you are brave enough to host a party in these troubled times; or while you're waiting impatiently for lobster at Red's Eats in Wiscasset in a line of customers that stretches nearly to the west bank of the Sheepscot River, with your collar turned up against the stinging wind.

The first edition of *This Day in Maine* was an outgrowth of a daily history column I wrote for the *Portland Press Herald* throughout 2020 to help commemorate Maine's two hundredth anniversary of statehood. The column also appeared in the company's other Maine daily newspapers—the *Sun Journal*, of Lewiston; the *Kennebec Journal*, of Augusta; the *Morning Sentinel*, of Waterville; and the *Times Record*, of Brunswick. After the book rolled off the press, my editors and I briefly congratulated each other for our success in informing the heretofore blissfully unaware public about topics such as the addled German saboteur who to tried to blow up a train bridge in Vanceboro during World War I, and who succeeded only in exploding many of the town's windows on a brutally cold day and giving himself a bad case of frostbite.

Then the entire press run of books vanished, and we realized we needed to update it quickly and set it loose again.

The saboteur story and many other oddities remain in the new version, but it also contains several vignettes that were developed in time for newspaper publication but too late for the book's first printing. In addition, the rampaging coronavirus prompted the revision or expansion of many of the original stories, and I seized the opportunity to correct some errors that had slipped unnoticed into the first version. Finally, a few of the items in this reworked collection have never seen the light of day in any publication.

Disregarding some occasional acerbic taunting—such as that from a reader who said my accidental misidentification of an expert in America's post-Civil War Reconstruction history made him laugh so hard that his butt almost detached itself from his body—I am grateful for the public's response to the book. It's a satisfying reminder that while Maine might be only a small part of our nation, its colorful past is worthy of close examination.

I'm also grateful for the chance to work with the crackerjack staffs at the *Press Herald* and Islandport Press, and for the fact that working on both editions helped me learn the history of my native state more intimately that ever before. Perhaps the resulting product will motivate others to dive more deeply into that history as well. There is still much to discover and interpret meaningfully.

—Joseph Owen
Augusta, Maine
May 2021

# JANUARY

## January 1, 1785
### Maine's First Newspaper Published

The premier issue of Maine's first newspaper, the *Falmouth Gazette*, is published. According to historian William D. Williamson (1779-1846), founders Benjamin Titcomb and Thomas B. Wait establish the paper to advocate for Maine's separation from Massachusetts. That goal of separation takes another 35 years to achieve, however.

## January 1, 1978
### Maine Anti-Billboard Law Enforced

A law banning the display of most roadside billboards takes effect throughout Maine, which becomes the third US state to enact such a ban.

Championed years earlier principally by Rep. Marion Fuller Brown (1917-2011), R-York, who later becomes a co-founder of a non-profit organization now known as Scenic America, the law survives multiple court challenges. It changes the appearance of Maine highways markedly, establishing a stark visual contrast with nearby states that do not enact such a ban.

## January 2, 2019
### Janet Mills Sworn in as Maine's First Female Governor

Janet Mills, a Democrat from Farmington who has been Maine's attorney general since 2013, becomes the state's seventy-fifth governor and the first woman to hold that office.

At the age of 71, Mills is the oldest person ever inaugurated as Maine's governor. She also is the first governor since 1966 to win election to a first term with more than 50 percent of the vote.

When elected the previous November, Mills identified expansion of Medicaid benefits and tackling the state's opioid addiction problem as two of her most important priorities.

She authorizes the Medicaid expansion almost immediately upon taking office, and on April 3 she announces that the federal government has approved the state plan under the federal Affordable Care Act, retroactive to July 2, 2018. Maine voters approved Medicaid expansion in a 2017 referendum.

As for opioid dependency,

1

Photo by Brianna Soukup; courtesy of Portland Press Herald
Janet Mills speaks after being sworn in as the seventy-fifth governor of Maine during her inauguration at the Augusta Civic Center.

she appoints Gordon Smith, of East Winthrop, a longtime doctors' lobbyist and public health advocate, to manage the administration's opioid crisis response. She also signs an order February 6 that boosts access to treatment and sets aside $1.6 million to increase the availability of an overdose antidote and recovery coaches in health care settings.

Nonetheless, the number of Maine's drug overdose deaths increases from 354 in 2018 to 380 in 2019, and to a record 502 in 2020, when the state is in the throes of a coronavirus pandemic.

The year 2021 starts out even worse, with 58 confirmed or suspected drug overdoses in January and 45 in February, yielding a monthly average that is higher than in all of 2020. Nonpharmaceutical fentanyl is cited as the most common cause of those January and February deaths.

### January 2, 2019
### Gov. LePage's Vetoes Total Five Times Those of Previous Record Holder

Two-term Republican Gov. Paul LePage, a former mayor of Waterville, leaves office after having issued 642 vetoes over eight years, breaking the record of 118 set by independent Gov. James

Photo by David Leaming; courtesy of Morning Sentinel
Republican gubernatorial candidate Paul LePage exits from a voting booth in
Waterville after casting his ballot on Election Day 2010.

---

Longley, who served a single term from 1975 to 1979.

LePage's veto habit—which prompted him to name his dog "Veto"—produces a veto total exceeding the combined total of all other Maine governors since 1917. His tendency to veto bills increased over his eight years as governor, especially after Republicans lost their monopoly on control of the Legislature.

The Legislature ultimately overturned about half of LePage's vetoes.

## January 3, 1989
### George Mitchell Chosen Senate Majority Leader

US Sen. George J. Mitchell, D-Maine, a Waterville native and former US attorney and federal judge, becomes Senate majority leader.

He later steps down on January 3, 1995, capping a fifteen-year Senate tenure, when President Bill Clinton appoints him US special envoy for Northern Ireland. In that job, the former federal judge helps negotiate a peace deal between the long-feuding Protestant and Catholic factions in Northern Ireland.

Mitchell also becomes the author or co-author of several books, mostly about politics and international peace negotiations.

## January 4, 1832
## New State House
## Opens for Business

The Maine Legislature convenes for the first time in the newly completed Maine State House. The building, located on Weston's Hill in Augusta, took three years to erect and was built of Hallowell granite.

Despite its construction, officials in Portland try unsuccessfully for decades to convince the Legislature to move the state capital to their city.

The State House later undergoes several expansions. It is added to the National Register of Historic Places in 1973.

## January 4, 1998
## Massive Ice Storm Batters Maine

A massive regional ice storm begins, eventually causing millions of dollars' worth of damage throughout central Maine and leaving nearly half the state's population without power, in some cases for weeks. The storm inflicts great damage in Quebec and Ontario and also affects New York, Vermont, New Brunswick, and Nova Scotia severely.

By daybreak on January 9, Central Maine Power reports about 275,000 of its customers—representing about 600,000 people—have lost electricity; and tens of thousands of Bangor Hydro Electric Co. customers also are in the dark. It is the worst storm to hit the area in a generation, and the costliest one in CMP's history.

Augusta Public Works Director John Charest notes that aside from freezing rain, "it was raining tree limbs, too, and they were pulling down all kinds of cables." Some rural residents describe the cracking and falling of ice-laden branches in the woods as sounding like occasional gunfire throughout the night.

The Augusta Civic Center, Colby College's Field House in

Waterville, and many other public buildings are opened as emergency shelters. Most city dwellers get their power back within a few days, but some people in rural areas have to wait a few weeks.

## January 5, 1786
### Convention Finds Boston Disregards Maine Interests

A report issued by the second convention to discuss the possibility of Maine separating from Massachusetts, held the previous day, asserts that Boston merchants benefit unfairly at Maine's expense because of trade regulations involving lumber.

It also says Boston officials don't represent Maine interests well and Maine residents are at a disadvantage in court proceedings because all the hearings are held in Boston and all the records are kept there.

The report cites several other reasons justifying statehood for Maine. A third convention is scheduled for the following September.

## January 6, 1854
### First Female American Writer of Gothic Fiction Dies at 95

Novelist Sarah "Sally" Sayward Barrell Keating Wood, known colloquially as "Madame Wood,"

Maine's first novelist and the first female American writer of gothic fiction, dies at 95.

Wood published four novels and a collection of stories, all under pseudonyms—either "A Lady," "A Lady of Massachusetts" (when Maine was part of that state), or "A Lady of Maine." A York native, she lived in Portland.

Although Wood was an early advocate of American independence and a trailblazer for female writers, she nonetheless believed that a woman's principal role should be a domestic one in service to her husband. She wrote only when she was a widow. Also, many of her characters were aristocratic single women who sometimes faced problems because they were not married. In a case of life imitating art, Wood herself then nearly married "a Spanish gentleman" who she later said proved to be a swindler interested only in her money. She called off that wedding and soon married a different man, who was a wealthy merchant and shipbuilder.

## January 7, 1991
### Old Town's Dick MacPherson Named Head Coach of Patriots

Following a successful run at Syracuse University, where he was named *The Sporting News* Coach of the Year in 1987, Old Town's Dick MacPherson is hired as the eleventh head coach of the New England Patriots.

MacPherson was born November 4, 1930, in Old Town, the second-youngest of twelve children. At Old Town High School, he played high school football, basketball, and baseball and graduated in 1948. He enrolled at Maine Maritime Academy and then served in the US Air Force from 1950 to 1954 during the Korean War.

"Coach Mac" arrived at Syracuse in 1981 and built the football program into a national championship contender during his tenure. His teams produced a 66-46-4 record, including a 4-1 mark in bowl competition, and were ranked as high as fourth in the national polls following an 11-0-1 season in 1987. He was inducted into the College Football Hall of Fame in 2009.

MacPherson, who was also an assistant coach for the Denver Broncos and the Cleveland Browns before coaching at Syracuse, took over a New England team in turmoil. He coached during a time of changing ownership and constant threats of mov-

ing the franchise and amassed an 8-24 record before he was replaced by Bill Parcells.

In later years, he said he felt he made a mistake by leaving college to coach for the pros. MacPherson died August 8, 2017. He was 86.

January 7, 1925
**Ralph Owen Brewster Wins Governorship with Klan Support**

Ralph Owen Brewster, a Republican supported openly by the Ku Klux Klan, takes office as Maine's governor, having been elected the previous fall.

The election campaign put the division in Brewster's party on full display. His predecessor, Gov. Percival Baxter, accused Brewster of being a sympathizer of the Klan, which had gained traction in Maine because of its anti-Catholic and anti-immigrant stances.

Brewster later is elected to the US Senate. Actor Alan Alda portrays Brewster in an unflattering light in the 2004 film *The Aviator*, about the life of aviation pioneer Howard Hughes.

January 7, 2003
**Journalist John N. Cole, Founder of *Maine Times*, Dies in Brunswick**

John N. Cole, author, writer, and co-founder of the groundbreaking *Maine Times* newspaper, dies in Brunswick following a battle with cancer. He was 79.

Cole, whose books include *In Maine*, a collection of his columns that detail his love affair with his natural surroundings, co-founded *Maine Times* with Peter Cox in 1968. The weekly newspaper kept a keen watch on government, chased stories that were not being covered by other papers, and was the first to truly cover the environment as an issue, closely reflecting Cole's personal interests.

Cole, almost universally described as "crusty," was also an avid fisherman and birdwatcher. He worked as a commercial fisherman before moving in the 1950s to Maine, where he worked as an editor at the *Kennebunk Star*, the *Brunswick Record*, and the Brunswick-based *Times Record* before founding the *Maine Times*.

## January 8, 1825
### First Issue of *Kennebec Journal* Published in Augusta

Having set up shop on the southeast corner of Bridge and Water streets in downtown Augusta, Russell Eaton (1800-1888) and Luther Severance (1797-1855) publish the first issue of the *Kennebec Journal*, which begins as a weekly newspaper. They were recruited for the task while working as printers in Washington, D.C.

In a front-page column introducing the newspaper, the partners state: "It may, we fear with too much truth, be urged that there are already a sufficient number of political publications in this state; but by an increase the public cannot suffer. Competition, in this as in all other cases, stimulates to exertion."

The debut issue appears less than five years after Maine achieved statehood, but before Augusta's selection as Maine's capital.

Eaton leaves the paper in 1833 and later buys the Winthrop-based *Maine Farmer* newspaper and moves it to Augusta, where it remains in business for another eight decades. Severance stays with the *Kennebec Journal* until 1850, when he is appointed US commissioner to the Kingdom of Hawaii. During his tenure at the *Kennebec Journal*, he also serves terms in the Maine House of Representatives, the Maine Senate, and the US House.

Despite their divergent later careers, the paper's two founders are buried literally a stone's throw apart from one another in Augusta's Forest Grove Cemetery.

The newspaper, later owned briefly by future US House Speaker and 1884 Republican presidential nominee James G. Blaine, becomes a daily in 1870. Today it is Maine's oldest newspaper still in publication.

## January 9, 1897
### Former Gov. Daniel Davis, Seated After Dramatic Standoff, Dies at 53

Former Republican Gov. Daniel F. Davis dies in the Penobscot County town of Corinth. He was 53. Davis became governor at the age of 36 following a weeks-long armed standoff between competing political factions, featuring threats of kidnapping and assassination.

Davis sought the governorship in the election of September 1879. In that election, no gubernatorial candidate received a majority of votes, so in accordance with state law at the time, the Legislature was directed to determine the winner. However, because of a controversial ballot certification process, the composition of the Legislature also remained in doubt. When reports began circulating that Democrats had tampered with the election results, a mob of armed Republicans surrounded the State House in Augusta. Mass meetings of indignation were held all over the state, and wide-scale violence seemed imminent.

Outgoing Gov. Alonzo Garcelon summoned Civil War hero Joshua Lawrence Chamberlain, then a major general in the state militia and the state's military commander, to Augusta. Chamberlain decided not to call out the militia, relying instead on help from Augusta Mayor Charles E. Nash, the city's police force, and his own reputation to keep order.

During the dispute, newspapers of both political parties railed against Chamberlain, calling him a traitor and a renegade. Police were assigned to him after the mayor learned of a plot to assassinate him. There were also rumors of plots to kidnap him, prompting him to change where he slept at night.

In the most dramatic moment, a crowd of twenty-five to thirty men, intending to kill Chamberlain, gathered outside the State House. Soon, Chamberlain walked to the rotunda, ascended the stairs, and told the mob, "Men, you wish to kill me, I hear. Killing is no new thing to me. I

Courtesy of Earl Brechlin

A postcard showing Portland Head Light, which was commissioned by George Washington.

have offered myself to be killed many times, when I no more deserved it than I do now. ... I am here to preserve the peace and the honor of this state, until the rightful government is seated, whichever it may be; it is not for me to say. But it is for me to see that the laws of this state are put into effect, without fraud, without force, but with calm and sincere purpose. I am here for that, and I shall do it. If anybody wants to kill me for it, here I am. Let him kill."

The dramatic gestured worked, and the mob stood down. The Maine Supreme Judicial Court finally ruled in the Republicans' favor on January 16, 1880,

whereupon the newly Republican-controlled Legislature elected Davis governor the next day.

Davis was the last governor elected before the length of Maine's gubernatorial terms was increased from one year to two. Since 1958, Maine governors have been elected to four-year terms.

## January 10, 1791
### Portland Head Light Begins Service

After more than three years of construction, Maine's iconic Portland Head Light, located in Cape Elizabeth, goes into service. The lighthouse, commissioned by George Washington, includes a seventy-two-foot tower and sixteen whale oil lamps. A renovation in 1865 increases the tower height twenty feet. A duplex home for the head lighthouse keeper, the assistant lighthouse keeper, and their families is built in 1891.

With the lighthouse fully automated, the US government turns the property over to the town of Cape Elizabeth in 1993. The town owns and manages the property and the adjacent Fort Williams Park. The park is open year-round from sunrise to sunset. A lighthouse museum operates during the warmer months.

### January 10, 1831
### Maine Rejects Border Proposal from Holland's King William IV

King William IV of the Netherlands, chosen four years earlier to arbitrate a dispute between Britain and the United States about where the boundary between Maine and what are now the Canadian provinces of New Brunswick and Quebec should be, submits a proposal to solve the problem. The British accept it, but the US Senate—at Maine's instigation—rejects it.

The boundary quarrel nearly breaks out into warfare in the late 1830s but is settled permanently by the Webster-Ashburton Treaty of 1842.

### January 10, 1854
### Maine-built Clipper *Red Jacket* Sets Transatlantic Speed Record

In the short-lived era of clipper ships, Captain Asa Eldridge sets sail from New York on a black-hulled, 251.2-foot, 2,305-ton *Red Jacket*, a clipper built in Rockland, Maine. The ship, making its maiden voyage, crosses the North Atlantic in snow, hail, and rain and arrives at a Liverpool dock thirteen days, one hour, and twenty-five minutes later, a record that still stands for sailing ships.

Eldridge's feat is all the more remarkable because when he reaches the mouth of northern England's Mersey River, bad weather has driven all the tugboats away, so he proceeds upriver with the ship at full sail. Thousands of people are awaiting the ship at the dock, and a grand ball is held within a week to celebrate the feat.

The ship is used later to carry passengers between England and Australia during the latter's gold rush period.

### January 10, 2000
### Libra Foundation Acquires Option to Buy Pineland Center

The Libra Foundation acquires an option to buy the crumbling

Pineland Center from the state with the idea of investing tens of millions of dollars to rehabilitate the property and create, among other things, a business campus. In tandem, Libra attempts to purchase a long-term lease to 1,100 acres of adjacent state-owned farmland. The Pineland property, a one-time school for people with mental disabilities, includes twenty-six buildings, although many are in disrepair and contaminated with asbestos and lead.

Later in 2000, Libra purchases the property for more than $200,000 and sets about creating a showplace in New Gloucester. It salvages nineteen of the buildings and over the next fifteen years invests more than $110 million by making repairs and infrastructure improvements. Along the way, it develops such projects as Pineland Farms-branded meat, cheese, and potatoes.

The Libra Foundation is a private foundation that was established by Elizabeth B. Noyce in June 1989. Noyce was the first wife of Robert Noyce, a founder of Intel and Fairchild Semiconductor and one of the inventors of the microchip. Elizabeth Noyce, who died in 1996, settled in Maine after her divorce in the

1970s and became a major benefactor of her adopted state.

While the Pineland Center development was dramatic, it was not the only place to benefit from Libra's largesse and attention. During its history, the foundation also developed the Fort Kent Outdoor Center and the Nordic Heritage Center in Presque Isle into world-class facilities that draw Olympians. It reinvigorated Black Mountain in Rumford and created an arts community in Monson. In its early years, it funded projects at Maine Maritime Academy, purchased the Nissen Bakery in Portland, and started Maine Bank & Trust, among its other activities.

### January 11, 1839
### Franklin Simmons, Creator of Longfellow Statue, Born in Lisbon

Sculptor Franklin Simmons, whose public works of art include the Henry Wadsworth Longfellow statue and the Soldiers and Sailors Monument in Portland and the Soldiers' Monument in Lewiston, is born in a part of Lisbon that later becomes the town of Sabattus.

Simmons, who grows up in Bath, begins working on sculpture models by using coarse clay from the banks of the Androscoggin River. He opens a sculpture studio in Portland after graduation from Bates College. He produces his first commercial statue, depicting Maj. Gen. Hiram Berry, for the city of Rockland.

His statues of William King, Maine's first governor, and Vice President Hannibal Hamlin, another Maine luminary, are on display in Washington, D.C.

He also creates the statue of President Ulysses Grant, shown in a Union Army uniform, that stands in the US Capitol rotunda.

He plans to do one of President Abraham Lincoln as well, but the day after the two meet in April 1865 to schedule a sitting, John Wilkes Booth assassinates the president.

Simmons moves to Rome in 1868, following in the footsteps of many American sculptors who want to gain exposure to and knowledge about the centuries-old Italian tradition of marble carving.

After the king of Italy decorates him three times for his work, he dies on December 8, 1913, in the Italian capital while taking a hot bath, according to *The New York Times*.

## January 11, 2012
### Twinkies Maker's Bankruptcy Leads to Closure of Maine Plant

For the second time in two years, Hostess Brands, which employs about 370 people at a bakery in Biddeford, appears in bankruptcy court because of insolvency. A spokesman for the company, whose cake products include Twinkies and Ding Dongs, says the filing will not result in job losses in Biddeford.

However, embroiled in a strike that includes workers at the Biddeford plant, the national company closes all thirty-three of its bakeries in November that year, and a bankruptcy judge issues a ruling the following March that authorizes the company to sell everything it owns. Flowers Foods Inc. buys most of Hostess' assets in July 2013, including the Biddeford bakery, but it puts that property up for sale the following year. The site never reopens as a bakery.

## January 12, 1858
### Nathan Clifford Sworn in as Supreme Court Justice

Nathan Clifford (1803-1881), a New Hampshire native who began his career as a lawyer in Newry, is sworn in as a US Supreme Court associate justice. His experience includes serving as both a Maine and a US attorney general, a member of both the Maine House of Representatives and the US House, and US ambassador to Mexico.

Clifford's nomination by President James Buchanan is hotly disputed because, although he comes from the North, he is a Democrat and favors continuation of slavery. The Senate barely confirms his nomination, 26-23. He serves on the court for more than twenty-three years. During the Civil War, he generally supports the Union, but afterward he seeks to limit the federal government's power.

By 1877, Clifford's mental abilities decline to the point that, according to Samuel Miller, a fellow associate justice, it is "obvious to all of the court," prompting Miller to assert that no judge on the court should serve past the age of 70. Clifford suffers a stroke in 1880 and dies in 1881. Miller remains on the court until his own death in 1890 at 74.

## January 12, 1922
### Portland's Helen Blanchard, Known as 'Lady Edison,' Dies in Providence

Inventor Helen Augusta Blanchard, a Portland native, dies in Providence, Rhode Island, after a lifetime of work that results in the issuance of twenty-eight patents to her, mostly related to sewing machines and needles. Blanchard's skill as a tinkerer became evident in childhood. After the Panic of 1866 wiped out her family's wealth and caused the loss of the Blanchard home, her inventive tendencies saved her family. She patented the zigzag sewing machine, which was especially useful for knitted fabrics.

Blanchard founded the Blanchard Overseam Machine Co. in Philadelphia, as well as the Blanchard Hosiery Machine Co. She continued to invent popular devices, earning for herself the nickname "Lady Edison." Royalties from her patents earned her enough money to buy back the family homestead in Portland.

She received her last patent at 74, then suffered a stroke in 1916 that rendered her unable to work. Her zigzag sewing machine is on display at the Museum of American History in Washington, D.C.

## January 13, 1629
### Pilgrims Obtain Land Patent Along Kennebec for 1.5 Million Acres

Pilgrims obtain a land patent along the Kennebec River, authorizing them to trade with local indigenous people. According to historian William D. Williamson, the patent, later called the Kennebec Patent or Plymouth Patent, "was intended as an express favor to her trade and fishery, and the propagation of religion."

The land grant consists of about 1.5 million acres stretching fifteen miles on either side of the Kennebec River and ranging from present-day Woolwich in the south to the Cornville area in Somerset County in the north. It also grants the patent holders the right of passage to the open sea. They are entitled to establish trading stations at what later becomes Fort Popham, the landing in Richmond, and Cushnoc—today's city of Augusta.

## January 14, 1943
### Pulitzer Prize Winner Laura Richards Dies in Gardiner

Author Laura E. Richards dies in Gardiner, where she spent most of her adult life. Richards won, with her sisters, a Pulitzer Prize in 1917 for *Julia Ward Howe, 1819-1910*, a biography of their mother, who wrote the words to the song "The Battle Hymn of the Republic."

Richards, a Boston native, moved in 1876 to Gardiner with her architect husband, Henry Richards. She wrote more than ninety books during her career. One of them, the 1890 novel *Captain January*, was made into a silent movie in 1924, then a 1936 movie with sound starring child actor Shirley Temple (1928-2014). Richards also founded several community institutions in Gardiner. An elementary school in the city is named after her, and her home is listed on the National Register of Historic Places.

## January 14, 2019
### Spinning Ice Disk Fascinates Maine, Nation

Three years after reports of a ten-foot-long snake eating a beaver near the Presumpscot River in Westbrook stimulated a lot of speculative chatter among the city's residents, another natural phenomenon on the river gives them even more to talk about. A rare spinning ice disk about three hundred feet in diameter forms in the river, drawing a parade of spectators from around the region and eventually garnering worldwide attention.

The disk, turning counterclockwise, lasts for several days, surviving bouts of warm weather and an attack by a chain-saw-wielding man from New Jersey who claims he is trying to carve the disk into a giant peace sign, before finally breaking up. At one point, a photographer noticed that the disk had become frozen to the riverbank, so he ventured out onto the river on a paddleboard and used that and an ice pick to set the ice disk free so that it could resume spinning.

In an apparent case of what goes around comes around, another ice disk forms January 17, 2020, in the same spot on the Presumpscot. This one is less circular and less robust that the 2019 version.

Also, a nonrotating ice disk forms in late January 2020 in the Kennebec River near the Great Eddy in Skowhegan. One resident says it is the first one he has seen there in his twenty-five years of living in a house overlooking the site.

## January 15, 2019
## Priests at Cheverus Accused of Abuse

The governing body of Jesuits—a religious order of the Catholic Church—for the Northeastern states makes public a list of fifty priests, including seven who were teachers or administrators at Cheverus High School in Portland, against whom credible allegations of child sexual abuse have been made.

That raises the total number of such accusations against Jesuits nationwide to 287, although some priests' names might appear on more than one list.

The accused priest who worked at Cheverus most recently, James Talbot, was fired in 1998 after nearly two decades. A former student said Talbot had abused him in the mid-1980s. Talbot later served six years in prison in Massachusetts for raping two students decades earlier in Boston. When the Jesuits release their list, he is serving a three-year term in Maine for the abuse of a boy in Freeport.

Five of the other Cheverus-linked priests on the list have died. The Rev. Richard Roos, who admitted abusing a minor in the 1980s, is listed as an administrator at a Massachusetts religious retreat center.

An eighth Jesuit priest, who was accused of having abused a minor outside Maine before he worked in the state, also has died.

## January 16, 2009
## Andrew Wyeth, Painter of *Christina's World*, Dies at 91

Realist painter Andrew Wyeth dies in Chadds Ford, Pennsylvania, his birthplace, at 91 after a seventy-year career.

He later is buried near his sum-

The Olson House in Cushing.

mer home in South Cushing, Maine, where he once observed Christina Olson (1893-1968) shuffling slowly up a hill toward her home, using her hands to propel herself because a genetic disease had robbed her of the use of her legs.

Wyeth depicted the scene in the 1948 oil painting *Christina's World*, which became an icon of American art. Painted from the viewpoint of someone watching her from the cemetery, it is in the collection of the Museum of Modern Art in New York. Olson is buried in the same cem-

etery. The Olson farmhouse now belongs to the Farnsworth Art Museum in Rockland and has been restored to look the way it did when Wyeth painted it.

Wyeth is one of the best-known American artists of the twentieth century. At his first one-man show of watercolors in 1937, the entire inventory of paintings sold out, foreshadowing his lifelong success.

His style contradicted the prevailing trend toward abstract art, and he drew inspiration from his neighbors and what he saw during solitary walks.

His father, N.C. Wyeth (1882-1945), a well-known artist and illustrator, died with his 3-year-old grandson when a freight train struck the car in which they were riding in Chadds Ford. Andrew later described the incident, in addition to being a personal loss, as a formative event in his artistic development. Andrew Wyeth's son Jamie Wyeth also is a well-known artist who paints in the realist tradition.

The Farnsworth Art Museum has one of the nation's largest collections of art by all three Wyeths.

## January 17, 2002
### Fires Rip Through Downtown Lincoln

Fire severely damages buildings on Main Street in Lincoln. Three days later, a second fire breaks out. The two blazes combined wipe out a quarter of the Penobscot County town's business district, including the three-story Lake Mall, and displace ten businesses. Firefighters manage to contain both fires and save other downtown businesses.

The town experienced a similarly destructive fire once before, in 1887. The 2002 fires were the worst disaster to hit the town since the 1968 closure of the Eastern Fine Paper and Pulp Division

of Standard Packaging Corp. and the accompanying loss of hundreds of jobs.

While that mill remained closed through the summer, the town scrambled to raise money from the sale of twenty-year bonds to meet the demands of a new owner, Premoid Corp., and the mill resumed operations in August that year.

## January 18, 2012
### Security Checkpoint Installed at State House

In Augusta, Capitol Police Chief Russell Gauvin reports that a new security checkpoint at the west entrance of the State House is complete and operational. Workers at that entrance run scanning machines similar to those found in airports.

The public no longer is able to enter the State House through any of the building's other doors.

The decision to install the checkpoint comes after the non-fatal shooting of US Rep. Gabrielle Giffords in Arizona and after a Maine House of Representatives member was charged for allegedly having pointed a gun at a man in a parking lot, both in 2011.

Even before those incidents, however, Republicans had been

urging the adopting of additional security measures at the State House. Democrats said the expense was unnecessary.

## January 19, 2014
### State Loses Track of Medicaid Overpayments

A *Maine Sunday Telegram* report says the state auditor found that the state Department of Health and Human Services lost track of millions of dollars in Medicaid overpayments to long-term care providers in fiscal year 2013, which ended the previous June 30.

The auditor found that DHHS computers were inadequate to track whether the money is repaid to the state and whether similar mistakes occur in the future.

A review of the period from September 2010 through June 2013 found that the total amount of Medicaid—or Maine-Care, as the state's program is known—overpayments during that time totaled $36.4 million.

The loss is of particular concern at a time when Maine's growing population of elderly people is expected to increase demand for Medicaid-funded long-term care.

Maine's median age is reported as being 43.5 years—the highest in all fifty states.

## January 19, 1929
### Lafayette Renamed Acadia National Park

The National Park Service changes the name of Lafayette National Park, on Maine's Mount Desert Island, to Acadia National Park.

The park became a public land preserve in 1916 as Sieur de Monts National Monument.

When it was elevated to national park status in 1919, it took the name "Lafayette" in honor of Gilbert du Motier, Marquis de Lafayette, the French aristocrat and military commander who led American troops in several battles of the American Revolution. When the US Interior Department chose the name, Americans were fighting to defend France from the Germans in World War I, and it seemed a fitting tribute to that alliance.

In 2018, more than 3.5 million people visit the park, the greatest total since 1989.

Visits decline to about 3.4 million in 2019, then to fewer than 2.7 million in 2020, when a coronavirus pandemic that starts early in the year dissuades many people from traveling.

The name was changed to Acadia National Park in 1929.

One of the carriage trails in Acadia National Park.

## January 20, 1998
### Cost of Restoring Power Soars Following Massive Ice Storm

Central Maine Power Co. submits to federal officials a report estimating that the cost of restoring electrical power to about 632,000 Maine residents who lost it in a regionwide ice storm would reach $55 million. The amount is more than double the $25 million figure the company cited on January 12, five days after the storm's peak.

Combined with the $27 million that state and local governments spent on cleanup and a $5 million estimate from Bangor Hydro Electric Co. for repairs in its service area, the new CMP estimate raises the statewide cost of contending with ice storm damage to about $87 million so far. A new, increased estimate from Bangor Hydro is expected within days.

At the time of the report, more than 14,000 Maine households remain without electrical power in the middle of winter.

## January 21, 1833
### First Issue of *Maine Farmer* Published

In Winthrop, editor Ezekiel Holmes (1801-1865) publishes the first issue of a long-running newspaper that eventually will become known as the *Maine Farmer*. *Kennebec Journal* co-founder Russell Eaton buys the newspaper in 1844 and moves it to Augusta, where it operates for another eight decades.

Holmes, dubbed "the father of Maine agriculture," also helps establish the University of Maine and serves multiple terms in the Maine House of Representatives and the Maine Senate.

"To Ezekiel Holmes more than to any other one man the University of Maine owes its existence as a separate institution, and to him more than any other one man Maine agriculture owes a debt for its progress before and for many years after the Civil War," writes his biographer, Clarence A. Day.

## January 21, 2013
### Richard Blanco Recites Poem at Presidential Inauguration

Poet Richard Blanco, 45, of Bethel, recites his poem "One Today" in the public phase of President Barack Obama's second-term inauguration in Washington, D.C.

Blanco, born in Spain as the son of Cuban exiles, moved to New York when he was only weeks old.

Educated as an engineer at Florida International University, he returned there to earn a Master of Fine Arts degree in creative writing in 1997. His first book of poetry, *The City of a Hundred Fires*, published in 1998, received the University of Pittsburgh's Agnes Lynch Starrett Poetry Prize.

Blanco traveled extensively after that, teaching along the way. He resumed his engineering career in 2004 in Florida, then moved to Bethel. Obama chose him as the fifth person—and first immigrant, first gay person, and first Latino—to deliver a presidential inaugural poem.

## January 22, 1981
### Marguerite Yourcenar, Author of *The Abyss,* Wins French Honor

Belgian-born novelist and essayist Marguerite Yourcenar (1903-1987), having lived for more than three decades in relative obscurity on Mount Desert Island, attends a ceremony in Paris at which she becomes the first woman inducted into the prestigious Académie Française.

Yourcenar is known best as the author of the novels *Memoirs of Hadrian* and *The Abyss*.

At a memorial service in 1988 in Northeast Harbor, her friend and translator Walter Kaiser, a Harvard professor, said of Yourcenar's death the previous year, "She herself had long since achieved immortality—not merely that conferred by the Académie Française but the ultimate immortality she had guaranteed for herself by her deathless writing. For, so long as men and women ask themselves what it means to be a human being in this sublunary, transient world, Marguerite Yourcenar is one of the authors to whom they shall turn for an answer."

## January 22, 2018
### Maine's Lobster Population Projected to Decline

A trio of agencies releases a report that predicts Maine's lobster population will drop 40 percent to 62 percent over the next thirty years because of rising ocean temperature.

The study, done by the Gulf of Maine Research Institute, the University of Maine and the National Oceanic and Atmospheric Administration, finds a decrease in the number of surviving lobster eggs and an increase in predators that eat lobsters at the root of the trend.

The study says the ocean

reached optimal temperature for lobster growth around 2010. At the end of the thirty-year period, lobster harvests should be comparable to those of the early 2000s, which were less than half as large as those of the late 2010s, it says.

In 2018, Maine lobstermen catch more than 119 million pounds with a value of more than $484.5 million. The volume drops to 100.7 million pounds in 2019, but the value of the catch is more than $485 million that year.

Fishermen begin 2020 expecting a gloomy market because of a global coronavirus pandemic that shutters many restaurants, but by September lobster prices are holding steady and sales are brisk. Final figures for the year are not available yet in March 2021.

### January 23, 2018
### Leader of New Albion Group Fired as Town Manager

Selectmen in the town of Jackman, near the Canadian border, fire the town manager, Tom Kawczynski, who they said compromised the town's image by publicly advocating racial segregation and condemning Islam.

Four days earlier, news reports identified Kawczynski, an Arizona native, as the founder and leader of New Albion, a pro-white group that says people from other cultures should stay out of northern New England. That prompted calls from many Jackman residents and outside groups for Kawczynski's ouster.

Kawczynski receives $30,000 in severance pay and agrees not to sue the town. Town attorney Warren Shay says the town did a good job vetting candidates for the town manager's job but that "some people just fly under the radar."

### January 24, 1692
### Wabanaki Warriors Commit Candlemas Massacre at York

In an event that comes to be known as the Candlemas Massacre, Chief Madockawando and Rev. Louis-Pierre Thury lead Wabanaki warriors in an attack on the English settlement at York during King William's War, killing about 100 inhabitants, taking about 80 as hostages, and setting many buildings on fire. The hostages are carried to New France (now Canada), where they are held until a Boston military commander pays ransom so they will be set free.

The violent incident is cited as evidence of God's displeasure and has a strong influence on the

Salem Witch Trials, which begin later that year.

## January 24, 1839
### Aroostook War Begins

The Maine Legislature authorizes newly elected Gov. John Fairfield to send a posse consisting of volunteer militia members led by Rufus McIntire, who is the state land agent and the Penobscot County sheriff, north to arrest New Brunswick lumbermen and confiscate their equipment for lumbering in disputed territory.

After they begin carrying out that mission, a New Brunswick posse arrests McIntire and other Americans and interrogates them at a jail in Woodstock, New Brunswick. The boundary dispute, now known as the Aroostook War, was finally settled by the Webster-Ashburton Treaty of 1842.

## January 24, 1908
### Fire Destroys Portland City Hall

The worst Portland fire since the city's Great Fire of 1866 burns City Hall and neighboring police buildings, endangering about 1,000 people who were gathered there for a Knights of Pythias celebration. There were no fatalities, but county offices, which also were located in City Hall, were destroyed. The fire also consumes one of the most valuable libraries in the state, the Greenleaf Law Library collection.

In the early stage of the fire, reported at 2:23 a.m., City Clerk A.L.T. Cummings runs from his home to the fire scene and, with the help of others, manages to save all the records in his office and the mayor's, as well as all the county records except those of the probate court.

Portland's previous City Hall also fell victim to a fire—the one in 1866.

## January 24, 1963
### B-52 Crashes Near Moosehead Lake

A vertical stabilizer falls off a US Air Force B-52 Stratofortress-C conducting a low-level navigation exercise, causing the plane to crash into Elephant Mountain, about five miles southeast of Moosehead Lake.

The crash kills six people aboard the plane, and the co-pilot, Maj. Robert J. Morrison, dies when he hits a tree while parachuting to the ground. Scott Paper Co. dispatches snowplows to clears roads leading to the crash site.

The pilot, Lt. Col. Dante E. Bulli, and the navigator, Capt. Gerald J. Adler, also eject themselves from the plane. They manage to survive despite severe injuries, the presence of five feet of snow on the ground, and a temperature of fourteen below zero at the time of the crash. The temperature reaches nearly thirty below before the two are rescued.

The crash site today remains strewn with wreckage from the plane and is accessible to hikers. A memorial made of slate from Monson commemorates the victims.

## January 24, 1997
### Cohen Named Secretary of Defense

William S. Cohen, a Bangor native and longtime Republican US senator from Maine, becomes secretary of defense under President Bill Clinton, a Democrat. Cohen serves for four years during a period of NATO expansion and tumult about the question of whether homosexuals should be allowed to serve in the US military.

## January 25, 1953
### Bangor-based WABI Becomes Maine's First TV Station

Bangor-based WABI-TV begins broadcasting as Maine's first television station, on VHF channel 5. Its first owner is Community Broadcasting Service, which was founded in 1949 by former Gov. Horace Hildreth, owner of WABI radio station, from which the TV station got its call letters.

The first full program aired is *Boston Blackie*, a detective drama about an ex-con turned private eye. WABI is a CBS affiliate, so early shows include *The Jack Benny Show* and *Your Hit Parade*. The first broadcast is a major event in Bangor, and stores can't keep up with demand for TV sets once the shows begin to air. In March, the station broadcasts the local boys' high school basketball tournament, the first sporting event ever televised in Maine.

Originally a multi-network affiliate, WABI-TV becomes a full-time CBS affiliate in 1959. The TV station adds digital channels WABI-DT2 and WABI-DT3 in 2007 and 2015, respectively. The station is purchased by Gray Television in 2014.

WABI is the local broadcaster of Maine's only local late-night talk show, *The Nite Show with Danny Cashman*.

## January 26, 1739
### Brunswick Incorporated as 11th Maine Town

The Massachusetts General Court, having received a petition

on the subject the previous year, incorporates Brunswick as the eleventh town in Maine, which then is part of Massachusetts.

The town holds six town meetings in 1739 and allocates 153 pounds and fifteen shillings for expenses in the town budget.

The town's voters also consider, but take no action upon, a proposal to control the local wolf population.

Brunswick, while still a town today, is Maine's eighth-most-populous municipality, according to the 2010 US Census, and therefore larger than several of Maine's incorporated cities.

## January 27, 1893
### James G. Blaine, Key Republican Leader, Dies in Washington

Former US House Speaker James G. Blaine, of Augusta, dies at 62 at his Washington home. Blaine was the Republican nominee for president in 1884, when he lost the general election to Grover Cleveland. During the latter 1800s, he was one of the most powerful men in the United States and one of the most powerful men in Maine history.

Blaine's body is buried in Oak Hill Cemetery in Washington's Georgetown neighborhood.

The remains of his wife, Augusta native Harriet Stanwood Blaine, are buried there after her death in 1903.

The remains of both Blaines are disinterred in 1920—Maine's statehood centennial year—and moved to the new Blaine Memorial Park, which overlooks a cluster of cemeteries and much of Augusta's West Side.

The park's landscaping is done by the Olmstead firm, which also designed Central Park in New York. According to Blaine's long-time secretary, Thomas Sherman, Blaine often enjoyed walking to that hilltop spot, a mere fifteen blocks from his house, when he was in Augusta.

## January 27, 1944
### Portsmouth Naval Shipyard Launches Four Subs in One Day

In World War II's penultimate year, the Portsmouth Naval Shipyard in Kittery launches four newly built submarines on the same day, three of them simultaneously. The USS *Ronquil,* the USS *Redfish,* and the USS *Razorback* rise from their blocks at 1 p.m., and a few hours later the USS *Scabbardfish* slides down Building Way No. 4 into the Piscataqua River.

Margaret Chase Smith arrives at the 1964 Republican National Convention in San Francisco.

January 27, 1964

## Margaret Chase Smith Becomes Presidential Candidate

Maine's US Sen. Margaret Chase Smith (1897-1995), a Republican, announces her candidacy for president. At the GOP convention in July near San Francisco, she becomes the first woman to have her name submitted for nomination at a major US party convention.

US Sen. Barry Goldwater wins the nomination but loses the November election to President Lyndon Johnson.

January 27, 1982

## Co-creator of *Bert and I* Killed by Hit-and-run Driver

Yale University graduate Marshall Dodge (1935-1982), co-creator with Robert Bryan (1931-2018) of the *Bert and I* stories of Maine humor, dies after being struck by a hit-and-run driver while bicycling toward Waimea on the island of Hawaii. He was 47.

*Courtesy of Islandport Press*

Marshall Dodge, co-creator of the Bert and I stories, emerged as the leading Maine humorist of his generation.

Dodge and Bryan released the first *Bert and I* record album of stories, told in a Maine accent, in 1958, when Dodge was a philosophy major at Yale University and Bryan was a Yale Divinity School student. Dodge had spent no more than a week in Maine when they did the recording.

Bryan's family owned a camp on Tunk Lake. Dodge and Bryan often took old, sometimes off-color stories they had heard, and rewrote them for a broader audience. The first album was a smash and *Bert and I* became a part of Maine's cultural history, creating iconic catch phrases such as "You can't get there from here."

Dodge and Bryan are now

considered the Godfathers of Down East humor, influencing everyone who laid claim to being a humorist in the region for the next sixty years.

While Bryan, a religious minister, used the money from record sales to purchase a plane and begin a mission in Quebec and Labrador, Dodge continued to record and perform and become the most popular Maine humorist of his generation.

Dodge, who also hosted a television show on Maine Public Television in the early 1970s, founded the Maine Festival of the Arts in 1976 at Bowdoin College in Brunswick.

## January 27, 2015
### Blizzard Sets Portland Snowfall Record

A blizzard featuring 50-mph wind dumps more than two feet of snow on parts of southern and central Maine, with downtown Portland's accumulation of 27.4 inches setting a record for that date.

The storm also drops twenty-seven inches in Lewiston and twenty-six inches in Sanford. Some communities in Connecticut, Massachusetts, and New Hampshire receive nearly three feet.

## January 27, 2020
### Maine Native Puts up $100 Million to Open Northeastern Research Center in Portland

Northeastern University announces it will create the Roux Institute at Northeastern University in Maine using a $100 million gift from Maine native David Roux. Roux, a technology investor and philanthropist, and his wife, Barbara, made the grant from their family foundation.

Northeastern, which will confer post-secondary degrees ranging from professional certificates to master's degrees and doctorates, announces it will enroll its first class in the fall of 2020 and will narrowly focus on artificial intelligence, including machine learning. Northeastern, even though it has not yet identified a permanent campus, expects to enroll 1,000 students within five years and up to 2,600 within ten years.

The institute, located temporarily in the WEX building on Fore Street in Portland, enrolls about 100 students in its first year despite the emergence of a global coronavirus pandemic. The initial classes are all on online, but in-person sessions are offered for courses that begin later.

## January 28, 1768
### Little, Bagley Receive Land Grant to Settle Future Site of Lewiston

Moses Little and Jonathan Bagley, both of Newbury, Massachusetts, receive from the Pejepscot Proprietors a grant for the land around the falls on the Androscoggin River. A condition of the grant is that fifty families live there in fifty houses by June 1, 1774. In the fall of 1770, Paul Hildreth becomes the first Colonial settler to move there. The settlement, named Lewiston, later becomes Maine's second-largest city.

## January 28, 1903
### Architect John Calvin Stevens' Augusta Masterpiece Debuts

Gov. John Fremont Hill and his wife, Laura, entertain hundreds of guests at their newly built home on State Street in Augusta. The house, still standing in 2021, is one of noted Portland architect John Calvin Stevens' signature achievements.

Hill (1855-1912), who made his fortune in the publishing industry, commissioned the design of the house at a time when Maine did not have a governor's mansion yet. His Colonial Revival mansion, made of St. Louis gray brick and Hallowell granite, was built by Waterville contractor Horace Purinton for $250,000—the equivalent of about $7.77 million in 2019.

The man Hill chose for the job, Stevens (1855-1940), is "the best documented figure in Maine architectural history," Maine State Historian Earle G. Shettleworth Jr. writes in a 2003 book about Stevens' work.

Stevens attained a national reputation beginning in 1880 for his drawings, and later photographs, that appeared in major architectural journals. Much of his work involved buildings on Portland's densely populated downtown peninsula.

Stevens grew up in Portland. He began his architectural career in the office of Francis H. Fassett, the architect responsible for rebuilding much of downtown Portland after the city's Great Fire of 1866. Stevens became Fassett's junior partner in 1880. After running a branch office in Boston, in 1882 he returned to Portland and set up his own firm.

He eventually receives more than three hundred commissions for designing or renovating homes and religious, business, and industrial buildings on Portland's downtown peninsula. Many of the homes are in Portland's West End, clustered on Bowdoin, Danforth, Neal, and Thomas streets. He also produced designs for other structures that never were built, such as an 1889 sketch of a proposed Maine State House, inspired by the city's unsuccessful effort to convince state government to move from Augusta back to Portland, where it had operated for several years after Maine achieved statehood in 1820.

### January 28, 1998
### Legendary Shoemaker Bass to Shutter Last Maine Plant

G.H. Bass & Co., announces it will shutter its plant in Wilton by summer, meaning that more than 122 years after George Henry Bass opened his first shop on Main Street and began peddling his leather boots to lumbermen and farmers, the company will no longer make shoes in Maine. The closing, which will put 350 people out of work, rocks the small town that is nearly synonymous with the Bass name.

"You think of Wilton and you think of Bass Shoe," says Wilton Selectman Norm Spencer, who termed the closing a "bombshell." Vicki Gordon, owner of Sassy Sizzors on Main Street, tells the *Portland Press Herald*, "This is just going to be devastating to the town. I can't imagine."

Phillips-Van Heusen Corp., parent of Bass, said it would keep a warehouse in Wilton and the Bass headquarters in South Portland; but in the coming years, they too will be closed.

The closing of Bass is one in a string of announcements that decimates the once-vital Maine shoe industry in a relatively short time.

In April 1999, Cole-Haan announces that it will close its last shoemaking plant in Livermore Falls, eliminating 255 jobs, while other job cuts are announced by Dexter Shoe and Etonic around the same time. More will come.

In 1983, more than 17,000 Mainers worked in footwear manufacturing, but by the time of the Cole-Haan announcement roughly sixteen years later, the number of jobs has dropped to fewer than 6,000.

By the early twenty-first century, nearly all shoe jobs would be gone from Maine after shoe manufacturers moved nearly all work out of the US to lower-wage countries.

January 28, 2019
## USM Announces $100 Million Revitalization Plan

The University of Maine System trustees approve the concept of a sweeping $100 million master plan for the revitalization of the University of Southern Maine.

The plan calls for a $25 million student center, new dormitories and a campus quadrangle in Portland, as well as other changes at the school's Portland and Gorham campuses. First proposed in 2016, the overhaul is expected to take years to achieve.

The plan is part of a major rebranding that USM President Glenn Cummings promised when he took over in 2015 during a fiscal crisis.

On November 27, the university releases a proposal from Alabama-based Capstone Development Partners to build 379 housing units for upperclassmen and graduate students, as well as a student center and green space. Those buildings would replace a bookstore and student center, a facilities management building and a parking lot that now exist on the corner of Durham and Bedford streets in Portland.

At the time of the proposal, the Portland campus has no dormitories. The university wants them because the cost of apartments in and around the city is more than many students can afford.

On January 27, 2020, the trustees give their unanimous blessing to the Capstone proposal. The expansion project is expected to get underway in the summer of 2020 and to be completed in 2022.

However, the 2020 coronavirus outbreak and delays in the issuing of permits cause a postponement in the construction of the combined 580-bed residence hall and student center. That part of the project now is scheduled for a "soft opening" in May 2023 and for a full opening in the fall of that year. Portland's Planning Board approved the project in November 2020.

January 29, 1890
## Powerful Thomas 'Czar' Reed Establishes 'Reed's Rules'

US House Speaker Thomas Brackett Reed, a Portland Republican, takes action to end the "disappearing quorum" tactic used by House Democrats to prevent House business from being conducted. He marks members "present" even if they refuse to respond to a roll call.

The procedure survives a court challenge and becomes part of what later are known as "Reed's Rules," a guide to procedure and parliamentary law that still holds sway today in the House and in many state legislatures.

Reed also abolishes the filibuster in the House. The stalling tactic still is used in the US Senate.

Reed serves as House speaker from 1889 to 1891 and 1895 to 1899, when he resigns from Congress. His iron grip on the chamber during those periods prompts his political enemies to give him the nickname "Czar Reed."

### January 30, 1649
### Dream of Gorges Family Dies with Beheading of King

The deposed King Charles I, whose forces were defeated in the English Civil War (1642-1651), is executed by beheading in London.

Charles' death essentially ends the dream of the family of Sir Ferdinando Gorges, who died two years earlier, of extending its control from the province of Maine to all of New England. In fact, the opposite happens. During the 1650s turmoil of changing governments in England, Massachusetts authorities gradually seize control of settlements in Maine.

After the restoration of the English monarchy, King William and Queen Mary present a charter in 1691 that makes Massachusetts' absorption of Maine permanent. Maine remains part of Massachusetts until it achieves statehood in 1820.

Gorges had a claim to Maine originally because the Plymouth Council for New England, acting under the authority of England's King James I, granted the first patent establishing the Province of Maine between the Merrimack and Kennebec rivers in 1622 to Gorges and John Mason. The two founders later split their territory, with Mason taking the section that is now mostly in New Hampshire, and Gorges retaining the section that now is in the state of Maine.

### January 31, 1945
### Fire Kills 17 People, Mostly Babies, at Unlicensed Nursery

A fire rips through a privately operated boarding home being used as an unlicensed nursery in Auburn, killing sixteen babies and a nurse. Three women and five children escape from the flames.

The state had cited the operator for code violations, and although the operator had delayed making improvements, state authorities failed to close the facility before the fire occurred.

## January 31, 2001
### Death of Logan Marr Prompts New Protection Laws for Children

Five-year-old Logan Marr dies of suffocation after her foster mother, Sally Anne Schofield, binds her with duct tape and straps her into a highchair in the basement of Schofield's home in Chelsea.

Schofield, a former Maine Department of Health and Human Services caseworker, is convicted of manslaughter in 2002 in connection with the child's death. She is released on parole in 2017.

The case, which becomes the subject of a PBS *Frontline* episode, results in an overhaul of child protection procedures in Maine. The state makes placement with family members a higher priority.

## January 31, 2006
### PMA Acquires Winslow Homer Studio in Prouts Neck

The Portland Museum of Art acquires the building and the surrounding grounds of the Winslow Homer Studio in Prouts Neck, a coastal community of summer residents that is part of Scarborough.

For the next six years, the museum works to restore the building's appearance to the way it looked when Homer used it.

The studio, which also was the famed artist's residence, was declared a National Historic Landmark in 1965. Homer (1836-1910), a Boston native, lived and painted in the studio from 1884 until his death.

## January 31, 2021
### First Commerical Rocket Using Biofuel Launched

A Brunswick company, blu-Shift Aerospace, Inc., launches the world's first commercial rocket using biofuel for propulsion.

The reusable rocket lifts off around 3 p.m. at the former Loring Air Force Base site in Limestone and reaches an altitude of slightly less than 5,000 feet, according to a report in Brunswick's *Times Record* newspaper. The flight occurs after a January 15 launch attempt failed because of weather-related problems and after technical glitches caused a five-hour delay of the later successful launch.

The rocket, called Stardust 1.0, is about twenty feet tall and fourteen inches in diameter. It carries three payloads and is a prototype demonstration intended to show investors what bluShift's capability is, the newspaper reports. A parachute deploys and slows the rocket and its payloads as they drop back to the ground, and a team of snowmobilers retrieves them.

Company CEO Sascha Deri declines to identify the rocket fuel but describes it as solid, nontoxic, carbon-neutral, capable of being obtained anywhere in the world, and less expensive than traditional rocket fuel.

Deri says the company hopes to conduct a second launch by the end of the year, possibly reaching the edge of outer space.

—30—

# FEBRUARY

## February 1, 1976
### Carter Wins Maine Caucuses

Former Georgia Gov. Jimmy Carter, relatively unknown nationally until a few months earlier, collects more delegates in the Maine Democratic Party's presidential caucuses than all the other candidates combined.

His victory contrasts sharply with a Gallup poll about a week earlier, in which only 4 percent of voters nationally identified him as their first choice as a presidential candidate. That changed dramatically when Carter won the Iowa caucuses on January 26.

Carter, the keynote speaker at the Maine Democrats' statewide convention in 1974, flies to Portland on the night of the Maine caucuses to celebrate his victory with supporters. Maine is the first state on the East Coast and the third nationally to hold its party caucuses.

Carter is elected president in November, defeating incumbent President Gerald Ford, a Republican. However, Ford wins a majority of Maine's votes in the general election, as does Ronald Reagan in 1980 when Carter is defeated in his re-election bid.

## February 1, 1991
### *Evening Express* Prints Final Edition

A Portland newspaper era ends when the *Evening Express*, the city's afternoon newspaper for 108 years, prints its last edition. The *Express* was started in 1882 by Arthur Wood Laughlin in a one-room office on Union Street. The original paper cost one penny and contained four pages.

The decision to merge the *Express* with the morning *Portland Press Herald* was made by the Guy Gannett Publishing Company the previous September. The two staffs were merged and news pages were added to the *Press Herald*.

## February 1, 1991
### Maine Savings Bank, State's Largest Bank, Collapses

On Friday evening, eighty-five FDIC regulators descend on once-high-flying Maine Savings Bank branches to seize the bank; and by the time the branches reopen, its deposits are controlled by Fleet

Bank of Maine. The 132-year-old Maine Savings Bank, a one-time symbol of Maine banking success, has failed.

The failure is not only symbolically devastating, but it is the largest and most costly bank failure in Maine history and comes during a time of massive problems in New England banking overall. Maine Superintendent of Banking H. Donald DeMatteis wrote, "Calendar year 1990 was the most difficult year to face the Maine banking community since the Depression."

Many of the problems were fueled by aggressive acquisitions and overly aggressive commercial lending and real estate. When suddenly the economy came crashing down, meaning a lot of loans soured, it took a lot of victims. By the end of 1992, either through acquisitions or failure, these venerable Maine banking names had disappeared during the preceding decade: Maine National Bank, Maine Savings Bank, Depositors Trust, Merrill Trust, and Merchants National Bank.

## February 2, 1915
### German Officer Attempts to Destroy Railway Bridge

Werner Horn, a German army lieutenant carrying out a sabotage mission on behalf of German officials in New York, plants a bomb on the Canadian side of an international railway bridge linking Vanceboro, Maine, and the village of St. Croix, New Brunswick.

Canada is fighting Germany in World War I at the time, but the United States is not yet involved in the war. Both nations, however, were providing war supplies to European powers fighting Germany, and some of that was being shipped across the Vanceboro bridge to the port at Saint John, New Brunswick.

Horn arrives in Vanceboro by train on January 30 and arouses suspicion when he is seen hiding a suitcase in a wood pile. When a local customs officer interrogates him, he says he is a Dutchman looking to buy farmland in the area. The agent lets him go. Horn checks out of his hotel on February 1 and hides in the woods until midnight, when the temperature is about 30 degrees below zero Fahrenheit and a strong wind is blowing. After midnight, he walks across the bridge, barely escaping being killed by oncoming trains.

Planted with a three-minute fuse, the bomb explodes, shattering shop windows in Vanceboro and St. Croix but doing little damage to the bridge. Horn suffers frostbite while walking back to his hotel, where US and Canadian officials detain him.

He is tried and convicted on a minor charge related to the window damage in Vanceboro. British and Canadian officials seek his extradition. After entering the war in 1917, the US extradites Horn to Canada, where he is tried, convicted and sentenced in New Brunswick to 10 years in Dorchester Prison. However, prison officials deem him in July 1921 to be insane, and he is deported to Germany.

## February 3, 1997
## New Bridge Across Fore River Named 'Casco Bay Bridge'

Portland and South Portland city councils vote to approve the name "Casco Bay Bridge" for the new $130 million span crossing the Fore River between the two cities.

Earlier, a committee of representatives from the cities and the town of Cape Elizabeth recommended the name after evaluating 137 naming proposals. The previous Portland-South Portland span was known as the Million Dollar Bridge because it cost about $1 million to build in 1916.

## February 3, 1999
## MBNA Dramatically Expands Maine Presence

Delaware-based MBNA, billed as the world's largest credit-card issuing corporation, announces a plan to expand its operations in Maine by opening telemarketing centers in Farmington, Fort Kent, Presque Isle, and Rockland and providing 2,300 jobs there.

Gov. Angus King calls the move "the single-biggest business expansion in the history of the state of Maine."

When the plan is complete, MBNA is expected to have five thousand workers in Maine, making it the state's fourth-largest employer.

When the company arrived in Maine in 1993, it hired about two dozen people for jobs in Camden. By 1999, it employs about three thousand in Belfast, Brunswick, Camden, Orono, Portland, and Presque Isle.

Company CEO Charles Cawley (1940-2015) was not unfamiliar with the state, having spent childhood summers with his grandfather in Lincolnville and having worked as a teenager in his grandfather's garment factories in Belfast and Camden. Cawley built an opulent summer home outside Camden.

Later he decides to move there year-round and to take most of the corporation to Maine with him. The company builds lots of infrastructure and donates generously to local institutions.

By 2005, its Maine workforce has shrunk to about 3,500 people. Then Bank of America buys MBNA. It keeps the Belfast operation going, but the other Maine offices close. Other companies have noticed MBNA's discovery of the financial and tax advantages of setting up shop in Maine, however, and they begin to do the same, thereby replacing many of the lost MBNA jobs.

## February 3, 2006
## National Register of Historic Places Adds Portland Church, Once on Underground Railroad

The Abyssinian Meeting House, the oldest African-American church building in Maine and the third-oldest in the United States, is listed on the National Register of Historic Places.

Because of its easy access by rail and sea, Portland became a northern hub of the Underground Railroad in the 1800s. The church played a critical role in providing safe houses and find-

ing escape routes to Canada and England. Speakers at the church during this era included Abolitionist leader Frederick Douglass.

The church building, located in the Munjoy Hill neighborhood of Portland, was built by free African-Americans in 1828-1831, after they formally organized the Abyssinian Religious Society in February 1828. The building was remodeled by the congregation after the Civil War and was used for religious, social, educational, and cultural events until it closed in 1916. Activity and membership declined rapidly following the wreck of the steamship *Portland* in November 1898, when nineteen adult male members, including two trustees, were killed.

In the 1920s, the building was renovated into tenement apartments, which were occupied until the building was condemned by the city of Portland in 1991. In 1998, the building was sold for back taxes to the Committee to Restore the Abyssinian. The church building is one of the few frame public buildings to survive the Portland fire of 1866, largely through the efforts of William Wilberforce Ruby (1824-1906), a Black fireman and son of Reuben Ruby, who, according to the

National Park Service, protected the building by draping the roof with wet blankets.

## February 4, 1953
### Ben Ames Williams, Author of Classic *Come Spring*, Dies at 63

Prolific writer Ben Ames Williams, author of *Come Spring* and *Leave Her to Heaven* and ardent chronicler of rural Maine life, dies in Brookline, Massachusetts, at 63.

Born in Macon, Mississippi, and raised in Jackson, Ohio, where his father owned the *Jackson Standard Journal* newspaper, Williams grew up in the news business, eventually writing and editing at his hometown paper. After graduating from Dartmouth College, he became a reporter for the *Boston American* and spent most of his spare time writing fiction. In 1912, he married Florence Trafton Tapley, of York, Maine.

Williams submitted short fiction to magazines, getting his first story into print in 1915. In 1917, the *Saturday Evening Post* printed another, and over the next quarter-century it published almost two hundred by him. More than 125 were set in the fictional town of Fraternity, Maine.

Fraternity was based at least partly on the Waldo County town of Searsmont. Williams said late in his life that the most important occurrence in his professional life was meeting farmer Bert McCorrison on a summer day in 1918 at Hardscrabble Farm in Searsmont. McCorrison and Williams became fast friends, with the former, a lifelong Searsmont resident, providing the inspiration for much of what the latter wrote and serving as a model for one of Williams' more memorable literary characters, Chet McAusland.

When McCorrison died in 1931, he willed his farm to Williams. Williams and his family spent summers there, and the rest of the year in the Boston area, until his own death in 1953. Hardscrabble Farm now is listed on the National Register of Historic Places because of its association with Williams.

## February 5, 1967
### Maine Icon L.L. Bean Dies at 94

Outdoorsman and Greenwood native Leon Leonwood Bean, age 94, dies in Pompano Beach, Florida, fifty-five years after having founded the iconic global company that bears his name.

L.L. Bean opened in Freeport selling a single product—the

Bean Boot, or Maine Hunting Shoe. Of the first hundred pairs sold, customers returned ninety of them because the soles separated from the body. Bean refunded their money, corrected the design problem and continued selling the boots, which are still among its signature products. An early fan of the Maine Hunting Shoe was Babe Ruth.

The founder's grandson Leon A. Gorman (1934-2015) is appointed company president upon his grandfather's death. The Bowdoin College graduate and US Navy veteran leads a transformation of the $2.25 million company of about a hundred workers into what by 2018 is an enterprise generating about $1.6 billion in net sales and employing about 5,200 year-round workers and about 3,700 seasonal ones.

Gorman and his wife, Lisa, both outdoors enthusiasts, also support efforts to protect the St. John River basin, the Hundred-mile Wilderness, and Katahdin Lake; and help fund a wide variety of youth organizations and cultural institutions.

Now one of Maine's most successful companies, L.L. Bean, led by Board Chairman Shawn Gorman—nephew of Leon Gorman and great-grandson of the company's founder—and President and CEO Steve Smith, operates a flagship store in Freeport that is open twenty-four hours a day, 365 days a year, as well as dozens of stores elsewhere in the United States. It also has stores in Canada, China, and Japan; and a brisk online sales operation.

## February 6, 1967
### *The Times Record* Rolls off Press

The first issue of *The Times Record*, a Brunswick-based daily newspaper, appears on newsstands.

The evening daily paper is a merger of the former *Brunswick Record* and the *Bath Daily Times*.

## February 6, 2007
### Old Town's Patty Griffin Releases *Children Running Through*

Old Town native Patty Griffin's album *Children Running Through* is released. It wins Album of the Year that fall at the 2007 Americana Music Honors & Awards ceremony in Nashville, and Griffin wins the Artist of the Year award.

The album also is nominated for a Grammy award. Griffin later wins a Grammy in 2011 for Best Traditional Gospel Album.

## February 7, 1827
### Waldo Becomes Maine's 10th County

Waldo County becomes Maine's tenth county, formed from part of Hancock County. It is the first Maine county formed after Maine achieved statehood in 1820. The county seat is Belfast. The county's population in 2010 was 38,876.

The county is named for wealthy merchant, soldier and land speculator Samuel Waldo, who in 1730 acquired title to the land in Maine between Muscongus Bay and Penobscot Bay and who settled German and Irish immigrants there.

Waldo County has a rich maritime history, much of which is on display in exhibits at the Penobscot Marine Museum in Searsport.

## February 7, 1978
### Historic Blizzard Slams New England

Wind, snow, and record high tides batter southern Maine, wiping away two-thirds of the three-hundred-foot Old Orchard Beach pier and many buildings and wharves that managed to survive a severe January 9 storm.

The storm causes much greater chaos in Boston and elsewhere in the Northeast, earning it the moniker "the Blizzard of '78." It is the worst blizzard to hit New England since 1888, eventually killing fifty-six people.

In Maine, while less brutal, the storm nonetheless forges a path of destruction. It damages or destroys about four hundred homes in York County, knocks the two-story Lord's Point Inn off its foundation and into the sea at Kennebunk Beach, rips away a sea wall and undermines the Silver Sands Motel in Scarborough, and destroys Steamboat Wharf on Bailey Island and the Riverside Inn and Marina in Christmas Cove, part of South Bristol.

The collapse of the Old Orchard Beach pier, a fixture in the resort town since the early 1900s, takes ten businesses along with it. "Planks, beams and pilings washed over the beach and into the town square," the *Portland Press Herald* reports the next day.

In York Beach, waves break over a burning house and knock firefighters to their knees as they try to get the fire under control.

Many people along the coast are forced to evacuate from their homes and take shelter in churches, fire stations and Salvation Army buildings.

## February 8, 2014
### Sound Engineer Bob Ludwig Wins Three Grammy Awards

Portland sound engineer Bob Ludwig, of Gateway Mastering, wins three Grammy awards for his work on new musical releases, after having won four the previous year.

His 2014 haul includes Album of the Year for *Morning Phase*, by Beck; Best Engineered Album, Non-classical, for *Morning Phase*; and Best Surround Sound Album, for Beyoncé's self-titled *Beyoncé*.

As of 2021, Ludwig has won a total of twelve Grammys and has been nominated thirty-two times.

In a 2017 *Portland Press Herald* interview, Ludwig, a former Utica (New York) Symphony Orchestra principal trumpet player, says he and his wife moved to Portland in 1992, thinking that "if the business fails, at least we'll be in a place that we like."

The only professional offer Ludwig claims to regret having turned town, just after splitting up with a girlfriend, was one to work on Pink Floyd's 1979 album *The Wall*.

His explanation: "I didn't think I could muster listening to depressing songs all day."

## February 9, 2019
### Brown Becomes First Openly Gay Bishop to Lead Episcopal Diocese of Maine

Rev. Thomas James Brown becomes the first openly gay bishop to lead the Episcopal Diocese of Maine and the third in the United States.

Brown, the husband of an Episcopalian minister who is rector of a church in Boston, is elected on the third ballot at a convention of clergy members and lay delegates at a convention in Bangor. He succeeds Rt. Rev. Stephen T. Lane.

Rt. Rev. Gene Robinson became the first gay and partnered Episcopalian bishop in 2003 when he was elevated to lead the Diocese of New Hampshire. Robinson's appointment sparked controversy among officials of the Anglican Communion, of which the Episcopal Church is a part. He retired in 2013.

Robinson joined his partner of twenty-five years in a civil union in 2008. They married in 2010 and divorced in 2014.

## February 10, 1886
### Steamship *Cambridge* Sinks off Port Clyde

At 4:45 a.m., the wooden passenger steamship *Cambridge* strikes Old Man's Ledge off Port Clyde and sinks in fifty feet of water.

The 248-foot vessel, carrying heavy freight, completely breaks apart, becoming the only Boston-to-Bangor steamer to be lost in more than a century of service.

All crew members and the forty passengers survive unharmed and are deposited on Allen Island, where the steamer *Dallas* picks them up and takes them to Rockland. Clusters of freight are found up and down the coast in the days after the wreck, in the possession of fishermen and others, and some items are returned to the owners.

The *Cambridge*, built in 1867 in New York, also was damaged in the last of a series of 1869 hurricanes, which came to be known as the Saxby Gale.

The storm, which killed at least thirty-seven people and caused extensive damage along the Bay of Fundy in Canada's Maritime Provinces, broke the steampipe and rudder on the *Cambridge*, which was off Monhegan Island at the time. The captain dropped anchor and secured the ship when it drifted to a point near the mouth of the St. George River.

## February 10, 1894
### *Dirigo* First Steel-Hulled Ship Built in United States

The Arthur Sewall & Co. shipyard in Bath launches the 312-foot-long, four-masted, square-rigged transport bark *Dirigo*, the first steel-hulled ship built in the United States.

Drawn by a British designer and using the contemporary British practice of building ships with steel plates, the *Dirigo* is owned by the Sewall company until 1915, when the company sells it to owners in San Francisco.

On May 31, 1917, during World War I, a torpedo from a German submarine sinks the *Dirigo* off the Irish coast.

## February 10, 1998
### Maine Repeals Gay Rights Law

In a statewide referendum, Maine becomes the first US state to repeal a law prohibiting discrimination based on sexual orientation.

The victory of the discrimination ban's opponents was short-lived, however.

In 2005, the Legislature amends the Maine Human Rights Act to include a ban on discrimination based on a person's sexual orientation or gender identity.

Petitioners put another referendum question on the ballot to challenge the amendment, but the question fails, 55 percent to 45 percent. The law remains on the books.

## February 11, 2016
### Garmin Buys DeLorme, Maker of Iconic *Maine Atlas and Gazetteer*

The *Portland Press Herald* reports that GPS giant Garmin has reached a deal to buy DeLorme, the Yarmouth-based maker of the *Maine Atlas and Gazetteer*.

At the time, DeLorme employs ninety-two people at its headquarters off US Route 1.

The company was founded in 1976 by David DeLorme, who, being frustrated over obsolete backcountry maps of the Moosehead Lake region of Maine, vowed to create a better map of Maine. His product, the *Maine Atlas and Gazetteer*, became iconic and beloved in the state to hikers, hunters, fishermen, and others.

By 2016, the trend was away from printed maps and toward satellite navigation technology, and the deal reflected that direction.

On March 3, Garmin, which has its US headquarters in Kansas, announces it has closed the deal.

## February 11, 1904
### Maine-built *Henry B. Hyde* Shipwrecked in Virginia

The transport ship *Henry B. Hyde*, the largest ship built in Maine to this time, is shipwrecked. It is recovered but sinks permanently on October 2 of that year.

The fully rigged three-masted sailing vessel, built in 1884 by Flint & Chapman in Bath and owned by the San Francisco-based California Shipping Co., is 268 feet long. It becomes a coal carrier in 1898.

The ship runs aground in 1904 in a gale off Cape Henry, Virginia. Workers trying to salvage it manage to get it afloat, but the ship breaks loose and becomes stranded again September 22 south of Dam Neck Mills Lifesaving Station, prompting abandonment of the salvage effort.

## February 12, 1959
### Paul Bunyan Stands Tall in Bangor as Gift From Builders

A New York group of builders gives the city of Bangor a thirty-one-foot-tall Paul Bunyan statue in commemoration of the city's 125th anniversary. The statue is placed in Bass Park on Main Street. The gift is designed to

A statue of Paul Bunyan looms over Bangor.

honor Bangor's former status as the "Lumber Capital of the World" in the mid-1800s. It was lumber and the Penobscot River that gave the Queen City and the regions north of Bangor much of their wealth and identity.

At the time of his visit in 1837, Henry David Thoreau recorded the presence of 250 sawmills along the Penobscot River and its tributaries.

February 12, 1834, also is supposed to be the fictional Bunyan's birth date.

The city clerk's office keeps what it calls his birth certificate on display.

February 13, 2019

## Guiness Confirms: Skowhegan Sets Moose-Calling Record

The town of Skowhegan and the Main Street Skowhegan organization receive confirmation from Guinness World Records that their community set the world record for moose calling on June 9, 2018.

On that date, 1,054 people, with registered Maine guide Robert Lambert leading them during the Skowhegan Moose Festival at the state fairgrounds grandstand, made a thunderous moose call that lasted thirty seconds.

Nonetheless, there is no record

*Photo by Derek Davis; courtesy of Portland Press Herald*
The US Navy's new stealth destroyer, the USS *Zumwalt*, passes Fort Williams on its way to Portland Harbor in 2015.

of an actual moose responding in any way to the call.

Attended by about 6,000 people, the moose festival also was the setting of the state's annual moose hunting permit lottery. Organizers drew 3,500 names of prospective hunters.

## February 14, 2008
### Navy Awards BIW Contract to Build *Zumwalt* Destroyer

Bath Iron Works wins a $1.4 billion contract to build the first ship in the US Navy's newest class of guided-missile destroyers. The USS *Zumwalt*, or DDG 1000, is due to be delivered in 2014.

The contract is expected to help BIW avoid layoffs when construction of the Arleigh Burke-class destroyers is complete.

The Zumwalt program originally was supposed to result in the production of thirty-two ships at a cost of about $1.34 billion each. Cost increases prompt the Navy to reduce the number of ships gradually. By the time of the *Zumwalt*'s christening in 2014, the number of *Zumwalt*-class ships is to be three, at a cost of about $7 billion per ship, when development costs are included.

Aside from the ballooning budget, several other problems—

USS *Maine*

engine testing difficulties, labor disputes at the shipyard and the fact that the Zumwalt is incomplete when delivered—bedevil the project. The Navy decides to revert to the Arleigh Burke class of destroyers for future construction.

In December 2019, the Department of Defense proposes reducing the number of new Arleigh Burke-class vessels planned for 2021-2025 from twelve ships to seven.

## February 15, 1898
### Remember the *Maine*! Cuba Blast Sours Relations with Spain

The battleship USS *Maine*, an armored cruiser commissioned in 1895, explodes in the harbor at Havana, Cuba, killing 266 of the 354 crew members and accelerating the decline in US relations with Cuba's parent nation, Spain. The United States goes to war against Spain later that year.

The ship was commissioned in 1895 as the first US Navy vessel named after the state of Maine. It was built at a time when, decades after the Civil War, the Navy and private industry no longer had significant shipbuilding expertise. By 1898, technical progress already had surpassed its design. The Maine arrived at Havana on January 25, three weeks before the blast. Its presence there in the midst of an ongoing war between Spain and Cuban revolutionaries is seen as a gesture of aggression toward Spain.

A naval court of inquiry determines on March 21 that the *Maine's* destruction is the result of two explosions, and that the cause of the first most likely was a mine placed outside the ship; the second was from an ignited magazine inside the ship.

In a study of the incident published in 1974, Adm. Hyman G. Rickover concludes that the court of inquiry was assembled hastily by a sick naval officer and that it failed to interview people with the proper technical expertise. The *Maine's* captain was alert to threats outside the vessel but had a spotty record for making sure his ships were in good working order, he writes.

"The strained relations between the two nations, the warlike and patriotic atmosphere in Congress and the press, and the natural tendency to look for reasons for the loss that did not reflect upon the Navy might have been predisposing factors in the court's findings," Rickover writes.

The court was aware that the configuration of damage inside the ship was consistent with that of an internal explosion, he said, adding, "Had the ship blown up in an American or friendly foreign port, and had the same type of damage occurred, it is doubtful that an inquiry would have laid the blame on a mine."

In any case, the United States, champing at the bit for war at any excuse, defeats the Spanish in three months. In the 1898 Treaty of Paris, Spain cedes Cuba, Puerto Rico, the Philippines and Guam to the United States, demonstrating convincingly the latter nation's evolution into a major world power.

The shield and scrolls are recovered from the *Maine* wreckage and placed in 1922 in Davenport Park in Bangor, where they are identified as the Battleship *Maine* Monument.

## February 16, 1804
### Commodore Preble Leads Fight Against Barbary Pirates

In a maneuver masterminded by Navy Commodore Edward Preble (1761-1807), of Portland, a group of sailors stages a surprise attack and sets fire to the frigate USS *Philadelphia*, which had run aground the previous year off Tripoli and had been captured by

Barbary pirates.

President Thomas Jefferson put Preble in charge of American efforts to stop the pirates from harassing shipping in the Mediterranean Sea despite the fact that Preble suffered from a longtime illness.

In the summer of 1804, buttressed by the loan of eight vessels from the Kingdom of the Two Sicilies, the commodore coordinates six attacks on Tripoli, the first of which results in hand-to-hand combat but also the capture of three Tripolitan gunboats.

Preble gained a reputation for being a firm commander who introduced many long-used Navy regulations and developing the officer corps that proved to be of critical importance to the United States in the War of 1812. Preble's grave is in Portland's Eastern Cemetery. Six US Navy ships have borne his name, the most recent being a guided-missile destroyer.

## February 16, 1816
### Penobscot Becomes Maine's Ninth County

Penobscot County, Maine's ninth county, is formed from part of Hancock County. It is the last one formed before Maine separates from Massachusetts and becomes a state in 1820.

The county seat is the city of Bangor.

The US Census lists the county's population in 2010 as 153,923, making it the third-most-populous of the state's sixteen counties.

At 3,556 square miles, it is the fourth-largest in area, larger than the states of Delaware and Rhode Island combined. It also comprises the only metropolitan statistical area in eastern Maine, with Bangor being its principal city.

The county envelops almost all of the Penobscot River watershed south of where the river's East and West branches meet, as well as more than half of the East Branch.

Penobscot County was a shipbuilding and lumber hub in the nineteenth century and a major producer of pulp and paper in the twentieth.

It is the home of the University of Maine, Husson University, Eastern Maine Medical Center, the Cross Insurance Center, the Penobscot Indian Island Reservation, the Old Town canoes and kayaks plant, and the 137-square-mile Katahdin Woods and Waters National Monument.

## February 16, 1952
### Loggers Trapped by Snowstorm

More than a hundred people emerge in Patten on foot and aboard snowmobiles, cars, and trucks, following snowplows and bulldozers that had freed them from northern Maine logging camps after a February 12 storm dumped thirty inches of wet, heavy snow on them.

The last to arrive are ten woodsmen who were trapped behind twelve-foot snowdrifts at an Eastern Corp. camp forty-five miles northwest of Patten.

Half of them trudge four miles on snowshoes through shoulder-deep snow to reach snowplows that are clearing the rest of the escape route.

Bush pilots dropped bundles of food at the camps to keep the stranded camp inhabitants fed until they could break out and reach civilization.

## February 16, 1956
### Movie Musical *Carousel*,
### Set in Boothbay Harbor, Premieres

The Rodgers and Hammerstein movie musical *Carousel*, starring Shirley Jones and Gordon Mac-Rae, is released.

The story is set in Boothbay Harbor, and much of the movie was filmed there and in Camden, Newcastle, and Augusta.

Some of the movie's scenes were filmed twice to accommodate two types of wide-screen processing methods. Frank Sinatra was supposed to play the male lead in the movie, and he even had recorded the songs; but on the first day of production in 1955 he walked out, claiming he wasn't being paid to act in two movies.

The movie's lead female star, Shirley Jones, said Sinatra told her years later that the real reason he left Maine was because his wife at the time, Ava Gardner, was shooting a movie with Clark Gable in Africa and was threatening to have an affair with Gable if Sinatra didn't join her immediately.

Gordon MacRae, fresh from his performance in the 1955 film version of the Rodgers and Hammerstein musical *Oklahoma!*, was hired to take the place of Ol' Blue Eyes, as Sinatra was known.

## February 16, 2006
### Seth Wescott Wins
### Snowboard Cross Gold

Seth Wescott, a Carrabassett Valley High School alumnus, wins a gold medal in men's snowboard cross in the Olympic debut competition of that event, in Bar-

Photo by John Patriquin; courtesy of Portland Press Herald
Olympic gold medalist Seth Wescott poses outside his home at Sugarloaf Mountain in 2010.

donecchia, Italy. The race is part of the 2006 Winter Olympics, hosted by the city of Turin.

Wescott wins a second gold medal in the event four years later at the 2010 Winter Olympics, held in and around Vancouver, British Columbia.

Wescott, who grew up in Farmington, began cross-country skiing at 3, alpine skiing at 8, and snowboarding at 10.

His pre-Olympics training included big-mountain drops in Alaska, in which he rode a helicopter to the upper reaches of a mountain that hadn't been ridden before, then rode his snowboard down uncharted slopes, including steep faces.

## February 17, 1927
## Opera Written by Edna St. Vincent Millay, *The King's Henchmen,* Opens in New York City

*The King's Henchmen,* an American opera written by Deems Taylor and Rockland native, poet, and playwright Edna St. Vincent Millay (1892-1950), opens successfully at the Metropolitan Opera in New York City.

The story becomes popular in book form as well.

## February 17, 1952
### Killer Blizzard Pounds Maine

A thirty-six-hour blizzard powered by high wind begins to envelop Maine, killing several people—including two lobstermen whose thirty-foot boat sinks in a stormy gale off Port Clyde—and leaving more than a thousand vehicles stranded on highways.

The *Portland Press Herald*, apparently combing a bookshelf literary anthology in search of mellifluous prose suited to the occasion, reports that "every city and hamlet in the southern two-thirds of the state was gripped in the deathly white hand of a winter vengeance beyond modern memory."

The storm dumps twenty-two inches in Portland, the most the city has received in a single storm since 1935, and greater amounts inland. Bangor endures its deepest snowfall since 1918 and is essentially cut off from the rest of the world. In Saco, Dr. Joseph M. Patane resorts to using a horse-drawn sleigh to travel to Old Orchard Beach to deliver a baby.

## February 18, 1795
### Lewiston Incorporated as Town

Lewiston is incorporated as a town. It becomes a city on March 15, 1861. Today it is Maine's second-largest city, as it has been since the 1880 Census. The US Census lists its population as 36,720 in 2010.

## February 19, 1988
### Ellsworth's Tim Scott
### Scores 13 Points in 58 Seconds

In the final two minutes of the Eastern Maine Class B boys basketball championship game at the Bangor Auditorium, Ellsworth High School senior Tim Scott scores thirteen points within fifty-eight seconds, leading the Eagles to a 65-64 victory. The fourth-seeded Eagles' opponent is third-seeded Mattanawcook Academy of Lincoln.

After Scott's thirteen-point run, which ties the game 63-63, the Eagles deliberately foul Mattanawcook player Mike Williams in a successful gamble to control the ball for the winning shot. Williams, a flawless shooter until this point in the game, lands only one of two shots from the foul line, making the score 63-64.

With the Eagles then in possession, Scott defies expectations. Rather than driving for the hoop himself, he passes the ball to senior forward Jason Sattler, who scores the winning two points with a layup.

The Eagles later lose the Class B state championship to Cape Elizabeth, 70-64.

Long after the Bangor Auditorium's demolition in 2013, Maine basketball fans savor the memory of Scott's "miracle minute" in the 1988 game there.

Scott would go on to play baseball for coach John Winkin at the University of Maine and for the Colorado Rockies organization. In 1999 he was selected for induction into the Maine Baseball Hall of Fame.

Scott is the youngest son of Jack Scott, also a former Ellsworth High School athlete and a member of both the Maine Basketball Hall of Fame and the Maine Baseball Hall of Fame.

### February 20, 1797
### Augusta Carved from Hallowell

The Massachusetts Legislature votes to partition the Maine town of Hallowell, with the northern part being incorporated as the town of Harrington, named after an English nobleman. Immediate dissatisfaction among residents prompts the selectmen to petition the Boston authorities for a name change.

The Legislature bows to the people's wishes, and on June 9, the new town is renamed Augusta. The town encompasses two-thirds of the former land of Hallowell and half its population and property valuation.

Hallowell long had consisted of two principal settlements—the Hook, where the Kennebec River bends near what is now downtown Hallowell; and the Fort, where Fort Western still stands today across from downtown Augusta. The separation of the two does not sit well with Hook residents.

"The imperialistic method of the Fort villagers in procuring the separation, and the haughty ignoring of the wishes of the Hook people as a party deeply interested," historian Charles E. Nash writes more than a century later, "laid the foundation of a petty enmity between the Fort and Hook which descended to the next generation and survived in the form of unfriendly pranks and sometimes rows between the neighboring youth long after the precise origin of the feud had faded from popular recollection."

Nash also cites Hook residents' use of the epithet "Herringtown" to mock the people of Harrington, especially Dr. Daniel Cony, a local benefactor who was in the fish trade. Cony also was in the Massachusetts Legislature, however, and was in a good position to make sure the request to rename the town received quick action.

Nash is unable to determine how the name "Augusta" is chosen as a replacement.

## February 20, 1799
## Kennebec Becomes Maine's First Inland County

Two years to the day after the incorporation of Augusta, Maine's future capital, Kennebec County, of which Augusta becomes the county seat, is set off from Lincoln County.

The new county, Maine's sixth, is the first to have no seacoast, which reflects the growth of the District of Maine's interior. The interior also is where the movement to separate Maine from Massachusetts is gaining the most traction.

Maine's population is growing rapidly at this time. The number of incorporated towns increases from seventy-one in 1790 to 126 in 1800.

Kennebec County's population in 2010 is 121,581, according to the US Census, giving it the state's fourth-largest number of inhabitants.

## February 20, 1893
## *Lewiston Daily Sun* Publishes in Blizzard

Amid a raging blizzard, Henry A. Wing, of Lewiston, produces the first edition of the *Lewiston Daily Sun* at a plant on Ash Street in Lewiston. The paper later becomes today's *Sun Journal* in a merger with the *Lewiston Evening Journal*.

## February 21, 1885
## Built From Maine Granite, Washington Monument Dedicated in Nation's Capital

The Washington Monument, the core of which consists of Maine granite, is dedicated in Washington, D.C., after construction that began in 1848 and was suspended for twenty-three years for a variety of reasons, including the American Civil War.

Maine's granite industry also supplied stone used in many other prominent late-nineteenth-century construction projects, including the Yorktown (Virginia) Monument, the Chicago Board of Trade Building, and San Francisco's Hibernia Bank Building.

Monopoly capitalism, new building techniques, and changing architectural styles drive the industry into decline in the twentieth century.

February 21, 2012
**Maine Gambling Control Board Approves State's First Full-fledged Casino in Bangor**

The Maine Gambling Control Board approves the state's first casino, allowing Hollywood Slots Hotel and Raceway to become Hollywood Casino Bangor.

The change means that the casino, located on the banks of the Penobscot River, can now offer table games such as roulette and poker, rather than just slot machines.

While the casino is the first, it is not the last. Oxford Casino, featuring more than five hundred slot machines and a dozen table games, celebrates its grand opening just a few months later.

February 22, 1864
**Wreck of *Bohemian* Kills 42 Off Cape Elizabeth**

The three-masted steamer *Bohemian*, an iron vessel owned by the Ocean Steamship Co. of Montreal, is bound from Liverpool, England, to Portland, when it strikes Alden's Rock, a ledge near Cape Elizabeth, at night in a dense haze. The accident kills forty-two people, including two crew members.

The ship was carrying 219 pas-sengers, most of them Irish immigrants traveling in steerage class; and nineteen crew members. It left Liverpool on February 4.

In that era, Portland is the winter port for passengers and freight heading to and from Montreal because about five months of the year, the St. Lawrence River in the Canadian city is too choked with ice to allow ships to pass.

When the *Bohemian*'s captain, Richard Borland, sees Cape Elizabeth through the haze on the night of the accident, he thinks he is farther at sea than he really is. The impact on the ledge tears a hole in the engine room, damaging it severely.

The crew sends up flares to summon a pilot boat, but none can be seen through the haze. Borland orders the firing of two guns as a distress signal. The first gun fires, but the second already is underwater. Two men in a pilot boat hear the lone shot. They wait for another, and hearing none, they assume someone has fired at random during an impromptu celebration of George Washington's birthday.

The *Bohemian* is equipped with six lifeboats. The first boat is launched without incident, carrying about eighty people. A pin holding the second boat breaks, and many passengers are heaved into the ocean. About sixteen men, women, and children are killed.

The other boats are released, but they are not full. Many people jump into the ocean from the steamer and drown.

Borland, the boatswain, three other crew members and seventy to eighty passengers remain on the ship. Most of them climb onto the foretop or into the rigging. Those who don't are swept out to sea when the ship settles in water twenty-four to thirty feet deep.

Lifeboats return to pick up people clinging to parts of the ship still poking up above the ocean's surface. Cape Elizabeth residents open their homes to shelter the survivors. Later, scavengers pilfer cargo from the half-sunken wreck.

A coroner's jury blames the accident on Borland's bad judgment, the lack of a bell on Alden's Rock, and inattentiveness of the men in the pilot boat. Unclaimed bodies are buried in a mass grave in South Portland.

A mural named *Shipwreck at Night* now graces a wall at the South Portland post office as a tribute to the disaster victims.

February 22, 1878

## Banker's Death in Dexter Robbery Becomes Enduring Mystery

Bank cashier John Wilson Barron is attacked fatally during a robbery in the Penobscot County town of Dexter. The robbers apparently expected to find an empty bank because it is Washington's Birthday, a national holiday.

The crime is discovered when Barron's wife reports him missing that evening. Barron, handcuffed and gagged, is found alive in the bank vault but dies the next morning. Bank robberies being a common occurrence in an age when Maine is experiencing a booming lumber trade, authorities question the usual suspects and offer handsome rewards for information leading to the killers. They get no results.

Ten years later, the case draws national attention when suspects David Stain and Oliver Cromwell, both of Medfield, Massachusetts, are arrested and put on trial in Bangor. East Coast newspapers cover the proceedings as relentlessly as the news media of the 1990s scrutinize the murder trial of actor and ex-professional football player O.J. Simpson. The defendants are tried by a jury, convicted and sent to the Maine State Prison in Thomaston.

The verdict is appealed to Judge John Peters, who presided at the trial. He rejects the appeal. A subsequent appeal to the Maine Supreme Judicial Court—of which Peters is the chief justice—also fails. While awaiting that final decision, the chief defense lawyer, Lewis Amasa Barker, 35, of Bangor, dies of illness and fatigue exacerbated by his defense work on the prisoners' behalf.

After several more years, a key witness—Stain's son—recants, admitting having fabricated a story about his father's participation in the robbery because he was angry with him.

Gov. Llewellyn Powers and his council consider the matter in response to a petition from Barker's son, Lewis Appleton Barker, who represents the prisoners after being admitted to the bar only months earlier. On December 31, 1900, two days before Powers leaves office, the governor and council agree unanimously to pardon Stain and Cromwell.

The two prisoners are freed, and the murder case remains unsolved to this day.

## February 23, 2009
### Storm Batters Brunswick; 130,000 CMP Customers Lose Power

A brief but intense storm dumps heavy, wet snow across much of Maine, knocking out electrical power to about 130,000 Central Maine Power Co. customers.

The storm hits the Brunswick area particularly hard, prompting Gov. John Baldacci to see the damage firsthand. By that evening, more than half of those who lose power still don't have it back.

The storm causes the third massive power loss within three months in the CMP service area. A storm around Thanksgiving in 2008 darkened about 35,000 homes, and more than 220,000 customers lost electricity in a December 12 ice storm that inflicted a blackout on about 1.5 million homes throughout the Northeast.

## February 24, 2012
### Mr. Paperback to Shutter All 10 Bookstores

Bangor-based Mr. Paperback announces it will close all ten of its bookstores, located mostly in eastern Maine, and will layoff 120 workers, leaving a huge bookselling void in a wide swath of the state.

The State House building in Augusta.

Mr. Paperback is the largest bookstore chain in the state, and in most cases the stores are never replaced by a new bookseller. The fifty-year-old chain operates stores from Augusta to Dover-Foxcroft to Ellsworth to Presque Isle. As part of the announcement, Magazines Inc., a sister company that distributes magazines and newspapers in Maine, is sold.

The companies were started in the 1960s by John and Evelyn Foss and handed down to their children.

The closing comes not long after Borders Books closes its stores in Bangor, Brunswick, South Portland, and Auburn, continuing the upheaval in the book industry.

## February 24, 1827
### Augusta Named Permanent Capital of Maine

Maine Gov. Enoch Lincoln

signs a bill determining that beginning January 1, 1832, "the permanent seat of government shall be established at Augusta." The bill makes Augusta the state's capital city, replacing Portland, which became the capital when Maine achieved statehood in 1820.

The bill, the latest of several on the subject, passed 81-38 in the Maine House of Representatives and 11-7 in the Maine Senate.

## February 24, 1838
### Congressman from Thomaston Killed in Duel

First-term US Rep. Jonathan Cilley (1802-1838), a Democrat from Thomaston, dies in Bladensburg, Maryland, at 35, having been wounded fatally by a rifle shot in a duel with US Rep. William Graves, a Whig from Kentucky.

Graves challenged Cilley to the duel, asserting that Cilley had insulted his honor by refusing to accept from him a letter containing a Whig newspaper editor's challenge to another duel. That initial challenge was a result of Cilley's public claim that the editor had changed his mind to favor re-chartering the Second Bank of the United States because the bank had granted him loans total-

ing $52,000.

Cilley graduated in 1825 from Bowdoin College, in Brunswick, in the same class that included writers Nathaniel Hawthorne, Henry Wadsworth Longfellow, and Horatio Bridge.

In 1839, reacting to Cilley's death, Congress passes a law strengthening a Washington, D.C., ban on dueling by making it a crime to issue or accept a challenge to a duel even if the duel itself is scheduled to take place outside the District of Columbia.

## February 24, 1989
### US Congresswoman, Governor Wed in Lewiston

Gov. John McKernan and US Rep. Olympia Snowe marry at the Greek Orthodox Church of the Holy Trinity in Lewiston. They become the nation's first case of a married couple holding both a governorship and a seat in Congress.

McKernan and Snowe, both Republicans, served together in the Maine House of Representatives, and together from 1983 to 1987 in the US House, where he represented Maine's First District and she held the Second District seat.

McKernan's tenure as governor lasts two terms, from 1987

*Courtesy of Portland Press Herald*

US Rep. Olympia Snowe and Gov. John "Jock" McKernan are wed in Lewiston on February 24, 1989. Snowe is later elected to the US Senate in 1994.

to 1995, during which Snowe is elected in 1994 to the first of her three six-year US Senate terms.

## February 25, 1791
### Surprise! It's Bangor, not Sunbury

The Massachusetts General Court approves a petition for the incorporation of the town of Bangor—which, like the rest of Maine, then is part of Massachusetts. The new town has about 170 residents. Rev. Seth Noble travels to Boston to incorporate the place as the town of Sunbury but either changed his mind or misspoke, and it becomes Bangor.

"We labor under many disadvantages for want of being incorporated with town privileges," Bangor clerk Andrew Webster writes in the petition in an effort to justify the request. "We have no Justice of the Peace for thirty miles on this side of the (Penobscot) River—no

Grand Jury, and some people not of the best morals."

Whatever the locals' morals are, they do not seem to inhibit the community's growth. By the mid-nineteenth century, it is Maine's second-largest municipality. It drops to third, after Portland and Lewiston, in the 1870 census and retains that status up to the present.

Bangor's population in 2010 was 33,039, according to the US Census.

## February 25, 1815
### Senate Rejects Call for Convention to Discuss Separation from Massachusetts

The Massachusetts Senate rejects, 17-10, a resolve submitted by Sen. Albion Parris, a Democratic-Republican representing the District of Maine's Oxford and Somerset counties, calling for a districtwide convention on the issue of separating from Massachusetts.

The vote probably was influenced by the fact that days before the vote, Massachusetts learned of the signing of the treaty that ended the War of 1812, which meant that the British military no longer would be threatening Maine's coast.

## February 26, 1972
### 'Tears' Damage Muskie's Presidential Chances

US Sen. Edmund S. Muskie, D-Maine, while running as a candidate in the March 7 New Hampshire presidential primary, delivers a speech in defense of his wife on the back of a truck outside the Manchester *Union Leader* newspaper offices.

The newspaper's editor, William Loeb, accused Muskie's wife, Jane, in print of drunkenness and using off-color language. Muskie, calling Loeb a "gutless coward," gives his speech during a snowstorm. Snowflakes melting on Muskie's face make him appear to be crying. Newspapers report that he actually was crying, which damages his image among voters who wonder whether he is stable enough to lead the country. That incident, as well as unrelated sabotage engineered by President Richard Nixon's re-election campaign, causes Muskie to fare worse than expected in the primary election, although he wins.

Muskie comes in fourth in the Florida primary in March, and he withdraws a month later from the race for the Democratic presidential nomination, which Sen. George McGovern, of South

AP photo

US Sen. Edmund Muskie denounces Manchester (N.H.) *Union Leader* publisher William Loeb in front of the newspaper's offices on February 26, 1972. The Rumford, Maine, native's run for the Democratic presidential nomination was derailed by a report that he had cried following the newspaper's attack on his wife. Snowflakes melting on his face made him appear to be crying.

Dakota, wins. McGovern then suffers a landslide loss to Nixon in November.

## February 27, 1813
### Future Colby College Established as Baptist School

The Commonwealth of Massachusetts, of which Maine then still is a part, establishes the Maine Literary and Theological Institution, which opens in Waterville. It becomes Waterville College in 1821; then in 1867, Colby University, to honor major donor Gardiner Colby; and finally, in 1899, Colby College, the name it retains today.

In 1871, the school becomes the first all-male college or university in New England to accept female students.

The college's Baptist origin influences its teaching for more than a century, but then its curriculum shifts to a more secular focus.

Also, because the college has little room for expansion in its downtown location, it begins

The oldest known photograph of Colby College, a daguerreotype taken in 1856 of the three central buildings on campus: South College, Recitation Hall, and North College.

moving during the Great Depression to the current Mayflower Hill campus on the western edge of Waterville.

In the 2010s, the college takes steps to strengthen its connection to downtown Waterville by launching a number of development projects.

Those projects include construction of a boutique hotel and the Bill & Joan Alfond Main Street Commons, a retail and residential building on Main Street.

## February 28, 1890
### BIW Wins First Navy Contract, Begins Building Two Gunboats

Bath Iron Works wins its first contract for the construction of complete ships—two iron gunboats for the US Navy. Flags are hoisted at the shipyard and the yard's whistles issue three loud blasts at noon to celebrate the occasion.

The award accelerates furiously an effort to convert the yard's South Division into a true ship-building facility.

Founded in 1884 by Civil War veteran Thomas W. Hyde, the storied Bath company would become a subsidiary of General Dynamics in 1995. It also would remain one of Maine's largest employers.

## February 29, 1820
### Final Pieces in Place;
### Maine to Become State

The Portland-based *Eastern Argus* newspaper reports that William King, soon to become Maine's first governor, led a successful effort to convince the Massachusetts General Court to grant a two-year extension to Maine on the terms of its separation from Massachusetts.

The Massachusetts action removed one of the final obstacles to Maine statehood, which will take effect March 15.

Some separation advocates had advocated that if Massachusetts didn't extend its March 4 deadline, Maine should declare itself an independent republic until Congress acted on the statehood question.

—30—

# MARCH

March 1, 1642
## Gorgeana, America's First City, Incorporated

Gorgeana, a Maine community named after Sir Ferdinando Gorges, a co-founder of the Colonial-era Province of Maine, becomes the first incorporated city in America. It is now the town of York.

Gorges sent his cousin Thomas Gorges in 1639 from England to Maine as his deputy. The latter, a trained lawyer who may have been the first from that profession in Maine, establishes Gorgeana—which is by no means a city in the twenty-first-century sense, although Thomas Gorges compiles an optimistic roster of positions to be filled, including that of a lord bishop. He also organizes the first English trek into the northern New England interior, reaching the White Mountains.

Back in England, when the English Civil War breaks out in 1642, the aged Sir Ferdinando takes to the battlefield alongside the royalists, or Cavaliers. Thomas Gorges returns the next year and sides with the parliamentarians, or Roundheads.

Thus distracted, they are unable to control the Maine settlement, which forms its own government at first and eventually is absorbed by the Massachusetts colony.

March 1, 1809
## Somerset Becomes Maine's Eighth County

Somerset County becomes Maine's eighth county, formed from part of Kennebec County.

The northwestern county, named after Somerset County in England, now bills itself as the nation's top producer of all things maple, and it celebrates that distinction by hosting two annual events—the Maple Festival and the Maple Madness basketball tournament, both held in March.

Travelers from coastal and central Maine heading to Quebec City usually spend about two hours crossing the county on US Route 201, passing through many of its larger communities.

The county seat is Skowhegan, which is also its most populous town. In 2010, the county's population was 52,228.

## March 2, 1797
### Samuel Adams Signs Bill Approving Separation Referendum

Gov. Samuel Adams signs a bill that the Massachusetts General Court, the state's legislature, approved calling for a referendum in the District of Maine about whether Maine should separate from Massachusetts.

The General Court acted in response to petitions received from Maine. The vote is scheduled for May.

Unlike a previous failed effort to achieve separation, this proposal includes all five Maine counties, rather than excluding Hancock and Washington counties.

In the May vote, the pro-separation side achieves a slight majority, but the General Court ignores the result because only about five thousand votes are cast. The anti-separation votes are clustered in seaport towns, which depend heavily on trade with other states.

Maine statehood still is twenty-three years away, awaiting historical events such as the War of 1812, which will convince Mainers more firmly of the need to govern themselves, instead of relying on government officials in Boston.

## March 2, 1896
### Flooding Washes Away Many Maine Bridges

Flooding across a wide swath of Maine sets high-water-mark records that will stand for years.

Several bridges in the Portland area are wrecked, as are a gatehouse and a power station at the S.D. Warren mill in Westbrook, putting 2,500 people out of work and depriving surrounding areas of electricity.

The flood washes away the East Turner Bridge and destroys twelve others in Turner.

In Hallowell, the Kennebec River rises and covers Water Street, site of the business district. The date of the high-water mark is carved into a granite corner of a building at Water and Wharf streets. The marking remains there today, as do markings of the high-water levels from other floods. In the 1896 flood, the river reaches the highest level ever recorded to that point, not to be surpassed until 1936.

## March 2, 1994
### Last Aircraft Leaves Loring Air Force Base in Limestone

The last aircraft from Loring Air Force base, a US Air Force KC-135R refueling tanker, roars away from the base, tipping its wings in salute to the community it leaves behind.

There was little fanfare, the Associated Press reports, with about two hundred spectators watching the event, another harbinger of the region's shaky economic future. "This is not something we want to observe or mark on the calendar," says Town Manager Troy Brown. "When that plane leaves, it's going to be a symbol of poor economic times."

The departure marks another milestone for the 11,000-acre base in northern Maine, which was home to fighters, bombers, and tankers for more than four decades. Loring was the largest employer in Aroostook County, providing as many as 3,300 military and 1,300 civilian jobs, along with an additional 3,900 spinoff jobs. By March, as the shutdown process continues, enrollment in area schools has dropped from 1,550 to 800 students and the school district is in the process of cutting 125 jobs. Meanwhile, a state report estimates that Aroostook County would lose a staggering 20 percent of its economic base, including 8,500 jobs, $152 million in annual earnings, and 15,000 residents.

A few months later, in September, the 42nd Bomb Wing flag is taken down in a ceremony that includes prayers and salutes and signifies the base's official end.

## March 3, 1820
### US Senate Approves Missouri Compromise; Maine to Become 23rd State

The US Senate's acceptance of a provision that slavery be permitted in Missouri (which would become a state in 1821) fulfills a compromise clearing the way for Maine to become a state twelve days later.

News that Maine's admission to the Union is linked to the slavery question sparks outrage among many Maine civic leaders and newspapers. Delegates to the Maine Constitutional Convention conclude that it might be better to wait another year for statehood than let Maine be used as "a mere pack horse to transport the odious, anti-republican principle of slavery" into Missouri, according to delegate George Thacher, of Biddeford.

Leading separation advocate and future Gov. William King opposes the slavery linkage at first, but comes to accept it. In the US House, Alfred resi-

Photo by Gregory Rec; courtesy of Portland Press Herald
Mount Katahdin as seen from Patten.

dent Rep. John Holmes (1773–1843), representing Massachusetts, becomes instrumental in pushing the Missouri Compromise through Congress.

March 3, 1931
### Gov. Baxter Donates Land to Create Baxter State Park

Former Gov. Percival Baxter's (1876-1969) donates Mount Katahdin and the land that surrounds it to the state, resulting later in the establishment of Baxter State Park in Maine's Piscataquis County.

In 1920, then president of the Maine Senate, Baxter climbed the mountain at 44. It left a lasting impression on him, and he was determined to preserve the mountain from development. He began developing proposals for the state to acquire it.

The next year, newly elected Gov. Frederick Parkhurst died unexpectedly a little more than three weeks after taking his oath of office. As Senate president, Baxter succeeded him. He won his own election to the job in 1922. At the beginning of each term, he laid out a plan to establish a Mount Katahdin State Park, but the Legislature rejected it repeatedly. When the independently wealthy Baxter left office, he offered to return his annual salary of $10,000 for the previous two years if the state would use it to acquire property for the park. The state never met the conditions of his offer.

Beginning in 1925, Baxter decided to fund the project himself. He made his first complicated purchase of six thousand acres, including Katahdin and most of its adjoining peaks, for $25,000 on November 12, 1930.

After he gives the land to the state in 1931, the state names it Baxter State Park in his honor and formally accepts it in 1933. Over three decades, Baxter makes a total of twenty-eight acquisitions and subsequent donations to the state, increasing the park's size to about 200,000 acres, all shielded from development. When it is done in 1962, he writes to then-Gov. John Reed and the Legislature to inform them. He applies all the subtlety he can muster to the message.

"This brings to an end an interesting incident in Maine history," he writes.

## March 3, 1904
### *Waterville Morning Sentinel* Debuts

The first issue of the *Waterville Morning Sentinel* appears. It is the

sixteenth newspaper to debut in Waterville; all of the others failed.

The *Sentinel*, at first a Democratic newspaper, competes during its first three years with the Republican-leaning *Waterville Evening Mail*, before the *Mail* goes out of business.

In another of the countless examples of how newspapers in those days rarely tried to avoid political conflicts of interests, the *Sentinel's* owner, Cyrus W. Davis, a Democrat, is elected mayor of Waterville. The election victory dominates the front page the next day, which bears six US flags and carries a cartoon of a rooster labeled "The Rooster that Crows for Waterville Democracy."

The *Sentinel's* name later is changed to *Central Maine Morning Sentinel*, and then to simply *Morning Sentinel*.

## March 3, 1977
### Cumberland County Civic Center Opens its Doors in Portland

The Cumberland County Civic Center, which cost $8 million to build, opens in Portland, featuring a performance by the rock band ZZ Top in the first concert held there.

The facility hosts concerts, shows, conferences and the newly arrived Maine Mariners minor league hockey team, part of the American Hockey League.

The county-owned project proves controversial. The town of Otisfield, where many people opposed it, petitions the Legislature in 1978 to be detached from Cumberland County and merged into neighboring Oxford County in order to avoid having to pay for the civic center, which Otisfield residents claim does not benefit them. The request is approved, and Otisfield shifts to Oxford.

ZZ Top proves to be one of most durable civic center bands, playing the venue eleven times. Other musical acts that perform there five times or more include Aerosmith, Disturbed, the Grateful Dead, Phish, and Carrie Underwood.

The Mariners, an expansion franchise, remain in Portland until 1992, when they move to Utica, New York. In 1993, the Baltimore Skipjacks, another AHL team, move to the civic center and become the Portland Pirates. They remain there for twenty-three years, then leave for Springfield, Massachusetts.

In 2018, the civic center becomes the home arena of a new Maine Mariners team, a temporarily inactive franchise most recently based in Alaska. The Mariners are an East Coast Hockey League franchise.

The Mariners suspend play after a game on March 10, 2020, in Portland because of the coronavirus pandemic, which eventually causes cancellation of the entire 2020-2021 season as well. However, the team announces in March 2021 that its home opener for the 2021-2022 season will take place on October 22, 2021, against the Worcester Railers.

After a $33 million renovation in 2012 and 2013, the fixed-seating capacity is 6,200. The renovation includes new sets, wheelchair-accessible seating, more restrooms, and additional concourse space.

The building's name changes in 2014 to the Cross Insurance Arena, after Cross Insurance buys the naming rights for $2.5 million.

## March 4, 1805
## Landlocked Oxford County Becomes Maine's Seventh

Oxford County, Maine's seventh county and the second one to have no seacoast, is formed from parts of York and Cumberland counties.

The county seat is Paris. The 2010 population recorded by the US Census is 57,833. Its long western boundary is the New Hampshire state line.

The home of many summer camps, the rural county is the most populous county in Maine to lack a portion of the interstate highway system. It also is the location of gemstone mining sites, paper manufacturing, the Fryeburg Fair, and Oxford Casino.

March 4, 1861
## Hannibal Hamlin Becomes Lincoln's Vice President, Highest-Ranking Political Figure in Maine History

Hannibal Hamlin (1809-1891), a Republican from Hampden, is sworn in as the fifteenth US vice president, serving under President Abraham Lincoln and reaching the highest political office ever achieved by a Maine resident.

Hamlin, a Paris Hill native, started his career as a lawyer, then entered politics as an anti-slavery Jacksonian Democrat. He served in the Maine Legislature, the US House of Representatives, and the US Senate before becoming vice president.

Hamlin grew disaffected with the Democratic Party as it became increasingly controlled by Southern power, at one point telling his wife, Ellen, it had become a "putrid mass of moral leprosy."

Finally, in 1856, after the Democrats at the Cincinnati Convention moved to divest the federal government of any power over slavery, he denounced his party and abandoned it in a fiery speech on the floor of the US Senate.

He was immediately courted by the fledgling Republican Party and just four years later was elected vice president. In some Maine circles, his bold decision prompted attacks such as one in the *Eastern Argus* of Portland, which proclaimed, "He has left a glorious renowned party, whose principles are ever young, and has united himself with a deformed monster whose embrace is destruction."

Hamlin was an early backer of emancipating slaves—a position that Lincoln, not prone to seeking Hamlin's advice, later adopts.

Lincoln gets a new running mate, Andrew Johnson, in 1864 and wins re-election.

Hamlin returns in 1869 to the Senate for twelve years, supporting radical reconstruction and

Hannibal Hamlin served as vice president of the United States under
Abraham Lincoln.

serving as chairman of the Foreign Relations Committee.

After a year of representing the country as minister to Spain, he retires to Bangor.

On July 4, 1891, Hamlin collapses while playing cards at the Tarratine Club in Bangor. The couch on which he dies is placed on display later at the nearby Bangor Public Library, where it remains today.

March 5, 1801
**Dearborn Named Jefferson's Secretary of War**

Army Maj. Gen. Henry Dearborn (1751-1829), a Revolutionary War veteran and longtime Gardiner resident, begins eight years of service as secretary of war under President Thomas Jefferson.

Previously, Dearborn participated in the Battle of Bunker Hill and was part of Benedict Arnold's ill-fated 1775 March to Quebec, where the British captured him. Released in a prisoner exchange, he fought at Saratoga and in the Battle of Monmouth, in New Jersey, and was at Valley Forge with George Washington's winter encampment there.

After the war, he became US marshal for the District of Maine—which then was part of

Massachusetts—and a two-term member of the US House of Representatives.

After his service to Jefferson, Dearborn takes a political patronage job as collector of the port of Boston. The War of 1812 puts him back in uniform, and as a senior Army commander he undertakes several attacks against the British in Canada. His efforts prove ineffective, and President James Madison removes him from command in 1813. He later serves as US minister to Portugal.

In 1812, a town in Kennebec County is named for him. The town eventually is divided among Waterville (later Oakland), Belgrade, and Smithfield and ceases to exist in 1841. Fort Dearborn, also named in the general's honor, is established in 1803 on Lake Michigan; but it becomes abandoned, and the site is now part of downtown Chicago. Dearborn, Michigan, hometown of Henry Ford and the Ford Motor Company, is also named for the general.

March 5, 1860
**Knox Becomes Maine's 16th and Final County**

Knox County, Maine's sixteenth and final county, is formed from parts of Lincoln and Waldo counties.

The county is named for American Revolutionary War general and Secretary of War Henry Knox, who lived in the coastal county from 1795 until his death in 1806. Knox, a Boston bookseller, is perhaps most famous for overseeing an arduous expedition that brought cannons from Fort Ticonderoga in upstate New York to Dorchester, Massachusetts, prompting the British, who had laid siege to the city of Boston, to withdraw their fleet, thus ending the siege.

At 365 square miles of land, Knox is the state's second-smallest county, after Sagadahoc, when only land is counted; and third-smallest when water is included. The county seat is Rockland. The county's 2010 population stood at 39,736.

## March 6, 2014
### Alfond Grant Provides $500 to All Maine Babies

The Harold Alfond Foundation announces that all Maine resident babies automatically will be awarded a $500 college grant.

The Portland-based foundation, which its namesake established in 1950, supports health care, education, youth develop-

ment and other causes in Maine. By 2003 it had donated more than $100 million to charity.

Alfond (1914-2007), a Massachusetts native and high school graduate, moved to Maine in 1934 to take a shoe factory job at the lowest rung of the corporate ladder, working his way up to factory superintendent.

In 1940, Alfond and his father founded a shoe manufacturing company in Norridgewock, which they soon sold, but Alfond stayed on as president for twenty-five years. He founded the Dexter Shoe Co. in 1956.

He sold the company and its affiliates in 1993 for $433 million to Berkshire Hathaway.

## March 7, 2019
### Skowhegan Drops 'Indians' as School Nickname

The Skowhegan-based School Administrative District 54 board votes 14-9 to discontinue the use of "Indians" in reference to the district's sports teams. The decision follows five years of bitter, high-profile controversy about the name.

The district consists of Canaan, Cornville, Mercer, Norridgewock, Skowhegan, and Smithfield.

Many Skowhegan-area residents oppose dropping the name, saying it is meant to honor indigenous people. Previous school board meetings drew representatives of Maine's four tribes who said use of the name harms them, although other Indians said they don't find it offensive.

"We've never been asked, and I think that we should all be asked," Passamaquoddy Tribe member Kathy LeBrun tells Maine Public. "I mean, we're all on the census."

Those who advocate dropping the name also include Gov. Janet Mills and ACLU of Maine, which says the school board's decision makes Maine the first US state to eliminate all Native American mascot names and imagery for school sports teams.

Before the March 7 decision—which reverses a 2015 board vote of 11-9 to keep using the "Indians" moniker—supporters of the nearly century-old name held boisterous rallies, conducted letter-writing campaigns, and held up large, home-made campaign-style posters at school board meetings to make their feelings known. Some called for a district-wide referendum on the issue, an idea that the board rejected.

By March 2020, the board has received 1,627 forms suggesting a new nickname and has narrowed the number of options to 305.

After much deliberation, the board votes 15-5 on October 8 to adopt "River Hawks" as the new nickname for the district's sports teams.

## March 8, 1957
### Wilhelm Reich Infant Trust Established

Four days before beginning a two-year prison sentence, Wilhelm Reich (1897-1957), an Austrian psychoanalyst and medical doctor who lives and works at his Rangeley estate, Orgonon, signs his last will and testament, creating an agency now known as the Wilhelm Reich Infant Trust.

Reich's many books and other writings influenced other professionals in the field of body psychotherapy, Gestalt therapy, biogenetic analysis, and primal therapy. He also espoused controversial theories about the role of the energy of orgasms in promoting and maintaining health, a force he called "orgone energy."

Reich, dogged by accusations of fraud, was sentenced for a criminal contempt of court conviction in connection with his violation of a court order banning the interstate shipment of orgone accumulators, devices the size of a small phone booth in which his patients would sit in an effort to connect with the energy force for therapeutic reasons. Newspaper reports described them as sex boxes designed to cure cancer. Filmmaker Woody Allen appears to parody the orgone accumulator in the 1973 movie *Sleeper*, calling the film's machine the "Orgasmatron."

Six tons of Reich's professional publications were burned in 1956 in accordance with a US federal court order.

Reich dies in prison before completing his sentence. His 175-acre Orgonon estate now is the home of the trust and the Wilhelm Reich Museum, open since 1960. The museum receives visitors from July through October.

## March 9, 1921
### *Wandby* Wrecks at Walker's Point

The British tramp steamer *Wandby* becomes shipwrecked when it runs aground on rocks at the Walker's Point ledge in Kennebunkport in dense fog.

The accident happens that morning because the ship's captain, David Simpson, mistakes a whistling buoy off Cape Porpoise for a buoy on Cashes Ledge,

southeast of the Portland Lightship, which marks the approach to Portland Harbor. When a lookout reports seeing breakers, the captain gives the engine room a "full astern" order to stop the ship.

The order comes too late. The 3,991-ton freighter grinds onto the rocks, thumping and scraping so loudly that it can be heard for miles around.

When the fog lifts around three o'clock in the afternoon, the crew can see that a large crowd has gathered on the beach to watch the spectacle. School is canceled in Kennebunkport so children can look at the wreck. When the tide recedes, the crew sees that rocks have penetrated three feet into the hull and caused a crack that extends thirty or forty feet toward the bow. Then the tide comes back in and floods the engine room, rendering any effort to refloat the ship pointless.

Although most of the ship is broken up for salvage, some parts remain on the ocean floor to this day.

The wreck occurs as future President George H.W. Bush's Walker ancestors already have owned their family estate at Walker's Point for a few decades, and less than five months before

Bush's parents marry in Kennebunkport. The only land-based eyewitness to the accident is William Goodwin, winter caretaker of the Walker estate.

## March 10, 1996
## Ocean Trading Route Established with Iceland

Portland entrepreneur James Finley announces a plan to set up an ocean trading route between Portland and Iceland, exporting hardwood to Iceland and importing frozen cod and lamb.

Finley, who operates three Portland-based fishing boats, said his first trading vessel, a 198-foot steel freighter, would arrive within the week at the Custom House Wharf in Portland. He calls prospects for Iceland-bound cargo so promising that he already has plans to expand with a second vessel.

He and his son Mark recruit sailors from Newfoundland, load a dismantled sawmill and a shipment of unprocessed trees onto the freighter and send them to Iceland, then fly to the country by plane. By that time, however, severe and unexpected legal and health problems are undermining Finley's efforts, his son says in a 2020 phone interview.

Finley, then in his mid-70s, sells the sawmill, the lumber, and his freighter and spends a year untangling the legal complications that result from his enterprise.

Finley's assessment of the prospect of business involving Iceland is not without merit, however. In 2013, a year after his death, the Icelandic shipping company Eimskip makes Portland, the site of Maine's only container shipping terminal, its American headquarters.

Container traffic at the port nearly triples over the following six years.

In 2018, the terminal handles 22,835 containers. In April 2019, Eimskip introduces the 461-foot *Pictor J*, which is the largest ship ever to use the terminal and can carry nearly twice the number of containers that Eimskip's next-largest ship can.

The company says it still sees room for growth in Portland, where the cargo traffic is greater than ever.

## March 11, 1936
## Flooding Ravages Maine, East Coast

A three-day rainstorm begins, causing a flood that results in major destruction and damage across New England.

In Maine, the Kennebec River

bridge linking the towns of Richmond and Dresden is washed away, and the Androscoggin River in Auburn is measured at its highest level ever.

More than 150 people are killed in the floods, which ravage the East Coast as far south as Virginia. The water bursts dams, wipes out roads, ruins businesses, and washes away homes.

## March 11, 1968
### Tribe's Attorney Gellers Arrested, Convicted, Later Pardoned

A state police detective arrests Donald Gellers, an attorney helping Maine's Passamaquoddy Tribe to assert its fiscal and land rights, at Gellers' home in Eastport and charges him with "constructive possession" of six marijuana cigarettes.

Gellers is convicted in May 1969 and sentenced to two to four years in prison, and he is subject to disbarment.

The case proves later to be the intended result of a conspiracy orchestrated by the Office of the Maine Attorney General, under the leadership of "law and order" conservative Attorney General James Erwin (1920-2005), to sideline Gellers in his defense of the Passamaquoddys.

At the time of his arrest, Gellers has just returned from filing a lawsuit in Boston to force the state of Maine to turn over land that the tribe claims belongs to it and to return $150 million the state stripped from a trust fund that had been set up for the Indians in 1794.

Gellers' work becomes instrumental in bringing about the landmark 1980 Indian land claims settlement with the state.

Gellers dies of cancer in 2014. His relatives, through their attorney, seek clemency for him several times, but the case never is granted a hearing.

On January 7, 2020, Gov. Janet Mills issues a posthumous pardon to Gellers.

## March 12, 1888
### 'Great White Hurricane' Kills More than 400

The Great Blizzard of 1888, also known as the "Great White Hurricane," locks up the East Coast from Chesapeake Bay to Maine, resulting in more than four hundred deaths, including those of about one hundred sailors.

The storm drops twenty-two inches of snow in New York City, but heavy wind forms snowdrifts that are dozens of feet deep. About

Chester Greenwood (see page 80)

fifteen thousand people become stranded on elevated trains. Much heavier snowfall is recorded in southern New England and upstate New York.

In Sanford, Maine, the snowfall is about twenty-six inches, according to local author Edwin Emery, writing at the time.

The storm, which causes more than $20 million worth of damage in New York City alone, helps convince some public officials of the value of placing electrical and telegraph lines and big-city public transit underground.

## March 13, 1877
### Chester Greenwood Patents Improved Earmuffs

Teenager and Farmington native Chester Greenwood (1858–1937) patents a type of earmuffs that he designed with his grandmother's help to cover his large ears while he goes ice skating.

While Greenwood does not invent earmuffs—contrary to popular myth—he does improve them by adding a V-shaped hinge that holds the earmuffs tightly to the ears. His earmuffs inspire mockery at first but eventually prove popular, prompting him to open an earmuff factory that employs many Farmington-area

residents. In its best year, the factory makes more than four hundred thousand pairs of earmuffs.

Greenwood later patents a number of other devices, including a tea kettle and a steel-toothed rake. He also operates a bicycle business and a heating system business, and he introduces one of the first telephone systems in Farmington.

The town celebrates Chester Greenwood Day every year with a parade on the first Saturday in December.

## March 14, 1909
### MacMillan Abandons North Pole Trek

Arctic explorer Donald Mac-Millan (1874-1970) drops out of Robert Peary's trek to the North Pole at 84 degrees, 29 minutes north latitude because of frozen heels, and he turns south again.

MacMillan, a Freeport High School and Bowdoin College graduate, also becomes a teacher, lecturer, researcher, sailor, and philanthropist. He eventually makes more than thirty expeditions to the Arctic, including one at the age of 79. After his marriage in 1935, his wife, Miriam, accompanies him on many of the trips. He compiles a dictionary of Inuktitut, the language of the

This design served as the flag of Maine from 1901 to 1909.

Inuit people. He also establishes a summer camp for boys to teach seasmanship and navigation.

Many of MacMillan's exploration and research accomplishments are on display at the Peary-MacMillan Arctic Museum in Brunswick.

March 15, 1820
**Happy Birthday, Maine!**

Maine is admitted to the Union as the twenty-third US state. It was part of Massachusetts until then.

William King (1768-1852), of Bath, is declared acting governor until elections can be held in April. King later wins that election.

Statehood was achieved in Congress through the Missouri Compromise, which allowed Maine to become a free state provided that Missouri be admitted as a slave state, thereby keeping the total number of free states equal to the total number of slave states, and keeping the number of US senators representing each group equal. Maine's US Rep. John Holmes proved to be a key force in moving the plan through Congress.

Linking Maine statehood to the slavery problem horrified many influential residents of the state, and the unexpected snag caused bitter political battles between strict abolitionists and pragmatists who could find no other means to achieve statehood.

Though Maine's population grows rapidly at the time of statehood, today it is the least densely populated state east of the Mississippi River. The state's population stands at 1.36 million in 2020.

*The Eastern Argus*, a Portland newspaper, publishes in its edition for that week the text of the law making Maine a new state. It reads: "Be it enacted by the Senate and House of Representatives of the United States of America in Congress assembled, That, from and after the fifteenth day of March, in the year one thousand eight hundred and twenty, the state of Maine is hereby declared to be one of the United States of America, and admitted to the Union on an equal footing with the original states, in all respects whatever."

## March 15, 2020
### Novel Coronavirus Spread Prompts Gov. Mills to Declare Emergency

Gov. Janet Mills, reacting to the news that the number of confirmed and presumptive positive cases of novel coronavirus infec-

tions has doubled in a single day from six to twelve, declares a statewide civil emergency.

By April 23, the number of Maine cases increases to 937. Infections are detected in every county.

The virus began spreading rapidly around the world in January from central China. By April 23, it has killed 50,236 people in the United States and nearly 191,000 worldwide, and the totals are expected to rise dramatically in the coming months. The virus has caused 44 deaths by this date in Maine.

The New England Small Colleges Athletic Conference already announced March 11 that interscholastic regular season and tournament play for the spring is canceled. Similarly, NCAA cancellations put an end to University of Maine teams' season.

The state announced Maine's first positive test result of a novel coronavirus case, involving a woman from Androscoggin County, on March 12. Colby College, in Waterville, announced that with the school's spring break about to begin, all students will be expected to move off campus, and classes for the rest of the semester and final examinations will be conducted online. Maine's other colleges and universities institute similar measures.

Mills' March 15 declaration gives her the authority to close schools, retail businesses and other facilities; but she stops short of that, instead making only recommendations for now. She calls for schools to suspend classroom instruction as soon as possible, says no meetings with fifty or more people should be held, and warns that high-risk people should take part in no gatherings of more than ten people.

President Donald Trump declares a national emergency March 13 because of the rapidly spreading infections. On March 16, he urges people to avoid going to restaurants, bars, and other public places; and to avoid gathering in groups of ten or more.

Dr. Nirav Shah, director of the Maine Center for Disease Control and Prevention, says the state is expecting delivery of thirteen thousand masks and seventeen thousand pairs of protective gloves from the federal stockpile by the end of the week. It also is preparing a request for ventilators.

On March 31, Mills issues an order that Maine residents remain in their homes except for trips to the grocery store, medical appointments, or other essential activities.

Mills renews the declaration monthly so that it remains continuously in effect.

While the virus spreads explosively in early spring in some parts of the United States, Maine is less affected. The state's number of daily new coronavirus infections remains relatively low—in double digits—until the fall of 2020, when the incidence grows to hundreds of cases daily. By late May 2021, when the daily numbers are declining again, Maine has recorded nearly 67,000 COVID-19 infections since the pandemic began, accounting for nearly five percent of the state's population. The coronavirus death tally in Maine rises to more than 800.

Even so, the state fares better than the vast majority of the nation. Its total number of infections and its infection rate are smaller than those of all but three other states. Only Alaska, Vermont, and Hawaii have lower COVID-19 death rates than Maine does. Also, by late May of 2021, the number of people fully vaccinated against the virus reaches more than 50 percent of the state's population and is growing quickly.

## March 16, 1839
### Aroostook Becomes Maine's 13th County

Land from Penobscot and Washington counties is set off to form Aroostook County, Maine's thirteenth county. In its final form, "The County" consists of 6,453 square miles and is geographically the largest county east of the Mississippi River. It is larger than the states of Connecticut and Rhode Island combined and is perhaps most known for its potato crop. The county seat is Presque Isle. The county's population stands at 71,870 in 2010.

Because of a long-running border dispute with the United Kingdom, the county's northern and eastern boundaries are uncertain at the time of its creation. The Webster-Ashburton Treaty of 1842, twenty-two years after statehood, finally establishes Maine's permanent border with Canada.

## March 16, 1855
### Future Bates College Established, Becoming First Coeducational University in New England

The Rev. Oren Burbank

Cheney and Benjamin Bates establish the Maine State Seminary—which later becomes Bates College—in Lewiston.

Started as a Freewill Baptist college, it is the first coeducational university in New England, admitting students regardless of their race, religion, national origin, or gender.

In 1864, it becomes a secular school and changes its name to Bates College to honor one of its co-founders, who donated a large sum of money to support the school's establishment.

## March 16, 1901
### 'Miracle City' Incorporated

The town of Millinocket, Maine's "miracle city in the wilderness," is incorporated. Much of the town was built seemingly overnight the previous year to meet the labor needs of Great Northern Paper Co., which establishes the world's largest newsprint mill there at the junction of Millinocket Stream and the West Branch of the Penobscot River.

The town rises from a single farm to a thriving community, becoming nearly synonymous with paper in Maine. By June 1900, Millinocket has one hundred homes; and when the plant

Photo by David MacDonald; courtesy of Portland Press Herald
Ricky Craven, right, talks with crew chief Andy Graves after a practice session for the NASCAR Winston Cup Jiffy Lube 300 at New Hampshire International Speedway in Loudon in 1997.

opens that fall, it already has two thousand residents.

The rise of Millinocket also marks the emergence of power for the pulp and paper industry in Maine and essentially heralds the end of the great lumber era of Bangor.

March 16, 2003
### Ricky Craven Wins at Darlington

PPI Motorsports driver Ricky Craven, 36, a native of Newburgh, wins the 2003 Carolina Dodge Dealers 500 stock car race before 55,000 fans at Darlington Raceway in Darlington,

South Carolina.

Craven defeats Kurt Busch by 0.002 second in what then was the closest finish in NASCAR Winston Cup Series history. (That margin is matched in 2011 when Jimmie Johnson grabs a victory over Clint Boyer at Talladega Superspeedway in Alabama.)

Craven, who began racing at 15 at Unity Raceway in Maine, eventually ends his career having won races in four series— the K&N Pro Series and three national series. His last full year of racing is 2005, after which he becomes a racing broadcaster for ESPN, from 2008 to 2018; and then for Fox Sports.

Craven is inducted in 2016 into the Eastern Motorsports Press Association Hall of Fame.

## March 17, 1912
### Camp Fire Girls Incorporated

The Camp Fire Girls, a national organization now known as Camp Fire USA, is incorporated. The organization traces its origin to 1910, when co-founders Dr. Luther Halsey Gulick and his wife, Charlotte Vetter Gulick, set up a girls' program at their camping complex on Sebago Lake in Raymond.

The Gulicks, cognizant of the fact that the Boy Scouts of America had been founded in 1910 to provide boys with outdoor opportunities, wanted to do the same for girls.

Dr. Gulick convened a meeting in 1911 at the Horace Mann Teachers College to discuss ways to do that. The organization comes into formal existence in 1912.

Chapters quickly blossom nationwide. By the summer of 1914, seven thousand to eight thousand girls are participating. Five years later, the number has grown to 220,000 girls meeting in nine thousand local groups.

The organization's name was changed to Camp Fire Boys and Girls in the 1970s, when boys were invited to participate; and to Camp Fire USA in 2001.

The Gulicks' summer camps, called Wohelo—short for work, health, and love—have remained in family ownership and are still operated by the Gulicks' descendants.

## March 17, 2018
### Fire Destroys Historic Chesuncook Lake House

Fire breaks out about one thirty in the morning at the historic Chesuncook Lake House hotel and burns it to the ground.

It takes the owners about two hours to contact the Greenville Fire Department. When department members on snowmobiles arrive around daybreak at the remote site about fifty miles north of Moosehead Lake, the fire is out.

Nobody is injured. The hotel, erected in 1864 in Chesuncook Village to supply northern Maine's logging camps, was added to the National Register of Historic Places in 1973, along with various outbuildings on the property.

Owners David and Luisa Surprenant say they plan to rebuild. Framing of the new structure is completed in November 2019.

Fuel sales to snowmobilers resume, but the lodge itself still is undergoing reconstruction in March 2021. A lodge representative says in a telephone interview that the owners have obtained all the permits they need and hope to finish rebuilding and to be fully back in business by the winter of 2021-2022.

## March 18, 1854
### Androscoggin County Becomes Maine's 14th County

Androscoggin County, Maine's fourteenth county, is formed from parts of Cumberland, Oxford, Kennebec and Lincoln counties.

The inland county, Maine's second-smallest in area after Sagadahoc, is the location of Maine's second-largest city, Lewiston. Like neighboring Kennebec County, Androscoggin County envelops only a small portion of the river after which it is named.

Androscoggin County is the home of Bates College, in Lewiston; Central Maine Community College, in Auburn; the annual Moxie Festival, in Lisbon; and the 2,675-acre Androscoggin Riverlands State Park, in Turner and Leeds.

The county seat is Auburn. The U.S. Census lists the county's 2010 population as 107,702.

## March 18, 1989
### USS *Philippine Sea* Commissioned

The USS *Philippine Sea*, a Flight II Ticonderoga-class guided-missile cruiser manufactured by Bath Iron Works, is commissioned in Portland.

The ship later takes part in 1999 in supporting NATO Operation Allied Force by launching Tomahawk cruise missiles against military targets in the former Yugoslavia. After the September 11, 2001, attacks on New York City and Washington, D.C., the vessel launches missiles that year against

Cornelia "Fly Rod" Crosby

al-Qaida and Taliban military sites in Afghanistan.

The cremated remains of Neil Armstrong, the first person to walk on the moon, are buried at sea from the ship on September 14, 2012. Armstrong was a Navy veteran.

March 19, 1897

**Hunting Guides Must Be Registered; 'Fly Rod' Crosby First in Line**

The Maine Legislature passes a law that requires hunting guides to register with the state. The first person to sign up is Cornelia "Fly Rod" Crosby (1854-

1946), a woman whose promotional activities and nationally circulated hunting and fishing stories of the Rangeley Lake area attract thousands of visitors to the Maine woods.

Crosby, who was six feet tall, left her job in a bank to work as a housekeeper in Rangeley hotels, where she befriended local guides. After a friend gave her a five-ounce rod in 1886, she became so skilled at fly-fishing that she once landed two hundred trout in a single day.

She also learned other ways to market the state to tourists. She organized a hunting display at the first annual Sportsmen's Show at Madison Square Garden in New York, appearing there holding a rifle and wearing a doeskin skirt. She became friends with famed sharpshooter Annie Oakley.

A knee injury in 1899 puts an end to her mobility, but she continues to write her columns.

## March 20, 1838
### Franklin Becomes Maine's 11th County

Franklin County, Maine's eleventh county, is formed from parts of Cumberland, Kennebec, and Somerset counties.

The northwestern county,

named for Benjamin Franklin, is Maine's second-least-populous county and one of its most mountainous. In 2010, the population is 30,768. The county seat is Farmington. It is the location of the Sugarloaf skiing complex.

## March 20, 1852
### *Uncle Tom's Cabin* Published

J.P. Jewett, a Boston publisher, begins its initial press run of a two-volume hard-bound edition of Harriet Beecher Stowe's anti-slavery novel *Uncle Tom's Cabin; or, Life Among the Lowly*.

Stowe wrote most of the book at her home in Brunswick, where she lived with her husband, Calvin, a Bowdoin College religion professor.

*Uncle Tom's Cabin*, which began appearing in print in serialized form the previous June in *The National Era*, a Washington, D.C.-based newspaper advocating the abolition of slavery, sells three hundred thousand copies in its first year and becomes what is widely regarded as the most popular novel of the nineteenth century. The story is reprinted in dozens of languages and becomes the inspiration for many stage renditions.

Stowe's tale uses the story of one

old slave to describe the cruelty of slave overseers, the terror experienced by escapees fleeing from slave hunters, and slave families ripped apart when they are sold to different owners. Stowe heard such stories from escaped slaves who had taken refuge in her parents' home in Ohio.

Stowe labored at the novel while her husband was away on business in Ohio, during a winter when her house was so drafty and cold that pails of water sometimes froze indoors, and while she was taking care of their seven children alone. She eventually ran out of regular paper and began writing parts of it on scraps of brown wrapping paper.

In November 1862, Stowe travels in Washington, D.C., in the midst of the Civil War and meets President Abraham Lincoln, only about six weeks before his Emancipation Proclamation takes effect, declaring all slaves in the Confederate States to be free. According to one of Stowe's biographers, Lincoln greets Stowe by saying, "So you're the little woman who wrote the book that made this great war." Other sources claim he said something similar to that. Lincoln scholars note that the president's supposed utterance is

part of Stowe family lore, however, and they have been unable to find any record that the president made such a statement. Even so, the anecdote has become, although with lesser prominence, as firmly entrenched in the American mythos as the story of George Washington admitting having chopped down a cherry tree.

In 1865, after the Confederacy is vanquished, the Thirteenth Amendment to the U.S. Constitution abolishes slavery everywhere in the United States.

## March 21, 2015
### Ski Lift Accident at Sugarloaf Injures 7

A ski lift at the Sugarloaf ski resort in Carrabassett Valley stops and rolls backward, injuring seven adults, four of whom require hospital treatment. The incident leaves about two hundred skiers and snowboarders dangling for an hour and a half on the lift.

On June 25, Sugarloaf announces $1.3 million in upgrades to lift safety, including a new Doppelmayr drive terminal for the one involved in the rollback.

It is the second such incident there within five years. On December 29, 2010, the Spillway East double chairlift derailed from a 30-foot-tall tower at Sugarloaf and five chairs dropped to the ground, causing eight people to be sent to hospitals.

The 35-year-old lift is required to undergo a comprehensive safety test every seven years. At the time of the 2010 accident, the seven-year deadline had passed a few weeks earlier without such a test, although the state tramway board's chief inspector had approved the test delay. The last legal claim stemming from that accident is settled in 2015.

The ski resort's owner, CNL Lifestyle Properties Inc., sells the resort to New York hedge fund manager Och-Ziff Capital Management in 2016. Och-Ziff sells it in 2018 to Michigan-based Boyne Resorts, which had managed it previously. New plans for capital improvements are announced in 2019.

March 22, 1848
### Doctor Convicted of Murder After Performing Victim's Autopsy

Dr. Valorus Perry Coolidge, of Waterville, is convicted of murder and is sentenced to hang for having killed Edward Mathews on the night of September 30, 1847. In Waterville, Coolidge killed Mathews in order to rob him of about $1,500 that Mathews had just withdrawn from a local bank to lend it to the debt-ridden Coolidge.

The case became a regional sensation because after Mathews' body was found, Coolidge was one of four people who took part in an October 1 autopsy on the body, and he tried during that procedure to cover up evidence of his crime.

Coolidge told his medical assistant, Thomas Flint, about Mathews' death but misrepresented the details, claiming that Mathews had died unexpectedly of natural causes. Flint remained silent until a second examination of Mathews' body, held October 3 without Coolidge present, revealed a fatal concentration of prussic acid in the victim.

After Flint's testimony for the prosecution, Coolidge is convicted. A long, melodramatic ballad titled "The Waterville Tragedy; or, Death of Edward Mathews by Dr. Valorus P. Coolidge" is posted on broadsides in public places.

Coolidge's sentence soon is reduced to life in prison, but then the Maine State Prison warden finds letters in which Coolidge conspired with an accomplice to murder Flint, again using prussic acid, and to make Flint's death look like a suicide.

Shortly afterward, prison officials report finding Coolidge dead in his prison cell. His brother claims the body but insists it is not that of Coolidge, fueling decades of public speculation about what happened to him.

## March 22, 1947
### Tiny Patten Academy's Eagles Shock Boston Latin, Claim New England Championship

The nine-member Patten Academy Eagles boys high school basketball team wins the unofficial New England Class B championship at the Boston Garden, beating Boston Latin in overtime, 35-32. The Patten school has eighty-eight students, including just twenty-nine boys; Boston Latin has about 1,800 students.

The Eagles earlier won the Maine state finals against Gould Academy of Bethel, also by three points—36-33. Before that, they edged out Fairfield's Lawrence High School, 43-42, to win the Eastern Maine Class B crown.

The 1946-47 Patten team is inducted into the Maine Basketball Hall of Fame in 2016, with a few of the surviving players attending the induction ceremony.

## March 23, 1838
### Piscataquis, Home of Katahdin, Becomes Maine's 12th County

Piscataquis County, Maine's twelfth county, is formed from parts of Penobscot and Somerset counties. The county is the location of Moosehead Lake, the state's largest lake; and Mount Katahdin, the state's highest mountain.

With a population of about 16,800 in 2018, it also is Maine's least populous county. The number of residents in 2018 is about the same that it was in 1900 and only about 30 percent greater than it was in 1840. The county seat is Dover-Foxcroft. The county's 2010 population was 17,535.

## March 23, 1870
### Thomas Begins Task of Recruiting Swedes to Settle New Sweden

The Maine Legislature appoints William Widgery Thomas Jr., of Portland, to be Maine's immigration commissioner.

Thomas quickly leaves for Sweden, where he lived for three years earlier, and recruits fifty-one immigrants to become the first European residents of a new settlement in Maine's far north.

The colony consists of twenty-two men, eleven women, and eighteen children. All the men are farmers, and some are skilled in carpentry and other trades. The Swedes settle in what becomes known as the town of New Sweden and eventually expand into the adjacent towns of New Stockholm, Perham, Westmanland, and Woodland.

In an 1895 address on the occasion of the colony's twenty-fifth anniversary, Thomas recalls that Maine entrepreneurs had tried once before, in 1864, to plant a Swedish colony in Maine. After they recruited about three hundred laborers and spent thousands of dollars to fund the immigrants' passage across the Atlantic, he said, those Swedes landed at Quebec and simply disappeared. Not one ever made it to Maine.

To prevent a second such failure, Thomas secures a state promise of land, then goes to Sweden in 1870 and sets up a recruitment office in the city of Gothenburg. Thomas travels all over the country to find candidates, who are required to submit documents testifying about their abilities and character.

On June 25, forty days after his arrival, he and the colonists leave Gothenburg on a steamer bound for England. In Hull, they take a train to Liverpool, then on July 2 board the steamship *City of Antwerp*, heading for Canada. The ship arrives in Halifax, Nova Scotia, where, barred from using any of the city's hotels and boarding houses, they spend the night in a warehouse. From there, they go to Saint John, New Brunswick, and board two flatboats to travel up the Saint John River.

Near Florenceville, one of the children, a 9-month-old baby girl, dies. The parents insist on taking their daughter's body to their new home.

The party reaches Tobique Landing on July 21, spends the night in a barn, and proceeds overland the next day across the US border to Fort Fairfield for a round of welcoming speeches by local dignitaries. After stopping for the night in Caribou, they arrive in the place that Thomas christens "New Sweden."

"All around us was an unbroken wilderness. A gigantic forest covered all the land, stretching away over hill and dale as far as the eye could reach," Thomas recalls twenty-five years later. Even so, the colony thrives.

Today, while the Swedes' descendants are thoroughly assimilated as

Americans, evidence of Swedish culture persists in New Sweden and its surrounding towns.

## March 24, 1958
### Sculptor Louise Nevelson Appears on Cover of *Life*

*Life* magazine's cover depicts sculptor Louise Nevelson (1899-1988) wearing a witch's hat and crouching behind one of her creations.

The magazine's cover article reveals to the nation Nevelson's "Moon Garden + One" exhibition at the Grand Central Moderns gallery in New York, which opened in January that year and elevates Nevelson, who grew up in Rockland, from the ranks of merely successful sculptors to a major innovative force in the art world.

The sculptor's exhibition work consists of 116 free-standing box-like platforms supporting wooden collages. Each box contains black-stained wood scraps that Nevelson collected in a variety of locations, including driftwood from the coast of Maine. The exhibition, shown in a darkened space, nearly envelops gallery visitors. Art critics' reactions vary, but they agree on the universally striking effect it has on those who see it.

The following December, Nevelson's similarly enveloping "Dawn's Wedding Feast" appears at the Museum of Modern Art, but it is all white. The change reflects Nevelson's lifelong habit of continually gravitating toward different styles, approaches and art media.

Nevelson, born in what is now the city of Kyiv, Ukraine, arrived in Rockland at the age of 6. As the daughter of Jewish immigrants, she spoke Yiddish at home and felt like an outsider in the community. She graduated from Rockland High School, having flourished in art classes and become convinced of her own talent. A short marriage to a rich New York City ship owner proved to be her admission ticket to the Big Apple's art world. Once there, she launched a career so diverse and attention-grabbing that she was elected at 80 to the American Academy of Arts and Letters.

She had a penchant for wearing stylishly flamboyant clothes, even before she became successful. In the 1930s and 1940s she became known as "The Hat" because of the many colorful hats she wore. Her biographer Laurie Wilson writes about Nevelson that "even when she was broke, she managed to look like a million dollars."

Her work is exhibited today in many major museums and galleries, including the Whitney Museum of American Art and the Museum of Modern Art, both in New York; and the Farnsworth Art Museum in Rockland.

Visitors to New York also can see some of her sculptures at Louise Nevelson Plaza, a triangular skyscraper-enveloped plot in the city's financial district that the city named in her honor in 1978 and that she designed.

## March 25, 1937
### More Than 4,000 Shoe Workers Strike Unsuccessfully

Lewiston and Auburn shoe workers initiate a strike that by early April involves more than four thousand workers. The strike draws widespread attention but ends three months later in failure.

In Maine, where many shoe manufacturers set up shop to flee the unions' organizing power in Massachusetts, shoemaking is concentrated largely in Lewiston and Auburn. Nineteen factories in the adjoining cities employ nearly six thousand workers.

Having conducted a failed strike in 1932, the cities' shoe workers sought help in 1937 from the Congress of Industrial Organizations (which today forms part of the AFL-CIO). CIO representatives promptly told them they were making less money than laborers with equivalent jobs in Massachusetts.

CIO organizer Powers Hapgood (1899-1949), a Harvard graduate, arrived on March 12 to coordinate the strike. A week later, the union petitioned the shoe manufacturers' association for recognition. The association didn't respond; that prompted the strike.

"For more than three months, thousands of shoe workers, many of them women and most of French-Canadian descent, battled manufacturers, courts, police, the press, and the Catholic Church in their quest for union recognition," writes Robert Bussell in his biography of Hapgood.

The workers demand higher pay, a shorter workweek, better employment conditions, and union representation. By early April, four thousand to five thousand workers are absent from their jobs.

About one thousand marching strikers defy a court injunction

April 21 by staging a march across a bridge linking the two cities and hoisting Hapgood on their shoulders. When a fight erupts between them and the police, Gov. Lewis Barrows calls in the Maine Army National Guard. On May 6, a judge finds Hapgood and seven other strike leaders in contempt of the injunction and sentences them to six-month prison terms.

Losing money and worker support and faced with unyielding opposition from the manufacturers, Hapgood and the union leadership call an end to the strike on June 28. The Maine Supreme Judicial Court overturns the union organizers' contempt convictions, and they are released.

One significant thing changes during the 1934 strike, according to cultural historian Mark Paul Richard.

"What distinguishes this strike from the others in the 1930s, something that other accounts have not emphasized," he writes in a 2008 book on French-Canadian culture in the United States, "is that some Franco-Americans became openly critical of their clergy." In the early stage of the strike, the strikers ignore parish priests who urge them to go back to work.

As for Hapgood, he acknowledges the union's mistakes in Maine and learns from them. He becomes a key figure in the CIO hierarchy, coordinating its national efforts to organize workers.

## March 26, 2009
### 22-year-old Old Town Man Convicted of Triple Homicide

Old Town resident Matthew Cushing, 22, is sentenced to life in prison for having stabbed his mother, his stepfather, and his half brother to death at their home in Old Orchard Beach and for having set their house on fire to cover his tracks. The court sentences him to three life terms for the murder convictions. He also is found guilty of arson.

Cushing offers no explanation for the February 20, 2008, crimes but acknowledges his guilt. Assistant Attorney General Lisa Marchese says he killed his family members because his mother, Carol Bolduc, and his stepfather, Christopher Bolduc, both 42 years old, were getting a divorce and Cushing didn't think his mother could support herself.

Marchese says Cushing's preparation and the timeline of events shows premeditation of each crime: Cushing traveled from his Old Town apartment carrying a stun gun and a knife, and he had plenty of time between the murders to consider stopping. He also used the internet to research ways to kill people.

## March 27, 1942
### Navy Task Force Commander Drowns After Armada Leaves Maine

A day after setting off eastward from Casco Bay, the US Navy's Task Force 39 plows through a heavy sea off Nova Scotia in the North Atlantic, heading for Scotland's Orkney Islands to reinforce the Home Guard while the British navy participates in a World War II invasion of Madagascar, then under the control of Vichy France, which is collaborating with Germany.

The thirteen-ship American task force's newly appointed commander is Rear Adm. John W. Wilcox Jr., whose flagship is the USS *Washington*.

At 10:31 a.m. the *Washington* reports seeing a man overboard. The USS *Tuscaloosa* spots a man in the water and moves aside to avoid running him down. The task force initiates a search-and-rescue operation. Officers conclude that Wilcox himself is the man in the water.

The aircraft carrier USS *Wasp*

launches four SB2U-2 Vindicator dive bombers to help look for the admiral. One of the planes crashes astern of the *Wasp*, killing both crew members.

Someone on the USS *Livermore* sees Wilcox's body floating face-down about an hour and twenty minutes after he went overboard, but rough weather prevents its recovery.

Wilcox, a Georgia native, had turned 60 five days earlier. He received the Navy Cross for his service in World War I and was the executive officer on a troop ship returning soldiers to the United States in 1919. Between the wars, he was on the US Naval Academy's teaching staff and, later, was acting president of the Naval War College in Newport, Rhode Island.

## March 27, 1980
### Rotten Potatoes
### Block Nine Border Crossings

Frustrated with US-Canada trade policies and low potato prices, Maine farmers dump rotting potatoes at nine border crossing points, preventing the transfer of goods between the two countries. The blockades and a standoff with police last two days.

The blockades are removed

when federal officials fly from Washington and meet with the farmers to talk about solutions.

The following November, some farmers say nothing was accomplished and the problem of New Brunswick farms exporting potatoes to the United States at unfairly low prices has gotten even worse.

## March 28, 2006
### Former US Defense Secretary 'Cap' Weinberger Dies in Bangor

Caspar Weinberger, US secretary of defense for seven years under President Ronald Reagan, dies at age 88 at Eastern Maine Medical Center in Bangor from pneumonia complications.

In the Reagan administration, Weinberger took the lead in directing a rollback strategy against Soviet communism. He was indicted in the Iran-Contra scandal, involving a violation of an embargo on weapons sales to Iran; but President George H.W. Bush pardoned him in December 1992, just before Bush left office. Weinberger maintained his innocence.

Weinberger also served in the administrations of President Richard Nixon and President Gerald Ford. In his 2001 memoir, Weinberger summed up his worldview by writing, "Those

who know anything about me know that I believe that lasting peace can be achieved only by American power and the will to use that power."

Weinberger was living on Mount Desert Island in retirement. His wife, the former June Dalton, grew up near where the Weinbergers bought their Mount Desert Island home in 1977.

## March 29, 1602
### *Concord* Anchors in York Harbor, Reignites Interest in New England Settlement

The *Concord*, a small vessel called a bark, sails from Falmouth, England, to establish a colony in North America. On May 14, five years before the establishment of the permanent English colony at Jamestown, Virginia, it anchors in what is now York Harbor after cruising along Maine's coast from Cape Elizabeth.

The ship, under Capt. Bartholomew Gosnold, sails the next day into what now is Provincetown Harbor. Gosnold names Cape Cod. The expedition later establishes a small post at what is now Cuttyhunk Island in Massachusetts, intending to leave some crewmen behind to found a colony; but the crewmen return with the ship to England when it becomes apparent that Bartholomew Gilbert, a co-captain of the ship, stocked only six weeks' worth of provisions for the would-be colonists.

While its colonizing goal remains unfulfilled, the trip renews English interest in the region, especially because of the bounty of fish observed off the New England coast.

## March 30, 1937
### 'State of Maine Song' Becomes Official State Song

The Maine Legislature adopts Roger Vinton Snow's "State of Maine Song" as the official state song.

Snow (1890-1953), a probate and corporate lawyer and frequent moderator of Falmouth town meetings, submitted the song for a 1931 competition sponsored by the Maine Publicity Bureau, and it won. Cressey and Allen, of Portland, published the sheet music in 1932. Snow's son, Roger Jr., later serves as a Republican in the Maine Senate, becoming chairman of the Education Committee.

The son recalls in a 1999 interview with Bates College researchers that another legislator, apparently dissatisfied with "The State of Maine Song," filed a bill to have it replaced. When a Democratic friend in the House, Herbert Payson, called it to his attention, Snow said he couldn't go to the bill's hearing because of a schedule conflict, and he asked Payson to attend.

"And he went and got up and said, 'Do you know that the father of the chairman of the Education Committee wrote this song?' And the sponsor dropped his bill. That was all that was necessary, an exercise of power," Snow says.

The tune remains Maine's official state song.

## March 30, 1999
### Skowhegan State Fair Grandstand Destroyed by Fire

Fire destroys the Skowhegan State Fair grandstand and nearby Constitution Hall, causing about $2 million worth of damage. The blaze takes fifteen hours to put out.

The cause is determined to be arson. Charles D. Miles confesses to the act two days later but is found not criminally responsible and is committed to Riverview Psychiatric Center in Augusta.

He later is sent to prison for damaging hospital property and threatening to harm the staff there.

A new Skowhegan grandstand

is built during the summer of 1999 and completed in time for that year's fair.

The first Skowhegan fair was held in January 1819 under the auspices of what then was called the Somerset Central Agricultural Society. The group changed its name to the Skowhegan State Fair in 1942.

## March 31, 1907
### West Gardiner Native Resigns From Panama Canal Project

An irritated US President Theodore Roosevelt reluctantly accepts the resignation of West Gardiner native John Frank Stevens (1853-1943) as chief engineer on one of the twentieth century's most challenging engineering projects—construction of the Panama Canal.

Stevens, who came on board when the project already was underway and plagued with problems, engineered major construction solutions and stopped work until a malaria epidemic among canal workers was brought under control.

Stevens' successor, US Army Lt. Col. George Washington Goethals, lauds Stevens as a genius and says the canal will be his monument. The canal opens to ship traffic on August 15, 1914.

Earlier in his career, Stevens, a graduate of Farmington Normal School (now the University of Maine at Farmington), was in charge of several railroad construction projects in the American and Canadian West. In the dead of winter, he personally found the Marias Pass through the Continental Divide in Montana; and he located what later was named Stevens Pass, in his honor, in the Cascade Mountains of Washington state.

—30—

# APRIL

**April 1, 1968**
**Dow Air Force Base Shuts Down After 27 Years**

Dow Air Force Base in Bangor officially closes. The city of Bangor obtains the airfield and reopens it the following year as Bangor International Airport.

Back in 1940, the city allocated $75,000 for development of the base. The Maine Military Defense Commission funded the purchase of the base's land. With construction of what then was called Bangor Army Air Field 90 percent complete and US participation in World War II looming, Army units began to occupy the base on April 19, 1941. (The US Air Force became a separate branch of the military in 1947.) The first military plane, an A-17 attack aircraft, arrived in May.

The installation's name was changed to Dow Air Field in 1942 to honor Army 2nd Lt. James Dow, an Oakfield native who died in a 1940 training accident in New York that killed twelve people.

Nearly one hundred thousand air combat crew members passed through Dow on their way to or returning from war assignments during World War II. As the war wound down, the military considered closing the base as early as 1944, but instead made it an Air Transport Command cargo service site.

A new plan to close the base emerged in 1950. Bangor moved its airport from Old Town to the base that year.

The military reactivated the site in 1951 as Dow Air Force Base, and the National Guard's 132nd Fighter Wing moved in.

President Dwight Eisenhower visited the base on June 15, 1955, and gave a brief speech, around the time construction of a base expansion took place.

To accommodate B-52 bombers, the longest runway east of the Mississippi River was built at Dow in 1958.

In 1964, the Air Force announced a plan to deactivate a Bomarc missile installation on the base, essentially meaning the base would close. The city began planning for the use of more than one hundred buildings there. Easy access to Interstate 95 beginning in the mid-1950s made locating a business there more appealing.

Today the Maine Air National Guard's 101st Air Refueling Wing, which flies KC-135 tankers, is located at the airport.

## April 1, 1980
### Maine Population Passes 1 Million Mark

The US Census conducted on this date shows that Maine's population exceeds one million for the first time. The 1.12 million inhabitants recorded represent a 13.4 percent increase in population since 1970, a greater increase than in any other ten-year period since 1850.

## April 1, 1987
### Heavy Rain Causes Severe Flooding; Fort Halifax Washed Away

Two heavy rainstorms and a quickly melting snowpack cause a regional flood in northern New England.

The damage from the first storm, estimated at more than $74.5 million, is most severe in the Kennebec River Valley, where Winslow's historic Fort Halifax blockhouse is washed down the river. A coal shed in Gardiner also floats away. Downtown Hallowell's streets are underwater,

and the river fills the first floors of buildings there. The water crests in Augusta at seventeen feet above flood stage.

The Androscoggin, Penobscot and Saco rivers also flood badly. Gov. John McKernan signs a disaster declaration covering every Maine county except Aroostook and Washington. It is the most severe flood in the state's history.

## April 1, 2013
### Down East Books Sold to Maryland-based Publisher

Down East Books, one of the largest book publishers based in Maine, is sold to Rowman & Littlefield, of Maryland. Owner Down East Enterprise sells the book business but retains the iconic publication Down East magazine, which continues to be published in Rockport.

The purchase also involves Shooting Sports Press, Fly Rod & Reel Books, and Countrysport Press. Ultimately, Rowman & Littlefield will lay off or move out of Maine all Down East Books employees except one. Down East Books is now an imprint of Globe Pequot Press of Connecticut, which is also owned by Rowman & Littlefield.

## April 2, 1865
### Hyde Leads Assault on Confederate Defenses at Petersburg

Union Army Col. Thomas W. Hyde (1841-1899), of Bath, leads an assault force that breaks through the defenses at Petersburg, Virginia, during the Civil War's Third Battle of Petersburg.

This successful gambit, following ten months of a frustratingly ineffective Union siege, prompts the Confederacy to abandon its capital at nearby Richmond, Virginia.

One week later, Confederate Gen. Robert E. Lee surrenders his Army of Northern Virginia to Lt. Gen. Ulysses S. Grant at Appomattox Court House.

Nearly two decades later, in October 1884, Hyde founds Bath Iron Works in his hometown.

## April 2, 1907
### Four-Masted Bark SV *Arthur Sewall* Disappears

The four-masted steel bark SV *Arthur Sewall*, built at the Arthur Sewall & Co. shipyard in Bath and launched there in 1899, leaves the Delaware Breakwater with a cargo of 4,900 tons of coal, bound for Seattle via Cape Horn, at the southern tip of South America.

The ship never is heard from again. Lloyd's Register posts it as missing on February 5, 1908.

## April 2, 1935
### Maine Poet's Pulitzer-Winning *Strange Holiness* Published

The Macmillan company publishes Brunswick native Robert P. Tristram Coffin's (1892-1955) book of poetry *Strange Holiness.* The book wins the 1936 Pulitzer Prize for poetry.

Coffin, a Bowdoin College graduate, Rhodes scholar and longtime Bowdoin professor of English, wrote dozens of fiction and nonfiction books, and he illustrated many of them. His nonfiction books include *Mainstays of Maine, Maine Ballads,* and *Kennebec: Cradle of Americans.*

He was the poetry editor at *Yankee* magazine.

## April 3, 1993
### Black Bears Hockey Team Wins First National Championship

The University of Maine men's hockey team, under the leadership of coach Shawn Walsh, wins the NCAA Division I Men's Ice Hockey Tournament in Milwaukee, defeating Lake Superior State University.

It is the team's first national title. Maine was down 4-2 after

Photo by Herb Swanson; courtesy Lewiston Sun Journal

Maine players celebrate winning the NCAA Division I hockey championship, the school's second, in 1999.

two periods in the championship game, but Maine's all-time leading scorer Jim Montgomery, who later will have a twelve-year playing career in the National Hockey League, scores a hat trick in the third period to put Maine ahead 5-4, the final score.

The team's members also include future NHL star and 2017 Hockey Hall of Fame inductee Paul Kariya, who notches an assist on each of Montgomery's three goals; and Garth Snowe, who also plays twelve years in the NHL.

UMaine ended the season with a 22-1-1 record in conference play and 42-1-2 overall.

The team wins a second national tournament championship under coach Walsh on the same date in 1999 in Anaheim, California, defeating the University of New Hampshire 3-2 in overtime in the Frozen Four final.

April 4, 1802
**Dorothea Dix, Champion for Mentally Ill, Born in Hampden**

Dorothea Dix, who becomes

Dorothea Dix

renowned nationwide as a reformer of treatment of the mentally ill and champion of their rights, is born in Hampden.

Teaching Sunday school lessons in the Cambridge House of Corrections in Massachusetts reveals to Dix the horrific conditions that people living in such places endure. She conducts an investigation from 1841 to 1843 of jails, plague houses and places where the mentally ill are confined. Then she publishes a report about them and petitions the Massachusetts Legislature for reform on behalf of patients who are confined in cages, closets, cellars, stalls, and pens, sometimes chained naked and beaten with whips and rods.

In the years from 1845 to 1852, she establishes or rebuilds psychiatric hospitals in Alabama, Maine, Maryland, Massachusetts, New Jersey, North Carolina, and South Carolina.

In the mid-1850s, on an extended tour of Europe, she visits facilities for the mentally ill in several countries and prompts a British government investigation of conditions of their treatment in the British Empire.

When the US Civil War breaks out in 1861, President Abraham Lincoln makes Dix superintendent of war nurses. She holds that post until the end of the war, then retires to the New Jersey State Insane Hospital, where she resides until her death in 1887.

A state hospital for the mentally ill in Bangor is named in her honor.

## April 4, 1854
### Maine Creates Sagadahoc County, State's Smallest by Area

Sagadahoc County becomes Maine's fifteenth county, formed from part of Lincoln County only seventeen days after neighboring Androscoggin County is established.

The southern part of the mid-coastal county consists chiefly of a complicated maze of peninsulas, coves, harbors, and inlets on the Atlantic Ocean.

In the north, the county's centerpiece is the freshwater yet tidal Merrymeeting Bay, which is at the confluence of the Abagadasset, Androscoggin, Cathance, Eastern, Kennebec, and Muddy rivers, as well as various brooks and streams.

The city of Bath is Sagadahoc County's seat. At 257 square miles, the county is Maine's smallest in area. With 35,293 residents in 2010, it is the fifth-smallest in population.

Of its nine towns, one city and one unorganized territory, only the town of Bowdoin has no frontage on either the Atlantic Ocean, Merrymeeting Bay, or the tidal section of the lower Kennebec River.

The county is the location of Bath Iron Works, the Swan Island Wildlife Management Area, and Popham Beach and Reid state parks.

April 4, 2013
**Elusive 'North Pond Hermit' Arrested in Rome**

Game warden Sgt. Terry Hughes apprehends Christopher Knight, 47, while Knight is breaking into the Pine Tree Camp in the town of Rome.

The news media later dub Knight "the North Pond Hermit" because of his claim to have entered the woods at the age of 20 in the North Pond area of the Belgrade Lakes and lived there almost without interruption for twenty-seven years.

Authorities find the makeshift camp where he has been living. They conclude that while in the woods, Knight survived by stealing food and supplies during about a thousand burglaries he committed at local summer residences and other properties.

The arrest confirms rumors that circulated for decades about a pilfering hermit living in the area of North Pond, which is in Belgrade, Rome, and Smithfield.

It also triggers a burst of inquiries from around the country, including a wedding proposal from the West Coast, as well as at least two bluegrass-style songs written as tributes to Knight's exploits.

Knight pleads guilty in August to seven burglaries and six thefts in two counties. He is sentenced to seven months in jail and payment of $2,000 of restitution, plus three years of probation.

April 5, 1974
**Horror Unleashed: Stephen King's Novel *Carrie* Published**

Horror writer Stephen King's novel *Carrie* is published. It is King's fourth novel but the first to appear in print. The book and a subsequent movie of the same name make King world-famous.

King was born in Portland and raised mostly in Durham, although he also spent part of his childhood in Indiana and Connecticut. His early writing includes a weekly column for the Maine Campus, the newspaper of the University of Maine, where he graduated in 1970 with a Bachelor of Arts degree in English; and "The Glass Floor," a short story that was the first one sold for publication, to *Startling Mystery Stories* magazine, in 1967.

He met his wife, Tabitha, in UMaine's Raymond H. Fogler Library, where they both worked as undergraduates.

King teaches at Hampden Academy in Hampden until it becomes clear that his income from the anticipated sales of *Carrie* will allow him to work full time as a writer.

A torrent of commercially successful works follows, including the novels *The Shining, Misery, It, The Green Mile, Dolores Claiborne* and *Under the Dome*; and the novella *Rita Hayworth and the Shawshank Redemption*. Many of them are outside the horror genre. Sales of his books, often set in a fictional Maine town, run into the hundreds of millions. Many of them are adapted for film or TV, including *Carrie*, which inspires three movies and a sequel; and *The Shawshank Redemption*, which *USA Today* listed in 2017 as one of the fifty best films of all time, and which has appeared on many other such lists.

His total novel count by early 2020 is eighty-three, including seven written under a pseudonym, Richard Bachman.

"He may write too much, but his best work endures," writes BBC culture reporter Jane Ciabattari in 2014. "He may be, at times, sophomoric, but he also can be superbly Gothic."

King and his wife live in Bangor and Center Lovell during the warmer months and in Florida during the winter.

## April 6, 1807
### Maine's Drive for Statehood Stalled by Referendum Loss

Advocates of the District of Maine's separation from Massachusetts suffer their worst referendum defeat—9,404-3,370. Of the district's 150 towns, most voters in one hundred of them oppose separation. The momentum for Maine statehood is at a low ebb, but that will change during and after the War of 1812.

## April 6, 1935
### Alna's Edwin Arlington Robinson, Three-time Winner of Pulitzer Prize, Dies of Cancer

Edwin Arlington Robinson, who won the Pulitzer Prize for Poetry three times, dies of cancer in New York City. He is 65.

Robinson was born in 1869 in Alna's Head Tide village and spent most of his childhood in Gardiner.

His biographer, Scott Donaldson, notes that Robinson grew up in the heyday of the so-called "Fireside Poets" such as Henry Wadsworth Longfellow, James Russell Lowell, and William Cullen Bryant, but he shunned that writing tradition.

"He was the first of our poets to write about ordinary people and events," Donaldson writes. "No one before his time would have thought it possible to write sonnets about an honest butcher consumed by grief, about a miser with 'eyes like little dollars in the dark,' about ancient clerks in a dry goods store measuring out their days like bolts of cloth."

As a young man in Gardiner, Robinson self-published his first volume of poetry, *The Torrent and the Night Before*, in 1896. Casting a pall over the whole enterprise, his mother died a few days before the printed copies arrived, and she never got to see it.

Robinson became friends with and was inspired by prolific local author Laura Richards, who was nearly twenty years his senior—and who also won a Pulitzer. He admired many other hardworking people in the small, blue-collar city on the Kennebec River; the "Tilbury Town" of his poems is based on Gardiner. He could not bring himself to live the way they did, however, so when he was about 30, he set off for Boston and New York.

A reticent man who spent a lot of time by himself, he courted women but never married. Though his poetry gained recognition, he lived in poverty as a young man. President Theodore Roosevelt, at the urging of his son Kermit, provided Robinson a civil service job at the New York Customs House so he could earn money but still have enough time to write poetry. However, Robinson suffered in destitution again after the job ended.

When he collected three Pulitzers in the 1920s, success finally lifted him out of his hardscrabble existence. He retained some of his reclusiveness, however. In 1933 he wrote to Richards that he had turned down several honorary degrees and expected "to turn down several more."

Donaldson summarizes Robinson's drive this way: "In the lifelong dedication to poetry, he was only fully alive when he was writing."

Robinson's childhood home on Lincoln Avenue in Gardiner is on the National Register of Historic Places.

## April 7, 2010
## Maine Apologizes for Malaga Island Evictions

Maine's Legislature issues a statement of apology for state officials' forcible eviction a century earlier of a largely interracial group of residents from Malaga Island, in Casco Bay.

The island lies off Phippsburg near the mouth of the New Meadows River. A racially mixed community of squatter fishermen's families lived there. Newspaper stories describing the "degenerate colony" on Malaga began to appear, troubling the wealthy summer residents of nearby mainland communities.

The state began placing some Malaga children in the Maine School for the Feeble-Minded—later known as the Pineland Center—in New Gloucester. Then Sagadahoc County decided that a family named Perry owned the island.

In 1911, Gov. Frederick Plaisted, a Democrat, and his whole Executive Council led an eviction force that removed forty-five people from the island.

"I think the best plan would be to burn down the shacks with all of their filth," Plaisted told a reporter then. "Certainly the conditions there are not credible to our state. We ought not to have such things near our front door."

State authorities kidnapped men, women, and children, separating them and incarcerating many of them in state institutions. Others were released on the mainland, where they lived in poverty.

In 1912, the state bought the island from the Perry family heirs for $400. The remaining residents were told to vacate by July 1. When a state agent visited the island on that date, he found that the residents had removed their buildings. The state dug up the remains of seventeen people from the island's cemetery and reburied them at the New Gloucester property.

Racial prejudice often followed the Malaga descendants, and many of them took pains to hide their origin and deny any connection to the island.

In addition to the Legislature's 2010 action, awareness of the travesty prompts apologies from two Maine governors; and in 2017 the state places a monument to the Malaga residents at Pineland.

## April 8, 1851
### 'Napoleon of Temperance' Elected Portland Mayor

Neal Dow (1804-1897) is elected mayor of Portland. He quickly uses his influence in that position to lobby successfully later that year for a state law generally banning the purchase and consumption of alcoholic beverages, earning Dow the nickname "the Napoleon of Temperance."

The law, which becomes known

nationally as "the Maine Law," provides for the search of places where the presence of alcohol is suspected, for confiscation of alcohol, and for fines and imprisonment for those convicted of trafficking in it.

Born in Portland as the son of Quakers, Dow organized the Maine Temperance Union in 1838. His controversial tenure as mayor lasts seven years.

In the Civil War, Dow is appointed colonel of the 13th Regiment, Maine Volunteers, and promoted to brigadier general in 1862. In the Battle of Port Hudson, he is wounded twice and taken prisoner. He remains captive for a year before being released in a prisoner exchange, and he resigns his commission in poor health in 1864.

Dow runs unsuccessfully for president in 1880 on the Prohibition Party ticket. He receives about 0.1 percent of the vote, winding up in a distant fourth place in the election that sends James Garfield to the White House.

### April 9, 1991
### Louise Dickinson Rich, Who Wrote of Life in Wilderness, Dies

Prolific author Louise Dickinson Rich, who often wrote about Maine, dies at 87 in Bridgewater, Massachusetts.

Rich, a Massachusetts native who worked as a teacher, met Ralph Rich, an engineer, in 1933 on a canoeing trip in the Rangeley area. They married, fled from their workaday world to Maine, and lived in a cabin at Forest Lodge on the Rapid River in Upton, cut off from the modern conveniences of more settled areas, from the late 1930s until Ralph Rich's death in 1945. His wife's success at marketing her writing supported the couple's growing family financially.

Rich described that experience in her best-known book, *We Took to the Woods*, published in 1942. She also wrote historical works and outdoor fiction for young adults, producing a total of twenty-four books and many magazine articles.

She is the subject of a biography by Alice Arlen, published in 2000.

### April 10, 1836
### Sensationalized Murder Sets Template for Tabloid Coverage

The matron in a New York City brothel discovers about three o'clock in the morning that somebody has killed Helen Jewett, a 22-year-old prostitute from Maine, and has set Jewett's bed on fire, partially charring her body.

One of Jewett's regular clients, Richard P. Robinson, later is arrested, tried, and acquitted amid a storm of lurid press reports about the case, which set a template for sensationalistic treatment of future criminal cases.

The case becomes a significant factor in the influence of the *New York Herald*, whose editor, James Gordon Bennett, proclaims Robinson innocent months before the trial begins and a mere two days after thrashing Robinson's reputation soundly in print.

Bennett bases his assertion on secret information gleaned from insiders. Other New York newspapers draw the opposite conclusion about Robinson, also claiming to have insider details. Both sides cite their duty to the public in reporting on the murder investigation.

"Yet for all their invocations of journalistic principle, for all their proclamations of civic duty, these furious editors were making up their stories as they went along," writes ABC News documentary producer Andie Tucker in a 1994 book on the case.

Jewett, whose real name was Dorcas Doyen, was born in Temple, Maine. She worked as a servant in the Augusta home of then-Associate Justice Nathan Weston, of the Maine Supreme Judicial Court, before becoming a prostitute in Portland and, later, New York.

Jewett appears as a character in a few prominent works of fiction and also is the subject of several historical books about the period, including Patricia Cline Cohen's 1998 book *The Murder of Helen Jewett: The Life and Death of a Prostitute in Nineteenth-century New York*.

## April 10, 1963
### USS *Thresher* Collapse Kills All Crew Members, Workers Aboard

The nuclear-powered Navy attack submarine USS *Thresher* (SSN 593), completed in 1960 at Portsmouth Naval Shipyard in Kittery, collapses and sinks during deep-diving tests about two hundred miles off the Massachusetts coast.

The catastrophe kills all 129 of the crew members and shipyard workers who are aboard, making it the world's worst submarine accident in terms of loss of lives.

The *Thresher's* hull collapses in a fraction of a second at a depth of about 2,400 feet. Its remnants are found later on the seabed at a depth of about 8,000 feet.

The disaster prompts changes in submarine design and quality control.

"We have not forgotten the lessons learned. It's a much safer submarine force today," then-Vice Admiral Bruce DeMars, the Navy's chief submarine officer, says in 1988.

The *Thresher* continues to be controversial, however.

After the accident, a Naval Court of Inquiry finds that major flooding probably doomed the vessel, but other experts challenge that conclusion.

Retired Navy Capt. Jim Bryant, who served on three *Thresher*-class submarines and commanded one of them, cites in his recent analysis of the sinking discrepancies between the court's findings and evidence available at the time.

Bryant claims the court finding disregards detailed acoustical data gathered by the Navy's underwater Sound Surveillance System that shows flooding was not occurring in the vessel.

Much of the testimony from the Navy's *Thresher* inquiry remains withheld from the public.

In 2019, fifty-six years after the sinking, Bryant sues the Navy in an effort to get the *Thresher* documents released.

On February 10, 2020, U.S. District Court Judge Trevor McFadden orders the Navy to provide the unclassified portion of its investigation of the sinking. As it releases documents incrementally over the following year, the Navy attributes the sinking to a failed seawater pipe and asserts that it has not covered up the accident.

However, Bryant and other experts say the disclosed files also identify other causes as contributing to the disaster, including malfunctioning ballast tanks, an inadequately trained crew, and overconfidence in the submarine's systems.

## April 10, 2012
### Soldier Loses Limbs, Establishes Foundation for Wounded Vets

An improvised explosive device detonates in Afghanistan, critically wounding US Army Staff Sgt. Travis Mills, of the 82nd Airborne Division, four days before he turns 25.

After amputation of parts of both his arms and both legs, and long treatment at Walter Reed National Military Medical

Center, in Bethesda, Maryland, Mills, together with his wife, Kelsey, establishes the Travis Mills Foundation.

The foundation opens a recreational center for wounded veterans in 2017 at the Maine Chance Lodge, the former Elizabeth Arden estate, in the Kennebec County town of Rome.

Mills also releases a best-selling memoir, *Tough As They Come*, on October 27, 2015.

## April 11, 1955
## Congressman Who Opposed Denying Citizenship to Naturalized Communists Dies

Former US Rep. John Nelson and Colby College trustee dies in Augusta at 80.

While in Congress, Nelson, a Republican, drew notice for refusing to sign a committee report calling for denying citizenship to naturalized communists.

A China native and Colby College and University of Maine School of Law graduate, Nelson worked four years as principal of Waterville High School before being admitted to the bar and practicing law.

He represented Maine's Third Congressional District from 1922 to 1933.

In 1931, Nelson served on a special House panel that conducted an eight-month study of communism in the United States. Most on the panel recommending outlawing the Communist Party, that all noncitizen communists in the US be deported and that no others be allowed to enter the country.

Nelson, while condemning communism, disagreed with his committee colleagues' notion of what to do about it.

"The solution to this problem," he wrote in a committee minority report, according to the *Kennebec Journal*, "lies in the wisdom of our legislators and the unselfishness of our industrialists. In proportion as we work our economic justice here in America and so order our social system that labor shall share in the economic life of the (nation) as fully and fairly and it now shares in its social and political life, in just that proportion will radicalism fail of its own inanition and the threat of communism cease to disturb us."

John Nelson's longtime home on Winthrop Street in Augusta was the nineteenth-century home of another prominent political leader—Lot Morrill (1813-

1883), who was Maine's governor, a US senator from Maine, and US treasury secretary in the Grant administration.

April 11, 2013
### Former UMaine Coach John Winkin Selected for National College Baseball Hall of Fame

Former University of Maine Baseball Coach John Winkin, who won 1,043 games at three colleges and led the University of Maine to the College World Series six times, is announced as a member of the National College Baseball Hall of Fame class of 2013.

Winkin (1919-2014), who played baseball at Duke University, coached Colby College from 1954 to 1974, the University of Maine from 1975 to 1996, and Husson University from 1997 to 2008. During his twenty-two years at the University of Maine, he compiled a record of 642-430-3 and took six teams to the College World Series, finishing third in the nation twice.

In addition to his coaching career, Winkin was also a lieutenant commander in the US Navy during World War II, was a founding editor of *Sport* magazine, and hosted the first Major League Baseball pre-game show

with Mel Allen and Curt Gowdy.

During World War II, 21-year-old Winkin was a crewman aboard the destroyer the USS *McCall*, which was assigned to protect the aircraft carrier USS *Enterprise*. Planes from the *Enterprise* had flown Marines to Wake Island and on the night of December 6, the aircraft carrier and its fleet of destroyers and cruisers were returning to Pearl Harbor, but they were delayed by a violent storm at sea and hadn't quite yet made Pearl on December 7, the morning of the Japanese attack.

"If it wasn't for the storm, we would have been docked right next to the battleship *Arizona* that morning," Winkin told the *Bangor Daily News*.

Instead, Winkin witnessed the Japanese air attack from a short distance away. "We were at the entrance of the channel leading to Pearl Harbor," Winkin said. "It was a gruesome sight. Seeing all those ships burning with all the men trapped inside them."

April 12, 1865
### Maine War Hero Chamberlain Witnesses Lee's Surrender of Troops at Appomattox

Following a series of skirmishes and battles from Petersburg west across Virginia, on Palm Sunday, April 9, Gen. Robert E. Lee surrenders his Army of Northern Virginia to Lt. Gen. Ulysses S. Grant, leader of the Union Army. Confederate troops farther south hold out for a short time, but in reality the Civil War is over. The Confederacy is dead.

A formal surrender comes three days later when Maj. Gen. John B. Gordon leads 20,000 Confederate troops to Union lines to stack arms and battle flags.

Grant chooses Brevet Maj. Gen. Joshua Lawrence Chamberlain, of Maine, to accept the formal surrender. The stately and eloquent Chamberlain had risen from college professor to war hero for his defense of Little Round Top at Gettsyburg, Pennsylvania and actions at other battles.

Chamberlain, who was wounded in combat twice, including a wound during the Richmond-Petersburg Campaign that was thought to be fatal, was deeply honored by Grant's choice. Chamberlain takes the proceedings seriously, understanding the gravity of the event and trying to strike a balance between victory and defeat and create the best atmosphere for both a surrender and the future of the reunited nation. Chamberlain later writes of that event, "On our part not a sound of trumpet, nor roll of drum; not a cheer, nor word, nor whisper or vain-glorying, nor motion of man . . . but an awed stillness rather, and breath-holding, as if it were the passing of the dead."

## April 12, 2019
### Joan Fortin Becomes First Woman to Head Maine's Largest Law Firm

Bernstein Shur, Maine's largest law firm, picks a female chief executive officer for the first time. Joan Fortin assumes her new duties in January 2020.

At the time of her selection, no woman holds the top job at any of Maine's fifteen largest law firms, according to a *MaineBiz* magazine annual survey. Bernstein Shur is the biggest firm when measured by the number of lawyers based in Maine.

Fortin grew up on a Benton dairy farm and went to Colby College. She earned a master's degree in educational administration, then worked at Bowdoin College. Then she got a law degree at Northeastern University to broaden her skills in the education field. However, her experience at Northeastern convinced her to become a practicing lawyer.

After several years at Bernstein Shur, she joined the board in 2008 and became director of attorney recruitment. She hired about half of the 120 attorneys who are working at the firm in the spring of 2019.

## April 13, 1976
### President Ford Establishes Exclusive 200-Mile Fishing Zone

President Gerald Ford signs the Fishery Conservation and Management Act of 1976, which affects Maine's fishing industry directly.

The law, which takes effect in 1977 and later is amended several times, establishes an exclusive fishing zone two hundred miles out to sea from all US coastlines. The law prescribes fishery management through eight regional councils. It is partly a response to declining fish stocks and overfishing by foreign vessels.

The State and Defense departments lobbied against the bill, but Ford promised lawmakers from New England that he would support it. Nonetheless, after signing, he says he hopes for an international agreement that would replace it in the coming months.

The law does not ban foreign fishing operations completely. They may catch fish not needed by US fishermen, provided they carry permits issued by the US Commerce Department.

## April 14, 1905
### Flames Gut Springvale Business District

Flames sweep through the business district in the York County village of Springvale, consuming two shoe factories, twenty commercial buildings, and fifteen residences.

The fire begins in the W.R. Usher & Son boot and shoe factory's boiler room and spreads rapidly. Local firefighting equipment proves inadequate to deal with the task. The arrival of Portland firefighters and their machines on a special train prevents destruction of the rest of the village.

When the fire is out, the buildings left in ruins include the Odd Fellows Block, the Western Union Telegraph office, the New England Telephone exchange, the Tibbets Hotel, and the Masonic Block. All the affected buildings were made of wood. Firefighters save the Springvale Hotel by blowing up a vulnerable harness shop next to the hotel.

Except for a firefighter who suffers from heat exhaustion,

nobody is injured. About eight hundred people are left homeless. Authorities say they expect to evacuate the entire population of Springvale, which is part of the town of Sanford.

The total value of the property lost is estimated at $300,000, which would be more than $8.6 million in 2020. The Usher factory's share of the damage is about $130,000.

## April 15, 1905
### Maine Acquires Kennebec Arsenal

The US War Department gives the state of Maine a deed that transfers ownership of the Kennebec Arsenal in Augusta from the federal government to the state of Maine.

The arsenal, located on the eastern bank of the Kennebec River within sight of downtown Augusta, is the northernmost nineteenth-century US arsenal and one of the best preserved. Eight granite structures built in the period from 1828 to 1838 still survive. They were built at a time when the lessons of British predation along the Maine coast during the War of 1812 were still fresh in the government's mind, and when the settlement of an ongoing, rancorous dispute about Maine's northern boundary still

was years away.

Some arsenal commanders later played conspicuous roles in the Civil War.

First Lt. Robert Anderson, the top officer there from 1834 to 1835, also was the commander at Fort Sumter in South Carolina when it surrendered to Confederate forces on April 13, 1861. When the war ended, Anderson, by then a major general, returned to the fort with the flag he had been forced to pull down at the war's outset.

Second Lt. Oliver Otis Howard, a Leeds native, commanded the arsenal from 1855 to 1856. He took part in key Civil War battles, including those at Antietam, Chancellorsville, and Gettysburg, losing an arm in the process and gaining promotion to major general.

After the war, he directed the Freedmen's Bureau for nine years and played a key role in the founding of Howard University, which bears his name.

The state uses the arsenal to expand the nearby Maine Insane Hospital, later called the Augusta State Hospital, and still later, the Augusta Mental Health Institute. The first patients move into the remodeled arsenal building in 1906.

By the end of the twentieth century, treatment of the mentally ill changes in ways that prompt the hospital to abandon many of the arsenal buildings. The state retains some for other uses for a while, but eventually it sells the whole complex in 2007 to North Carolina developer Nieman Capital, which proposes to turn the buildings into condominiums and retail shops.

By February 2021, none of that has happened, and Augusta city officials are unaware of any pending efforts to make it happen.

The private nonprofit group Maine Preservation, apprehensive about potential degradation, places the arsenal on its 2013 list of most endangered historic properties.

The undergrowth that once choked the arsenal's granite riverside wall is now cut away, affording a clear view of the grounds from several vantage points around the city.

## April 15, 1943
### Brunswick Naval Air Station Commissioned

Brunswick Naval Air Station is commissioned in the midst of World War II on the site of what was a municipal airport since the mid-1930s.

Naval auxiliary airfields are commissioned on the same day in Auburn, Owls Head, and Sanford; and another is opened later that year in Trenton, near Bar Harbor. The Navy relinquishes all four of those auxiliary airfields after the war, and they become municipality- or county-owned regional airports.

During the war, the Brunswick base provides Atlantic air and surface patrols to protect the US coast. It is in caretaker status after the war, but in 1951 the Navy recommissions it to support fleet reconnaissance and anti-submarine aircraft operations. That prompts an expansion that includes building two 8,000-foot runways. For a half-century until 2009, the station's planes patrol the North Atlantic using P-3 Orion aircraft.

In 2005, the Defense Closure and Realignment Act commission decides to close the Brunswick station. The last squadron leaves in 2009, and the station is decommissioned on May 31, 2011.

At the time of its closure, the Navy's Brunswick property consists of 3,372 acres—3,162 at the main base and the rest at outlying facilities including two housing com-

A vintage postcard image of "Big Jim," a sign that once stood over the sardine cannery in Prospect Harbor.

plexes and a radio transmitter site.

The station—now called Brunswick Landing—and the Navy's Topsham property now are managed by the Brunswick-based Midcoast Regional Redevelopment Authority.

April 15, 2010
**Maine's Last Sardine Cannery Shuttered**

San Diego-based Bumble Bee Foods closes its Stinson Seafood sardine cannery in Prospect Harbor, ending an era.

The industry once consisted of dozens of sardine plants in Maine. Bumble Bee's was the last sardine cannery not just in Maine, but in the entire United States.

The cannery dates to 1906. It burned in 1968 but was rebuilt and back in operation in 1969.

Bumble Bee cites federal restrictions on the allowable catch of herring, which are called sardines when canned, as the reason for the shutdown.

As of 2020, the only sardine cannery left in North America is run by the Connors Bros.' Clover Leaf Seafoods, which cans the fish under the Brunswick label in Blacks Harbour, New Brunswick, a scant ten miles by water from Eastport, Maine.

April 16, 1996
**Landslide Cuts Rockland House in Half**

A landslide in Rockland tears a cliffside house in half in the early morning darkness and prompts authorities to evacuate five other houses.

The slide, which occurs after heavy rain, sends half of the home of Dorothy Smalley, a woman in her 90s, tumbling toward Rockland's harbor. Her garage and her car also fall.

A police officer breaks down a door to enter the rest of the house, awakens Smalley, and removes her.

Nearby, Smalley's neighbors Susan and Douglas Gerrish discover about one o'clock in the morning that their backyard has vanished, as has the concrete floor of their garage.

Officials cite a total damage estimate of $700,000.

In January 1997, the Rockland City Council imposes a temporary building moratorium in the area of the landslide. The harbor's north shore, lined with fifty-foot cliffs composed mostly of clay, has experienced slides in the past, the most recent of which occurred twenty-five years before the 1996 incident.

## April 17, 2014
### Engineer Behind Moon Landing Method Dies in Scarborough

Aerospace engineer John C. Houbolt, who convinced NASA to use the lunar-orbit rendezvous method to land American astronauts on the moon, dies at 95 in Scarborough, where he has been living in retirement.

Houbolt, who grew up in Iowa and Illinois, was the key figure in a rancorous, protracted, behind-the-scenes debate in the late 1950s about how to send space travelers to the moon and back safely and efficiently.

The debate was fractured into three camps—those who favored shooting a big rocket directly at the moon, landing it, and taking off again; those who advocated Earth orbit rendezvous, in which the lunar vehicle would be fired at the moon from Earth orbit; and those who, like Houbolt, favored putting two small vehicles into lunar orbit, sending one to the moon's surface, and then launching it to meet and dock with the other capsule before returning to Earth.

All three plans were riddled with risky elements. The first option's biggest flaw is that it required the use of an enormous rocket, much larger than a Saturn V, that had not been developed yet. The second proposal would need at least two Saturn Vs to get all the necessary parts into Earth orbit. The lunar rendezvous plan—proposed long before the United States had even launched a manned capsule, let alone conducted a docking exercise—called for two in-space vehicle dockings. If a crisis ensued, the crew would be too far away to be rescued.

Arguments about which method to choose became especially heated because although Houbolt worked at NASA's Langley Research Center, he was not on the moon landing project team. German-born Saturn V rocket designer Wernher von Braun became incensed when Houbolt circumvented the supervisory chain of command and made a direct, blunt pitch directly to NASA Associate Administrator Robert Seamans.

Seamans forced consideration of a lunar rendezvous, and by 1962, von Braun became convinced of its merits.

Houbolt left NASA in 1963. Von Braun invited him to the mission control room in Houston to observe the Apollo 11 moon landing in 1969. When Neil Armstrong and Buzz Aldrin's lunar capsule touched down on the Sea of Tranquility, Houbolt recalled decades later, von Braun turned to him and said, "Thank you, John. It is a good idea."

Houbolt spent his final days in a Scarborough nursing home, suffering from Parkinson's disease.

According to his obituary, as "a scientist to the end," Houbolt, with his family's help, arranged to donate his brain to Massachusetts General Hospital for study of the disease.

## April 18, 1983
### Joan Benoit Wins Boston Marathon, Sets World Record

Foreshadowing her gold-medal triumph the following year at the Los Angeles Summer Olympics, Cape Elizabeth native Joan Benoit wins the Boston Marathon for the second time and notches a women's world-record finish—2:22:43.

Greg Meyer, of Michigan, wins the men's race that year, finishing at 2:09:00. After that, through 2020, only one other American man and two other American women win the Boston Marathon.

After she won the 1979 Boston race, also in record time —2:35:15—Benoit endured an appendectomy and, in December 1981, surgery on both feet, causing her to wonder whether she ever would race again.

Before the 1983 marathon, however, she won several races and was running one hundred miles per week.

Decades later, she steps up to the challenge again in 2019 as Joan Benoit Samuelson at age 61.

Stating that her goal was to come within forty minutes of the time of her first marathon win, she runs the Boston Marathon at 3:04:00, less than twenty-nine minutes short of her 1979 finish. She wears a Bowdoin College singlet, having graduated from the Brunswick school in 1979.

## April 19, 2013
### Disbarred Celebrity Lawyer F. Lee Bailey Denied Reinstatement in Maine

Maine Supreme Judicial Court Associate Justice Donald G. Alexander rules that former celebrity lawyer F. Lee Bailey, of Yarmouth, is "almost fit to practice law, except for an outstanding tax debt of nearly $2 million," essentially clearing a path for Bailey to return to the profession.

The Maine Board of Bar Examiners disagrees. It decides that Bailey, who was disbarred in Florida and Massachusetts over his representation of a marijuana dealer, does not demonstrate the "requisite honesty and integrity" to practice law.

On June 20, the board appeals Alexander's decision to the entire state supreme court.

The court decides in a 4-2 ruling on April 10, 2014, not to grant Bailey a law license, saying he has "failed to demonstrate that he is sufficiently rehabilitated."

"Maine has spoken," Bailey tells the *Portland Press Herald* after the ruling. "I gave it the best shot I could."

Bailey moved to Maine in 2010. He is best known as having represented clients Albert DeSalvo, who confessed to being the Boston Strangler; newspaper heiress and bank robber Patricia Hearst; Dr. Sam Shepperd, who was acquitted in Ohio of having murdered his wife; and former football and movie star O.J. Simpson in his 1995 double murder trial.

## April 20, 1775
### York Militia Marches Toward Boston after Concord, Lexington Battles

Sixty militiamen from the town of York begin marching to Massachusetts to confront the British after receiving news about the opening battles of the Revolutionary War at Lexington and Concord.

Other groups of fighters from Biddeford, Scarborough, and Falmouth soon follow them, but all are turned back because they no longer are needed.

The quick response demonstrates, however, that the Maine men have more loyalty to Massachusetts than they do to Britain.

## April 20, 1783
### Court Decision Helps Outlaw Slavery in Massachusetts, Maine

During an assault case that results in the defendant's conviction and a fine of 40 shillings, Massachusetts Supreme Court Chief Justice William Cushing announces while giving instructions to the jury that slavery is incompatible with the principles enshrined in the new Massachusetts Constitution.

To the extent that the judge's utterance has an effect, it is valid in Maine, which is still part of

Massachusetts.

The assault case actually is the third of three cases involving the same parties—Quock Walker, a slave; and his owner, Nathaniel Jennison.

James Caldwell had bought Walker in 1754. Caldwell died, and his widow married Jennison, who became Walker's new owner. Walker escaped in 1781 and fled to some of Caldwell's relatives. Jennison found, beat, and re-enslaved him.

In the first court case, Walker sued Jennison for assault and battery. He said his original owner had promised he would be freed at age 20. A jury agreed and awarded him fifty pounds as damages.

In the second case, heard in the same session, Jennison sued the Caldwells, alleging they had interfered with his property by convincing Walker to leave for their benefit. Jennison won that case and was awarded twenty-five pounds, but the Caldwells succeeded in getting the ruling overturned on appeal.

In the last case, the state attorney general prosecuted Jennison on charges of criminal assault and battery on Walker. Jennison was indicted in 1781. The case went before the state's high court in 1783.

That's when Cushing gives his interpretation of the state constitution. He notes that the document states that all men are born free and equal and are entitled to liberty, and that all are entitled to have it guarded by law.

"In short," Cushing says, "without resorting to implication in constructing the constitution, slavery is as effectively abolished as it can be by the granting of rights and privileges wholly incompatible and repugnant to its existence."

The jury convicts Jennison and fines him forty shillings.

Some historians trace the Bay State's prohibition of slavery to this decision. Others say news about the Jennison and Walker cases was not disseminated widely at the time, and other influences were eroding support for slavery in Maine and Massachusetts anyway.

## April 21, 1951
### David Mallett, Influential Folk Singer, Born in Sebec

Maine singer-songwriter David Mallett, the originator of seventeen albums, is born in the Piscataquis County town of Sebec. One of his early compositions, "Garden Song," is recorded by

125

Louis Sockalexis

John Denver; Pete Seeger; Peter, Paul and Mary; and many other acts.

Mallett begins performing at the age of 11 in a county-and-folk duo with his older brother, Neil. Singer-songwriters Gordon Lightfoot and Bob Dylan inspire him to begin writing his own songs while he is a theater stu-dent at the University of Maine.

After gaining experience by singing in bars and gradually turning his set list into songs that are exclusively his own, he meets Noel Paul Stookey, of Peter, Paul and Mary, in 1975. Stookey, who owns a Blue Hill recording stu-dio, produces Mallett's first three albums there.

Aside from a stint in Nashville in the 1980s, Mallett makes Maine his home and often his stage as well, although he also performs around the world.

The internet-based folk music fan group FolkWax picks his release *Artist in Me* as Album of the Year in 2003.

"You know, it's an interesting life," he says in a 2018 interview about his career. "You live like a farmer. Some years you have good seasons and some years you don't, and you've got to always come up with something new to keep things interesting. It's a challenge, but there's nobody else I'd rather be, you know? Maybe a little smarter would be good."

## April 22, 1897
### Sockalexis Makes Major League Debut as First Documented Minority in National League

Professional baseball player Louis Sockalexis (1871-1913) makes his major league debut as an outfielder with the National League's Cleveland Spiders. He is often claimed to be the first American Indian in the big leagues and first recognized minority in the National League.

Sockalexis, a member of the Penobscot Nation who was born at the tribe's Indian Island reservation in Maine, had a stellar college baseball career at Holy Cross and Notre Dame, often in the face of racist taunts from other players, sports writers, and fans.

He becomes an overnight sensation as a major leaguer. In his first season, he bats .338 with three home runs and sixteen stolen bases. However, alcoholism and injury hobble his playing, and Cleveland releases him just after the start of the 1899 season after only ninety-four major league games. (For other reasons, the team racks up the worst win-loss record in the history of the majors—34-120—then disbands at the end of the season.)

Sockalexis dies in 1913 of a heart attack while cutting down a pine tree during a logging operation in the Maine woods in Burlington. He is 42.

Cleveland's recollection of him gets a boost when its American League team, founded in 1900 and called the Naps, is renamed in 1915. Its new name is the Indians, the same name that a Cleveland newspaper tried to impose on the Spiders in 1897 after Sockalexis' arrival.

More than a century later, Cleveland's team still is called the Indians.

## April 22, 1922
### WMB, Maine's First Radio Station, Begins Broadcasting

WMB, a radio station owned by the Auburn Electrical Co., makes Maine's first radio broadcast by transmitting an Arbor Day speech. The station, one of only twenty-four government-licensed stations in the nation, goes off the air after a few years.

## April 22, 1976
### Bomb Blast Injures 22 in Boston; Other Blasts by Domestic Terrorist Group Follow

A bomb explosion injures twenty-two people at the Suffolk County Courthouse in Boston. That blast, three others in the Boston area that year, one in 1975 at the Massachusetts Statehouse in Boston and many others over the following years in the Northeast are attributed to a domestic terrorist group that calls itself the United Freedom Front, co-founded by Maine native Raymond Luc Levasseur, originally from Sanford.

The group's members eventually are arrested and convicted of conspiracy, murder, attempted murder and other charges. Levasseur and his wife, Pat, are arrested November 4, 1984, in Deerfield, Ohio. Raymond Levasseur, sentenced to forty-five years in prison, is released on parole in November 2004, having served nearly half that time.

## April 23, 1945
### Navy Patrol Boat Explosion Kills 54 Off Cape Elizabeth

Two weeks before the German surrender in World War II, the USS *Eagle PE-56*, a Navy patrol vessel taking part in a bomber training exercise five miles off the coast at Cape Elizabeth, explodes and sinks.

The incident kills fifty-four of the *Eagle's* sixty-seven crew members. A passing Navy vessel picks up the thirteen survivors and takes them to shore.

American authorities initially attribute the sinking to an accidental boiler explosion. After re-examining historical evidence, however, the Navy reclassifies the sinking in 2001—fifty-six years later—as having been caused by torpedoes fired from Germany's *U-853* submarine. The service bases its revision on research by local lawyer and naval historian Paul Lawton.

The wreck site remains undetected until June 2018, when civilian divers find relics from the *Eagle* five miles off the coast. They make fifteen to twenty dives, preparing a documentary film about the ship, "The Hunt for *Eagle 56*," for the Smithsonian Channel.

According to a plaque placed on shore near the wreck site, the sinking constituted the war's greatest loss of Navy personnel in New England waters up to that time.

The families and friends of the officers and crewmen of the PE-56 were planning to hold a dedication of a monument in 2020 at Fort Williams Park, just south of the cliff walk overlooking the part of the ocean where the ship exploded and sank. The ceremony was postponed because of the coronavirus pandemic, however.

## April 24, 1816
### Pro-Statehood Convention Draws up to 500 People

Four hundred to five hundred people show up at the courthouse in Augusta in response to an invitation to attend a convention, moderated by Judge Daniel Cony (1752-1842), an Augusta physician and Revolutionary War veteran, about a proposal to separate Maine from Massachusetts.

The crowd, composed of residents of Kennebec, Lincoln, and Somerset counties, is so large that the meeting location is changed to the town house, then

to the Congregational Church meeting house, to accommodate the attendees.

The convention appoints a committee of twenty-six members to draft a report and recommendations for the entire convention to consider. The panel, with some members dissenting, proposes Maine's separation from Massachusetts for reasons that often have been cited in recent years.

The Augusta convention on separation precedes a May 20 vote throughout Maine on the issue. It will be the latest of several, and not the last.

Cony's convention effort comes a few months after trustees of a girls' school accept a gift of a building he arranged to have built near his home on Augusta's east side. The new school, the Cony Female Academy, is the predecessor of today's Cony High School.

Separation and Maine statehood finally arrive in 1820. Unlike many of the people who began agitating in 1785 for that result, Cony lives to see it happen.

## April 25, 1906
### John Knowles Paine, Pioneer in Orchestral Music, Dies at 67

Portland-born John Knowles Paine, one of the first Americans to achieve recognition for large-scale orchestral music, dies at 67 in Cambridge, Massachusetts.

Paine's father owned a music store, led Portland's band, and published music. The son also drew inspiration from Hermann Kotzschmar (1829-1908), a German musician, conductor, and composer who settled in Portland and is best known as having inspired the name of the Kotzschmar Organ, the largest organ in Maine, which resides in Merrill Auditorium in Portland City Hall. Kotzschmar gave organ and composition lessons to Paine.

After training in Berlin's Hochschule für Musik with organist Carl August Haupt and composer Wilhelm Wieprecht, Paine returned to the United States and began a long career as an organist, composer, and music professor. He joined the Harvard University staff in 1862 as a vocal instructor and organist, became the school's first music professor in 1875, and established the first music department at an American university there.

His musical works include two symphonies, a violin sonata, many piano and organ works, many choral compositions, and a song collection.

In the last fifteen years of his life, Paine worked on composing a three-act opera, *Azara*, according to a May 2000 *Harvard Magazine* biographical article by then-Harvard choirmaster and organist Murray Forbes Somerville.

"Acclaimed a masterpiece in concert performances," Somerville wrote, "*Azara* was scheduled at the Metropolitan Opera in the 1905-06 season, the year of his retirement, but the company's Italian singers refused to learn a full-length opera in English and it was dropped, to his bitter disappointment."

The opera, although published, never has been staged, he wrote.

## April 26, 1879
### Madame Nordica Blossoms as One of World's Great Opera Singers

Madame Nordica (1857-1914) takes nine curtain calls after a stunningly successful performance in Verdi's *La Traviata* at Brescia, Italy, during the opening phase of her long singing career.

The singer, who spent the first eight years of her life in Farmington, Maine, as Lillian Norton, changed her name to make it more pleasing to the ears of prospective opera fans in Italy.

Her critical breakthrough occurs in 1894 in Bayreuth, Germany, where she sings the role of Elsa in Wagner's *Lohengrin*.

For the next fifteen years, she is recognized as one of the world's greatest opera singers. In 1911, past her prime, she returns to Farmington and performs for fans in her former hometown.

Three years later, Nordica is shipwrecked while on a concert tour of the Pacific. As she lies dying of pneumonia in Batavia (now Jakarta), her accompanying violinist, Francis Holding, of Lewiston, plays some of her favorite music for her.

### April 26, 1983
### Manchester Girl, 10, Writes to Soviet Leader, Visits Russia, Becomes Emissary of Peace

In December 1982, Samantha Smith (1972-1985), a 10-year-old Manchester girl, writes a letter to Yuri Andropov, leader of the now-defunct Soviet Union, telling him she is worried about a potential U.S.-Soviet nuclear war and asking Andropov what he would do to prevent one. Her letter initially is printed in the newspaper *Pravda*. Then in April, Smith becomes world-famous when Andropov replies and invites her and her parents to tour the Soviet Union for two weeks at his government's expense.

The Smiths accept the invitation.

In July 1983, they take a two-week tour of Russia. They go to the Bolshoi Ballet and visit Leningrad—now St. Petersburg. Samantha Smith spends five days at Artek, a Soviet children's camp, swimming, dancing, and putting peace messages in bottles and setting them adrift in the Black Sea.

Some critics deride the trip as a Soviet publicity stunt that exploits the Smiths, but others praise the girl as a symbol of hope for peace.

The girl's fame leads to high-profile TV interviews; a ten-day trip to Japan, where she delivers a speech at the Children's International Symposium; political appearances; and other television work, including hosting *Samantha Smith Goes to Washington* on the Disney Channel. She is cast as a regular in an action-adventure TV series, *Lime Street*.

On August 25, 1985, she and Arthur, her 45-year-old father, are returning from a trip to England, where she was filming an episode of *Lime Street*. En route from Boston, they are aboard a Bar Harbor Airlines commuter plane that

Samantha Smith (1972-1985), 10, of Manchester, holds a letter she received from Yuri Andropov, general secretary of the Soviet Union, in which he assures her that he does not want war.

crashes near the Auburn-Lewiston Municipal Airport, thirty miles from her home. None of the eight people aboard survive. Samantha dies at 13.

Despite her early death, her legacy survives in a number of ways, including contacts between Russians and Americans.

"It was amazing to see," former Artek camp director Valery Kostin says thirty years after Smith's death, having met her at the camp in the summer of 1983. "She was very natural. Some men in the State Department were working so hard to deliver a good message through diplomacy, but this girl arrived like an angel and changed the way Russian people viewed the United States. With her childish, naive voice, she delivered a very powerful message."

Both Soviet leader Mikhail Gorbachev and US President Ronald Reagan send condolences to Smith's mother, recognizing the girl's impact during the final stages of the Cold War.

"Perhaps you can take some measure of comfort in the knowledge that millions of Americans, indeed millions of people, share the burdens of your grief," Reagan writes. "They also will cherish and remember Samantha, her

smile, her idealism and unaffected sweetness of spirit."

## April 27, 1973
### Saint John River Floods; Hundreds Evacuated

A storm system stalls over the Saint John River Valley, unleashing the worst flood ever recorded there. The flood causes severe damage in northern Maine and a crisis in next-door New Brunswick, where 1,450 people are evacuated. In and around the provincial capital, Fredericton, water pervades older neighborhoods and spills into the basement of the legislative building.

## April 27, 2003
### Poisoned Coffee Kills One, Sickens Others in New Sweden

One man dies and more than a dozen other people become ill after drinking coffee at the Gustaf Adolph Lutheran Church in the Aroostook County town of New Sweden, a small town noted for its Swedish character stemming from a mass migration of Swedes to the area in 1870. Investigators discover the coffee has been poisoned with arsenic.

Five days later, on May 2, church member Daniel Bondeson, 53, is found shot in the chest with a rifle

*Photo by David MacDonald; courtesy of Portland Press Herald*
University of Maine star senior Cindy Blodgett readies for a foul shot during an exhibition game at Alfond Arena in Orono.

at his home in nearby Woodland. A note left on a table convinces state police that Bondeson was involved in the poisonings. He dies later at Cary Medical Center in Caribou, the same facility that treats many of the poisoning victims. Police say later that Bondeson's death is ruled to be a suicide.

A local waitress who knew Bondeson describes him as a shy, quiet, frugal man who worked as a substitute teacher, nursing assistant, and seasonal raker of blueberries. Many people in New Sweden say the events are out of character for Bondeson.

In 2006, the state attorney general's office and the state police release a statement saying that while they investigated the possibility that others could have been involved in the poisonings, they became convinced that Bondeson acted alone and that the arsenic had been stored at his farm.

The case influences public health policies and medical research, including a change in the way federal money designated for fighting bioterrorism is distributed.

### April 28, 1780
### War General Complains about Treatment of Troops in Maine

Brig. Gen. Peleg Wadsworth, Revolutionary War commander of the American forces fighting the British in Maine, writes a letter describing the deplorable condition of his troops.

Maine still is part of Massachusetts then. Wadsworth's letter is addressed to the Massachusetts Council, the upper chamber of the Provincial Congress. In it, he says he has not yet received the number of soldiers he expected. "The Consequence of this Delay is very Dangerous, & is the cause of frequent desertions from the Inhabitants to the Enemy," Wadsworth writes.

Wadsworth says the troops also are underpaid and unmotivated, their officers are incompetent, and local inhabitants are helping the enemy.

This last trend frustrates the general so much that a few months later he orders the execution of a civilian aiding the British, which sparks outrage among Maine residents.

### April 28, 1998
### Cindy Blodgett Drafted Sixth by WNBA's Cleveland Rockers

Maine schoolgirl legend Cindy Blodgett is drafted sixth by the Cleveland Rockers in the second-ever WNBA draft following four years at the University of Maine, where she led the Black Bears to the NCAA tournament four times.

Blodgett, of Clinton, led Lawrence High School to an 84-4 record and four Class A State Championships, scoring 2,596 points. At the University of Maine, she scored 3,005 points and averaged 25.5 points for her career, twice leading the nation in scoring.

She plays four years in the WNBA—one for the Rockers and three for the Sacramento Monarchs. She also plays internationally and later becomes a college coach, including a stint at her alma mater, when her playing career ends.

## April 29, 2013
### Arsonist Keeps Lewiston on Edge

Deliberately set fires destroy three buildings in downtown Lewiston, depriving seventy-five people of a place to live.

The fires are the first of three arson cases within a week that occur in Lewiston's city center, keeping the city's residents on edge as police try to figure out who committed the crimes. In all three instances, the fires are set in condemned buildings, then spread to buildings next door. In all, nine apartment buildings are destroyed.

Two adults and two 12-year-olds are charged in connection with the blazes. Later, charges against one of the adults and one of the juveniles are dismissed— in the juvenile's case because of a police procedural error.

However, Brian Morin, a homeless man, pleads guilty in 2014 to three counts of arson in connection to fires set on May 6, 2013. He is sentenced to five years in prison and twelve years of probation. The other juvenile pleads guilty in 2015 to criminal mischief and is sent to the Long Creek Development Center in South Portland until the age of 17.

The city was blighted by abandoned, dilapidated buildings for several years before the fires began. In the five years after them, Lewiston tears down sixty-three buildings, including the nine that burned.

In some cases, banks that foreclosed on the loans of absentee owners didn't even know what they owned.

"We had a bank that tried to sell a property after we had torn it down," City Administrator Ed Barrett said.

*Courtesy of Bangor Public Library*

Flames engulf Bangor Savings Bank, the Bangor Public Library, and the Bangor Historical Society on April 30, 1911, along State Street in Bangor.

## April 30, 1911
### Massive Fire Ravages Historic Downtown Bangor

The Great Fire of 1911 begins in a hay shed on Broad Street in downtown Bangor. Over two days, the fire ravages the city's core on both sides of Kenduskeag Stream, destroying 285 homes, one hundred businesses, the public high school, two fire stations, six churches, and a synagogue. The city library burns after barely having escaped destruction in two previous fires, the most recent in 1910. It is Maine's worst downtown fire of the twentieth century.

Old Town and Brewer firefighters arrive as fast as possible to help fight the flames, but it is not enough. Because the telephone exchange is one of the first buildings to burn, Mayor Charles W. Mullen races in his car to a train junction to send word to other cities around the state that Bangor needs help. He later places the city under martial law.

One man escapes injury from a falling building, but another building's collapse kills him. A falling chimney on Penobscot Street strikes a Brewer firefighter fatally.

"The downtown area resembled a bombed city after the conflagration, with steam and smoke rising from the ruins," author Trudy Irene Scee writes in her 2010 history of the city. Hundreds of people are left homeless.

—30—

# MAY

## May 1, 2008
### Record Flooding Swamps Northern Maine

Rising rivers throughout northeastern Maine and northwestern New Brunswick drive area residents out, force bridge closures and submerge many businesses and homes in the worst inundation in living memory, caused by five inches of rain and a rapidly melting snowpack.

The Aroostook River in Masardis crests at 18.33 feet, a record level. The St. John River peaked at 30.17 feet at Fort Kent—three feet higher than the record level of 1979—the previous night.

Some international bridges to New Brunswick are closed until they can be inspected for damage. Six hundred people are evacuated and 140 homes are flooded.

In Van Buren, the water knocks the US Customs port-of-entry building off its foundation. Evacuations also are ordered there, as well as in Mattawamkeag, where the Penobscot and Mattawamkeag rivers are bursting over their banks.

In New Brunswick, the flooding causes more than $23 million (Canadian) worth of damage.

The flood also causes pollution concerns because overtaxed treatment plants are releasing untreated sewage into the river, and heating oil tanks break free, spilling oil into the floodwater.

There are no reports of death or major injuries.

## May 2, 1994
### Homegrown LaVerdiere's Sold to National Pharmacy Chain

LaVerdiere's Super Drug, a Maine-based chain with seventy-two stores in northern New England, reaches an agreement to sell all its stores to industry behemoth Rite Aid Corp.

LaVerdiere's, a homegrown chain based in Winslow, was founded in 1922 and grew to include fifty-five stores in Maine, many in rural areas, but still maintained a quirky general store look and feel that was beloved by many customers.

"I am really very upset this state has not been able to hold and foster businesses that are unique and home-grown," Janice Carpenter tells the *Kennebec Journal.*

Margaret Urquhart, an industry

consultant, says, "LaVerdiere's was a unique chain not only in Maine, but in the whole drugstore industry. They really marched to their own drum. ... I think you are going to see that flavor disappearing in Maine."

LaVerdiere's employs 1,500 people at the time of the sale. Rite Aid is the nation's largest chain, with more than 2,600 stores and annual sales of $4.05 billion. It entered the Maine market only two years earlier by purchasing thirty-four Wellby Super Drug Stores from Hannaford.

Stephen LaVerdiere, grandson of founder Evariste LaVerdiere, provided reasons for the sale that would be heard again in the state. He cited factors that included a weak Maine economy, the decline of sales to Canadians, the impending closing of Loring Air Force Base, increased competition from Walmart and other national chains, and the squeeze on prescription drug profit margins by insurance companies.

## May 2, 2018
### Lawmakers Override LePage Veto of Pot Legalization Bill

The Maine Legislature overrides Gov. Paul LePage's veto of a bill that would bring about the sale of recreational marijuana, which voters decided to legalize under state law in a November 2016 referendum.

The House votes 109-39 and the Senate, 28-6 to secure the bill's final passage.

The next step is the rulemaking process, which a Maine Department of Administrative and Financial Services spokesman says would take no less than nine months.

The Legislature approves the rules, and Gov. Janet Mills signs that bill June 27, 2019. The Office of Marijuana Policy adopts them in final form in November.

The bill is amended from a previous version by prohibiting marijuana social clubs and reducing from six to three the number of plants that may be grown for personal use.

Maine legalized the prescribing and use of marijuana for medical purposes in 1999. Marijuana possession and use remain illegal under federal law, but the law is generally unenforced.

## May 3, 1903
### Fire Devastates Kennebunk Business District

Nearly all of Kennebunk's business district is wiped out in a three-hour fire of unknown origin that starts in the town's four-story, wooden, electric lighting station.

The loss includes the lighting station, two mills, five business blocks, two tenement buildings, and seven other wooden buildings.

The burned buildings cover an area of about two acres. The merchandise and equipment of fourteen stores is destroyed.

Firefighters and fire equipment from Biddeford and Portland arrive to render assistance, but the Kennebunk fire squad has the blaze under control by the time they arrive.

Unlike many other major fires of the period, this one occurs when there is no wind to spread the flames further, and the local firefighters have enough water pressure to apply full force to their efforts.

The town of Kennebunk suffers the greatest financial loss through the destruction of the power station, valued at $35,000, which would be about $1.01 million in 2019.

The fire does not cross to the other side of the Mousam River, where the Kennebunk Manufacturing Co.'s large mills, the Mousam Hotel, and several residences are located.

May 4, 1837
## Slave Escapes from Georgia as Stowaway on Maine Schooner

The Maine schooner *Susan* departs from the harbor in Savannah, Georgia, where the ship stopped for repairs. The crew apparently is unaware that a local slave named Atticus, trained as a ship's carpenter, has sneaked aboard the vessel to escape from his masters, James and Henry Sagurs.

Atticus comes out of hiding once the ship has been underway for several days.

Back in Georgia, aware of the escape, James Sagurs boards a pilot boat and gives chase. After both vessels arrive in East Thomaston, Maine, Sagurs goes to court and gets a warrant for Atticus' arrest. Two local men betray the slave, who is recaptured, put aboard the pilot boat, and taken back to Georgia.

Sagurs then presses successfully for a warrant for the arrest of Daniel Philbrook, captain of the *Susan*, and his first mate, Edward Kelleran, as "fugitives from justice."

Exemplifying a national divide over slavery that would lead to the Civil War twenty-four years later, two successive Maine governors refuse to comply with the order.

## May 5, 2017
### Katahdin National Monument Targeted for Possible Size Reduction

The newly designated Katahdin Woods and Waters National Monument, in northern Penobscot County, is added to a national list of twenty-two sites that President Donald Trump's administration is considering for possible reduction in size.

Maine Gov. Paul LePage lobbied hard to get the site added to the list, having opposed the 87,000-acre monument's establishment in 2016. The federal government first said it would consider alterations only to monuments of 100,000 acres or more, but it made an exception in Katahdin's case.

Even so, nothing changes. US Interior Secretary Ryan Zinke visits Katahdin Woods and Waters in June 2017. Months later, he recommends leaving its boundaries as they are.

LePage refuses at first to authorize highway signs directing travelers to the monument. Then a state government shutdown interferes with awarding contracts for the signs.

Their installation finally begins October 30, 2019, about nine months after LePage leaves office.

## May 6, 1964
### Rev. Martin Luther King Jr. Speaks in Brunswick

On his only visit to Maine, Rev. Martin Luther King Jr. (1929-1968) speaks at First Parish Church in Brunswick at the invitation of the Bowdoin Political Forum at Bowdoin College.

King comes to Maine with Bayard Rustin (1912-1987), another nationally prominent civil rights leader, who was the chief organizer of the 1963 March on Washington. The event is so well promoted that college officials have to move it from the Pickard Theater, where it originally was scheduled to take place. About eleven hundred people attend the speech.

In his address, King talks about the need for an organized civil disobedience campaign to maintain public awareness of the civil rights issue.

"The realist," King tells the crowd, describing race relations in the United States, "would agree with the optimist that we have come a long, long way; but he would seek to balance that by agreeing with the pessimist that we have a long, long way to go before this problem is solved."

Bowdoin's radio station,

WBOR, records King's entire hourlong speech. The recording is lost for many years, but Bowdoin archivist Caroline Moseley rediscovers it while sorting through uncatalogued material.

King is assassinated in Memphis, Tennessee, in 1968. The United States makes his birthday an annually observed federal holiday in 1986.

## May 7, 1812
### Midwife Martha Ballard Records Final Diary Entry

Kennebec Valley midwife Martha Moore Ballard (1735-1812), gravely ill, records in her diary that the day is clear, very cold, and windy. Her daughter, grandchildren, two friends, and a minister stop by to greet her and to pray with her.

It is her final diary entry after twenty-seven years of chronicling weather patterns, gardening results, local politics, criminal cases, births, deaths, health care, family matters, and other activities, providing perhaps the most vivid firsthand description ever written about daily life in early post-Colonial New England. She dies a few weeks later at 77.

Born in Oxford, Massachusetts, Ballard married husband Ephraim and gave birth to all but one of the couple's nine children in Massachusetts. She joined her husband in Hallowell in 1777. Her diary that survives covers the years 1785 to 1812.

The diary, while cited in excerpts in at least two historical works written more than a century ago, flies largely under the cultural radar until 1990, when University of New Hampshire professor Laurel Thatcher Ulrich's book *A Midwife's Tale: The Life of Martha Ballard, Based on Her Diary, 1785-1812* is published. The book wins a Pulitzer Prize.

## May 7, 1933
### Arsonist Sets Fire That Consumes 130 Buildings in Ellsworth

An arsonist sets fire to the Bijou Theater building in Ellsworth. By the time the flames are put out, the fire consumes about 130 buildings, including three-quarters of the business district and most of the houses south of Main Street. Many others are damaged.

Firefighters, in an effort to save municipal records, dynamite a burning house next to Hancock Hall, where those records were kept; but the explosion sends flaming lumber into Hancock Hall, and it is lost as well. The flames spread so quickly that some fire squads abandon their flowing hoses and run for their lives.

The city's fire department has only two pumpers and a hook-and-ladder truck, so it requests help from other communities. Firefighters from as far away as Bangor, Bar Harbor, and Belfast come to assist, hindered by highway traffic consisting of would-be spectators who hope to get a close look at the unfolding catastrophe.

As the wind-blown blaze spreads along sides of Main Street, residents deploy garden hoses and bucket brigades in an unsuccessful effort to contain it. They also haul furniture from buildings in the fire's path and store it in barns or simply pile it up outdoors. By the morning of May 8, most of the center of Ellsworth has simply disappeared, replaced by a smoldering mile-long trail of ruins.

Police arrest Norman Moore, a dishwasher at Tracy's Restaurant, and interrogate him. Moore confesses to the crime. At his trial, the court finds him not guilty by reason of insanity and commits him to the state hospital for the mentally ill in Bangor.

The Ellsworth insurance firm now known as the Brown Holmes & Milliken Agency, founded in the 1860s, pays out many insurance claims in connection with the fire. The firm is still in business in Ellsworth.

## May 8, 1980
### Longtime Maine Senator Begins Term as US Secretary of State

US Sen. Edmund Muskie (1914-1996), a Democrat from Maine, becomes US secretary of state under President Jimmy Carter. He serves until January 18, 1981, two days before the end of Carter's presidential term.

Under Muskie, the State Department holds its first high-level talks with the Soviet Union, trying in vain to convince the Soviets to withdraw from Afghanistan and end the 1979-1989 Soviet-Afghan War. It also negotiates the release of fifty-two American hostages who have been held in Iran since November 1979.

Muskie was governor of Maine from 1955 to 1959, a US senator from 1959 to 1980, the unsuccessful Democratic nominee for vice president in 1968, and a candidate for president in 1972. After his service as secretary of state, he returns to private law practice.

As a US Navy veteran of World War II, he is buried in Arlington National Cemetery.

## May 9, 1775
### Brunswick Militiamen Capture British Navy Lieutenant

With the onset of the Revolutionary War, Brunswick militiamen sneak into Falmouth (now Portland) and capture British Navy Lt. Henry Mowatt, captain of the sixteen-gun sloop-of-war HMS *Canceaux*, on land.

In an incident that becomes known as Thompson's War, the *Canceaux's* crew threatens to shell the city unless Mowatt (also spelled "Mowat" or "Mowett," depending on the source) is released. Six hundred militiamen from nearby towns gather while Falmouth residents negotiate to prevent bloodshed and destruction.

The militiamen hand Mowatt over to his crew but force the *Canceaux* to leave port on May 15.

Mowatt returns five months later aboard the *Canceaux* with four other ships and, in a nightmarish assault that haunts Maine residents for generations, destroys much of Falmouth with incendiary cannonballs.

## May 9, 1894
### Fire Ravages Norway

A conflagration reduces almost all of the south side of Main Street in the Oxford County town of Norway to ashes.

The fire begins early in the afternoon in the C.B. Cummings mill, just across Pennesseewassee Stream from the town's business district.

Driven by an unusually strong, hot wind, it consumes the town's opera house, the post office, a tannery, a church, two banks, two barber shops, and several other retail businesses, as well as several homes.

## May 10, 2005
### Moxie Named Official Soft Drink of Maine

The Maine Legislature designates Moxie as the official soft drink of Maine.

The bitter concoction, first marketed as medicine, sprang to life around 1876 in Lowell, Massachusetts; but its inventor, Dr. Augustin Thompson, was born in Union, Maine. He originally called it "Moxie Nerve Foods."

While the company that produced the drink also cobbled together fanciful fables about how Moxie got its name, Maine's many lakes and streams identified by the Abenaki word "Moxie" ("dark water") probably inspired the name of the soft drink—which now is made in

A sign advertising Moxie.

New Hampshire.

A Moxie Festival, founded in 1982 by the late Frank Ancetti, is held annually in Lisbon to celebrate Mainers' passion for the beverage.

Even Ancetti, however, known as "Mr. Moxie," once acknowledged that the bitter soft drink is an acquired taste.

May 11, 1966

## New Legislation Protects Allagash River

The Maine Legislature passes the Allagash Wilderness Waterway statute, providing protection for northern Maine's Allagash River, contingent on passage of a bond issue intended to supply funding for the protection.

Courtesy of E. J. Johnson Photography/Shutterstock.com
Chamberlain Bridge, crossing over Chamberlain Lake on the Allagash Wilderness Waterway in northern Maine.

Maine voters approve the bond on November 8.

In 1970, the US Department of the Interior designates the ninety-two-mile, northward-flowing water way as the first state-run component of the National Wild and Scenic River System.

The nineteenth-century writer Henry David Thoreau explored the Allagash in 1857 in the company of his Concord, Massachusetts, friend Edward Hoar and Penobscot guide Joseph Polis.

## May 12, 1999
### Linda Greenlaw's First Book, *The Hungry Ocean,* Released

Linda Greenlaw's book *The Hungry Ocean,* the first of many books by the swordfishing boat captain, is published. It remains on the *New York Times* bestseller list for three months.

The book recounts the day-to-day perils and personality clashes that emerge during a monthlong swordfishing voyage. It describes racial prejudice, drug use, unexplained illness, and other problems that bedevil a crew of six living on a hundred-foot boat that, at the end, is loaded with fish.

In the book *The Perfect Storm,* writer Sebastian Junger calls Greenlaw "one of the best captains, period, on the entire East Coast." As captain of the *Hannah*

Performer Susan Poulin as her alter ego, Ida LeClair.

*Boden,* Greenlaw plays a substantial role in Junger's book.

In a review of Greenlaw's book, *Publishers Weekly* says: "Greenlaw's narrative should foster an abiding respect in anyone who has tossed a swordfish steak on the grill, and it is certain to induce jaw-dropping admiration among personnel managers everywhere."

Acknowledging the dangers inherent in her chosen profession, Greenlaw nonetheless confesses in the preface to her book: "Writing has proven to be hard work, often painful. I can honestly say I would rather be fishing."

Greenlaw, a Connecticut native who settled in Isle au Haut in 1997, also is portrayed by actor Mary Elizabeth Mastrantonio in the 2000 film *The Perfect Storm.*

## May 12, 1958
### Susan Poulin, Creator of Ida LeClair, Born in Jackman

Future author and performer Susan Poulin is born in Jackman. Poulin will eventually create her alter ego Ida LeClair, a feisty, groundbreaking, straight-talking, and oh-so-familiar figure from fictional Mahoosuc Mills, Maine, who bills herself as the funniest woman in Maine.

Originally introducing her character in 1996 at a Yankee storytelling festival, Poulin, through LeClair, emerges as a trailblazing iconic figure of Maine culture—the first female counterpart to the likes of storytellers Marshall Dodge, John McDonald, and Kendall Morse.

Poulin takes her character even further by creating a fully developed life and world for Ida, one more personal and familiar, perhaps more similar to Lake Wobegon than the decks of Dodge's *Bluebird*. She continues to perform on stages throughout Maine.

## May 13, 1803
### Capt. Preble Recommissions 'Old Ironsides' for First Barbary War

US Navy Capt. Edward Preble (1761-1807), a Portland native, recommissions the USS *Constitution*—"Old Ironsides"—as his flagship during the First Barbary War. Given a promotion to commodore, Preble sets sail August 14 on the *Constitution*, heading for the Mediterranean Sea.

The painting *Bombardment of Tripoli*, by Michele Felice Corné,

depicts the *Constitution* in action during that war against the Barbary pirates on Africa's north coast. The painting hangs in the Maine Historical Society library in Portland.

The *Constitution*, built from 1794 to 1797, is used in combat with the British during the War of 1812. Several overhauls and retrofits later, it now is docked at the Charlestown Navy Yard in Boston, about a block away from the USS *Constitution* Museum. It is the world's oldest commissioned naval vessel still afloat.

## May 14, 2006
### 'Mother's Day Flood' Swamps York County

Gov. John Baldacci declares a state of emergency for York County in the midst of a three-day deluge that drops more than fifteen inches of rain and turns streets into rivers.

Across New England, rising water floods homes, forces dozens of schools to close because the buses can't use the roads, and threatens dams and communities.

The governors of Massachusetts and New Hampshire also declare states of emergency.

A presidential disaster declaration for Maine occurs May 25.

Measurements in nine streams in York County reveal peak flow rates in eight of them that exceed what could be expected once every five hundred years.

Damage in the county from what sometimes is called the "Mother's Day Flood" is estimated at $7.5 million.

## May 15, 1933
### Fire Destroys Nearly 250 Buildings in Auburn

Eight days after a massive fire destroyed about 130 buildings in Ellsworth, another fire starts in the early afternoon in Pontbriand's Garage on Mill Street in Auburn's New Auburn district.

The southwesterly wind drives the fire in three directions. "A triangular space containing nearly twenty buildings was a roaring furnace almost before the first hose line was laid," the Associated Press reports the next day.

The conflagration destroys 249 buildings, causes about $1 million (nearly $20.3 million in 2020) worth of damage, and leaves about 1,500 people homeless in the midst of the Great Depression.

Most of those affected are French Canadian, Greek, and Italian immigrants who work on the other side of the Androscoggin River in Lewiston's mills.

Many of the lost structures are closely packed tenement buildings that house several families each.

The flames also consume two schools and a synagogue. Embers rising from the disaster zone float across the river and set three smaller fires in Lewiston, one of which destroys a house.

On the Auburn side of the river, the fire finally stops when it reaches a cemetery, which harbors nothing for it to burn. No serious injuries are reported.

At an anniversary gathering eighty years later, in 2013, Auburn Fire Chief Frank Roma says the fire not only changed the face of the city, it also helped shape fire codes and building ordinances.

"The area was a classic for a conflagration—low humidity, high winds, warm weather, debris, wooden buildings with cedar-shake roofs," Roma tells the *Sun Journal* newspaper at the commemoration event. "Much of what happened here in Auburn has actually gone into the fire codes that [have] made the United States a better place to live. We learn lessons from these disasters."

Sen. William Pitt Fessenden

May 16, 1868
**Maine Senator Key Vote in Acquitting President Johnson Following Impeachment**

In the last of three US Senate votes on whether to convict President Andrew Johnson after the US House impeached him in connection with Johnson's attempt to fire Secretary of War Edwin M. Stanton, Sen. William Pitt Fessenden (1806-1869), a Republican from Portland, and six other Republicans break ranks with their party and vote against Johnson's conviction.

Johnson is acquitted by a single vote in all three voting sessions, and he serves out the remainder of his term. Fessenden's action later earns him a mention in future President John F. Kennedy's 1957 book *Profiles in Courage*.

Before the vote, Fessenden, who admired Stanton and found Johnson wanting as a leader, wrote that he nonetheless "would rather be confined to planting cabbages for the remainder of my days" than vote in contradiction to his own judgment.

"It is rather hard at my time of life, after a rather long career, to find myself the target of rather pointed arrows from those whom I have faithfully served. The public, when aroused and excited by passion and prejudice, is little better than as wild beast. I shall at all events retain my own self-respect and a clear conscience, and time will do justice to my motives at least," Fessenden wrote.

## May 17, 1605
### *Archangel* Lands on Monhegan; Five Wabanakis Seized, Taken to England

The English ship *Archangel*, under the command of George Weymouth, lands around noon on the north side of Monhegan island, which he names for St. George.

The ship's voyage was organized by the Earl of Southampton, who wanted to establish a colony for discontented English Catholics. The ship left England on March 31 and arrived May 14 at Nantucket Island. Then, although Weymouth tried to go south to the intended destination, strong wind blew the *Archangel* northeast, to what is now Maine.

After reaching Monhegan, the crew explores the nearby coast and stocks up on salmon, cod, haddock, lobsters, and shellfish, extracting fourteen pearls from one specimen. Crewmen plant peas and barley, which produce plants eight inches tall in sixteen days. Weymouth explores much of Penobscot Bay and the rivers that lead to it.

Trade relations with local Wabanaki Indians begin well, but an unexplained difference of opinion prompts Weymouth to seize five of them as captives. When the ship departs in June, he takes them back to England.

In England, Weymouth gives three of the Indians to Sir Ferdinando Gorges, governor of Plym-

Photo by Kevin Bennett; courtesy of Islandport Press
Gerry Boyle, author of mysteries featuring his iconic character Jack McMorrow.

outh Fort and future founder of the English colony in Maine, who teaches them English.

## May 17, 2016
### Gerry Boyle's Jack McMorrow Returns for Eleventh Mystery

Former *Morning Sentinel* reporter and editor Gerry Boyle releases *Straw Man*, his eleventh Maine-based novel featuring Jack McMorrow, perhaps the most iconic running character in Maine literature. *Straw Man* wins a Maine Literary Award for Best Crime Fiction.

Boyle, a graduate of Colby College, took his first reporting job in Rumford, before moving on to the (Waterville) *Morning Sentinel*. His experiences as a reporter inspired his first novel, *Deadline*, which was published in 1993.

## May 18, 2018
### Trucker Who Dodged More Than $1,300 in Tolls Arrested

A Turner man is charged for allegedly having dodged about $1,300 in Maine Turnpike tolls systematically over six years.

State troopers charge Danny Olson, 61, a long-haul trucker and owner of Olson Transportation, with one count of felony theft of

Molly Spotted Elk (Mary Nelson Archambaud) circa 1930.

services and several misdemeanor offenses, including failing to take a legally prescribed rest after long trips, failing to retain his truck's previous logbooks, illegally attaching registration plates, theft of registration plates, and failing or neglecting to pay tolls.

Police stopped Olson in Auburn after he drove onto the turnpike, coming from New Hampshire. They said he is suspected of failing to pay thousands of dollars' worth of tolls in other jurisdictions as well.

Troopers said before passing through Maine tollbooths, Olson put license plates on his truck and trailer that did not belong to him.

Olson is convicted in 2019 of theft by unauthorized taking or transfer, as well as forgery, and given a suspended sentence of sixty days in jail, according to the *Portland Press Herald*. The court orders him to pay restitution of $1,788.83. Seven other charges against him are dismissed.

The Maine Turnpike Authority tells WGME-TV in July 2018 that toll-evading truckers are a problem for the agency. The turnpike's top ten toll violators owe a total of $13,000, they say, including $7,000 owed by a trucking company in Rhode Island.

## May 19, 1930
### Molly Spotted Elk Stars in *The Silent Enemy*

*The Silent Enemy*, a silent movie, gets its premiere at the Criterion Theater in New York with Indian Island, Maine, native Mary Nelson Archambaud (1903-1977) in one of the key roles.

The film wins critics' praise but is a box office failure, probably because in an era when the industry is in transition from silent movies to "talkies," moviegoers quickly are gravitating toward pictures with sound. Nonetheless, the experience creates opportunities for Archambaud.

Better known as Molly Spotted Elk, Archambaud, a writer, chorus line dancer, and performer of traditional Native American dances, entertains audiences in the United States and in Europe. Her wide-ranging experience includes studying journalism and anthropology at the University of Pennsylvania, starring in a documentary drama about Ojibway Indian life, dancing topless in New York, and lecturing at the Sorbonne in Paris.

"She had an anthropologist's eye and in her travels frequently recorded culturally based values, habits, and tastes that were different from her own," biographer Bunny McBride writes.

While living in France, Archambaud marries a French journalist.

She and her 6-year-old daughter flee the 1940 Nazi invasion, escaping on foot over the Pyrenees, the mountain range along the border with Spain. She returns to Indian Island and learns a year later that her husband has died in a French hospital.

Apart from a year in a mental institution, she spends the rest of her life living either in New York or on Indian Island.

## May 19, 1946
### Booth Tarkington, Two-time Winner of Pulitzer Prize and Inspiration of Kenneth Roberts, Dies at 76

Booth Tarkington, novelist and longtime Maine summer resident, dies at 76 in Indianapolis. Tarkington wrote much about Maine characters and places.

In 1903 Tarkington contracted scarlet fever, and a doctor recommended that he go from his native Indiana to Kennebunkport, Maine, to recuperate. It changed his life. Eventually, he spent the warmer months there annually.

He wrote most of his more than thirty novels after the age of 50. The best known include *Alice Adams*, *The Magnificent Ambersons*, and the children's book *Penrod*. He became close friends with Kennebunkport neighbor Kenneth Roberts, a historical novelist who dedicated three of his novels to Tarkington.

Tarkington's own novels were blockbuster successes. He won the Pulitzer Prize twice and a metaphorical wheelbarrow full of other honors, including being listed in 1922 on *The New York Times'* list of the twelve greatest contemporary American men.

Tarkington was a workhorse, even when eye operations robbed him of his sight for five consecutive months. "(E)ven the calamity of blindness," biographer Robert Gottlieb writes, "did not keep him from writing—the only thing he not only knew how to do but needed to do."

Tarkington hired a secretary to read him his correspondence and take copious dictation until his eyesight returned.

## May 20, 1676
### Jacques de Chambly Restored as Governor of French Colony of Acadia

Jacques de Chambly is re-established as governor of the French colony of Acadia, the capital of which is Fort Penta-gouet, at the site of the present Maine town of Castine.

A Dutch force under the command of Capt. Jurriaen Aernouts and sailing aboard the corsair *Flying Horse* seized the fort two years earlier and imprisoned de Chambly.

The French had been trading cooperatively with Indian tribes in the region before the Dutch take-over, and the loss of Fort Penta-gouet disrupted the Indians' supply line. Some historians interpret that development as one of the causes of the relatively short but highly destructive King Philip's War, which broke out in 1675.

The 1678 Treaty of Nijme-gen ends the Franco-Dutch War (1672-78) and Holland's claim to Acadia.

## May 20, 1690
### French, Indian Attackers Seize Fort Loyal, Kill 200

During King William's War, English colonists at Fort Loyal, where downtown Portland is today, surrender after a four-day battle with French and Indian attackers under the command of Joseph-François Hertel de la Fresnière (1642-1722) and Jean-Vincent d'Abbadie de St. Castin

(1652-1707)—the latter being the namesake of the modern town of Castine.

During the siege, the attackers burn all the houses and kill or wound most of the defenders.

After the surrender, the French agree to spare the survivors. Then, according to an account by the surviving fort commander, Indians kill about two hundred of the English, especially the wounded. They leave the corpses stacked in a pile, where at least some of them remain unburied for more than two years.

The French take the fort commander and a few other Englishmen to Canada.

## May 21, 1847
### *Lewiston Falls Journal* Published; Later Part of *Sun Journal* Merger

William H. Waldron and Dr. Alonzo Garcelon (1813-1906) publish the first issue of the weekly *Lewiston Falls Journal*.

Waldron, a printer, also is a co-founder of the *Boston Herald*. Garcelon is a medical doctor who also serves as a surgeon general of Maine during the Civil War and is elected Maine's governor in 1878. He serves several terms in the Maine House of Representatives and the Maine Senate, and he convinces the founders of

The Porteous, Mitchell & Braun department store on Congress Street in Portland.

Bates College to place the school in Lewiston.

The paper's first home is on lower Main Street in Lewiston. Subscriptions cost $1.50, but almost anything is accepted as payment, including sheepskins and pumpkins.

Nelson Dingley Jr., another future Maine governor, buys a half-interest in the newspaper in 1856 and the rest in 1857. Also in 1857, the *Journal* publishes a twenty-seven-day run of daily editions to cover the murder trial of George Knight, of Auburn, who is accused of having stabbed his wife while she slept. The paper becomes a full-fledged evening daily in 1861, then merges with the *Lewiston Daily Sun* in 1989 to form today's *Sun Journal*.

Among the *Evening Journal's* more illustrious employees is Holman Day (1870-1935), who works there for seventeen years and becomes a poet and prolific writer of novels, several of which become movies in the silent film era of the early twentieth century.

## May 22, 1990
### Porteous, Mitchell & Braun to Close Its Downtown Portland Department Store

Venerable Portland department store Porteous, Mitchell & Braun, the grand anchor of retail on Congress Street for eighty-four years, announces it will close the downtown store in early 1991, a painful blow to the city's core.

Porteous, at the time still owned by members of the founding family, operates six other locations, including one at the Maine Mall, but no others located in downtown areas.

"I feel like jumping off the tallest building in Portland," says Peter Spano, operator of Global Village Imports across the street. "I was told that Porteous would be here forever and that this area was being revitalized."

In truth, family-owned department stores everywhere were being crushed by the move to enclosed shopping malls and competition from national chains. Freese's Department Store in downtown Bangor already closed in 1985.

Porteous would follow a path similar to that of its independent brethren. In May 1992, the family announces it will sell all six of its stores to Texas-based Dunlap Corp. At the time, Porteous has about six hundred employees and operates stores in South Portland, Brunswick, Auburn, and Bangor; Burlington, Vermont; and Newington, New Hampshire.

Just ten years later, in 2002, the company announces it will close its Bangor Mall location, leaving a lone store in Presque Isle at the Aroostook Centre Mall to carry the flag. But that doesn't last long. PMB Inc., a subsidiary of Dunlap, announces about a year later, in August 2003, that it will close the last Porteous store.

## May 23, 1759
### Provincial Governor Stakes Claim to Eastern Maine Territory for Britain

Province of Massachusetts Bay Gov. Thomas Pownall, accompanied by a British military detachment of 136 men, climbs a hill on the east side of the Penobscot River north of Brewer and affixes a leaden plate asserting Britain's claim to the territory.

The British Empire—and its American subjects—then are in the midst of the French and Indian War (1754-1763). Pownall's gesture is an effort to rebuff

French claims to what now is eastern Maine. An unforeseen consequence of his claim is that at the close of the American Revolution, US negotiators are able to secure British agreement that the St. Croix River, not the Penobscot, would form the eastern border between the United States and the new British colony of New Brunswick.

May 23, 2012
## Shipyard Worker Sets Fire on Submarine; Seven Injured

Shipyard worker Casey James Fury sets a fire aboard the nuclear-powered submarine USS *Miami* at Portsmouth Naval Shipyard in Kittery, injuring seven other workers and causing about $450 million worth of damage. He pleads guilty the following year, is sentenced to seventeen years in prison and is ordered to pay $400 million in restitution.

He tells the judge that he set the fire because he was having an anxiety attack and needed to go home.

The submarine is decommissioned in 2014.

May 24, 1977
## The King in Augusta! Elvis Plays Civic Center Months Before Death

It's 10:15 p.m., and the per-former at the Augusta Civic Center is long overdue on the stage. The waiting crowd is on edge.

Suddenly, a bus rolls up to a back door and a double line of police officers creates a shielded exit path to the building. Inside, the lights grow dim and a loud-speaker blares the portentious opening strains of Richard Strauss' "Thus Spoke Zarathus-tra," the theme music to the 1968 movie *2001: A Space Odyssey.*

Elvis Presley, the King of Rock 'n' Roll, bounds into the arena and onto the stage amid high-pitched screams and staccato camera flashes for what later turns out to be the only concert appearance he ever will make in Maine.

Less than three months later, on August 16, he dies at his home, Graceland, in Memphis, Tennessee—one day before he is scheduled to perform in Portland at the Cumberland County Civic Center, now called the Cross Insurance Arena.

In Augusta, sporting a trade-mark spangled white jumpsuit, he draws the most enthusias-tic response with some of his early-career tunes—"Heartbreak Hotel," "Don't Be Cruel," "It's Now or Never"—but the crowd is so wired up that it doesn't really matter what he sings. He could have read an L.L. Bean catalog to them.

"All he had to was stand there and move something—a finger, a leg, a shake of the head," the *Kennebec Journal* reports the next day. "Every time he struck a different pose, the flashbulbs and the screaming would start again."

He tosses a scarf to the crowd. Someone throws roses onto the stage. Someone else throws a fake lobster. There's another song, another scarf. And another. With each jettisoned piece of fabric, a cluster of women washes toward the footlights and back again, like the tide.

And suddenly it's over.

Grainy, shaky video of the concert still is available online for those who want to experience the atmosphere of that frantic night.

## May 25, 1995
### Richard 'Dick' Curless, 'Baron of Country Music,' Dies

Dick Curless, one of Maine's most popular and famous country music stars, dies of stomach cancer. He is 63.

Curless, born in Fort Fairfield, rose to fame in 1965 when he released his biggest hit, "A Tombstone Every Mile," which describes the dangers of hauling potatoes through the Haynesville Woods in northern Maine. Other hits included "Big Wheel Cannonball" and "Hard, Hard Traveling Man." Curless was known for his eyepatch and his popular truck driving songs.

His career was interrupted by the Korean War, and he served from 1952 to 1954. In the late 1950s, he performed frequently on the West Coast, appeared on such television shows as *Arthur Godfrey's Talent Scouts* and toured with Buck Owens.

His final album, *Traveling Through,* was released posthumously in 1995. Famed music critic Peter Guralnick called it "the final, definitive statement from Dick Curless, the eyepatch-wearing cowboy from Bangor, Maine, and one of the most versatile singers in the history of country music."

## May 25, 1965
### Down Goes Liston!
### Ali Wins with 'Phantom Punch'

In a bout lasting little more than two minutes, Muhammad Ali (1942-2016) defeats Sonny Liston (about 1930-1970) in the only world heavyweight championship fight ever fought in Maine.

The lightly attended match at

Photo by John Ewing; courtesy of Portland Press Herald

Richard "Dick" Curless, 1984 (see page 161)

what then was known as the Central Maine Youth Center, in Lewiston, is notable for accusations by many witnesses that the outcome was rigged in favor of Ali. The two boxers had faced one another the previous year in Florida, when Ali—then still using his birth name, Cassius Clay—took the crown away from Liston.

Ali fells Liston with a punch to the chin, which seems to some observers so minor that it becomes known as the "Phantom Punch." Even so, Liston lies sprawled on the canvas for the first time in his career. In the absence of a count from referee Jersey Joe Walcott, Liston eventually stands up and resumes fighting. Walcott then breaks up the fight and declares Ali the winner.

The Lewiston venue was an emergency backup that was used because of legal problems in Massachusetts, where the fight originally was scheduled to be held.

*Phantom Punch* is a Sonny Liston biographical film that is released in 2008.

## May 26, 2015
### Penobscot Nation, Passamaquoddy Tribe Withdraw Representatives to Protest State Policies

The Penobscot Nation and the Passamaquoddy Tribe withdraw their nonvoting representatives to the Maine Legislature, saying state policies fail to respect the tribes' sovereignty, deny members sustenance fishing rights, and ignore tribal culture.

The Penobscots' Rep. Wayne Mitchell and Rep. Matthew Dana, of the Passamaquoddys, walk out of the House of Representatives chamber, saying the state tries to deal with their tribes the way a guardian treats a ward.

"Our hope is that one day the state will recognize us for who we are and value the tribes as sovereign partners and engage in a relationship of mutual respect, "Dana says, according to the *Portland Press Herald*. "Until then, we must simply decide our own future. If history has taught us anything, it certainly is that lesson."

Gov. Paul LePage's office said the tribes have not been cooperative in working with the state or each other.

The Houlton Band of Maliseet tribe's representative retains a House seat.

In 2016, the Penobscots widen the gulf further, terminating the 150-year-old arrangement under which its group is represented at the State House. Penobscot Chief

Wayne Francis says the Penobscots want to convert their discussion with Maine's government, or any other government, to something more like nation-to-nation talks.

"The idea that stuck the most with everyone has been to create an ambassador of the tribe," he tells a Maine Public reporter. Later, the Penobscots do that.

The Passamaquoddys, on the other hand, change their minds. They send a representative to the Legislature again in 2017, and they still have one there in 2021.

Then the Maliseets' chief, Clarissa Sabattis, elected in 2017, sends a letter on November 28, 2018, notifying the Legislature that her tribe will not send a representative for the 2019-2020 Legislature. The letter gives no explanation for the decision.

"Basically, we were finding that the relationship really wasn't working the way it was built," Sabattis, of Houlton, says in a January 23, 2020, phone interview. She notes that the Maliseet representative, like the other tribal delegates, was not allowed to vote. "It was just a token seat at the Legislature."

Sabattis says she spends a lot of time at the State House representing the tribe's interests as chief.

The old arrangement perpetuated a paternalistic system, she says. Now the tribe, which consists of about eight hundred members in Aroostook County and one thousand elsewhere, is weighing whether to set up an ambassadorial arrangement similar to that of the Penobscots.

## May 27, 1692
### Maine Native Orders Convening of Salem Witch Trials

In accordance with an order signed by newly arrived Sir William Phips (1651-1695), a native of Nequosset (now Woolwich), a court convenes at Salem, Massachusetts, to deal with the cases of more than 125 people who have been arrested on charges of witchcraft and are being held in prison in Salem and Boston.

By the time Phips returns in September from a trip to Pemaquid, in Maine, where he is overseeing the construction of Fort William Henry, twenty executions have occurred and more people have been arrested. His own wife, having secured the temporary release of a witchcraft suspect, also has been accused.

Phips exonerates by proclamation eight defendants who have been convicted, the pro-execution chief justice storms out of the court in protest, and Phips replaces him with a less volatile judge. The discredited witch trials soon end, but their notoriety maintains an unyielding grip on Americans' imagination to this day.

Phips, who grew up in Maine as one of twenty-two children, was a shepherd and a shipwright. After moving to Boston, he made three trips to the Caribbean and made a significant recovery of sunken Spanish treasure, for which he received a knighthood. He also led a failed 1690 expedition to attack Quebec.

In Massachusetts, he sometimes becomes physically violent in his confrontations with rival authorities. England's Privy Council eventually summons him to London to account for himself. He dies there of fever.

## May 28, 1821
### Gov. William King Resigns

Maine's first governor, William King, resigns from office to become a special minister appointed by James Monroe assigned to negotiate a treaty with Spain.

Maine Senate President William D. Williamson, who later becomes Maine's first state historian, succeeds King as governor.

## May 28, 2005
### Film Adaptation of Richard Russo's *Empire Falls* Debuts on HBO

The two-part TV miniseries *Empire Falls*, based on a 2001 Pulitzer Prize-winning novel of the same name by Colby College professor Richard Russo, debuts on the HBO cable TV network.

The miniseries, shot in 2003 in Waterville and Skowhegan and directed by Fred Schepisi, is set in the fictional Maine town of Empire Falls. It stars Ed Harris, Paul Newman, Helen Hunt, Aidan Quinn, Robin Wright Penn, Philip Seymour Hoffman, Joanne Woodward, and Danielle Panabaker.

The show wins a Golden Globe for Best Miniseries or Motion Picture Made for Television. Paul Newman wins both a Golden Globe and a Primetime Emmy for his work in a supporting role. Also, Harris, the miniseries' lead actor, returns to Waterville in July 2004 to accept the Maine International Film Festival's Mid-life Achievement Award.

In May 2019, Harris donates $75,000 to the development of the planned Paul J. Schupf Arts Center in downtown Waterville.

"Ever since living in Waterville and working on *Empire Falls* some 15 years ago, the town and the people in it have held a fond place in my heart," he says in a news release about the donation.

## May 29, 2001
### Supreme Court Rules Seavey's Island Belongs to Pine Tree State

The US Supreme Court delivers a decision asserting that Seavey's Island, which is in the Piscataqua River and is the site of Portsmouth Naval Shipyard, is part of Maine, not New Hampshire, based on an ill-defined 1740 decree by Britain's King George II.

The court dismisses a claim by New Hampshire, and it later refuses to reconsider the ruling after New Hampshire appeals.

The court disregards new information about the king's intent and instead rules that the two states' 1976-77 effort to determine the border's location applies to the entire length of the river and out through the harbor.

Justice David Souter recuses himself from voting because he was involved in the issue in the 1970s as a New Hampshire assistant attorney general and later as the state's attorney general.

The decision means, among other things, that New Hampshire residents who work at the shipyard must pay Maine income tax. Enforcement of that requirement resulted in the lawsuit that the Supreme Court ended up resolving. New Hampshire does not have a state income tax.

## May 30, 1979
### Owls Head Airplane Crash Kills 17

Seventeen of the eighteen people aboard a Downeast Airlines commuter plane from Boston die when the plane crashes into a heavily wooded area on Otter Point in Owls Head.

The pilot, trying to land at Knox County Regional Airport in Owls Head, made a request for a diversion to Augusta because of poor weather. Then the plane, a de Havilland DHC-6-200, loses its left wing when it hits two trees about eighty feet above the ground. It strikes several more trees, losing parts, and the fuselage comes to rest nearly vertically, standing against a tree.

A National Transportation Safety Board investigation of the accident attributes the crash to the flight crew's failure to stop the plane's descent when it reached the minimum altitude for a landing approach not guided by precision instruments without the runway in sight.

The NTSB report said it was unable to discover why the crew acted as it did, but it said "inordinate management pressures, the first officer's marginal instrument proficiency, the captain's inadequate supervision of the flight, inadequate crew training and procedures, and the captain's chronic fatigue were all factors in the accident."

The only survivor was John McCafferty, of Searsmont, who was 16 at the time and suffered several injuries. McCafferty, now retired, still lives in Searsmont.

## May 31, 1820
## First Maine Legislature Convenes in Portland

The Maine Legislature convenes its first session at the original Cumberland County Courthouse in Portland. The session lasts until June 28.

The legislators meet there because the state offices in a nearby two-story Federal-style structure at the corner of Congress and Myrtle streets don't have enough space to accommodate the House and Senate sessions.

Gov. William King opens his June 2 message to the legislators with this observation: "The political connexion, which had so long subsisted between Massachusetts and Maine being dissolved, it is a source of much satisfaction to reflect, that the measures, adopted for its accomplishment, have effected the object in the most friendly manner."

With that breezy remark, the governor seems to paper over thirty-five years of pitched battles about political and religious differences, animosity about Maine statehood being dependent on allowing slavery in Missouri, resentment about how Massachusetts was unable to defend its Maine territory effectively during the War of 1812, and the impediment once posed by customs duties imposed by the recently repealed federal Coasting Law, which would have been a heavy post-statehood burden for Maine businesses selling goods in other states.

The state government's sojourn in Portland is temporary. After competition among a variety of places to host the new capital, the Legislature passes and the governor signs in 1827 a bill selecting Augusta as the capital. The government is directed to begin operations there on January 1, 1832.

Arguments in Augusta's favor, according to historian James

North, include the fact that it is more centrally located in the state, its inland location would make public records and public offices more secure in the event of war, and that by moving to a small town, "the business of legislation might be carried on with less embarrassment and more purity than in a large town."

## May 31, 2011
### Brunswick Naval Air Station Shuts Down

Brunswick Naval Air Station is decommissioned, sixty-eight years after it opened in the middle of World War II on the site of a former municipal airfield.

The closing leaves New England without an active-duty military airfield. Navy patrol aircraft, which monitored the Soviet Union's submarine activity in the North Atlantic during the Cold War, now fly from Jacksonville, Florida.

The Midcoast Regional Redevelopment Authority, established to find new uses for the base and a Topsham housing annex, reconfigures the base as Brunswick Landing: Maine's Center for Innovation, a business park; and Brunswick Executive Airport, which uses the former base's two eight-thousand-foot runways.

By 2020, according to the redevelopment agency, the property it controls hosts 135 businesses employing two thousand people and has generated $3 million in property taxes.

—30—

# JUNE

June 1, 1849
**Stanley Brothers, Inventive Businessmen, Born in Kingfield**

Inventors, businessmen and identical twins Freelan Oscar Stanley and Francis Edgar Stanley are born in Kingfield.

After becoming wealthy through pioneering work in manufacturing and marketing dry-plate photography equipment, they turn their attention to transportation—partly because their factory in Watertown, Massachusetts, is next to a bicycle factory.

Francis Stanley's wife, Augusta, tries riding a bike but finds that she keeps falling off, so her husband vows to devise something similar that would enable her to get around in comfort and safety. He produces a steam-driven

*Courtesy of the Stanley Museum*

Francis Edgar Stanley and Freelan Oscar Stanley ride in a steam-powered car in 1897.

169

automobile in 1897. Its enthusiastic reception the following year at the Boston Auto Show prompts him and his brother to turn to making cars. Locomobile, a company they start and quickly sell, produces more than two hundred steam-powered cars in 1898 and 1899, the most in the nation.

In 1899, Freelan Stanley and his wife, Flora, ride one to the top of New Hampshire's Mount Washington. In the same year, he gives President William McKinley a tour of Washington in one of the vehicles, making McKinley the first sitting US president to ride in a car.

In 1902, the brothers found the Stanley Motor Carriage Co.; its products become known as "Stanley Steamers" or "flying teapots." After Francis Stanley dies in 1918 in a car accident, his brother sells his own interest in their car company. Overtaken by technological improvements in cars powered by internal combustion engines, the Stanley company ceases production in the 1920s.

Freelan Stanley plays a significant role in the 1915 creation of Rocky Mountain National Park and development of Estes Park in Colorado. He builds the Stanley Hotel in Estes Park. The hotel later becomes the inspiration for and the setting of Stephen King's novel *The Shining*.

## June 1, 1950
### Margaret Chase Smith Delivers 'Declaration of Conscience' Speech

US Sen. Margaret Chase Smith (1897-1995), a Republican from Skowhegan, delivers what later becomes known as her "Declaration of Conscience" speech on the Senate floor, chastising key Republican leaders for the tactics they employ in trying to root out communists in US government. Smith upholds Americans' right to criticize their government and to protest against its actions.

The speech is regarded widely as a stand against powerful US Sen Joseph McCarthy (1908-1957), a Republican from Wisconsin, from whose name the campaign against communists becomes known as "McCarthyism." Six other Republican senators support Smith's declaration, prompting McCarthy to label the group "Snow White and the Six Dwarfs." For years afterward, McCarthy tries, mostly unsuccessfully, to undermine Smith's political career.

Smith's declaration is re-enacted by actress Patricia Neal in the 1977 made-for-TV biographical movie about McCarthy, *Tail Gunner Joe.*

## June 1, 1978
### Bottle Deposit Law Takes Effect

A state law commonly known as the Bottle Bill, requiring that consumers pay a deposit on all soft drink, beer, wine cooler, and mineral water containers takes effect in Maine.

Proponents of the Bottle Bill cited the need to reduce litter, an increasing problem because of the growing use of disposable cans in the marketplace. Following a heated campaign in 1976, voters approved a referendum in support of the deposit law, 58 percent to 42 percent. The law is expanded in 1990 to include other types of beverage containers.

## June 2, 1851
### Maine Law Bans Sale of Alcohol

Gov. John Hubbard signs what becomes known as the Maine Law, which bans the sale of alcoholic beverages except for "medicinal, mechanical, or manufacturing purposes."

The law, for which Portland Mayor Neal Dow lobbied furiously, also includes a search-and-seizure provision that enables any three voters to obtain a search warrant if they suspect someone of selling liquor.

The bill's enactment earns Dow the nickname "the Napoleon of Temperance," but also many enemies.

Dow travels for three years after that as a temperance crusader in other states and in Canada. Versions of the Maine Law are enacted in Indiana, Massachusetts, Michigan, Rhode Island, and Vermont.

Maine's groundbreaking prohibition law engenders the Portland Rum Riot on June 2, 1855, in which one person dies and several are injured, leading to the law's repeal in 1856. Later, other state laws are passed having the same effect, however, and prohibition is added to the state constitution in 1884.

The Portland Rum Riot and its legislative aftermath foreshadow in microcosm the national battle about Prohibition in the early twentieth century, and the ultimate repeal of the constitutional amendment that puts it in place.

## June 2, 2017
### Visitor Dumps 100 Live Bedbugs at Augusta Office

Augusta City Center, the headquarters of the city's government,

Courtesy of Lone Stag Studios/Shutterstock.com

A draft horse at Maine's Fryeburg Fair.

closes unexpectedly early when an unhappy visitor dumps a cup full of about a hundred live bedbugs on a counter about two o'clock in the afternoon in one of the offices.

The bugs start moving around and spreading out. The city evacuates the building and summons an insect-control specialist.

Officials said the bug carrier came to City Center to seek General Assistance money. When he was told he didn't qualify for it, they said, he unleashed the bugs.

Weeks later, police charge 74-year-old city resident Charles Manning with assault and obstruction of government administration in connection with the incident.

Over the following three years, three of four lawyers assigned to represent Manning withdraw from the case, citing a breakdown in communications with Manning. The fourth lawyer withdraws because of scheduling conflicts. Kennebec County Superior Court Judge William Stokes assigns a fifth lawyer to the case in September 2020. In May 2021, Manning's case is unresolved but no further court dates are scheduled.

June 3, 1851

**Agricultural Society's Founding Sets Stage for Future Fryeburg Fair**

Ten towns join to incorporate the West Oxford Agricultural Society and establish an annual exhibition. They hold their first fair October 23 in Hiram.

The event moves from town to town in its initial years, but eventually settles permanently in the town of Fryeburg and becomes known as the Fryeburg Fair. It uses one site beginning in 1858, then moves to the current location to accommodate its growth. The first fair is held there beginning October 4, 1885.

In modern times, the agricultural fair lasts eight days, and its organization has about one hundred buildings on more than 180 acres.

The contributing towns today consist of sixteen in Maine and six in New Hampshire. The fair, which employs about six hundred people annually, hosts more than three thousand animals, including draft horses, ponies, racing horses, oxen, dairy and beef cattle, sheep, goats, pigs, poultry, and rabbits.

The Fryeburg Fair is held the first week of October as the capstone event of the Maine fair season, which stretches from summer into fall and includes numerous weeklong fairs such as those in Blue Hill, Bangor, and Skowhegan.

Organizers announce in June 2020 that the fair planned for that fall, like other agricultural fairs in Maine, is canceled because of the coronavirus pandemic. As of late May 2021, the fall 2021 fair is scheduled to take place October 3 through 10, but tickets are not available yet.

June 4, 1942

**USS *Nicholas* Commissioned, Later Plays Role in Japanese Surrender in Tokyo Bay**

The USS *Nicholas*, a US Navy Fletcher-class destroyer built at Bath Iron Works in Bath, is commissioned.

The second ship to be named for the Marines' first commandant, Samuel Nicholas (c. 1744-1790), the destroyer receives thirty battle stars—more than any other US Navy ship—for its service in World War II, the Korean War, and the Vietnam War.

The *Nicholas* is also present in Tokyo Bay for the Japanese surrender ceremony on September 2, 1945, at the end of World War II. The destroyer carries the

American delegation to the USS *Missouri*, where the ceremony takes place.

The ship participates in the *Apollo 7* and *Apollo 8* spacecraft recovery missions in 1968 before being decommissioned in 1970 and scrapped.

The *Nicholas* is the first Fletcher-class destroyer to be commissioned and one of the last of them to be taken out of service.

## June 5, 2015
### Murder Launches 68-Day Manhunt, Longest in Maine History

Abbott resident Robert Burton shoots his former girlfriend, Stephanie Gebo, 37, at her Parkman home, killing her. The discovery of her body later that day launches a manhunt that lasts sixty-eight days, the longest and costliest in Maine history.

Gebo was afraid of Burton, so she slept with a gun under her pillow. When Burton climbs through her bedroom window carrying a knife and duct tape, she shoots him in the neck. He seizes the gun and shoots Gebo three times in the back, leaving without seeking medical attention for her or himself.

Burton commits the crime a day after completing his proba-

tion on a domestic violence conviction that put him in prison for ten years.

The manhunt for Burton, during which several people report seeing him, costs the state police about $500,000. The FBI, the Maine Warden Service, and the local sheriff's office also incur expenses in the operation.

The presence of lighted, flashing "manhunt under way" signs along area highways around the Fourth of July unnerves people who live in the area and seems to put a damper on local business.

The manhunt ends August 11 when Burton walks into the Piscataquis County Jail in Dover-Foxcroft and turns himself in. A jury convicts him in October 2017 of the murder. The court sentences him in December to fifty-five years in prison.

## June 6, 1944
### Charles Shay Takes Part in D-Day Invasion, Earns Silver Star

Nineteen-year-old Charles Norman Shay, a Penobscot Indian, rescues drowning and wounded soldiers while under enemy fire as he takes part on D-Day in the first wave of attackers to land on Omaha Beach in France. His actions there earn him a Silver Star.

Shay, who grew up on Indian Island in the Penobscot River, is an Army combat medic assigned to 2nd Battalion, 16th Regiment, 1st Infantry Division, a division also known as the Big Red One.

After D-Day, he takes part in the battles of Aachen, Huertgen Forest, the Ardennes (Battle of the Bulge), and the Rhine, near Remagen, Germany. The Germans capture him in the Sieg Valley, and he spends nearly a month in prisoner-of-war camps until his liberation on April 18, 1945.

Shay joins a military police company in Vienna, Austria, in 1946, and meets his Austrian wife during his four-year assignment there. In November 1950, he lands in North Korea, with the 7th Regiment, 3rd Infantry Division, and takes part in combat against the invading Chinese army. Shay is promoted to master sergeant and picks up a Bronze Star.

After a stint in the Air Force that takes him to atomic bomb tests in the Pacific and hospital work in Germany, Shay moves with his wife to Vienna, where he works for the International Atomic Energy Agency and, later, the United Nations High Commissioner for Refugees.

In 1988, while vacationing in the Penobscots' Indian Island village, he inherits a house there. He and his wife spend the next fifteen years gradually improving it, then move there in 2003 from Austria. Shay dedicates himself to promoting and preserving Penobscot cultural heritage there. He publishes booklets by or about Penobscots, operates a small museum, and facilitates the republication of a book by his grandfather, *Life and Traditions of the Red Man*.

## June 6, 1944
### John Martin 'Bull' Feeney, aka John Ford, Films D-Day Invasion

Charles Shay wasn't the only versatile Mainer on Omaha Beach during the D-Day invasion. Another was Portland native John Martin "Bull" Feeney, better known as Hollywood movie director John Ford (1895-1973).

Working as the photographic branch chief of the Office of Strategic Services, a US intelligence agency, Ford arrived April 19 in London and began gathering camera crews and equipment to make a filmed record of the invasion.

He coordinated a plan for photographic coverage in separate meetings with the Navy, the Coast Guard, the Army, and

Legendary Hollywood director John Ford, who was raised in Portland as John Feeney, around 1920.

Canadian and British forces, including the use of blackboard diagrams. Ford arranged to have a crew, supervised by Naval

Reserve Lt. Mark Armistead, install 152 movie cameras on mounts aboard the landing craft, set to begin filming automatically when the third man or third vehicle left the boat; 500 movie cameras attached to the front of landing craft; and fixed cameras mounted to tanks.

In midmorning on the day of the landing, Ford is aboard the destroyer USS *Plunket*. He clambers into an amphibious truck and heads to Omaha Beach with others as the Germans continue to fire at advancing Americans. He reminds his cameramen, who are unarmed, to lie behind cover while filming, not stand up.

When the landing is complete, Ford sends his photographers back to the ship while he proceeds inland. He makes his way to a house being used as an Army Air Forces combat camera unit's headquarters. Then, according to biographer Joseph McBride, Ford "began drinking Calvados. He drank steadily for days on end." The combat photo chief eventually gets somebody to take him away.

Prone to such lapses though he was, Ford's efforts result in some of the best photography to emerge from the war. Among other famous battles Ford filmed was the Battle of Midway.

The saloonkeeper's son and Portland High School graduate got his start in movies early. He went to the University of Maine for a while, but soon made a beeline for Hollywood, following his older brother Francis, an actor.

Ford worked as an extra in several films, including *Birth of a Nation*, but he began directing quickly, in the silent movie days.

He became one of the most influential movie directors in history, eventually winning six Academy Awards for his films, including four as best director for *The Informer, The Grapes of Wrath, How Green Was My Valley,* and *The Quiet Man*; and two for his World War II documentary work. He also is known for directing John Wayne and other marquee names of the era in groundbreaking Westerns.

When asked what brought him to Hollywood, he often responded, "The train."

## June 7, 1985
### South Portland's Billy Swift Drafted Second by Seattle Mariners

Billy Swift, a four-year pitching star for the University of Maine Black Bears, is the second overall pick in the Major League Baseball Draft by the Seattle Mariners.

Swift was a star at South Portland High School and was recruited as an outfielder. However, at Maine he was converted to pitcher and helped lead the Black Bears to four consecutive College World Series appearances. He also pitched for the US Olympic Team in Los Angeles in 1984, carrying the US flag into Dodger Stadium.

He makes his major league debut on June 7, 1985, in Cleveland and would go on to play thirteen seasons in the majors with Seattle, San Francisco, and Colorado. A reliever for some of his career, he compiles a 94-78 record with a 3.95 earned run average. His best season is 1993, when he is a starter, has a 21-8 record with a 2.82 ERA, and finishes second in voting for the 1993 National League Cy Young Award, losing out to Greg Maddux. In 1992, he leads the majors with a 2.08 ERA. He retires in 1998 and becomes a member of the New England Baseball Hall of Fame.

## June 7, 1909
### Wind-driven Fire in Presque Isle Leaves 1,000 Homeless

Fire aggravated by high wind wipes out the entire northeast-ern section of Presque Isle. Several people are injured and nearly 1,000 are homeless.

The loss includes about 100 houses, a Congregational church, a Masonic hall, a Canadian Pacific Railroad freight station, ten potato storehouses, and several other buildings.

The houses are not close together, but wind-driven embers landing on dry, shingled roofs are enough to ignite many buildings almost simultaneously.

Volunteer firefighters from Fort Fairfield and Houlton arrive to help local firemen contain the damage, which is a nearly impossible task, given the wind.

The fire breaks out in the kitchen of John Brown's boardinghouse on North Main Street. When the fire burns out at midnight, it has destroyed part of the electrical grid, leaving the town in darkness.

The initial damage estimate is $300,000—about $8.8 million in 2020 dollars.

Meanwhile, about ten miles to the north, Caribou firefighters are preoccupied with a fire of their own. The foundry and machine shops of J.S. Getchell & Son, as well as manufactured goods awaiting shipment in a storehouse, burn about the same time the Presque Isle conflagration is underway. That fire causes about $30,000 worth of damage, or about $877,000 in today's property value.

Three days later, Presque Isle endures a risk of further destruction, this time from fires in the woods outside the town. Barely rested from its earlier exertions, the town's fire squad patrols the parts of town still standing, dousing flaming embers wherever they appear until the wind finally changes direction.

## June 8, 1864
### Andrew Johnson Replaces Hamlin as Lincoln's Vice President

The National Union Convention, held in Baltimore, nominates Republican Abraham Lincoln for a second term as president. Then, with Lincoln's support, it rejects Vice President Hannibal Hamlin, of Maine, in favor of War Democrat Andrew Johnson, of Tennessee, as Lincoln's running mate.

Lincoln wins re-election in November. Six weeks after his inauguration in 1865, he is assassinated. Johnson becomes president.

Hamlin was the first of a series of Maine Republicans to hold key federal posts in the second half of the nineteenth century. They hold the offices of secretary of state (twice), secretary of the treasury (twice), House of Representatives speaker (twice), and president pro-tempore of the Senate. Also, Augusta resident James G. Blaine is the Republican nominee for president in 1884.

## June 8, 2016
### Ringo Starr, Former Beatle, Performs in Bangor

Ringo Starr & His All Starr Band perform a packed concert at the Cross Insurance Center in Bangor. It is the first Maine concert appearance by any former member of the Beatles.

The ex-Beatles drummer's stage mates include performer, multi-instrumentalist, and record producer Todd Rundgren; singer, keyboardist, and Santana and Journey co-founder Greg Rolie; singer, guitarist, record producer, and Toto co-founder Steve Lukather; and several other longtime musicians.

The Liverpool, England-born Starr was scheduled to perform a second Bangor concert—again, his only tour stop in Maine—on June 9, 2020, two months short of his 80th birthday, at the same venue. However, in March 2020, Starr cancels his entire spring concert schedule because of the worldwide coronavirus pandemic.

## June 9, 1820
## Maine Approves Design for State Seal

The Maine Legislature adopts a design of the state seal about three months after Maine's admission to the Union as the twenty-third state.

Designed by committee—a foreboding circumstance in itself—the image shows a farmer resting on a scythe and a seaman leaning on an anchor, with a moose and a pine tree gracing a shield in the middle. The North Star, an allusion to the fact that Maine is the northernmost state at that time, is fastened at the top, like an angel on a Christmas tree. The Latin word "dirigo," meaning "I direct" or "I guide," hangs under the star.

The design does not meet with universal approval, and for more reasons than the fact that the "moose" looks like a deer.

One committee member expresses disappointment that the aurora borealis and a quote from St. Paul, "I saw in the way a light,"

could not have been shoehorned into the existing menagerie of parts.

Historian William D. Williamson, a former governor, writes about the seal in 1832 that although some kind of state symbol was needed urgently for use on official documents, "no part of it was very ingeniously wrought or executed; hence people of taste and judgment have not been altogether pleased with the devices, or emblems."

The seal undergoes revision from time to time throughout the nineteenth century, but those revisions always incorporate the elements prescribed in 1820.

Finally, in 1919, the Legislature approves the version used today, and the state moves on to more pressing matters, such as selecting an official state bird, tree, flower, song, soft drink, and treat.

Photo by David A. Rodgers; *courtesy of Portland Press Herald*
Gov. Angus S. King Jr. in 1998.

---

June 10, 2002
**Apple CEO Steve Jobs Joins Gov. Angus King to Promote Value of School Laptop Plan**

Apple CEO Steve Jobs visits Maine to promote Gov. Angus King's groundbreaking plan to distribute thirty-three thousand Apple iBooks to seventh- and eighth-grade students in Maine.

Jobs appears with King to tout the value of laptops for students. At the time, King is battling the Legislature to save the program in face of a $180 million budget deficit.

"I'm here to report on the progress of the largest educational technology project in the history of the world, here in the state of

Maine, and it hasn't been easy, has it?" King asks.

Maine signed a four-year, $37.2 million contract with Apple in January that would provide thirty-three thousand students and three thousand teachers with iBooks, wireless networks training, and technical support. The much-watched and debated program survives all attempts to scuttle it and begins statewide that September. It would not only continue, but expand in scope in the years ahead.

Students' increased access to computers and the internet proves to be unexpectedly beneficial during the coronavirus pandemic that erupts statewide—and worldwide—in 2020. Many schools conducted instruction only remotely for part of the year, with students taking classes online.

## June 10, 2019
### New Law Protects Maine Waterways

The Legislature approves a bill that strives to settle disputes between the state and Indian tribal representatives about sustenance fishing rights.

The Senate votes 35-0 to approve the bill, which would designate dozens of Maine waterways as sustenance fishing areas. Those waterways, including several in northern and eastern Maine, would be subject to tighter water quality standards than others. Gov. Janet Mills signs the bill into law on June 21.

The measure is intended to improve tribal members' health and to end legal battles with the tribes about river water quality.

Mills' administration worked with representatives of the Maliseet, Micmac, Passamaquoddy, and Penobscot tribes to draft the bill.

Maine Department of Environmental Protection officials testified that private companies and nineteen municipal wastewater treatment plants that discharge into the waterways already are meeting the standards, so the bill should not affect them.

## June 11, 1775
### Machias Residents Seize HMS *Margaretta* After Battle at Sea

The Battle of Machias, the first naval engagement of the Revolutionary War, begins, resulting in Machias residents' seizure of British vessels and the death of the British commander of the armed sloop HMS *Margaretta*.

The conflict arose from British

This illustration, titled "Hand-to-Hand Engagement on the deck of the *Margaretta*, June 12, 1775," is from the book *Life of Captain Jeremiah O'Brien, Machias, Maine*, by Andrew M. Sherman (1902).

efforts to obtain lumber to build barracks for their troops in Boston. Underlying that is the privation the people of the Down East coast have suffered because of trade disruptions. Reports of children starving to death in some coastal towns are circulating.

In a May 25 letter to the Massachusetts provincial congress, thirty-eight residents pledge their loyalty to the revolutionary cause but cite the hardships they have had to endure.

"(W)e must add, we have no country behind us to lean upon, nor can we make an escape by flight; the wilderness is impervious, and vessels we have none," they write.

The *Margaretta*, accompanied by two other ships, arrived on June 2 in the Machias River. The British, acting through a local merchant, Ichabod Jones, circulated a document asking the locals to agree to allow the lumber shipment, in exchange for which they would receive the provisions they need. After a few false starts, most residents agreed, but the British then gave supplies only to those people who signed, increasing the resentment the locals felt about being forced to flout the Continental Congress' order not to trade with the British.

On June 11, a group assembles with intention of kidnapping Jones and the British officers while they are attending church. The British notice their movement, however. Midshipman James Moore, captain of the *Margaretta*, flees with his officers to their ship and repositions it downriver. Moore threatens to burn the town.

After dark, the ship pulls closer and engages in an exchange of gunfire with locals on the shore, then withdraws downriver again. About sixty men armed with guns, swords, and pitchforks use two vessels, including a sloop they steal from Jones, to catch up to the *Margaretta*, which is heading for the open sea.

A pitched battle at close quarters wounds Moore fatally. The *Margaretta* surrenders. Four others on the British side are killed, and five sailors are wounded. The Americans suffer three fatalities and three wounded.

The battle prompts Machias residents, after consulting the provincial congress in Watertown, Massachusetts, to take other measures to improve their security, including arming one of the sloops they commandeer.

They use it July 15 in a successful effort to capture two more British ships in Machias harbor.

## June 12, 1800
### Future Site of Portsmouth Naval Shipyard Purchased

Congress allocates $5,500 for the purchase of Fernald's Island in Portsmouth Harbor. The island becomes the site of what is now Portsmouth Naval Shipyard, now located in Kittery.

Originally one of a close group of five islands, Fernald's is merged through construction and now is part of the much larger Seavey's Island.

## June 12, 2019
### 'Death With Dignity' Law Enacted

Gov. Janet Mills signs a bill into law letting terminally ill patients obtain prescriptions for lethal doses of drugs to end their lives, calling it her hardest decision as governor so far.

She cites her awareness of the moral dilemma between seeking to establish a path to death with dignity and sanctioning state-sponsored suicide.

The measure, fraught with emotional testimony and debate in the Legislature, passed by a single vote, 73-72, in the Maine House of Representatives; and by three votes in the Maine Senate.

More than a hundred people came to Augusta to speak about the issue. The *Portland Press Herald* cited one in particular, Terry Moore, of Stetson, who has lost thirty relatives to a genetic form of amyotrophic lateral sclerosis, or ALS. She said having watched their slow deterioration and ultimate death, she realized that if it happens to her, she wants the option of ending her life, even if she chooses not to use it.

Bishop Robert Deeley, of the Roman Catholic Diocese of Portland, takes the opposite view in a statement released after Mills signs the bill. "Allowing doctors to prescribe deadly medications to hasten a person's death is a horrendous wound to the dignity of the human person," he says.

## June 13, 1897
### John B. Curtis, Inventor of Chewing Gum, Dies at 69

Maine businessman John B. Curtis (1827-1897), considered the inventor of chewing gum and the first person to commercialize it, dies in Portland.

Curtis, who was born in Hampden, developed his first batch of State of Maine Pure Spruce Gum on his family stove. He boiled spruce gum and then poured it into a tub of ice water and strained it. The gum was sold in sticks one centimeter wide and two centimeters long in tissue paper.

Eventually, Curtis added flavors to his gum, which increased its popularity, and moved the business from Bangor to Portland so he could better expand his production and markets. His company, Curtis & Son, developed a machine to mass-produce gum. Eventually, the company employed more than two hundred people and turned out eighteen hundred boxes of chewing gum a day.

### June 14, 1834
### Readfield Native Invents Improved Diving Suit

Leonard Norcross, of Dixfield, patents a diving suit made of rubber with a metal helmet attached to it with a water-tight seal.

Norcross (1798-1865) experimented with the suit in the Webb River in Oxford County. A set of bellows provided an air supply to the helmet through a hose. The test diver's boots were filled with lead shot to offset buoyancy. He was able to walk on the riverbed comfortably and remained

relatively dry.

Other diving suits had been invented, but the Norcross suit was different in that its rubber composition allowed the diver to move about freely and bend over, or even lie down underwater.

Norcross apparently was happy with the result; he named his son "Submarinus."

Hardly a one-trick pony, Norcross, born in Readfield, also was a millwright and a mechanic. He invented a threshing and separating machine, a nail-making machine, an accelerated wool spinner, and a stump lifter. He also lectured on astronomy and temperance and was a gospel preacher.

### June 15, 1781
### Revolutionary War Officers Escape from Jail in Castine

Brig. Gen. Peleg Wadsworth (1748-1829) and Maj. Benjamin Burton, both US Army officers being held prisoner by Loyalists during the Revolutionary War and confined at Fort George in British-controlled Castine, escape by cutting a hole in the roof of their jail cell.

They were captured and imprisoned for their role in the court-martial and execution of a Loyalist guide who had helped a group of people travel from Falmouth (now Portland) to Castine.

The incident is the second time the British take Wadsworth prisoner. He also was captured during the disastrous—from the Americans' perspective—Penobscot Expedition of 1779, and he escaped then as well.

Although the British are defeated in the war in 1781 and concede American independence in the 1783 Treaty of Paris, their forces remain in Castine until 1784.

Wadsworth later lives in Portland and serves in the U.S House of Representatives. He also becomes an overseer of Bowdoin Colllege. One of his grandchildren is famed poet Henry Wadsworth Longfellow (1807-1882), a Portland native.

## June 15, 1901
## Stage Play Marks Birth of Lakewood Theater

The stage play *The Private Secretary* opens at a swampy amusement park on the shore of Lake Wesserunsett in East Madison, constituting what now is regarded as the birth of the Lakewood Theater.

The theater later serves as a summer proving ground for many career singers, Broadway performers, and Hollywood stars.

Myrna Loy, Mama Cass Elliott, and John Travolta are among the luminaries who perform there.

## June 16, 1745
## Colonial Fighters Seize French Fortress on Cape Breton Island

New England Colonial fighters under the command of William Pepperrell (1696-1759), a wealthy Kittery merchant, seize control of the French Fortress of Louisbourg after a six-week siege during King George's War. One-third of the attacking Colonials are from Maine.

The fortress stands on Cape Breton Island. The island remained under French control under the terms of the Treaty of Utrecht, which ended Queen Anne's War (1702-1713). The French quickly built the fort, and it later served as a staging area for French raids against English settlements.

After the New Englanders' 1745 conquest of the fort, Pepperrell is made a baronet in recognition of his victory, becoming the first English colonist to be elevated to the ranks of nobility.

At the end of King George's War, the 1748 Treaty of Aix-la-

Chappelle restores the fortress to French control, but the French lose it permanently after the 1756-1763 French and Indian War.

Today, Cape Breton Island is part of the Canadian province of Nova Scotia. The fortress at Louisbourg, once destroyed, has been reconstructed partially. Parks Canada historical interpreters in clothing resembling that of the eighteenth century play the roles of French fort inhabitants when they tell visitors about the fortress's history.

## June 16, 1987
### Jay Mill Workers Begin Strike

About 1,250 employees walk off the job at the International Paper mill in Jay, beginning an ultimately unsuccessful 16-month strike that results in permanent replacement of the striking workers.

The strike begins after the rejection by Local 14 of the United Paperworkers International Union of a labor contract offer from IP, which was seeking major concessions from its workers at a time when its financial condition was sound. IP—the world's largest paper company and the nation's largest landowner—then spends lavishly on a public relations campaign to discredit the union. The workers, many of whom live in Jay or neighboring Livermore Falls, maintain a 24-hour-per-day picket line outside the mill and conduct a series of well-attended and well-publicized rallies, including a picket line at the governor's mansion in Augusta.

As the strike persists, IP hires replacement workers who become the targets of vandalism and threats of violence. The rift draws national attention and divides the region, causing people who once were close friends in the Androscoggin River towns to become bitter adversaries of one another.

"They threw a two-by-four through my windshield the first day I drove my truck into the mill, but it's been worth it," replacement worker Jay Clement tells the *Los Angeles Times*. "My wife's behind me one hundred percent and the kids think it's great. I can buy them things I could never afford before."

Around the state, the dispute arouses little sympathy either for the strikers, who were earning wages far greater than those of the average Maine worker; or for the company, which is seen as arrogant in its demands and its tactics.

The union's national office finally capitulates to the company in October 1988, offering to tell its members to return to work with no conditions attached. Embittered local members, feeling betrayed by union leaders, are demoralized further when the company, having found and trained enough replacements, announces that it has no jobs available for them.

"The strike helped to convince organized labor that the traditional strike weapon was ineffective, led to a major but unsuccessful effort to amend the National Labor Relations Act, and signaled the demise of adversarial collective bargaining that had dominated labor relations since World War II," University of Texas Law School professor Julius Getman concludes in his 1998 book on the strike.

Labor organizer Peter Kellman, hired by the Maine AFL-CIO to work with Local 14 during the strike, reflects on the event in his own book, published in 2004. Kellman describes labor unions as being fairly democratic at the local level but structured nationally in a way that discourages members' participation and often produces results that don't align with local members' interests.

"The result is that only a handful of people decide who speaks for labor in this country. And that handful is generally pretty far removed from the everyday life and pressures of the actual rank-and-file union members," Kellman writes.

Two years after the strike's end, about one hundred former mill-workers have been rehired at the mill. More than one thousand have not.

Despite severe contractions in the paper industry, the mill remains in production in the early twenty-first century. CMP Holdings LLC, a subsidiary of Ohio-based Verso Corp., buys the Jay mill from International Paper in 2006. Verso sells it to Pennsylvania-based Pixelle Specialty Solutions LLC in February 2020 as part of a $400 million deal that also includes a mill in Stevens Point, Wisconsin.

The Jay mill, established in 1885, employs about 500 workers today.

## June 17, 2019
### Single-Use Plastic Bags Banned

Gov. Janet Mills signs a bill into

law banning single-use plastic shopping bags. Maine becomes the fourth state to do so, after California, Hawaii, and New York.

The law is scheduled to take effect April 22, 2020, which is Earth Day, allowing businesses time to adjust to the change.

However, on March 17, 2020, Mills announces a delay of the ban's start until January 15, 2021, because of the coronvirus pandemic. Then the Maine Department of Environmental announces in December that it will delay enforcement of the ban until July 1, 2021, again because of the pandemic.

By the time of Mills' signing, twenty-four Maine municipalities already have adopted bag bans of their own, in an effort to prevent the bags from contaminating the environment.

According to co-sponsor Rep. Nicole Grohoski, D-Ellsworth, the Retail Association of Maine and the Maine Grocers and Food Producers Association requested the law to create a uniform statewide policy on the bags.

The law prohibits retailers from distributing the single-use plastic bags at the point of sale. They can offer customers paper bags but must charge at least five cents

each for them.

The law exempts certain kinds of bags, such as those used for prescription drugs, laundry, newspapers, and live animals.

## June 18, 1812
### War! America Again Battles British

The US Congress, citing continued British harassment of American shipping, declares war on the United Kingdom.

New England states refuse to contribute militias or money to the war effort. They continue trading with the British, and they come to regard Washington as a greater threat to their security and prosperity than London. In response, the federal government withdraws its troops from New England.

The War of 1812, which actually lasts until early 1815, results in an eight-month British occupation of all of Maine east of the Penobscot River, in the form of the short-lived crown colony of New Ireland.

The failure of the federal and Massachusetts governments to expel the British from that territory provides a fresh impetus to the decades-old movement to separate Maine from Massachusetts, a dream that finally is fulfilled in 1820.

June 18, 1864

## Chamberlain Suffers Grievous Wound on Virginia Battlefield

A ricocheting bullet penetrates the right thigh of Col. Joshua Chamberlain and tears through his whole body to his left hip while he is directing his troops in at attack on a Confederate battery during the Second Battle of Petersburg. He is told his wound probably is fatal.

On the same day, the First Maine Heavy Artillery, recruited mostly from Maine's Penobscot Valley, suffers 632 casualties of about 900 men engaged in combat in a hopeless attack on the defenses at Petersburg, about twenty-five miles south of the Confederate capital at Richmond, Virginia.

Chamberlain, whose troops helped turn the tide against the Confederacy in the 1863 Battle of Gettysburg, at this point in the Civil War is the commander of First Brigade, First Division, Fifth Corps.

After being shot, he thrusts the point of his sword into the ground to steady himself, then stands rigidly upright in full view of his troops, to keep them motivated while they are under relentless fire from Confederate infantrymen and cannons. Eventually he collapses because of his loss of blood.

Rescuers remove him from the battlefield as his men are being cut down and blown to bits all around him. Doctors at a field hospital three miles away remove the bullet and patch him up, but they have little hope for his recovery.

"My darling wife," Chamberlain writes the next day to Fanny Chamberlain, who is at home in Brunswick Maine. "I am lying mortally wounded the doctors think, but my mind & heart are at peace ... God bless & keep & comfort you, precious one, you have been a precious wife to me."

On June 20, Gen. Ulysses Grant, commander of the Union armies, gives Chamberlain a battlefield promotion to brigadier general. He is transferred the next day to the naval hospital at Annapolis, Maryland. Defying expectations, he begins to recover and is furloughed home to Brunswick on September 20. On November 18, he returns to duty at Petersburg.

Petersburg eventually falls to Union forces in April 1865 after a ten-month siege. Confederate Gen. Robert E. Lee signs the Army of Northern Virginia's surrender document April 9 at Appomattox Courthouse, Virginia. Chamberlain presides over the Confederates' surrender of their arms there on April 12.

## June 18, 1889
### Bangor Daily News Debuts; Competes with Whig & Courier

The *Bangor Daily News* begins publication after Bangor shipping magnate Thomas J. Stewart failed to convince another Bangor daily, the *Whig & Courier*, to back his candidacy for a congressional seat. He establishes the *Daily News* as a way to promote his run for office. Stewart loses his political race, but his newspaper outlasts its two daily competitors in the Queen City.

Under new ownership, the *News* buys the *Whig & Courier* in 1900 and merges the two operations into one. The other Bangor daily, the *Evening Commercial*, continues operating until 1956, when diminishing circulation and a fire put it out of business.

The *Bangor Daily News* initially is modeled on the format of the *New York Herald*, even using the same typeface. Its chief editor, George Miner, comes from the *Herald*; and the *News* is the first paper in New England to receive *Herald* reports by cable and publish them.

The *News* grows to become northern New England's largest newspaper by the late 1940s. More than 130 years after its founding, the paper is still in business and is the only one of Maine's six daily newspapers that remains independently owned.

## June 18, 1964
### Brewer's Joe Ferris Named Most Outstanding Player at College World Series

University of Maine sophomore pitcher Joe Ferris, a Brewer native, wins the Most Outstanding Player Award at the end of the 1964 NCAA University Division Baseball Tournament's College World Series, held in Omaha, Nebraska. His team, the Black Bears, places third in the series among eight teams.

UMaine also appears in the series in 1976, 1981, 1982, 1983, 1984, and 1986.

As for Ferris, he becomes a lawyer who, after decades of practicing in Brewer and Bangor, still is engaged in that profession. He also still holds the UMaine season pitching record for winning percentage—1.000 with nine straight victories, including two College World Series wins, in 1964; and the UMaine career

Photo by John Patriquin; courtesy of Portland Press Herald
US Sen. Susan Collins is flanked by US Sen. Olympia Snowe and Collins' mother, Patricia Collins, in Portland in 1996.

record, .842, with a 16-3 win-loss tally over three seasons.

## June 18, 2019
### Susan Collins Casts 7,000th Consecutive Senate Vote

US Sen. Susan Collins, a Republican who grew up in Caribou, casts her seven thousandth consecutive Senate vote, never having missed a vote since she took office in 1997.

At the time of the achievement, Collins has the third-longest skein of consecutive votes in Senate history, behind those of U.S. Sen. William Proxmire (1915-2005), a Wisconsin Democrat, with 10,252; and Republican Sen. Charles Grassley, of Iowa, who amasses a total of 8,927 consecutive votes from 1993 until November 2020, when he goes into quarantine after testing positive for a COVID-19 infection.

Collins went to great lengths to keep the streak alive. Once a vote was scheduled unexpectedly when she had boarded a plane that was preparing to take off. She got off the plane immediately and went to the Senate chamber. Another time she broke an ankle while rushing to the chamber, but she voted anyway.

"Mainers are known for their work ethic and diligence, and by showing up for every vote, I hope that I am carrying out that Maine tradition," she tells an interviewer on the day of her landmark vote.

During her successful 2020 quest for election to a fifth six-year Senate term, Collins notes that her consecutive voting streak remains unbroken.

### June 19, 1760
### Cumberland, Lincoln Counties Created

York County, which has comprised all of Maine since the late seventeenth century, is carved into sections to create Cumberland and Lincoln counties. Those new counties later will be reduced in size to create additional counties.

Cumberland County, with a population of 281,674 recorded in the 2010 census and location of many of the state's larger communities, is the most populous of Maine's sixteen counties.

Lincoln, with 34,457 people, is the fourth-smallest in population in 2010.

### June 19, 1936
### Twelve Children Die in Boating Accident Down East

Twelve children from four rural schools taking part in an outing to celebrate the end of the school year drown when wind capsizes a boat in which they are riding on Gardner Lake, near East Machias.

It was the last boat trip of the day. Three other children and a 70-year-old man are rescued.

One of the children, Miriam Kelley (1926-2018), escapes death when high school student Wyman Ramsdell grabs her by the hair to hold her head above water. In the early twenty-first century, Kelley, by then known by her married name, Miriam Doherty, and having worked twenty-six years as a teacher in the Lubec school system, winds up being the Gardner Lake accident's last living survivor.

### June 19, 1939
### Little Deer Isle Connected to Mainland Via Bridge

The Deer Isle-Sedgwick Bridge

is dedicated, sixteen months after the start of its construction, then opens December 31 of that year. It constitutes the first fixed link across Eggemoggin Reach between the mainland and Little Deer Isle.

The bridge sustains severe damage when unusually intense storms in the winter of 1942-43 cause it to move in a way resembling the movement of the Tacoma Narrows Bridge in Washington state, which collapsed in 1940 shortly after opening. As a result, the Maine bridge is strengthened extensively during its repair.

June 20, 2011
### Uganda Native Kakande Sentenced for Sham Wedding Scheme

Rashid Kakande, a 37-year-old native of the African nation of Uganda, is sentenced in US District Court in Bangor to two years in prison for masterminding a series of sham weddings involving Americans who marry Africans with expiring US visas.

He was convicted March 24 of conspiring to defraud the US government. The case, adjudicated at US District Court in Portland, was part of a US Immigration and Customs Enforcement probe that lasted more than four years.

Kakande, listed as living in Lexington, Massachusetts, is implicated in nine of the bogus marriages. He tells the court he received $1,000 to $1,500 for arranging each of them. The American spouses were paid at least $1,500 for going through with the scam, and up to $5,000 if they agreed to meet with lawyers and immigration officials to make the marriage look more convincing.

Wedding photos were taken of each couple, with the bride wearing a wedding gown and floral arrangements prominently displayed, the prosecutor said, and they were used to make the marriages appear to be legitimate.

Kakande is sentenced in June to two years in prison.

Many of the participants in the plot also were tried and convicted before Kakande's conviction, and others are prosecuted successfully afterward.

June 21, 1979
### Original Jordan Pond House Building Destroyed by Fire

The original Jordan Pond House, an historic and popular Acadia National Park attraction, is destroyed by fire.

It was built as a farmhouse in

*Courtesy of Mr. Klein/Shutterstock.com*
Jordan Pond and The Bubbles near the Jordan Pond House at Acadia National Park.

1847 and eventually converted to a restaurant. It was famous for its tea and popovers served beside Jordan Pond and in the shadow of the rounded hills known as "The Bubbles."

John D. Rockefeller Jr. bought the Seal Harbor building in 1928 and donated it to Acadia National Park in 1940. A replacement building is completed in 1982 and is accessed by the Park Loop Road.

June 21, 1954
**US Sen. Margaret Chase Smith Wins Republican Primary**

US Sen. Margaret Chase Smith (1897-1995), running for election to a second Senate term, defeats Robert L. Jones in a Republican primary election by a five-to-one margin, even though US Sen. Joseph McCarthy, a Wisconsin Republican noted for his accusations about communists infiltrating the federal government, surreptitiously backs Jones.

Smith aide William C. Lewis Jr., writing later about McCarthy's failed effort to make a dent in Smith's popular support, says, "Suddenly his paralytic power over the United States Senate was lifted and destroyed."

Smith eventually serves four six-year Senate terms, leaving office in 1973 after losing a re-election bid to Democrat William Hathaway. She retires to her home in Skowhegan.

After Smith's death, her house becomes the Margaret Chase Smith Library, which features both a library and museum exhibits about Smith's life and congressional career.

## June 22, 2013
### Final Class Graduates from Bangor Theological Seminary

The Bangor Theological Seminary graduates its final class after nearly two centuries of operation.

Founded in 1814 in the Congregational tradition of the United Church of Christ, it was northern New England's only graduate school of religion.

The school had announced in 2011 that it was planning to close.

Forty-seven students receive degrees at the final graduation ceremony, held at Husson University's Gracie Theatre in Bangor.

"There is rejoicing and weeping," seminary President Robert Grove-Markwood tells the five hundred attendees, according to the *Bangor Daily News*. "There

is weeping in our rejoicing and rejoicing in our weeping."

In July, the campus becomes the home of the nonprofit BTS Center, which bills itself as "a think tank and incubator for twenty-first-century ministry" that carries on the seminary's mission. The institution consolidates its activities soon after that in Portland, where it remains in operation in 2021.

## June 23, 1862
### Portland Daily Press Published

The first issue of the *Portland Daily Press* appears. The four-page tabloid newspaper is published on Exchange Street. Subscriptions cost fifty cents a month or five dollars per year. The *Press* later is merged with *The Portland Herald* in 1921 to form the *Portland Press Herald*.

## June 23, 2017
### Fire Destroys Vacant Mill; Boys Charged with Arson

About 100 firefighters combat a blaze that breaks out in the five-story, vacant former Stenton Trust Mill in Sanford. Three boys are charged in the case.

The mill complex, built in 1922, was where the Goodall Worsted Co. manufactured Palm

Beach cloth, a lightweight fabric used in making men's suits.

Two of three boys charged with arson in the case plead guilty to lesser charges in October. The River Street mill building, which was used for textile manufacturing, is demolished in 2019.

On October 19, 2017, four months after the mill fire, another Sanford blaze destroys six buildings on Island Avenue, in the heart of the city, and sends four people to the hospital.

Witnesses say they smelled smoke, then eventually saw flames in a pile of trash on the back porch of one of the buildings.

The fire put firefighters in danger because it burned through power lines, which were falling into the street, according to the fire chief.

The fire crews used a drone equipped with a video feed to see the fire's scope fully and to figure out the best ways to direct water from their hoses.

## June 24, 1794
### Bowdoin College Chartered; Named for Massachusetts Governor

The Massachusetts State Legislature charters Bowdoin College, which is named after the late Massachusetts Gov. James Bow-

doin II, an amateur scientist and influential advocate of American independence.

At the time of its founding, Bowdoin is the easternmost college in the United States.

The Massachusetts state government and the governor's son, James Bowdoin III, provide the college with an endowment.

The college expects to acquire money for operations from the sale of wilderness land it receives from towns and the state, but those sales take longer than expected. The college finally opens on September 2, 1802. Its first building is Massachusetts Hall.

The college is located in Brunswick as a compromise between Portland interests and people who live in the Kennebec Valley and farther east.

Bowdoin strongly identifies with the Congregationalist Church. It also becomes a center of support for the Federalist Party and of opposition to separating Maine from Massachusetts. On the threshold of Maine statehood, however, separation advocates succeed in inserting an article into the Maine Constitution that gives the Legislature the authority to regulate colleges, which tempers the school's partisan leanings.

June 24, 1970
## Four Killed in Interstate 95 Bridge Construction Accident in Kittery

A construction platform on the Kittery side of the Piscataqua River Bridge, then being built as part of Interstate 95, collapses shortly after seven o'clock in the morning, dropping four workers to their deaths.

The accident also inflicts a range of injuries on nine other workers. Three others avoid death by grabbing a girder and clinging to it for an hour until they can be rescued.

The workers are cleaning girders on the bridge when the staging collapses. The platform on which they stand is about eighty feet long and ten feet wide and is suspended on steel tracks between the bridge piers.

Construction of the $21 million bridge began in 1968 and is completed in 1971.

June 25, 1789
## Hancock, Washington Become Maine's Fourth, Fifth Counties

Hancock and Washington counties, the fourth and fifth Maine counties, are set off from Lincoln County, temporarily making the map of Maine counties look like five north-to-south zebra stripes.

Hancock County, located on Maine's eastern coast, is the home of Acadia National Park and the Maine Maritime Academy. It also is a major hub of the state's lobster industry.

The county is recorded as having 54,418 residents in the 2010 US Census. The county seat is the city of Ellsworth.

Next-door Washington County, which shares a border with the Canadian province of New Brunswick, is the state's easternmost county and the one with the highest tides. Most of Maine's lowbush blueberry crop is harvested here, as are cranberries.

Washington County's 2010 population was 32,826, making it Maine's third-least-populous county. Its county seat is the town of Machias.

British forces occupied parts of both counties during the War of 1812.

June 25, 1955
## President Eisenhower Visits Maine, Fishes on Magalloway River

Exit the plane, then immediately grab a fishing rod. That's President Dwight Eisenhower's prescription for relaxing when he arrives to spend a few days at Parmachenee Camps in Lynch-town Township, in far northern Oxford County.

Fly-casting on the Magallo-way River at Little Boy Falls, and using flies tied by his guide, Don Cameron, of Wilson's Mills, the 64-year-old president lands three trout in fifteen minutes in full view of a clutch of photographers, who then are released—as are the fish.

Because of his job, Eisenhower has to set aside a few moments to keep tabs on his administration's handling of an incident involving a Soviet fighter jet that shot at a US Navy plane in international waters of the Bering Strait.

Then it's back to casting flies.

Later he enjoys a baked-bean supper with ham, salad, and pie, followed by a game of bridge with GOP national commit-teeman Fred C. Scribner Jr., of Portland, state Sen. James L. Reid, of Hallowell, and Sid-ney W. Thaxter, of Portland. At 10:30 p.m. it's lights out.

The next morning, with more privacy, he scores a three-pound landlocked salmon, also on the Magalloway. Then, with his entourage, Eisenhower leaves the fishing camp, with welts from blackfly bites encircling his wrists.

In Skowhegan, introduced to a crowd of 7,500 by local

icon US Sen. Margaret Chase Smith, Eisenhower talks about the importance of world peace. Then he broils a steak for himself at a cookout with Smith, Gov. Edmund Muskie, and other dig-nitaries before trundling off to Dow Air Force Base in Bangor to meet US Secretary of State John Foster Dulles, who accompa-nies him on Eisenhower's plane, *Columbine III*, for the 8:15 p.m. flight back to Washington.

The departure ends a six-day New England tour by the president, who has not said yet whether he plans to seek re-elec-tion the following year. He does run, and he wins.

### June 26, 1871
### Train Accident Damages Track; One Killed, Others Injured

An axle breaks in Freeport on a railroad tender on a Maine Central Railroad train bound for Portland, causing the tender to fall and rip up sections of track east of Freeport.

The six cars behind the tender overturn, killing baggage master George Chase, of Skowhegan, who is crushed beneath the demolished baggage car in which he was riding; and injuring many other people, including a brakeman, Alfred Barron, whose leg is trapped and bleeding severely. Dr. F.N. Otis, of New York, who happens to be on board the train, removes the crushed part of Barron's leg with a knife and a saw.

The train departed Bangor earlier in the day and stopped in Augusta. It was carrying cars from Farmington and Skowhegan that had been attached en route.

"In all the wreck and crush of matter that we have described it may almost be counted as a miracle that no passenger was materially injured," the *Portland Daily Press* reported the next day, after a long recitation of how each of the derailed cars burrowed into the ground or lay askew on the tracks.

The next day, June 27, two other Maine Central trains collide head-on south of Hallowell, causing the death of engineer David H. Berry, of Brunswick, who was working aboard the southbound train, which left Augusta just before three o'clock in the afternoon. Several others aboard the trains are injured severely.

The wife and child of Chase, who died in the Freeport accident, also are aboard the southbound train in the Hallowell crash. After the collision, the woman grabs her child and leaps out of the car,

despite other passengers' efforts to restrain her, and falls down an embankment.

## June 26, 1943
### Bomber on Training Flight Crashes in Fort Fairfield, Killing Nine

A twin-engine Army bomber plane crashes into a potato field in Fort Fairfield, killing the pilot, 1st Lt. Bernard M. Robertson, of Greenville Junction, and the other four people on the plane, as well as four people on the ground.

One of the plane's wings strikes the ground, causing the plane to cartwheel end over end and fling off parts that cut down the workers in the field.

The plane was in the midst of a training flight.

Robertson was a former Maine State Police officer. The crash site is partly on farmland owned by Robertson's father-in-law, Carl Rasmussen. The victims on the ground, including a 9-year-old boy, were picking rocks out of the potato field for Rasmussen.

The crash shows that while many Americans are putting their lives on the line in World War II—at that time, the bloody Italian campaign is front-page news—military operations in the United States carry their own share of risk.

Courtesy of Islandport Press

Helen Hamlin, author of *Nine Mile Bridge*.

June 26, 1917

### Author Helen Hamlin Born in Fort Kent; Teaches at Churchill Depot

Helen Leidy, who would go on to teach school in a remote lumber camp and write the classic book *Nine Mile Bridge* about her adventures in the northern Maine wilderness after marrying game warden Willis "Curly" Hamlin, is born in Fort Kent.

Helen Hamlin attends Mada-waska Training School in Fort Kent (now the University of Maine-Fort Kent) and becomes fluent in French.

Her first teaching job is at the remote lumber camp settlement of Churchill Depot, an outpost along the Allagash River on Churchill Lake, some sixty miles southwest of Fort Kent. The camp is nearly all men and she is initially told she can't go because she is a woman.

Her descriptions of the region and the depot, now a ghost town but once a bustling community of twenty or so families that processed thousands of people annually, help preserve a way of life that has vanished from the state.

## June 27, 1820
## Medical School of Maine Established

Maine's first Legislature establishes the Medical School of Maine and puts it under the control of the trustees and overseers of Bowdoin College.

Legislators supply $1,500 for initial expenses and authorize a $1,000 annual payment after that, although that ceases in 1834. The school opens in 1821 in Bowdoin's Massachusetts Hall, then moves in 1862 to Seth Adams Hall.

The school's establishment is important in a heavily forested, thinly populated state that otherwise gives medical practitioners few chances to exchange ideas with their professional peers. It has the added utility of giving physicians a platform from which to influence the development of public policy concerning their field. It also serves to boost public

confidence in the profession.

"A medical degree was becoming important in distinguishing the serious physician from others involved in the field—the practitioners trained in the apprenticeship method, the homeopaths, and the quacks and charlatans," Dr. Thomas Keating, of Portland, writes in a 2016 article about the school.

The Medical School of Maine grows rapidly at first, from an enrollment of twenty-one in 1821 to more than eighty in 1834. It begins to suffer in the late nineteenth century, however, from its relative remoteness from medical facilities in Portland, at a time when medical colleges depend more and more on close interaction with hospitals and related institutions. Although some schools of that era are far worse, Keating writes, the Maine school "was unable to keep pace with modern developments."

Philanthropist Andrew Carnegie funds a movement in the early 1900s to improve medical education and shut down substandard schools. His investigators, through a report by Abraham Flexner, give Maine's school a poor rating. After the faculty and the enrollment shrink during World War I, and with the school running a $7,000 annual deficit, the trustees vote to close the school, but the overseers refuse.

The Medical Council's decision to reduce the school from a Class A ranking deals the final blow. The school graduates its final class in 1921, then goes out of existence.

## June 27, 1863
### Confederate Sailors Steal Schooner, Capture Revenue Service Cutter

Confederate Navy sailors under the command of Lt. Charles Read sneak into Portland Harbor aboard the fishing schooner *Archer*, which they captured three days earlier.

Read and his crew have spent the previous three weeks capturing or destroying a series of Northern vessels along the Atlantic coast. Their goal in Portland is to seize either the sidewheel steamer *Chesapeake* or the *Caleb Cushing*, a US Revenue Service cutter. Evading detection by the Union soldiers on duty at the three forts, they enter the inner harbor late on the night of June 26.

Read's engineer tells him he would need several hours to get the *Chesapeake's* engine running, and the cover of darkness doesn't

last long in late June, so Read decides to seize the *Caleb Cushing* instead. Two boarding parties on small boats take the cutter's crewmen by surprise, put them in irons and hold them prisoner below deck, promising to free them after the cutter clears the outer harbor.

Getting away presents many obstacles. First, the rebels are unable to discard the *Caleb Cushing's* anchor chain, so they have to haul it aboard. Then the cutter is discovered to be aground, so they attach a line to another ship to pull the cutter to deeper water. Finally, the wind dies down, making the sails useless, so rebel crewmen use small rowboats to tow the cutter out of the inner harbor.

When the port's customs collector learns about 8 a.m. that the cutter is missing, he charters four vessels and asks local Army units for help. The *Chesapeake*, with the 7th Maine Union Wharf soldiers aboard, and the paddle-wheel-driven steamer *Forest City* quickly leave to pursue the purloined cutter. They catch up with it near Green Island Reef, near the outer edge of the outer harbor.

Read and his rebel crew have guns and plenty of gunpowder, but they are unable to find a secret compartment where most of the *Caleb Cushing's* shot and shells are stored. They begin firing scrap metal at the *Forest City*, which pulls back to avoid damage to its vulnerable paddle wheels. When the *Chesapeake* arrives, the firing stops. The Confederates have run out of ammunition.

The *Chesapeake* crew votes to ram the *Caleb Cushing* amidships, or, if that is unsuccessful, to board it.

Read sees both steamers approaching, so he gives the order to burn the cutter. Then he, his crew, and the prisoners flee separately in smaller boats.

Seeing the cutter ablaze, the *Chesapeake* starts to turn away, knowing it is about to explode. However, some men from the *Chesapeake* take a small boat to fetch another boat tied to the side of the doomed cutter.

They free the empty boat and are about halfway back to the *Chesapeake* when the fire reaches the *Caleb Cushing's* powder magazine and blows the cutter to pieces, sending flaming shards of masts, spars, and other objects hundreds of feet into the air.

The cutter sinks almost immediately.

The *Chesapeake* picks up the *Caleb Cushing's* crew members, still in irons. The *Forest City* takes Read and his men prisoner. It also finds the *Archer* and tows it back into the harbor.

It is the last time the Confederacy infiltrates Portland Harbor.

Read ends up in an island prison in Boston Harbor, from which he nearly escapes. Later he is exchanged in a prisoner swap and returns to the Confederacy.

## June 27, 1900
### Gift Establishes Site of Future Theater at Monmouth

Cumston Hall, a striking Romanesque revival and Queen Anne-style building on the east side of Main Street in the center of Monmouth, is dedicated, the gift of Dr. Charles Cumston, after construction that lasted a year.

The new building houses the town library, an auditorium, and town offices. Later it becomes—and remains—well-known regionally as the longtime home of the Theater at Monmouth, a year-round repertory company of professionals performing Shakespeare plays and other stage productions.

The building is added to the National Register of Historic Places in 1973.

## June 28, 1991
### Lewiston's Gamache Wins WBA Featherweight Title

Joey Gamache, 25, of Lewiston, wins the World Boxing Association's super featherweight title by achieving a technical knockout against Jerry Ngobeni, 24, of South Africa, at the Lewiston Raceway.

Gamache later wins the WBA lightweight title on June 13, 1992, in a fight against Chil-Sung Jun, 31, of South Korea. He remains the only person from Maine who has won a world boxing title.

At the age of 10, when Gamache was having trouble mastering some baseball skills, his father encouraged him to work out in a boxing gymnasium to strengthen his throwing arm. That led to a fascination with boxing that exceeded his interest in baseball. Trained by Tony Lampron and Teddy Atlas, he turned professional in 1987 and won his first twenty-nine pro bouts.

Gamache's pro career record is fifty-five wins—including thirty-eight knockouts—and four losses in fifty-nine professional bouts, of which the first seven and two others take place in Maine. Six of them are held in France.

In a February 26, 2000, match at Madison Square Garden in New York, Italian-Canadian boxer Arturo Gatti (1972-2009) knocks Gamache out in two rounds with such force that it puts Gamache in a hospital for days and prompts him to end his career. Gamache says he suffered a brain injury during the bout with Gatti.

He later files a lawsuit against the New York State Athletic Commission, claiming that Gatti weighed too much for the fight and that a failure to monitor Gatti's weight properly played a role in Gamache's loss of both the bout and his career.

In 2010, Judge Melvin Schweitzer rules that based on the evidence, he concludes that boxing commission official Anthony Russo allowed Gatti to step off a scale before ascertaining that the boxer had met the weight limit. Schweitzer says he cannot conclude, however, that the flawed maintenance of boxing standards caused Gamache to lose the bout and stop boxing.

HBO Boxing unofficially weighed Gatti at 160 pounds and Gamache at 145 pounds.

Gamache now works as a boxing trainer.

## June 29, 1914
### Interurban Trolley Service Established Between Lewiston and Portland

The Arbutus, an electric car on the Portland-Lewiston Interurban trolley, makes the system's initial run from Lewiston to Portland with inspecting railroad commissioners on board.

The system starts with six cars and eventually expands to nine. Shortly after it starts operation, the Portland-Lewiston Interurban becomes an electric railroad subsidiary of the Androscoggin Electric Company. When it starts regular operation, the service offers runs every two hours between Monument Square and Union Square in Lewiston and makes eleven stops for a fare of seventy-five cents. The running time is ninety minutes and the last train leaves Portland at 10 p.m. Within short order, additional cars are added and service is offered every hour. Eventually, an express run making stops only in West Falmouth, Gray, New Gloucester, Upper Gloucester, and Danville is added, as is a run making additional local stops.

The increasing popularity of cars and construction of a modern highway between the two cities in the late 1920s reduces demand for the Interurban, and the line goes out of service on June 29, 1933—nineteen years to the day after its opening. Parts of the Maine Turnpike are built over the right-of-way for the Interurban.

## June 29, 1941
### Boat Accident Kills 14 Picnickers Bound for Monhegan Island

The 40-foot cabin cruiser *Don*, loaded with picnic-bound passengers from the towns of Rumford and Mexico, heads from Harpswell to Monhegan Island.

The motorboat stops briefly at West Point, near Phippsburg's Cape Small, before beginning its three-hour crossing to the island at 10 a.m. Then it disappears.

A search reveals that the worst maritime catastrophe in sixteen years has killed everyone aboard. Two of the dead are found floating off Bailey Island. A total of fourteen bodies are recovered by mid-July. Some are wearing wristwatches, which are stopped at times ranging from 11:35 to 11:43. None of the bodies is wearing a life jacket, even though the vessel was equipped with forty of them, suggesting that the emergency developed quickly.

The *Don's* wheelhouse and

some other wreckage float ashore. A board of inquiry concludes that a groundswell caused the boat to capsize because of instability and the weight of the passengers. Other observers theorize that the boat exploded, noting that it had a history of gasoline tank repairs, and that it was carrying 150 gallons of gasoline on the Monhegan trip.

A state official says the vessel had sunk three times before and was raised again each time.

## June 30, 1818
### United States Regains Eastport, Relinquishes Claims to Eastern Islands

As a result of successful negotiations with the British in 1817, the United States regains control of Eastport, which the British had occupied since seizing it—and the rest of eastern Maine—during the War of 1812.

The Americans relinquish claims to islands east of Eastport that now are part of the Canadian province of New Brunswick.

The British occupied Eastport and the rest of Moose Island for four years. During that time, both the British and American governments seemed to disown the area in terms of recognizing its residents as full citizens.

Maine was still part of Massachusetts during the war and remains so until 1820. The Massachusetts government levied state taxes in Eastport, as it did everywhere else, and sued to collect them; but its legislature refused to seat a senator elected from there, calling it a conquered district.

Peace with England reduced the tension somewhat, but the 1814 Treaty of Ghent, which ended the war, left the issue of which country owned Moose Island and outlying areas in the hands of peace commissioners. It took three years for the commissioners to determine that Moose Island belongs to the United States, and another six months to bring British martial law there to an end.

On June 30, US Army Brig. Gen. James Miller and Army Col. Henry Sargent, representing US President James Monroe and Massachusetts Gov. John Brooks, respectively, meet with Capt. R. Gibbon, the British commandant, to exchange flags and accept the territory's formal restoration.

—30—

# JULY

July 1, 1950
## Scarborough Downs Opens for First Horse Races

The newly constructed Scarborough Downs racetrack opens for its first horse races in Scarborough.

The facility includes a grand-stand that has a capacity of sixty-five hundred spectators, stables for a thousand horses, and parking for six thousand cars.

The million-dollar complex was carved from a patch of woods in seventy-three days. The track was built despite opposition from anti-

Courtesy of Portland Press Herald
Opening day at Scarborough Downs in 1990.

gambling groups and harness racing fans who thought the Scarborough track could harm the nearby Gorham Raceway and local agricultural fairs, which also sponsor races. Legal battles between the two factions last for years.

Alfredo Montiero, riding the horse Fighting Foot in the $2,500 Governor's Cup opening day feature, claims victory in the first race.

It is apparent within weeks that the number of fans is not enough to justify afternoon races, so the racetrack installs lights and becomes the first track in the nation to hold races at night.

In 1959, the track draws an attendance of about 260,000 for a forty-eight-day season, and betting tops $9 million. The track begins to falter financially in the 1960s, when other venues arise to compete with it and vacation visitors' preferences start to change. Then the New York-based Ogden Corp. buys the track in 1969, makes about a million dollars' worth of improvements and introduces harness racing.

In the 1970s, the track abandons thoroughbred racing and turns exclusively to harness racing. It also hosts horse shows, a rodeo, band concerts, a square dance convention, a snowmobile show, and fairs in an effort to stay in the black.

In 1985, Joseph Ricci, who bought the track in 1979 and continues to own it until his death in 2001, spends three million dollars to expand and renovate its facilities.

Maine voters approve a referendum in 2003 authorizing the track to offer its customers access to slot machines, subject to local approval. Voters in Scarborough and Westbrook, which track officials were considering as an alternate site, shoot down the idea, however.

State law grants Scarborough Downs a share of the proceeds from racetrack-connected slot machines in Bangor.

The added revenue proves to be insufficient. After suffering financial losses for about 15 years, the track ends live racing on the premises on November 28, 2020.

On February 3, 2021, a 30,000-square-foot mass vaccination clinic opens at the former racetrack to inoculate people against the coronavirus, which has been spreading worldwide for more than a year. The clinic is expected to vaccinate up to 2,000 people per day.

## July 1, 1999
### Edwards Dam Breached; Kennebec Flows Freely Again

Reggie Barnes, an employee of demolition contractor H.E. Sargent, uses a giant backhoe to break through the Edwards Dam in Augusta at 9:21 a.m., allowing the Kennebec River to flow freely there for the first time since 1837.

"I thought of wearing a tuxedo, but I also thought better of it," Barnes, sporting a hard hat, tells the *Kennebec Journal.* "This shouldn't take more than ten minutes, once we get underway."

The first breaching of a functioning hydroelectric dam comes about because, also for the first time, the Federal Energy Regulatory Commission, against the owner's wishes, declined in 1997 to renew the dam's license.

Interior Secretary Bruce Babbitt says the Edwards Dam's demise sets a national precedent that will and should be followed, given the appropriate circumstances. The dam's removal helps to restore the fish population in the river and set a template for dam removal projects elsewhere in the country.

The *Kennebec Journal,* through the repeated urging of editor Luther Severance, played a role in getting the dam built in the first place. In 1825, the year he co-founded the paper, Severance began agitating for the dam's construction to provide a power source and encourage industrial development.

The Legislature granted a dam charter in 1834, and a corporation headed by Reuel Williams built the dam from 1836 to 1837.

## July 2, 1855
### Portland Rum Riot Kills One, Injures Seven

Portland Mayor Neal Dow calls out the militia to use lethal force against rock-throwing participants in the Portland Rum Riot. On Dow's order, militiamen fire into the crowd of more than a thousand people, killing one person and wounding seven.

The crowd gathered because police were resisting an effort to carry out a court-ordered search at City Hall, where the prohibitionist mayor was storing alcohol.

The city's Irish residents take Dow's campaign against booze as an attack on them, and some of them initiated the court proceeding that resulted in the issuance of the search warrant.

The crowd reacts violently when the police keep the searchers at bay. Some call the mayor a

Col. Joshua L. Chamberlain

hypocrite, unaware that the alcohol was being reserved for medicinal purposes.

## July 2, 1863
### Chamberlain's Troops Stand Firm During Battle of Gettysburg

Col. Joshua Chamberlain (1828-1914), of Brunswick, while suffering from malaria and dysentery, successfully leads the Twentieth Maine Regiment in fending off a Confederate attack by Col. William Oates' Fifteenth Alabama Regiment at the extreme left of the Union Army's line at Little Round Top, helping enable the Union forces to win the Civil War's Battle of Gettysburg in Pennsylvania.

On the same day, and in another action of the Battle of Gettysburg, Brig. Gen. Adelbert Ames (1835-1933), a native of what now is Rockland and the Twentieth Maine's previous commander, takes part in hand-to-hand combat alongside his Eleventh Corps division troops while successfully fending off a Confederate assault on Cemetery Hill.

Chamberlain, a former Bowdoin College professor, approached the strategic boulder-strewn prominence known as Little Round Top with two of his brothers, Tom and John. When a Rebel shot whizzes past all of their faces, he suggests the brothers split up, or another such shot "might make it hard for Mother."

Late that afternoon, Chamberlain's brigade commander, Col. Strong Vincent, shows him the spot on the hill that his men must defend. Failure to do so would imperil the entire Union force at Gettysburg.

With his men interspersed among trees and boulders to give them good firing positions, Chamberlain notices suddenly that the enemy artillery has stopped firing. He knows that means the Confederate infantry is coming up the hill, and that the Confederate battery wants to avoid striking its own troops.

Firing breaks out all along the line formed by Vincent's brigade. Chamberlain steps up onto a boulder and sees that Oates' Alabama troops are rushing to his left to try to make an end run around his regiment and attack it from the side and rear. He bends his line into a hook so the Twentieth Maine units on the far left will be in position to face the attackers dead on. When the Rebels emerge from cover, they face a well-positioned Union line firing at them.

The ensuing fight lasts nearly two hours at great cost to both sides. The line of skirmish moves backward and forward in waves. Oates' brother is killed, shot from multiple directions. The Rebels withdraw, then advance a second time without breaking through the Union line.

When a third charge seems imminent, and with many of his men having run out of ammunition, Chamberlain orders a bayonet charge with his front line wheeling about to the right, like a gate swinging shut.

The sight of 200 screaming Union soldiers racing down the hill, with Yankee sharpshooters behind them firing into the Confederate lines, throws the Rebels into panic. Many run away. Those who are not shot down or bayonetted are captured en masse. When Oates orders a retreat, his entire force flees in disorderly panic.

With that costly burst of courage, Little Round Top remains in Union hands; and after the Confederates fare no better during Pickett's Charge and other combat the following day, Confederate Gen. Robert E. Lee's army withdraws from Pennsylvania and back to Virginia, never to set foot on Northern territory again.

Actor Jeff Daniels portrays Chamberlain in the 1993 film *Gettysburg*, and he does so again in the 2003 film *Gods and Generals*, the plot of which precedes that of *Gettysburg*.

After the war ends in 1865, Chamberlain serves four consecutive one-year terms as Maine's governor. He dies in 1914 from complications of a wartime wound suffered during combat in 1864 at Petersburg, Virginia.

Adelbert Ames eventually becomes the last surviving permanently promoted Civil War general officer. Like Chamberlain, Ames becomes a governor, although appointed provisionally by Congress, not elected. He serves as governor of Mississippi while it is under post-Civil War martial law, then as a US senator from that state after it is readmitted to the union in 1870.

## July 3, 1847
### President Polk Visits Maine

Cannons boom and bells ring in Augusta as President James K. Polk (1795-1849) pays a call in the city at the invitation of the Legislature, which had learned Polk was planning a New England tour.

The president and several officials traveling with him—including Secretary of State and future President James Buchanan (1791-1868) and US Attorney General Nathan Clifford, who is from Maine—ride to Augusta after arriving around 1 a.m. in Hallowell aboard the steamer *Huntress*.

The State House, the hotels, and most other buildings on State Street are ablaze with light for the occasion and remain so after Polk and his party proceed to the home of former US Sen. Reuel Williams, like Polk a Democrat, on the town's east side.

Late the next morning, the president joins a procession that forms at the west end of the Kennebec Bridge—the location of the today's Calumet Bridge at Old Fort Western—and moves through Augusta's principal streets to the State House, greeting well-wishers from a barouche, which is an open carriage. At the State House, Gov. John Dana introduces him to legislators, who have gathered in the House of Representatives. Polk addresses them at length, emphasizing the importance of the Union in those pre-Civil War days, and calls for adherence to what he calls the compromises of the Constitution.

The House and the Senate adjourn. The president speaks to a crowd of spectators outside briefly, is introduced to a dizzying variety of people, then proceeds two blocks north to the Augusta House hotel, where he eats dinner among a torrent of local, state, and national dignitaries.

One of the diners is an Army captain named Stein who was wounded four and a half months earlier at the Battle of Buena Vista, in Mexico. The Mexican War, which began the previous year, still is underway and will continue until the following February.

After the meal, the president leaves for Gardiner, where he visits civic leaders, then boards the *Huntress* again to continue his journey, this time heading for Portland to spend Sunday there.

## July 3, 1933
### Edna St. Vincent Millay Visits Ragged Island, Plans Purchase

Pulitzer Prize-winning poet and playwright Edna St. Vincent Millay (1892-1950) enters just four words in her diary for this and the following day—"Ragged Island / Garnet Rocks," apparently implying that she and her husband, Eugen Boissevain, have just traveled to the island, the

Edna St. Vincent Millay

outermost one in Casco Bay, four miles out to sea.

Two weeks later, their purchase of the island is complete, enabling Millay, a Rockland native, to reconnect with Maine in a substantive way by using the island's lone house as a summer home.

She later concludes her poem "Ragged Island" this way: "Oh, to be there, under the silent spruces, / Where the wide, quiet evening darkens without haste / Over a sea with death acquainted, yet forever chaste."

## July 4, 1786
### Portland Separates from Falmouth

Ten years to the day after the signing of the Declaration of Independence, the residents living in a section of Falmouth called the Neck achieve some independence of their own when their home area becomes incorporated as the separate community of Portland.

What is now downtown Portland remained largely in ruins for many years after a British bombardment destroyed much of it in 1775. Many people who lost their homes left the settlement, never to return. Others hesitated to settle there because the Revolutionary War with Britain continued until 1783, and nobody knew whether the British might strike again during that period.

When peace was declared, however, an amicable meeting in May 1783 determined the terms of the settlement's separation from the rest of Falmouth, and new settlers began to arrive rapidly.

In 1784, the year after the signing of the Treaty of Paris, forty-one homes, ten stores, and seven shops were built.

The first brick house, the home of Brig. Gen. Peleg Wadsworth, was built in 1785. The childhood home of nineteenth-century poet Henry Wadsworth Longfellow, it is still standing and is the property of the Maine Historical Society.

Because of an economic crisis,

it takes three years from the time of the 1783 meeting for the actual separation of Portland to occur. The General Court in Boston—Maine still was part of Massachusetts—approved the separation in May 1786, and it takes effect July 4. A month later, residents hold their first town meeting in the old meetinghouse.

The first federal census, conducted in 1790, records 2,240 residents in the new municipality. It is still smaller than York, Gorham, and the remainder of Falmouth at the time, but it quickly becomes Maine's largest community and it remains so today. In 2010, 66,194 residents are counted in Portland.

The new town needs a name, of course. Some residents advocate calling it "Falmouthport"; others lobby for "Casco." In the end, residents take the name that has long been used to describe the headland in Cape Elizabeth and the channel leading to the harbor, and they call it "Portland."

## July 4, 1829
### Cornerstone Laid for Maine State House on Weston's Hill

The cornerstone of the Maine State House is laid on Weston's Hill in Augusta. The 150-by-50-foot building is completed

three years later at a final cost of $138,991.

The project is dogged by cost overruns and a continuous effort on the part of Portland legislators to move Maine's capital back to Portland.

## July 4, 1866
### Great Portland Fire Destroys 1,800 Buildings; 12,000 Homeless

A fire, apparently accidental and possibly caused by a firecracker, starts in a boathouse on Commercial Street in Portland. It destroys about 1,800 buildings, leaves about 12,000 of the city's residents homeless, and kills four people.

It is considered the largest urban fire in American history up to that date. Portland at the time is a city of about 30,000 people, ranking fourth in imports and fifth in exports among the nation's seaports. The fire leaves most of it in ruins. It is the third time in its history that the community endures general devastation.

"The Fourth of July that year was celebrated with extraordinary fervor, with ringing of bells, firing of cannon, decoration of buildings, public and private, and a very long procession of military companies, fire department, civic bodies, floats and organizations making an imposing array," historian Augustus F. Moulton writes decades later in his history of the city.

The fire, fanned by wind from the south and first reported about four o'clock in the afternoon, quickly ignites a row of wooden houses on Fore Street. Wind carries embers to the Brown Sugar House complex on Maple Street, which is amply supplied with barrel parts and other combustible material. "The conflagration was soon beyond control" after that, Moulton writes.

Many factors hamper efforts to stop the flames' advance. The city's firefighting equipment consists only of a few steam engines and hand tubs, or hand pumpers. Firefighters can't get to the crisis zone on the Commercial Street side, and flames and smoke on Fore Street make it dangerous to tackle from that direction. Wells and cisterns in the area soon run dry.

The fire creates a vacuum that sucks in more air, increasing the wind strength and prompting everything to burn with greater intensity. The draft fills the air with flaming objects, which spread out and set new fires, widening the area of destruction.

Some people try to save their furniture by dragging it into the streets, but it quickly catches fire there.

The fire's heat warps the iron horse car tracks embedded in the streets. Helpless fire crews try to limit the disaster by tearing down buildings or exploding them with gunpowder to create fire breaks. The inferno carves a wide path diagonally across the city from Commercial Street to Back Cove, roughly the same area that burned during the British bombardment ninety-one years earlier, at the start of the Revolutionary War.

The fire burns through the night until it runs out of material to burn. The next day, from the Portland Observatory on Munjoy Hill, which escaped destruction, the scene looking westward, toward downtown, Moulton writes, is "a wilderness of chimneys, portions of brick walls that had not fallen and blackened remains of shade trees, while westerly, beyond were the green tree-tops, spires and houses of the undestroyed portion."

The ruins cover about three hundred acres. Buildings lost to the flames include the Custom House, the post office, the six-year-old City Hall, eight churches, eight hotels, all newspaper offices, and every bank, lawyer's office, wholesale outlet, dry goods retail shop, and bookstore.

The fire also destroys half the city's factories. Structures surviving the fire and still standing today include the Henry Wadsworth Longfellow house on Congress Street and the Abyssinian Meeting House on Newbury Street.

Monetary aid pours in from around the country, much of which still is recovering from the ravages of the four-year Civil War, which ended in 1865. Munjoy Hill, on the eastern end of the downtown peninsula, becomes a tent city housing refugees. Barracks are built quickly in various places for the same purpose.

The net financial loss is estimated at $6 million—about $107.6 million in 2020 dollars—or about a quarter of the city's assessed valuation in 1866. The inability of insurance companies to meet their obligations resulting from such a large fire hampers reconstruction efforts, but rebuilding commences almost immediately.

Streets are relocated, widened and straightened. Noted Portland architect Francis H. Fassett, treating much of the ruined city as an unexpected gift of a blank canvas,

designs a majestic new City Hall and many other public and private buildings that exude more grandeur than those they replace.

As a reaction to the water shortage during the fire, the Portland Water Co. is established in 1867 to bring water to the city from Sebago Lake. With the blasting of rock and laying of pipes complete, the first gravity-fed lake water arrives in the city amid great celebration on July 4, 1870, four years to the day after the fire.

## July 4, 1975
### Fire Destroys Historic Poland Spring House

Fire breaks out about quarter to ten in the morning and levels the storied Poland Spring House in Poland just as its owners are planning to sell most of it to a Boston corporation that has been leasing it since 1972.

The building's electrical system has been shut off for several years, so the sprinkler system is not functioning. Firefighters from Poland and eight other communities fight unsuccessfully to stop the five-story landmark's destruction, but they prevent the flames from spreading to other buildings.

The hotel site was a tourist

A postcard image of the historic Poland Spring House.

magnet for mostly wealthy vacationers since immigrant Jabez Ricker opened a boardinghouse in 1827 to exploit the fame and purported curative properties of Poland Spring mineral water. The hotel was built in 1876 and expanded later. In its heyday it had 325 guest rooms.

Vacant since 1969, the building is uninsured. The sale price is reported to be about two million dollars. The sale closure deadline was to have been September 1.

The last time the building was used was in 1970, when the Maharishi Mahesh Yogi and 1,200 of his adherents occupied the building for a month.

## July 5, 1906
### Colby's Jack Coombs Makes Major League Debut for Philadelphia Athletics

John Wesley "Jack" Coombs, a former baseball star at Freeport High School and Colby College, debuts for the Philadelphia Athletics, pitching a seven-hit shutout to defeat the Washington Senators 3-0.

Coombs would play fourteen seasons in the major leagues, compiling a 158-110 pitching record with a career ERA of 2.78. He pitches for three teams—the Philadelphia Athletics, the Brooklyn Robins, and the Detroit Tigers—and plays in three World Series, notching five wins and no losses. In the 1910 World Series, Coombs pitches three complete games in a span of six days, all victories.

Coombs was born in Iowa but moved to Kennebunk when he was 4 years old. He played baseball for Freeport High School and was a captain at Colby College, where he also played basketball and other sports. Following his major league career, he was a college coach at Duke University for twenty-four years. The baseball fields at both Duke and Colby College are named for Coombs.

At Colby, he was the first student to graduate with a Bachelor of Science degree in chemistry in 1906. Coombs also received an Master of Arts degree in 1946 and had been accepted to the Massachusetts Institute of Technology for graduate work when he was signed to a baseball contract. Legendary University of Maine baseball coach John Winkin plays for Coombs at Duke, and Coombs recommends Winkin for his first coaching position at Colby Col-

lege, where Winkin coaches for twenty years before leaving for Orono.

## July 6, 1854
### Anti-Catholic Mob Burns Church Used by Irish Residents

A mob incited by a street preacher named Brown burns the Old South Meeting House in Bath, which was bought by Irish Catholics to serve as a church.

The incident is one of several violent anti-Catholic crimes that occur in the 1850s in Maine, including the tarring of Rev. John (or Johannes) Bapst on October 14, 1854, in Ellsworth, in association with the rise of the xenophobic Know Nothing Party.

Around eight o'clock in the evening, several hundred men charge up Meeting House Hill and burst through the doors of the church. They hang an American flag from the belfry, ring the church bell, then burn the church to the ground while police officers watch.

Bath firefighter John Hilling later depicts the church's destruction in a series of paintings now in the possession of the Maine Historical Society.

After the church fire, the police follow the mob back

into town, where it threatens to drag a prominent Catholic out of the Sagadahoc House, but the mayor intervenes. The agitated crowd storms through the streets, firing weapons into the air and yelling that all Irishmen should leave town to avoid being burned to death in their own houses. The rioters then haul some Irish occupants out of nearby shanties and demolish their dwellings.

The next night, the mob still is spoiling for a fight. Several men attach a rope to a house on Bowery Street, intending to pull it down because its owner, Oliver Moses, rented the house to a Catholic family. Moses steps to the front of the crowd, holding an ax. He cuts the rope, then turns and quietly faces the crowd, members of which curse at him and threaten to kill him.

A marshal steps to Moses' side, and soon others join in his quiet resistance to the mob.

Otherwise, Bath town officials essentially do little to contain the rioting during the two-day period, according to author James Mundy, a former executive director of the Maine Historic Preservation Commission.

"The Bath Riot showed above all else that the cancer of nativism had become, not only politically acceptable, but politically institutionalized in Maine," Mundy writes in his 1990 book *Hard Times, Hard Men: Maine and the Irish, 1830-1860.*

## July 7, 1833
### Mob Violence Fuels Drive to Make Bangor a City

Several Irishmen beat a sailor severely near Carr's Wharf in Bangor. Hundreds of other sailors disembark from ships along the waterfront and burn Joseph Carr's pub and a nearby tenement house to the ground. The next night, sailors destroy Irish shanties and attack local Irishmen. The town calls out the militia. Several homes are set ablaze.

In spite of the incidents, Irish immigrants become increasingly numerous in the community; and partly because of the violence, a movement to incorporate Bangor as a city gains steam and achieves fruition in 1834, with the goal of establishing a stronger police force.

## July 7, 1876
### Augusta Man Named Treasury Secretary by President Grant

Lot Morrill, of Augusta, having served as a Maine governor

and a US senator from Maine, becomes US treasury secretary under President Ulysses Grant. Morrill (1813-1883), born and raised in what now is the town of Belgrade, serves eight months in that post, with his tenure in office overlapping briefly that of President Rutherford B. Hayes.

Morrill's older brother Anson Morrill (1803-1887) also was a Maine governor, serving from 1855 to 1856 as the first Republican to hold that office; and he was a member of the U.S. House of Representatives from 1861 to 1863. Both Morrills are buried in Augusta's Forest Grove Cemetery.

## July 8, 1524
### Verrazano Becomes First Known European to Visit Maine

Italian explorer Giovanni da Verrazano arrives in France after a sea voyage that took him to North America, including, in early May, the coast of Maine. His trip is the first clearly documented European visit to the Maine coast.

Verrazano later will describe Maine as the "land of the bad people," reporting that local inhabitants waved his ship away from shore and would trade goods with his crew only by means of transferring them on a rope to and from a

cliff where the locals stood.

## July 8, 1908
### Nelson Rockefeller Born in Bar Harbor

Nelson Rockefeller, a future US vice president, is born in Bar Harbor. Rockefeller, a corporate president, author, assistant secretary of state, fifteen-year governor of New York, and three-time presidential candidate, becomes in 1974 the second person—after Gerald Ford in 1973—appointed to the vice presidency under the terms of the Twenty-fifth Amendment to the US Constitution. He serves from 1974 to 1977.

## July 8, 1916
### President Wilson Designates Sieur de Monts National Monument

President Woodrow Wilson designates a large tract of land on Mount Desert Island as Sieur de Monts National Monument, whose name honors a French explorer and colonizer. Composed of donated tracts of land, it is the embryonic form of what later will become Acadia National Park.

The site becomes Lafayette National Park in 1919, named after Gilbert du Motier, Marquis de Lafayette, the French aristocrat and military commander who led

American troops in several battles of the American Revolution. When the US Interior Department chooses the name, Americans are fighting to defend France from the Germans in World War I, and it seems a fitting tribute.

Interior Department legal assistant Horace Albright (1890-1987) and George Bucknam Dorr (1853-1944), who oversee Acadia's formation, don't like the name, but they go along with it until Albright becomes National Park Service director in 1929. "Then I pushed through the name we had chosen years before, Acadia National Park," he says. On January 19, 1929, President Calvin Coolidge signs a bill authorizing the name change.

"Acadia" was a name that had been in use among local Indians long before English and French explorers arrived in the area, so that seemed a more appropriate moniker to Albright.

Ronald H. Epp, in a 2016 biography of Dorr, concludes that the park's "admission into the rapidly evolving park system was based on a novel concept—that private land donated by a conservation organization was entitled to be federally protected public land. This decision irrevocably altered

the concept of a national park."

By the time of Dorr's death, the park has expanded to five times the size it was when the national monument was designated, and it includes mainland property.

## July 9, 1806
### Augusta Man Murders Wife, Seven Children With Ax, Commits Suicide

In one of the worst domestic-violence crimes in Maine history, Capt. James Purrinton, 46, assaults his entire family with an ax sometime between two and three in the morning at their farm on Belgrade Road in Augusta.

His wife, Betsey, 45, is killed immediately, as are their children Polly, 19; Benjamin, 12; Anna, 10; Nathaniel, 8; Nathan, 6; and Louisa, 18 months. Daughter Martha, 15, dies of her wounds on July 30. Only James, 17, also wounded, survives the attack. He flees the house and reports the attack to a neighbor.

Back at the farmhouse, his father slashes his own throat with a razor and dies. The following day, the victims' bodies are laid out in the town house, with the killer's body remaining on the porch. The ax and the razor are set on his coffin. A stage is set up for a funeral on Market Square in front of the meeting house. The funeral draws such a large crowd of mourners that the nearby houses are filled and people are standing on the roofs.

The victims' remains are buried in a cemetery on what now is Winthrop Street. The killer's body is buried, without a gravestone or other marking, in the road with the ax and the razor.

## July 9, 1968
### Earthen Dam's Smelly Water Helps Doom Sugar Beet Refinery

A former mayor of Centerville, New Brunswick, organizes a group of his friends to create an earthen dam on Prestile Stream, causing its fetid, smelly water to rise across the border in Aroostook County, Maine.

The highly publicized dam protest is one of the blows that kills a controversial, scandal-plagued effort by businessman Fred H. Vahlsing to establish a sugar beet refinery in the county. Vahlsing's existing potato processing plant was dumping pollutants into the Prestile.

## July 10, 1962
### First Transatlantic TV Signal Beamed from Andover Via Telstar 1

The newly built Andover Earth Station successfully transmits a television image from Andover to the Pleumeur-Bodou Ground Station, on the Brittany coast in northwestern France, via the Telstar 1 satellite, which was launched that morning in Florida.

It is the first transatlantic transmission of a TV signal via satellite. The first image transmitted shows the American flag waving on a pole outside the Andover station.

The signal follows telephone and domestic TV experiments conducted that day by American Telephone and Telegraph Co. and Bell Laboratories, which designed the satellite. The remote station in rural Oxford County is chock-a-block full with AT&T and Bell representatives, Federal Communications Commission members, and other VIPs.

The Associated Press and United Press International immediately use the satellite to send news dispatches across the ocean, including stories about the satellite's history-making debut.

Telstar, the property of AT&T, is the world's first privately owned satellite. It inspires the name of nearby Telstar High School in Bethel, which still exists today.

The Andover Earth Station

The Telstar ground station in Andover.

proves to be an economic boon to the area, drawing tourists and providing jobs for local residents. However, overcome by advancing technology, the station's large horn antenna and its signature dome are dismantled and removed in the 1990s. The main facility and its large-dish antennas, which Verizon buys several years later, remain in operation.

## July 11, 1814
### British Capture Fort Sullivan, Seize Eastport

During the two-and-a-half-year War of 1812, a British fleet under the command of Commodore Sir Thomas Hardy arrives off Eastport and demands the surrender of Fort Sullivan.

Hardy gives the occupants only five minutes to reply.

Maj. Perley Putnam, the fort's commander, responds by saying his men will defend it at any cost. Eastport residents beg him to reconsider, however, and he does, striking the colors and giving up without a shot.

The British seize the American guns, place all the surrendering American enlisted soldiers on a prison ship, dispatch their 102nd

Regiment of Infantry and an artillery battalion to the shore, occupy the fort, and hoist the Union Jack.

The conquest constitutes a step in the ultimately unsuccessful British effort to re-establish the crown colony of New Ireland in eastern Maine.

The conquerors also order Eastport residents to take oaths of allegiance to the British crown on May 16 or to leave the settlement within seven days. Two-thirds of the residents take the oath.

The war ends the following year, but the British remain in Eastport until 1818.

## July 11, 1944
### Plane Crash in South Portland Kills 19 People, Including 17 on Ground

Maine experiences its worst-ever airplane disaster when 2nd Lt. Philip Russell, of South Portland, a US Army Air Forces pilot, accidentally crashes his Douglas A-26 Invader in that city while on his way home to visit his family.

The plane cartwheels into a cluster of government-run trailers housing shipyard workers, killing seventeen residents there and destroying sixteen trailers. Russell and his navigator also die in the crash.

The crash comes on the heels of another military plane disaster a few hours earlier.

A B-17G Flying Fortress that left Nebraska that morning, bound for Dow Army Air Field in Bangor, crashes on Deer Mountain, northwest of Rangeley, killing all ten members of its crew.

It is by far the deadliest day in Maine aviation history.

## July 12, 1896
### Bath's Sewall Runs for Vice President, Sharing Ticket with Populist William Jennings Bryan

Arthur Sewall, of Bath, is nominated for the vice presidency at the five-day Democratic National Convention in Chicago, running for election with populist and presidential nominee William Jennings Bryan.

Sewall is a wealthy shipbuilder and industrialist, but the only elective office he ever held was that of alderman and councilman in Bath. At the 1896 convention, Bryan delivers his famous Cross of Gold speech.

The ticket goes down to defeat in the November election, losing to Republican William McKinley, a former Ohio governor; and his running mate, corporate lawyer and New Jersey politician

227

A bald eagle soaring.

Garrett Hobart.

Vice President Hobart dies in office in 1899; Sewall dies at 64 on September 5, 1900, at a time when he still would be vice president if the Democratic ticket had won the 1896 election.

## July 12, 1995
### Bald Eagle Removed from Endangered Species List

The bald eagle is removed from the federal endangered-species list. When the species was put on that list in 1972, Maine had only twenty-nine nesting pairs and eight eaglets—a steep 97 percent decline from the amount estimated to have been present in the state 150 years earlier.

Much of the drop was attributed to environmental pollution. After environmental controls and improvement in land-use management are imposed, the number rises quickly. In 2013, a survey finds 633 nesting pairs in Maine.

Today, a visitor to the Hatch Hill Landfill in Augusta can see eagles there at almost any time of year, but especially in winter.

## July 13, 1658
## Massachusetts Bay Colony Extends Authority in Maine

Twenty-nine men in the town of Spurwink, now part of Portland, sign a document submitting to the authority of the Massachusetts Bay Colony.

Massachusetts authorities already seized Saco, Biddeford, Cape Porpoise and Kennebunk earlier. At this point, it has taken seven years for Maine to lose its autonomy. Maine won't get it back for another 162 years.

## July 13, 1925
## WCSH Becomes Maine's First Commercial Radio Station

WCSH, Maine's first commercial radio station—that is, one that earns its income by selling advertising—is born.

The station is the brainchild of Henry Rines, president of the Congress Square Hotel Co. (hence the last three call letters, "CSH"), in Portland; and Bill Foss, who sells and repairs home radio receivers.

It was warm the evening of the first broadcast, with Gov. Ralph Owen Brewster, the Fifth US Infantry Band, several soloists, and announcer Linwood T. Pitman assembled in one relatively small room at the hotel. Foss sold sponsorships to WCSH's and Maine's first radio advertiser, the John J. Nissen Baking Company. Early advertisers bought program sponsorships rather than commercial announcements and used institutional copy rather than detailed descriptions of products or services.

Children's programming was one of the first genres of shows to be developed. Bill Foss became "Uncle Billy" on the *Kids Klub* program begun in the late 1920s. He was aided by "Uncle Jimmy" Nicholson, who eventually took over the program.

## July 14, 2013
## Motorcyclist Dies Trying to Set Speed Record; Clocked at 285 mph Before Crash

Bill Warner, 44, of Wimauma, Florida, dies as a result of a crash at the former Loring Air Force Base in the Aroostook County town of Limestone while trying to set another land speed world record on his motorcycle.

His bike is clocked at 285 mph before the accident occurs. He is participating in the Maine Event, a racing event organized by the Loring Timing Association.

In 2011, Warner set a record, at

Loring, for driving his motorcycle faster than any person on the planet ever had done before—311 mph—over 1.5 miles.

The Loring Timing Association uses Loring because its runway is available and 14,200 feet long—almost 2.7 miles. On July 14, Warner is trying to hit the 300-mph mark in less than a mile.

Warner is conscious and talking after the crash, which happens about quarter to ten in the morning, but he dies about an hour and a half later at Cary Memorial Hospital in Caribou.

## July 15, 1980
### Winners Drawn at First Moose Lottery

Cub Scout Todd Rogers draws the first winning entry from a giant rotating drum during Maine's inaugural moose lottery at the Bangor Civic Center.

The state was reviving moose hunting, which had been discontinued in 1935. The number of hunters authorized for 1980 was about seven hundred—less than one-fourth the total of most recent years.

The Maine Public Broadcasting Network puts the event on live television as uniformed Cub Scouts pick names out of the bin.

While most of the thirty-two thousand people seeking a permit wind up empty-handed, all six applicants from the Clemens family on Ocean Avenue in Portland hear their names selected while watching the drawing at home.

Alfred Clemens Sr., a 50-year-old plumber, says people started calling his house right away to offer congratulations.

"The phone's been right busy," he tells the *Portland Press Herald*. "Every time I set it down, it would ring."

The hosts for the drawing are Inland Fisheries & Wildlife Commissioner Glenn Manuel and Bud Leavitt, a *Bangor Daily News* outdoors columnist, who opposed Manuel's appointment to the commissioner's job.

Leavitt says moose hunting opponents might have submitted some of the permit applications, paying the five-dollar fee in hopes that if they win, that would be one less dead moose.

The six-day moose hunting season that year is September 22-27.

## July 15, 2009
### Lewiston's Cowan Mill Burns When Arsonist Strikes

A suspicious fire destroys the 159-year-old Cowan Mill on the east bank of the Androscoggin River in Lewiston, causing chaos in the city and imperiling other buildings.

Thousands of people watch from the sides of Main Street as the mill fire intensifies, most failing to notice that a second building right behind them, Bates Mill No. 5, is beginning to smolder.

"There's another fire," a police officer yells to the crowd, according to the *Sun Journal* newspaper. "Get out of here!" That provokes many to start running up the center of Main Street, away from the river.

Flames start penetrating the Cowan Mill's roof about four in the afternoon, and within fifteen minutes it collapses, spewing flaming embers that float across the street and land on No. 5, setting it alight. Auburn firefighters rush to the scene and snuff out the flames. Police climb onto rooftops to get a better view of what else might be catching fire.

Investigators later rule the fire to be a case of arson and offer a $5,000 reward for tips that lead to a conviction. A judge orders the mill's shell demolished.

In October, the Office of State Fire Marshal detains a 13-year-old boy at the Long Creek Youth Center in connection with the fire, but he is released later. No charges are filed.

The four-story Greek Revival-style Cowan Mill was built in 1850 on the site of a previous mill, which dated to 1836 and also was destroyed by fire. The remains of the later mill are demolished July 21 in accordance with a court order.

## July 16, 1915
### Gorham-born Ellen White, Co-founder of Seventh-day Adventist Church, Dies in California at 88

Ellen Gould Harmon White, 88, a co-founder of the Seventh-day Adventist Church who was born in Gorham and grew up in Portland, dies in California.

Raised in the Methodist church, she suffered permanent disfigurement at the age of 9 when another girl threw a stone, hitting her in the face and breaking her nose. White was knocked unconscious, and though her wound healed, she endured health problems throughout the rest of her childhood.

White and her family were swayed to the Adventist cause when they heard William Miller, a Baptist minister, deliver lectures in 1840 in Portland about the expected second coming of Jesus Christ. In 1843 the Methodist church adopted a resolution condemning the Millerite views. White's congregation expelled her family.

She suffered a further blow on October 22, 1844, the day of the Great Disappointment, a day when the long-awaited second coming predicted by Miller didn't occur. The letdown drove many people away from Miller's teachings, but White said she had a vision from God that December in South Portland that convinced her she was on the right track. The message of a second vision inspired her to go out in the cold of a Maine winter and visit Adventists up and down the coast to tell them what she had seen.

In 1846, she married James White. They met a Millerite movement follower named Joseph Bates who introduced them to the idea that the Sabbath, or holy day, should be observed on Saturday rather than on Sunday, in accordance with biblical tradition. They came to accept the idea, and Ellen White said she had a vision in 1847 that confirmed the belief.

The group adopted the name Seventh-day Adventists in 1860.

White became a world traveler, writer and what Seventh-day Adventists today regard as a prophet.

Missionary work is a key component of Adventist faith. So is education, and White was instrumental in arranging for the establishment of Bible-centered schools, including medical training.

She also established Seventh-day Adventist churches in Europe and Australia and helped found the denominational headquarters in Washington, D.C.

## July 16, 2004
### Martha Stewart, Summer Resident of Mount Desert Island, Sentenced to Five Months in Prison

Homemaking mogul Martha Stewart, a part-time Maine resident, is sentenced to five months in prison for lying about a stock sale.

She also is ordered to spend five months in home confinement after the prison term, is fined thirty thousand dollars and is allowed to remain free pending the result of an appeal. She had pleaded not guilty to the charge.

Her stockbroker, Peter Bacanovic, who also was convicted of lying in connection with the Stewart case, receives the same prison and home confinement sentence.

Stewart then approaches a microphone outside the courthouse, denounces the insider-trading scandal, and encourages her fans to buy her magazines and homemaking products.

When she was indicted, Stewart resigned as CEO of Martha Stewart Living Omnimedia. After her conviction, she resigns her board seat in the organization.

Her court appeal notwithstanding, she later asks to be allowed to begin serving her prison term. She reports on October 8 at a minimum-security federal penitentiary in West Virginia.

Asked in 2017 on NBC's *Today* show about her prison time, she says, "It's a horrible experience. Nothing is good about it, nothing."

Stewart's Mount Desert Island summer estate, named Skylands and built by Edsel Ford, the only son of Henry Ford, is featured in the July 2015 issue of *Architectural Digest*.

## July 17, 1939
### Donn Fendler, 12, Separated from Family on Mount Katahdin, Survives Nine Days in Wilderness

Twelve-year-old Donn Fendler (1926-2016), of Rye, New York, becomes separated from his family while hiking during a storm near the summit of Maine's Mount Katahdin. Putting his Boy Scout skills to use, he survives nine days without food or proper clothing, then finds his way back to civilization in the town of Stacyville, having shed sixteen pounds.

The search for the missing boy generates nationwide attention. Fendler later writes a book about the experience, *Lost on a Mountain in Maine*, which becomes a classic children's book.

Fendler serves in the military during World War II and the Vietnam War, retiring as an Army lieutenant colonel and settling in Clarksville, Tennessee.

## July 17, 1991
### $3.2 Billion Budget Deal Ends State Shutdown

After sixteen days of intense negotiations, the Legislature approves a $3.2 billion state budget for the 1992 and 1993 fiscal years, breaking a deadlock that caused a state government shutdown and sidelined about ten thousand state workers since the start of the fiscal year on July 1.

When the previous fiscal year

ended without a budget deal, Republican Gov. John McKernan ordered the closure of most state offices and the layoff of state workers except those in emergency services.

Sticking points in the budget impasse were spending, taxes, and proposed revisions to workers' compensation laws. McKernan and other Republicans had insisted on reforms to the compensation laws because Maine workers' compensation insurance rates were among the nation's highest.

When the tumult about the budget reached its peak, crowds of outraged state workers using whistles, drums, and bullhorns gathered in the State House in protest of McKernan's layoffs, shouting repeatedly, "We want his head!"

The shutdown, which included state parks, occurred in the midst of Maine's tourist season, which is critically important to the state's economy.

The budget approved by the Legislature cuts $500 million from workers' compensation costs.

McKernan signs the bill around three o'clock in the morning. The shutdown ends.

## July 18, 1864
### Confederate Officer Fails in Attempt to Rob Calais Bank

Three men in civilian clothes walk into the Calais Bank in Calais. Just as they begin to draw revolvers to rob the bank, armed federal agents who have been tipped off about the plan catch the would-be robbers off-guard and arrest them.

The ringleader of the robbers, William Collins, is a Confederate army captain who plans to turn the money from the robbery over to the Confederacy. Four months later, he escapes from the Maine State Prison at Thomaston and returns to the South via New Brunswick to resume fighting for the Confederacy.

## July 19, 1969
### Fire Destroys Two Blocks, Part of Pier in Old Orchard Beach

A fire breaks out in the amusement area known as the White Way in Old Orchard Beach, destroying about two blocks and one-third of the town's famous pier, from which many visitors are evacuated by ladder.

The fire, striking at the height of the tourist season, inflicts severe burns on one person and minor injuries on several others, including a police officer and a firefighter who suffers burns when he pulls somebody out of the flaming Noah's Ark funhouse.

About one hundred thousand people were estimated to be at the beach during the previous week, and motel owners said that all available rooms were rented for the weekend.

According to witnesses, the blaze consumes about one hundred feet of the pier, including small booths and refreshment stands, then stops. Many amusement rides also go up in flames. A power failure casts some streets in darkness, and minor looting ensues.

Spectators flocking to the fire scene intensify the normal summer weekend traffic congestion, clogging roads all the way to US Route 1 in Saco and Scarborough.

Fire damage is estimated initially at $500,000, the equivalent of $3.58 million in 2020.

The Blizzard of 1978 destroys what remains of the pier. A new pier is built in 1980.

July 19, 1984
### Bailey Island Bridge Dedicated as National Historic Civil Engineering Landmark

The Bailey Island Bridge, built in 1927, is dedicated as a National Historic Civil Engineering Landmark.

The crib bridge was built using granite slabs to calm the effect of ocean tides in the adjacent Will's Gut. It has been listed on the National Register of Historic Places since 1975.

Route 24 crosses the bridge from Orr's Island and ends on Bailey Island. Both islands are part of the town of Harpswell.

July 19, 1989
### CBA Commissioner Jay Ramsdell Among 111 Killed in Plane Crash

Continental Basketball Association Commissioner Jay Ramsdell, who grew up on Mount Desert Island, is among 111 passengers killed when United Airlines Flight 232 crash lands in Sioux City, Iowa. He is 25.

Ramsdell, who at 24 became the youngest commissioner in professional sports history in 1988, was on his way from league headquarters in Denver to the CBA player draft in Columbus, Ohio. An hour into the trip an engine blew out, causing a complete hydraulic failure. There are 296 people on board the DC-10 and 111, including Ramsdell, are killed. Ramsdell declined an earlier flight so he could travel with his friend and CBA colleague Jerry Schemmel, who survives the crash and later calls play-by-play for the Denver Nuggets and the Colorado Rockies.

Ramsdell, a relentless worker, parlayed a job as a 14-year-old statistician for the CBA's Maine Lumberjacks, of Bangor, into the commissioner job. Ramsdell took a job in the league office after graduating from Mount Desert Island High School and, save for one year when he served as the 20-year-old general manager of the CBA's Maine Windjammers, made a quick and steady ascension to the position of commissioner.

In 1989, the CBA league championship trophy is named the Jay Ramsdell Trophy to honor his memory.

Ramsdell is posthumously inducted into the Maine Basketball Hall of Fame in 2019.

## July 20, 1970
### Fire Destroys B-52 Valued at $7.7 Million at Loring Air Force Base

A fire of unknown origin destroys a B-52 Stratofortress bomber on the ground at Loring Air Force Base in Limestone.

The $7.7 million (about $51.4 million in 2019) jet burns down to the tarmac in less than an hour. Small explosions occur when fuel tanks rupture and the plane's tires burst.

Two Air Force specialists are doing maintenance work on the plane when the fire starts. Both are taken to the hospital, examined, and released.

One of the firemen who arrives at the scene is hospitalized for treatment of smoke inhalation. Four other airmen working nearby are treated for minor injuries.

Investigators are unable to determine what caused the fire.

When it occurs, the plane is parked on a "stub"—a parking strip attached to a taxiway.

## July 21, 1903
### Ruth Moore, Author of *Spoonhandle*, Born on Gotts Island

Ruth Moore, a *New York Times* best-selling author and widely considered one of the best regional novelists of her era, is born on Gotts Island, a tiny fishing village in Frenchman Bay where her ancestors had lived for generations.

Moore specializes in detailed fiction of the Maine coast, drawing upon her heritage and firsthand knowledge to paint vivid pictures and realistic characters often struggling to survive

Ruth Moore

against constant change to their way of life. In her time, she is called "New England's answer to Faulkner."

Her debut novel, *The Weir*, is based on her childhood experiences on Gotts Island. It chronicles the disintegration of a fishing and farming community on the fictional Comey's Island. The book is well received, but it is her second book, *Spoonhandle*, that establishes her reputation. The novel spends several weeks on *The New York Times* bestseller list and is made into the 1948 movie

*Deep Waters*, by 20th Century Fox. Although Moore doesn't like the movie, it provides her enough money and fame to build a house on Mount Desert Island and spend the rest of her life writing novels.

July 21, 1957
### Kenneth Roberts, author of *Northwest Passage*, dies in Kennebunkport

Kenneth Roberts, known chiefly for his many historical novels, dies at the age of 71 in Kennebunkport, where he was born and where he lived for many years.

Roberts' best-known works include *Northwest Passage*, a French and Indian War-era tale that was published in 1937 and made into a 1940 movie starring Spencer Tracy; *Arundel*, a 1929 novel about Benedict Arnold's 1775 march to Quebec; and *Rabble in Arms*, the 1933 sequel to *Arundel*, which chronicles the unfolding of the American Revolution up to the 1777 Battles of Saratoga.

Roberts recently had won a Pulitzer citation for his books, which had been on best-seller lists for twenty years.

A Cornell University graduate,

Roberts participated as an Army captain in the Intelligence Section of the little-remembered Siberian Expeditionary Force, part of an unsuccessful, ill-equipped, multinational invasion of Russia immediately after World War I intended to reverse a communist takeover.

In Kennebunkport, he became fast friends with novelist Booth Tarkington, a summer resident who often provided useful critiques of his work.

Roberts was known for his reclusiveness as a writer, going so far as to rent a cottage in Italy's rural Tuscany region so he could avoid visitors and telephone calls and concentrate on his work— only to be distracted by braying donkeys, shouting fishermen, and the racket generated by Italian military pilots who conducted training maneuvers outside his bedroom window.

"Perhaps I may be regarded as allergic to noise," he concluded in his 1949 memoir.

Nonetheless, he persisted in striving for seclusion.

"I have been accused of hermitcy or recluse-ism because I stay at home and work while others sit in the sun on a beach: because I shun cocktail parties and large gatherings of distracto-maniacs," Roberts asserted in his memoir. "If that's being a hermit or a recluse, I plead guilty.

"I'm also a writer, and it's my unalterable belief that writers should stick to writing: not argue world affairs over radio programs, or act as ballyhoo men (and most offensively so) during presidential campaigns, or kill valuable hours at noisy gatherings of gin drinkers who have nothing better to do, or try to collaborate with the editorial staffs of moving picture companies. In addition to wasting time, such things are ruinously destructive to a writer's peace of mind."

## July 22, 2010
### Financial Backer Withdraws; LNG Gas Terminal Project Dead

The only financial backer of a proposed $1 billion liquefied natural gas terminal in Calais, a tiny Washington County city on the Canadian border, withdraws from the project.

The pullout of investment bank Goldman Sachs and its subsidiary, GS Power Holdings, LLC, is but one of many nails to be hammered into the controversial proposal's metaphorical coffin.

A group called Calais LNG

wanted to build the terminal on about 330 acres along the St. Croix River, seven miles south of the middle of Calais, featuring a 1,000-foot pier and two or three storage tanks. It also would have had twenty miles of underground pipes connecting to the Maritimes & Northeast Pipeline. It would have been built with the capacity to move one billion cubic feet of gas daily.

Critics say such a terminal could endanger coastal wetland and the livelihoods of local fishermen, and they consider the prospective presence of large LNG tankers in Passamaquoddy Bay and the St. Croix River a great risk.

The US Federal Energy Regulatory Commission dismisses Calais LNG's application in 2012, leaving only Downeast LNG, one of three organizations originally seeking to build a terminal, still ostensibly striving toward that goal.

In May 2016, Downeast puts its project up for sale. The plan accumulates another obstacle when the Canadian government prohibits LNG tankers from using Head Harbor Passage, the only route ships of that size could use to enter Passamaquoddy Bay.

Finally, in August 2016, the US Federal Energy Regulatory Commission dismisses an application from Downeast to build an LNG terminal in Robbinston, which is near Calais and across the mouth of the St. Croix River from St. Andrews, New Brunswick.

In a statement about its decision, FERC said, "There has been essentially no progress at all toward completion of an application in the past nine months, and Downeast has presented nothing to persuade us that its situation is likely to change in the immediate future."

Maine's unemployment rate in August 2016, when FERC dismisses the last LNG proposal, is 3.1%. In Washington County, where any of the terminals would have been built, it's 4%, the fourth-highest of Maine's sixteen counties. In January 2021, after a coronavirus pandemic's yearlong battering of the Maine economy, the statewide unemployment rate is 6.4 percent and Washington County's is 8.4 percent, the state's highest.

## July 22, 2013
### Removal of Veazie Dam Reopens Penobscot River to Salmon

A jackhammer-equipped backhoe pounds its way through the 10-year-old Veazie Dam, which is being demolished as part of a river restoration project.

The dam was built on the Penobscot River to generate hydroelectric power.

As they could before the dam was built, migrating fish now will be able to swim upstream past the dam site.

In 2012, the Great Works Dam was removed 7.3 miles upriver from the Veazie Dam. The first river obstacle fish will meet when the Veazie Dam is gone is the Milford Dam, but a work crew is building a modern fish ladder there. The restoration project costs $62 million. When it's done, fish will have direct access to the Piscataquis, Mattawamkeag, and Pleasant rivers; and the East Branch of the Penobscot River.

For similar reasons, the Edwards Dam was removed in 1999 from the Kennebec River in Augusta, a precedent-setting action.

The Penobscot River project is considered a model for others because it is based on a cooperative agreement among environmental groups, federal agencies, an Indian tribe, and a power company.

## July 23, 1849
### Augusta Incorporated as City

Gov. John Dana signs a bill permitting the incorporation of Augusta, Maine's capital, as a city. At a special meeting held the following December 31, voters approve the incorporation, 586-196. City government and its departments are organized in 1850.

In the first mayoral election, candidates run on a partisan basis, unlike the nonpartisan system used in the twentieth and twenty-first centuries. The Whigs assume they will claim the mayor's job, especially since the opposition to Augusta's incorporation as a city came largely from Democrats.

The Democrats say the city at large should decide the matter, and they propose Reuel Williams, a former US senator, as mayor. The Whigs agree he would make a fine choice, but they doubt he would be willing to do it. They schedule a meeting to nominate their own candidate.

On February 2, a large, ostensibly nonpartisan meeting nominates Williams by acclamation. He declines the honor. Then the gathering nominates Rev. William Drew by acclamation, and he accepts.

The Whigs, dissatisfied, nominate George Morton, who declines. The Whigs then turn to

Courtesy of Sean Pavone/Shutterstock.com

Downtown Augusta reflected in the Kennebec River.

John Pettingill, who accepts. The Democrats hold their own meeting and put up Alfred Redington (1802-1875) as a candidate.

In a three-way contest held March 11, 1850, no candidate achieves a majority, which is needed to win. Drew gets 517 votes; Pettingill, 430; and Redington, 291. Pettingill withdraws. The Whigs nominate Thomas Little, and another vote takes place March 21. Drew, who perhaps peaked too early, gets 416 votes; Redington, 440; and Little, 275. Little then withdraws.

The final showdown pits Drew, one of the organizers of the February 2 meeting, against his right-hand man, Redington. Redington wins, 668-582, showing that a city of 8,225 inhabitants, as

241

recorded in the 1850 census, can have politics as complicated as that of a major metropolis.

Redington, a Vassalboro native, arrived in Augusta in 1822. He made a fortune in real estate speculation linked to the construction of the Kennebec Dam—which, later known as the Edwards Dam, is demolished in 1999—then lost his wealth when in 1840 both an economic bubble and the dam burst, the latter because of a flood. Redington organized the dam's repair and later became the agent for the company that owned the dam's water power. He also serves as Maine's adjutant general.

The Democrats renominate Redington for mayor in 1851, and he defeats the Whig candidate, James W. North (1810-1882), who, nearly two decades later, writes a history of Augusta. That detailed book chronicles, among other things, North's and Redington's part in that history.

The following year, on the heels of the Gold Rush, Redington moves to Sacramento, California, where he becomes a steamboat company's agent and builds flour mills. He never looks back.

Today, Augusta is Maine's thirteenth-most-populous municipality, based on 2010 census figures.

It is also the third-least-populous of America's state capitals, having a larger population than only Montpelier, Vermont, the smallest; and Pierre, South Dakota.

## July 24, 1927
### Aviation Hero Lindbergh Lands in Old Orchard Beach on Goodwill Tour

Two months after his pioneering solo transatlantic flight in the *Spirit of St. Louis*, aviator Charles Lindbergh lands the same plane in Old Orchard Beach while on a goodwill tour. His intended landing site—Portland's new airfield in Scarborough—is fogbound, so he touches down right on the beach instead.

"You see, we cannot land in fog," the world-famous aviator later tells about twenty-five thousand people gathered in Portland's Deering Oaks park to hear him to advocate for increased use of air mail and commercial aviation.

Lindbergh's visit also draws thousands of people to the cordoned-off Scarborough airfield. Looking into the mist expectantly, hoping to catch a glimpse of the *Spirit of St. Louis* landing, they are surprised to see Lindbergh chauffeured up to the enclosure that was set aside for the plane. He is riding in the car of the state highway police chief, who brings him there from Old Orchard Beach.

Lindbergh also is the feature attraction of a parade that winds its way through downtown Portland.

That evening, seven hundred people attend a banquet given at Portland's Eastland Hotel in Lindbergh's honor, with hundreds more trying unsuccessfully to storm the doors outside.

## July 25, 1722
### Massachusetts Bay Colony Declares War on Wabanakis; Dummer's War Begins

Massachusetts Bay colony Gov. Samuel Shute declares war on the Wabanaki Confederacy. This begins what is referred to variously as Lovewell's War or Dummer's War, and it has several other names as well.

It is during this three-year conflict that English raiders in 1724 destroy the Indian settlement at Norridgewock, killing and scalping Rev. Sébastien Râle, a French Jesuit priest who is head of the Catholic mission there, and twenty-six others. The scalps are sent to Boston to claim a bounty. Scalping is encouraged on both sides of the conflict.

Also, Lovewell's Fight occurs the following year in Fryeburg, although this time the English suffer heavy casualties.

Unlike other conflicts of the period, Lovewell's War is not part of a larger European conflict. Much of the fighting takes place in the interior of New England, demonstrating that English colonials are becoming more aggressive about protecting their existing settlements and pushing the French and what they consider to be enemy Indians back.

The Indians, suffering badly from the war, take part in peace talks in November 1725 in Boston.

The peace terms entrench local English property rights further. It is signed in 1726 on Casco Bay.

## July 26, 1819
### Maine Votes Overwhelmingly for Separation from Massachusetts

Maine residents vote overwhelmingly for separation from Massachusetts, 17,091-7,132, in contrast to the two much closer referendums held in 1816.

The pro-separation result is strongest in Kennebec County, where the "yes" tally exceeds 75 percent in all but six towns. A majority of voters in each other county opts for separation as well.

Before the vote, the anti-separation Federalists and allies of Bowdoin College tried unsuccessfully to convince voters that Maine is growing so fast that its population soon will eclipse that of the rest of Massachusetts, so Maine's delegation to state government will be in a position to control that as well. Perhaps the capital could be moved from Boston to a point that is more centrally located, they said.

The argument fails. While other obstacles await the pro-separation side, they will be overcome. Less than eight months later, Maine becomes a state.

Today the population of Massachusetts is more than five times that of Maine.

## July 27, 2011
### Deteriorating Memorial Bridge Linking Maine, New Hampshire Shuts Down

Transportation officials from Maine and New Hampshire agree to close the Memorial Bridge across the Piscataqua River permanently—about a year ahead of what was expected.

The announcement essentially puts US Route 1 businesses on either side of the eighty-eight-year-old bridge, in Kittery and Portsmouth, New Hampshire, on dead end roads until another bridge is built to replace it, at a projected cost of $90 million. That bridge is forecast to open to traffic in June 2014; it actually will beat that deadline, however, opening in August 2013, and costs only $81.4 million.

George N. Campbell Jr., commissioner of New Hampshire's Department of Transportation, says in a news release that a recent bridge inspection revealed an accelerating rate of deterioration, forcing the decision to close the bridge to motor vehicles. It would remain open temporarily to pedestrians and bicyclists, and the lift span still would be raised to accommodate commercial vessels in the river.

A department spokesman says the bridge, which is part of US Route 1, carried about twelve thousand vehicles per day.

Two other bridges, both upriver from the Memorial Bridge, link the two communities—the Sarah Mildred Long Bridge, which carries the US Route 1 bypass; and, farther upstream, the Piscataqua River Bridge, with carries Interstate 95.

The replacement bridge also will be called Memorial Bridge.

Like its predecessor, it will be named to honor New Hampshire members of the military who played a role in the United States' 1917-1918 participation in World War I.

Also, the new bridge will have a lift span used to let ships pass and will be accessible to bicyclists and pedestrians.

When the original Memorial Bridge opened in 1923, a 5-year-old girl, Eileen Foley, cut the ribbon at the dedication ceremony. She later became Portsmouth's mayor. In 2013, Foley, by then 95 and an ex-mayor, dedicates the new bridge.

## July 28, 1759
### Britain Builds Fort Pownall in Stockton Springs

Britain's construction of Fort Pownall, in what now is the town of Stockton Springs, is completed. It is named for Massachusetts Bay provincial Gov. Thomas Pownall, who oversaw its construction.

The fort is intended to make the area safe for European settlement and to drive off Norridgewock and Penobscot Indians. It is destroyed in the Revolutionary War by both American colonists and British forces who want to prevent it from being used.

## July 28, 1911
### Collision of Trains in Grindstone Kills Nine

The head-on collision of an excursion train and a regular passenger train in violent weather in the Penobscot County community of Grindstone kills nine people and injures two dozen others.

The excursion train departed from Kidders Point on Penobscot Bay, near Searsport, and is headed to Caribou. The passenger train left Van Buren and is bound for Bangor.

The crash occurs just as musicians in one train lift their instruments to serenade an injured baseball team member who is aboard the train.

Rail commissioners release an investigation report in August concluding that the southbound passenger train had the right of way, and that the northbound excursion train should have stayed out of its way. It says the actions of conductor H.G. Dibblee and engineer Frank W. Garcelon aboard the excursion train "constituted a grossly reckless disregard of duty amounting to criminal carelessness, and were the sole cause of the accident."

Garcelon dies in the crash. Dibblee, who jumped to safety

before the crash, admits his role in causing it. He pleads guilty a few months later to a charge of manslaughter, is sentenced to sixty days in jail, and is fined $500.

## July 28, 1973
### Author Mary Ellen Chase Dies in Massachusetts

Blue Hill native Mary Ellen Chase, author of more than thirty books, dies in Northampton, Massachusetts, at the age of 86.

Chase, a 1909 University of Maine graduate, is considered to be one of the most important regional literary figures of the early twentieth century.

Her novels are set largely on the Maine seacoast and involve seafaring families. Her best-known works of fiction are *Mary Peters*, *Silas Crockett*, and *Windswept*.

Chase also wrote history, children's books, literary criticism, biblical studies, essays, and writing instruction. One of her books, *Jonathan Fisher: Maine Parson, 1768-1847*, is based partly on a diary that Fisher, a Congregational minister from Blue Hill, wrote in a code that he had devised when he was a student at Harvard. The diary was deciphered more than 160 years after his death.

From 1926 until her retirement in 1955, Chase taught at Smith College in Northampton.

## July 29, 1931
### Charles Lindbergh, Anne Morrow Lindbergh Land on North Haven

The monoplane *Sirius* lands on the island of North Haven. Charles Lindbergh, famous after having flown across the Atlantic four years earlier, steps out, as does his wife, Anne Morrow Lindbergh.

They visit Anne Lindbergh's parents—New Jersey's US Sen. Dwight Morrow and poet Anne Cutler Morrow, soon to become top administrator at Smith College—who are spending the summer there. (Charles Lindbergh also is the son of a member of Congress. His father, Charles Augustus Lindbergh, represented Minnesota's Sixth District for ten years in the US House of Representatives.)

The next day, the Lindberghs board the plane again and soar off into the clouds, resuming their pioneering flight on the Great Circle route to Asia.

Wearing flying suits heated by electricity and stopping at prearranged fuel depots, they cross Hudson's Bay, Alaska, eastern Siberia, and Japan, then land on the plane's pontoons on the flooded Yangtze River in China.

Anne Lindbergh, who serves as radio operator on the flight, describes the trip later in her best-selling 1935 book, *North to the Orient*. The Lindberghs return to North Haven occasionally after that.

## July 30, 1898
### Gold Scam in Lubec Prompts Issuance of Arrest Warrant

Authorities in Boston issue an arrest warrant for Rev. Prescott Jernegan in connection with a factory in Lubec, Maine, that Jernegan's investors were told was extracting gold from seawater.

Jernegan, a Bowdoin College graduate and Baptist minister, and fellow Martha's Vineyard native Charles Fisher convinced two gullible investors that the process is real by manipulating a seaside experiment that seems to confirm the two entrepreneurs' claims. Thus armed with start-up capital, the swindlers cobbled together the Electrolytic Marine Salts Co. and established offices in New York, London, and Boston. Jernegan solicited investment from his acquaintances and former schoolmates.

Jernegan and Fisher then went to Lubec. They began retrofitting a grist mill, saying they picked Lubec because of its extreme tides; their real reason was that Lubec is so remote that it is unlikely to receive many prying visitors. They set up underwater "gold accumulators" and hired one hundred men to work on the project.

For the few visitors who did arrive, Fisher repeated his earlier sleight-of-hand trick. According to some versions of the story, it consisted of going underwater to place gold in the accumulators when nobody was looking. Others say he inserted gold surreptitiously in advance into mercury samples that were added to seawater, supposedly to draw the gold from the water. In either case, the company sent the staged result to Boston for verification, giving the duo a chance to lure even more investors. Some of the money was used to develop the Lubec project further and to buy more gold for the contrived demonstrations; Jernegan and Fisher kept the rest.

By the summer of 1898, investors had provided the company almost $1 million—the equivalent of about $31.5 million in 2020. Then a disgruntled former partner spilled the beans to the *New York Herald*, and the scheme began to collapse. When investors arrived in Lubec to find out what had happened, Fisher had disappeared and Jernegan had taken his wife to Paris.

With his lawyers managing to keep him out of court, Jernegan first says he took only his fair share from the money, that Fisher fled with all the company's money, and that he is looking for Fisher to get the plant running again. Nonetheless, Jernegan later sends $85,000 to the United States to help reimburse cheated investors. After the money arrives and the company's assets are sold off, the investors receive 36 cents per dollar invested. With that, the great gold swindle of Lubec is over.

## July 31, 1779
## William D. Williamson, Maine's Second Governor, Born in Connecticut

William D. Williamson, Maine's second governor and a scholar who laid much of the foundation for Maine historical research, is born in Canterbury, Connecticut.

Williamson's *The History of the State of Maine: From Its Discovery, A.D. 1602, to the Separation, A.D. 1820, Inclusive* is a standard reference work for modern researchers.

A Brown University graduate, Williamson studies law and becomes the Hancock County attorney. He serves in the Massachusetts legislature at the end of the period when Maine still is part of that state, and he plays a prominent role in the successful effort to separate Maine from Massachusetts and secure its admission to the Union in 1820.

Williamson, as president of the Maine Senate, becomes governor when the state's first governor, William King, resigns in May 1821. Williamson himself steps down in December that year to take a seat in the US House of Representatives.

—30—

# AUGUST

August 1, 1931
## Commercial Air Passenger Service Begins in Portland

The first commercial air passenger service at Stroudwater Airport—now Portland International Jetport—begins with a Boston-Maine Airways flight from Boston.

Boston-Maine is one of two carriers to start serving Maine that day. Its flights will leave Boston and land in succession in Portland, Rockland, and Bangor.

The company says it will operate two round-trip flights daily on that route, with an additional round trip only between Boston and Portland.

The other company is Pan-American Airways, which operates an international run from Boston to Calais; Saint John, New Brunswick; and Halifax, Nova Scotia.

The *Portland Press Herald* describes the emergence of the services as "marking the greatest event in the history of passenger railroading in New England," which seems odd from a twenty-first century vantage point; but the paper explains that Boston-Maine Airways is a subsidiary of the Boston and Maine and Maine Central railroads.

None of those companies is in business today.

Ironically, however, although Pan-American collapses in 1991 as a business, in 1998 Guilford Transportation Industries buys the right to use the name and renames its rail assets Pan-American Railways.

The company also revives Pan American Airways Corp. as a regional air carrier, but the airline subsidiary ceases operations in 2008.

In December 2020, CSX Corp. announces it has reached a deal to buy Pan Am Railways, Inc., which would add Maine, New Hampshire, and Vermont to its railway network, expanding that network to cover twenty-three U.S. states.

August 2, 1909
## Tradition of Boston Post Cane, Given to Oldest Resident, Begins in 700 Towns

Edwin A. Grozier, publisher of the *Boston Post* newspaper, sends a gold-headed ebony cane to the Board of Selectmen in each of seven hundred towns in New England, asking each board to present the cane to the oldest living male resident of that town.

Upon that man's death, the cane is to be transferred to the next-oldest man in town. The tradition is expanded to include women starting in 1930.

J.F. Fradley and Co., of New York, manufactures the canes from seven-foot lengths of ebony shipped from Africa.

Grozier does not send the canes to cities, only towns.

Also, current research suggests that no towns in Connecticut or Vermont are included in the distribution.

More than a century after the distribution of the canes, many Maine towns still carry on the tradition by giving it to their oldest residents.

Historians in Maynard, Massachusetts, maintain a Boston Post Cane Information Center on their town's website. Having sent out an appeal for information about the canes' whereabouts, the group reports that as of 2016, 517 of the canes have been tracked down, and 227 of them are in towns in Maine.

## August 3, 1924
### The Hillcrest, Summer Hotel on Chebeague Island, Destroyed by Fire

Fire caused by a carelessly discarded cigarette butt consumes the Hillcrest, a summer hotel on Chebeague Island, and nearby buildings, killing three guests and injuring others.

The fire also burns up a neighboring dance hall and two residences, one of which was being used as a hotel annex; as well as the personal belongings of about ninety guests.

Several women are reported to have fainted, and guests try to enter the burning hotel to fetch their property from their rooms.

Cyril York, who lives on the island in Casco Bay, suffers burns on his hands and his face when he puts out flames on the burning clothing of a man jumping from a second-story window in the annex. The jumping man, John A. Cady Jr., dies of injuries that night in a hospital.

The cigarette butt was thrown under the front steps leading to the hotel's front door.

The Hillcrest was a popular tourist getaway spot in the late nineteenth and early twentieth centuries. Its burning is the worst fire in the island's history.

Afterward, a new hotel is built to replace it. Called the Chebeague Island Inn, that hotel still is in business.

## August 4, 1914
### Giant German Ocean Liner SS *Kronprinzessin Cecilie* Diverts to Bar Harbor as World War I Starts

The North German Lloyd ocean liner SS *Kronprinzessin Cecilie*, headed from New York to Plymouth, England, diverts to Bar Harbor. The great ocean liner arrives at six o'clock in the morning in a town that usually sees nothing but small coastal ships off its shore.

The captain was approaching England when he learned that World War I had begun. He reversed course, lest the British or the French confiscate the German vessel.

The crew turned the ship—carrying 1,216 passengers and more than $13 million worth of gold and silver—and headed for the closest port in then-neutral America, which was Bar Harbor.

On November 7 the ship is moved to Boston while civil lawsuits are resolved in federal court. In 1917 the United States, having declared war on Germany, commandeers the ship, renames it the USS *Mount Vernon* and uses it as a troop transport ship.

A German submarine torpedoes the ship on September 5, 1918, killing dozens of sailors and injuring others, but failing to sink the *Mount Vernon*, which is repaired. It eventually is scrapped in 1940.

## August 5, 1948
### Army Veteran First Person to Document Walking Entire Length of Appalachian Trail

World War II Army veteran Earl Schaffer, who later says he was trying to "walk the war out of my system," climbs to the peak of Maine's Mount Katahdin, which is the northern terminus of the Appalachian Trail.

He becomes the first person to lay claim to having hiked the entire 2,200 miles of the trail from Georgia, and he supplies a diary—now in the Smithsonian Institution archives—and photographs as proof.

The diary page that wraps up the hike says, "In morn climbed Katahdin in leisurely fashion, reached summit of Baxter peak about 1:30. Had pic taken by sign. Talked a while with several fellas come on down to campground. finis."

Joan Benoit statue in Cape Elizabeth.

---

August 5, 1984

**Cape Elizabeth's Joan Benoit Wins First-ever Women's Olympic Gold Medal in Marathon**

Taking the lead and keeping it for the rest of the race, Cape Eliza-beth native Joan Benoit, 27, wins the first-ever women's Olympic marathon with a time of 2:24:52 in Los Angeles.

After breaking a leg at age 15 in a skiing accident, Benoit began running as rehabilitation therapy, then became a star on her school track team.

Benoit won the women's Boston Marathon in 1979 in record time, 2:35:15, even though she had become stuck in a traffic jam and was forced to sprint two miles to arive on time at the start of the race in Hopkinton, Massachusetts.

Despite surgery on both Achilles tendons in 1981, she won the Boston Marathon again in 1983, this time with a world-record finish of 2:22:43.

Surgery in April 1984 to repair a knee injury appeared likely to imperil her bid to compete in the first Olympic women's marathon, but she captured the lead at the trials on May 17, following that feat by winning the gold medal in the Los Angeles Olympics with a time of 2:24:52.

Benoit, who by marriage in 1984 becomes Joan Benoit Samuelson, continues to race selectively after her Olympic achievement, right up to the present. In 1998 she establishes a new race in her home state—the Peoples Heritage Beach to Beacon 10K, now known as the TD Beach to Beacon 10K.

She still lives in Maine.

## August 6, 1899
### Slip Collapses at Hancock Point; at Least 20 Dead, 50 Injured

At least twenty people drown and more than fifty are injured at Hancock Point when a moveable slip leading to a steamship collapses, dropping about two hundred boarding passengers fifteen feet into the ocean.

The people in the water are hemmed in on three sides by dock pilings and on the fourth by the steamer, and mass panic ensues.

Most of the victims are from eastern Maine.

When the accident happens, the steamer *Sappho* is waiting to transport the passengers on a Sunday excursion to Bar Harbor, eight miles away on Mount Desert Island.

Many of the travelers were trying to go to the island to see the warships of the Navy's North Atlantic squadron, which are at anchor off Bar Harbor. A train that rolls onto the wharf has just delivered hundreds of people a few steps from where they would board the steamer.

The dock features no gate or fence to protect people who might find themselves pushed by a crowd or to encourage them to wait until passengers in front of them board the steamer.

The Maine Central Railroad train that brought the passengers had left Bangor at 8:25 a.m.—fifteen minutes late—and arrived at 10:25 at the ferry landing. A large crowd of other would-be passengers had been left standing on the train platform in Bangor because the train was full, like others before it that day.

When the train arrives at Hancock Point, the disembarking passengers, fearful of being left without a seat on the already crowded boat, begin bypassing a gangplank and going down the slip to board. The crowd surges forward, moving like a single organism. Then the slip, built only two months earlier, breaks, plunging the crowd into a watery, rectangular enclosure about forty feet long and twelve feet wide.

Many travelers still standing on the wharf play a role in hauling out those who fell, especially Chester W. Robbins, of the *Oldtown Enterprise* newspaper, who strips off his clothes, goes into the water, and rescues about thirty people, according to witnesses.

The jury at a coroner's inquest rules on August 8 that the slip's construction was defective.

## August 7, 1823
## Maine's First Recorded Meteorite Falls in Nobleboro

Maine's first recorded meteorite falls between four and five o'clock in the afternoon in Nobleboro, startling a nearby flock of sheep when it hits the ground.

Mr. A. Dinsmore, who looks for the rock after hearing what he later says sounded like musket fire, digs down about six inches and recovers five or six pounds of a mass that smells like sulfur. The fallen object—only the second reported in the United States—proves to be achondrite, a type representing only 3 percent of all recovered meteorites. Samples of it are now in museum collections around the world.

The sky unleashes another surprise at 4:15 a.m. May 20, 1848, in Castine. Charles Blaisdell finds a single stone about the size of a hen's egg, composed mostly of olivine, pyroxene, and nickel-iron. The American Journal of Science carries an account of the find, and once again, parts of it are distributed around the world.

Maine's next extraterrestrial gem plops into a field at 8:15 a.m. May 21, 1871, in Searsmont—oddly, not far from Nobleboro and Castine, and almost equidistant between the two. This one, about two pounds, is about 90 percent iron, 9 percent nickel, and a trace of cobalt.

As if the state had signed up with some cosmic book-of-the-month club—except the book is a stone and the month is actually about a quarter-century—another meteorite falls on August 5, 1898, on Lincoln Dresser's farm in Andover, generating a noise like a buzz saw as it falls. Dresser recovers a seven-plus-pound chunk and some smaller ones that fragmented when they hit a stone wall.

Finally, a 1978 newspaper report tells of Mark L. Smith, who was fixing a shed roof at his father's poultry farm in North Yarmouth when he noticed a hole in the roof. A small black stone was nestled inside. He and his father take it to the University of Southern Maine, where it is identified as a meteorite.

The five meteorites recovered so far in Maine come from at least three parent bodies. The Maine Geological Survey theorizes that many more have fallen in the state without being recovered or even observed.

According to the agency, the largest recorded meteorite to fall anywhere on Earth is a sixty-ton monster called the Hoba Meteorite, which is found in 1920 in what now is the African country of Namibia.

## August 8, 1901
### Photography Pioneer Chansonetta Stanley Emmons Opens Exhibit in Farmington

Chansonetta Stanley Emmons (1858-1937) opens a two-day exhibit of her photography in Farmington. Emmons is the sister of the Stanley brothers, who invented and marketed the Stanley Steamer car. The brothers turned to transportation technology after becoming wealthy through pioneering work in manufacturing and marketing dry-plate photography equipment, but their sister stuck with cameras.

Emmons is among the early practitioners of photography as an art form. She carefully stages each of her photographs and controls each step of their development. She takes frequent painting-and-photography trips with her daughter, Dorothy, who is a painter.

## August 8, 2015
### American Indian Sculpture Relocated to Langlais Park

Langlais Park, a new home for the newly restored sixty-two-foot-tall 1969 American Indian sculpture by Maine artist Bernard Langlais (1921-1977), is dedicated in Skowhegan.

The restoration was needed because the sculpture had deteriorated from exposure to the elements. It also was the subject of vandalism threats linked to a controversy about whether the local school district should cease using the term "Indians" as the name of its sports teams.

## August 9, 1842
### Treaty of Washington Ends 'Aroostook War'

The US signs the Treaty of Washington, or Webster-Ashburton Treaty, with the United Kingdom, establishing what is now the boundary between the US and Canada, including the boundary in northern and eastern Maine.

The treaty resolves a dispute known as the "Aroostook War," a disagreement that led to deployment of militia units to the northern frontier and almost resulted in armed conflict.

The 1783 peace treaty that ended the Revolutionary War between the United States and Great Britain had failed to define adequately the border separating Maine and what later became the Canadian province of New Brunswick, resulting in confusion and dangerously competing land claims.

## August 9, 1911
### Augusta Park Hosts Maine's First Plane Flight

Aviator St. Croix Johnstone, 24, of Chicago, makes Maine's first plane flight, taking off in a Moisant monoplane in Augusta for a half-hour, twenty-five-mile trip up and down the Kennebec Valley. About 10,000 people watch the exhibition. The event occurs about eight years after the Wright brothers' famed first flights in North Carolina.

Six days later, Johnstone dies in a flying accident during the 1911 Chicago International Aviation Meet.

The Augusta demonstration begins on the baseball diamond at the Augusta Driving Park, a horse-racing venue located about where the local YCMA stands today, on the west bank of the Kennebec River and immediately south of Capitol Park. It is part of Governor's Day activities, which also include several horse races.

Johnstone's initial attempt at about five p.m. fails to get the speeding aircraft off the ground, so he shuts off the motor in centerfield and the plane rolls to a stop. He tries again at 5:20 p.m., and the plane floats aloft by the time it reaches second base, drawing a roar from the crowd, according to a story in the next day's *Daily Kennebec Journal.* The southbound aircraft creeps steadily higher, gliding along "as steadily as a ship at sea, with the buzz of the engine and the whirr of the propellor audible to everyone," the newspaper reports.

The plane turns east, crosses the river, circles the state hospital's tall chimney, then flies back over the racetrack, still ascending. It crosses the river again, returns to the hospital, then flies north over the Augusta Lumber Co. mill, which emits a whistle blast to celebrate the pilot's achievement. Johnstone's plane, within sight of the spectators through all of this, then disappears briefly over the city's northeastern section. It reappears over Capitol Park, then touches down without incident on the baseball diamond, only a few feet from where it had started, and rolls into the outfield.

"The crowd then made a grand rush for the plucky and skilled aviator and he was repeatedly cheered and congratulated," the

*Daily Kennebec Journal* reports.

On Aug. 15 in Chicago, Johnstone is one of two pilots killed in separate crashes, both of which are attributed to mechanical failure. In Johnstone's case, the pilot is over Lake Michigan when his plane's engine fails, and the plane plunges into the lake. Trapped under the motor, Johnstone drowns when it drags him into deep water. His body is recovered an hour later.

## August 10, 1674
### Dutch Capture French-controlled Fort Pentagouet, Rename Colony

A Dutch force commanded by naval Capt. Jurriaen Aernouts, aboard the frigate *Flying Horse,* overruns the thirty lightly armed French soldiers at Fort Pentagouet during the Franco-Dutch war of 1672-78. The Dutch also seize the French military headquarters there.

Pentagouet, located on the Bagaduce River at the current site of the town of Castine, at the time is the capital of the French colony of Acadia. The Dutch rename the colony "Nova Hollandia," Latin for "New Holland."

The French quickly regain control of the area, although the Dutch continue to claim it and

Courtesy of Presque Isle Historical Society

The *Double Eagle II* prepares to launch in 1978 from Presque Isle.

attack Pentagouet again in 1676. Holland finally gives up its claim to Acadia under the terms of the 1678 Treaty of Nijmegen, which ends the war. The French lose it again in 1713 to the British.

A roadside sign explaining the brief Dutch presence in the area stands in Castine.

## August 11, 1978
### First Manned Transatlantic Balloon Flight Launches from Presque Isle

Ben Abruzzo, Maxie Anderson, and Larry Newman, riding in the helium-filled balloon *Double Eagle II*, launch at 8:42 p.m. from Presque Isle. After 137 hours and six minutes, they land in a barley field in Miserey, France, about sixty miles northwest of Paris, completing the first successful manned transatlantic balloon flight.

Their gondola, *The Spirit of Albuquerque*, carries a twin-hull catamaran for an emergency water landing. It also carries a glider intended to be used to aid in the balloon's descent, but that is jettisoned during flight to reduce the balloon's weight.

The flight is the fourteenth known attempt to accomplish such a feat, and it occurs 205 years after Étienne Montgolfier became the first person in history to take a balloon flight, also in France.

A one-acre park on Sprague-ville Road in Presque Isle, located where the *Double Eagle II's* flight began, contains a balloon-shaped monument commemorating the feat.

## August 12, 1901
### George Dorr Visits Seal Harbor, Laying Groundwork for Future Acadia National Park

George Bucknam Dorr receives a letter from Charles W. Eliot, president of Harvard University, asking him to attend a meeting the next day at Seal Harbor about setting aside land on Mount Desert Island for the public's perpetual use.

Sowing the seeds that eventually will grow into Acadia National Park, they form a corporation, with Eliot its president and Dorr its vice president.

After a few minor acquisitions, the corporation's trustees receive their first major land gift—the Bowl and Beehive tract on Newport Mountain. This forms the nucleus of what in 1916 becomes Sieur de Monts National Monument; and in 1919, the national park.

## August 13, 1607
### *Gift of God* Arrives at Kennebec After Eleven-week Voyage from England

Colonists led by George Popham and traveling on the ship *Gift of God* arrive at the mouth of the Kennebec River after an eleven-week voyage from Plymouth, England. An accompanying ship, the *Mary and John*, arrives a few days later.

The colonists, who number about 120, build Fort St. George in what is now Phippsburg. They also build the *Virginia*, the first English vessel built in North America, and it crosses the Atlantic Ocean twice. By December, the *Mary and John* and the *Gift of God* depart for England, leaving some colonists to spend the winter.

The colonists split into two competing factions, after which Popham, the head of one of them, dies on February 5, 1608. The other leader, Raleigh Gilbert, 25,

*Courtesy of Maine Historical Society*

This illustration showing a fleet of British warships and frigates approaching Penobscot Bay in 1779 appeared in the *Naval Chronicle* of London in 1814.

then becomes the entire colony's leader. Gilbert and the remaining forty-five colonists return to England that summer aboard the *Virginia*.

Knowledge of Fort St. George's precise location becomes lost until Jeffrey Brain, a researcher from the Peabody Essex Museum, discovers it in 1994.

## August 13, 1779
### American Armada Destroyed by British on Penobscot River

After unsuccessfully attacking British defenses since July 28 at the newly built Fort Majabigwaduce—the site of modern Castine—by unleashing the Revolutionary War's largest amphibious assault, an American forty-four-ship armada known as the Penobscot Expedition is attacked by a British relief fleet.

The fleet, under the command of Sir George Collier, drives the American ships up the Penobscot River to their destruction.

The Revolutionary force's fleet had a seemingly overpowering numerical advantage in men, firepower and ships when it first arrived; but its commander, Adm. Dudley Saltonstall, of Connecticut, is accused later of letting the attack falter by inaction. Having failed to destroy the first group of British ships in the harbor, he is dismissed from the Navy.

American survivors are forced

to make their way over land to safety in other settlements in the District of Maine, which then is part of Massachusetts.

A noteworthy participant among the fort's British defenders is Lt. Henry Mowatt, who commanded the ships that firebombed Falmouth—now Portland—in 1775, causing great destruction there.

On the American side, Paul Revere, not to become nationally famous until decades after his death, was in charge of Saltonstall's artillery. Accused later of failing to follow orders during the attack, he is placed under house arrest September 6, shortly after returning to Boston. A long-postponed court-martial in 1782 absolves him of the two charges against him.

### August 13, 1922
### Fire Destroys Fifteen Locomotives at Portland Railroad Yard

A fire destroys fifteen train locomotives and damages nine more cars and a railroad roundhouse in Portland.

The fire, reported about half past seven in the morning because deputies working there heard an explosion, starts in a small outbuilding composed of two discarded rail cars and used by air brake repairmen. It is so saturated with grease and oil that it goes up in flames immediately, as does the engine house.

Low tide prevents a fireboat dispatched to the waterfront near the fire scene from being used effectively. Also, firefighters find it impossible to move their apparatus close to the roundhouse because it is surrounded by railroad tracks. Explosions occur throughout the morning as the fire ignites acetylene gas tanks on the engines.

The locomotives are lost because when railway workers try to move them out, one breaks down on the turntable, trapping the others.

A Boston & Maine railway official estimated the damage would top $1 million—more than $15.7 million in 2020.

### August 13, 2016
### Elle Logan Makes History with Third Consecutive Olympic Gold in Rowing

Elle Logan, who grew up in Boothbay Harbor, becomes the first woman to win a gold medal in rowing in three consecutive Summer Olympics.

Her first medal came when she won the women's eight event at the 2008 Beijing Olympics as a 20-year-old Stanford University undergraduate.

Next, she was on the team that won the same event at the 2012 London Olympics. Finally, in 2016, she wins the same event in Rio de Janeiro.

## August 14, 1777
## Royal Marines Seize Machias Battery

Landing in Machias under cover of fog, Royal Marines fighting for England seize an American battery during the American Revolution. The Revolutionary forces, aided by a group of Penobscot, Passamaquoddy, and Maliseet Indians, repel the attackers.

## August 14, 1935
## Roosevelt Signs Social Security Act, Frances Perkins Plays a Key Role

President Franklin Roosevelt signs the Social Security Act, a landmark piece of legislation that was drafted by U.S. Labor Secretary Frances Perkins, a Boston native who spent much of her time at the family homestead in Newcastle, Maine.

Perkins also did much of the groundwork for other important New Deal programs, including workman's compensation, and the 40-hour workweek.

Perkins' remains are buried in the family plot at the Glidden Cemetery in Newcastle.

The nonprofit Frances Perkins Center in Damariscotta educates the public about Perkins' life and legacy. In 2020, the organization buys the Perkins family homestead, which is a national historic landmark, to operate it as a public educational resource.

## August 14, 1945
## Victory over Japan Announced; World War II Ends

On a quiet August evening, workers at the *Bangor Daily News* scrawl a note in blue crayon on a white placard and place it in the window. It says, simply: "War Ends." President Harry Truman announces at 7 p.m. that the Japanese have accepted terms of surrender.

In Bangor, thousands of people surge into downtown. Church bells ring, whistles blow, fire alarms sound. Thousands of cars, two and three abreast, circle through Bangor, blasting their horns. Fireworks, confetti, beer bottles, and flags are everywhere, while the high school band descends on downtown Bangor in joyous pandemonium. Businesses close for two days.

In the war against Nazi Germany and Japan, more than 8,000 men and women from Maine served and more than 1,600 died. More than 110 Bangor men were killed. The final months were particularly deadly for Maine, as more than 580 Maine men were killed from January to April alone.

## August 14, 1779
### Residents of Belfast Flee Following Destruction of Penobscot Expedition by British

With the remaining ships of the destroyed Penobscot Expedition armada burning off the coast or fleeing, residents of Belfast hide their valuables and evacuate their town as the British forces fighting the Americans in the Revolutionary War approach from the east.

The refugees arrive at a defensive timber breastwork at Clam Cove, between Rockland and Camden, the next day. When they return to Belfast the following year, they find almost everything in ruins.

## August 14, 1870
### Adm. David Farragut, Hero of Battle of Mobile Bay, Dies in Kittery

Adm. David Farragut, the Civil War officer to whom the command "Damn the torpedoes, full speed ahead!" is attributed, dies in Kittery while on vacation. He is 69.

Farragut was in command of Union forces during the Battle of Mobile Bay. Commodore Foxhall A. Parker, in his 1878 book about the battle, claims that Farragut actually said, when told that the bay was seeded with tethered mines, or "torpedoes," "Damn the torpedoes! Jouett, full speed! Four bells, Captain Drayton." His son Loyall Farragut's biography of 1879, however, cites the elder Farragut's exclamation as "Damn the torpedoes. Four bells, Captain Drayton, go ahead. Jouett, full speed."

In any event, most of the fleet succeeded in entering the bay, closing off the last major Confederate port on the Gulf of Mexico.

## August 14, 1947
### All the Lobster You Can Eat for $1

A front-page story in the *Camden Herald* announces an event called the Camden-Rockport Lobster Festival, using the headline "All the lobster you can eat for $1."

The low price causes the festival to lose so much money that it is never repeated in that form. The next year, however, the Rockland Junior Chamber of Commerce revives the idea, and the result is what today is known as the Maine Lobster Festival, held for five days around the first weekend in August.

It is one of Maine's premier summer events. A worldwide coronavirus pandemic prompted cancellation of the festival in both 2020 and 2021.

## August 15, 1635
### 240-ton English Galleon Destroyed by Storm

The Great Colonial Hurricane of 1635 tears the 240-ton English galleon *Angel Gabriel* from its anchors off Pemaquid Point in Bristol and destroys it.

The ship—similar to the *Mayflower* but eighteen feet longer and containing more gun ports—was carrying settlers to America. Many of them disembarked at Pemaquid before the sinking, but the ship's crew members and the passengers remaining on board die.

Centuries later, descendants of the wreck survivors gather in 2010 at Pemaquid Point to dedicate a plaque commemorating the event on its 375th anniversary.

Today researchers still are trying to find the wreckage, which is believed to be covered by mud on the ocean floor.

## August 15, 1907
### Firestorm Ravages Old Orchard Beach

A firestorm devastates Old Orchard Beach, burning up seventeen hotels, sixty cottages, several commercial buildings—all of wooden construction—and the first hundred feet of the resort town's pier on the Atlantic Ocean, all within three hours.

The fire starts in an annex of the Olympia House hotel and is well underway, fanned by a southwest wind, by the time somebody discovers it. Fire squads from Portland, Saco, and Biddeford arrive within an hour to help, but they are hampered by the fact that their hose couplings don't fit properly on the Old Orchard Beach hydrants.

Firemen use dynamite to blow up buildings and create a gap that slows the fire's progress, and by midnight it is under control.

The disaster results in two deaths and the injury of at least five people. One of the deaths occurs when a soda tank explodes at Horgan's Pharmacy on Old Orchard Avenue and shoots across the street like a rocket, decapitating the victim instantly and throwing two other people violently up against a building. It also shatters a post, flying fragments of which inflict minor scratches on Boston Mayor John F. "Honey Fitz" Fitzgerald, the maternal grandfather of future President John F. Kennedy. Fitzgerald happens to be walking along Old Orchard Avenue at the time.

The disaster leaves hundreds of summer guests with no place to stay, because train service is interrupted and hotels in nearby communities are full anyway. Many of them cluster on the beach with their belongings, struggling to douse flaming embers that drift toward them and trying to ward off thieves. Fitzgerald, a longtime summer resident of the town, sends the police a message begging them to do something about criminals swooping down on helpless victims at the beach.

Many of the town's hotel guests pack up their luggage while escaping from the flames, and the bags are carried to the beach and deposited on the sand at low tide. When the tide comes in, it drags many of the bags into the ocean.

When the fire is over, fifty acres of beachfront property have been reduced to ashes. The damage is estimated at $500,000 to $800,000, which equates to $13.9 million to $22.2 million in 2019 dollars.

## August 16, 1941
## President Franklin Roosevelt Stops in Rockland after Drafting Atlantic Charter with Winston Churchill

President Franklin D. Roosevelt arrives in Rockland aboard the presidential yacht *Potomac*, recently returned to the United States from a shipboard meeting off the coast of Newfoundland with British Prime Minister Winston Churchill.

At that meeting, Churchill and Roosevelt drafted the Atlantic Charter, which mapped out the Allied World War II and postwar strategy. (The United States is aiding Britain but would not become one of the fighting nations until the Japanese attack on Pearl Harbor in December.)

At Rockland, Roosevelt is evasive at a news conference on his yacht about exactly where he met Churchill or what subjects they discussed.

When Maine's state police chief lurches forward at the wharf to shake the president's hand, Secret Service agents who don't know

Courtesy of DigiCommons

Harry Goodridge and Andre the seal.

him nearly knock him into Rockland Harbor.

The president then travels by motorcade to the train station, waving to a cheering throng of people in a city that had voted mostly for his opponent in the previous election.

## August 17, 1994
### Andre the Seal Movie Released

Paramount Pictures releases a film titled *Andre* about an orphaned seal in Rockport that grows up in the care of a girl and her father. The film is based on a real orphaned seal pup named Andre (1961-1986) that was rescued and raised by Rockport's harbormaster, Harry Goodridge, and that chose to stay with Goodridge rather than return permanently to the wild.

Andre began attracting crowds when Goodridge built a waterfront pen in which the seal could frolic. The New England Aquarium in Boston offered to take Andre in during the winters, and when it released the seal each spring, it swam 150 miles back to Rockport.

Newspapers began covering Andre's annual trip so comprehensively that in 1979, newly inaugurated Maine Gov. Joseph Brennan complained that his policy proposals were getting too little coverage.

"There should always be a place on the front page for the interesting, bright, human interest story," he said at a news conference. "But in the end, it won't affect the progress of our state government, it won't change your local property tax rate, or the quality of your local fire department one bit if Andre reaches Rockport."

Brennan's remark unleashed a firestorm of angry letters from Andre's fans. The continuing uproar eventually prompted Brennan to say that his criticism of the Andre news coverage "was the worst thing that I've done since I've been governor." In the run-up to his 1982 re-election campaign, he went to Rockport and finally met the seal face-to-snout.

The movie, based on a book by Goodridge and filmed in Bristish Columbia and Mississippi, stars Tina Majorino, Keith Carradine, and Chelsea Field. It garners $16.8 million at the box office worldwide.

## August 17, 1995
## General Dynamics Buys
## Bath Iron Works for $300 Million

General Dynamics, one of the world's largest defense contractors, announces that it will buy Bath Iron Works for $300 million in cash.

The corporation still owns BIW in 2021.

BIW, established in 1826 as an iron foundry and reorganized as a shipyard in 1884 by Civil War veteran Thomas Hyde, is Maine's largest private employer and the oldest private shipyard in the United States.

Its primary business is designing and building vessels for the US military.

General Dynamics originated in 1952 as the merger of Electric Boat and Canadair, a Canadian aircraft builder. In New England it is known best for its Electric Boat division, which is headquartered in Groton, Connecticut, and produces and repairs nuclear submarines.

At the time of the 1995 acquisition, BIW has about 8,300 employees. Its peak employment occurred in 1944, the penultimate year of World War II, when 12,000 people worked there.

The frigate USS *Oliver Haz-*

*ard Perry*, now out of service, was one of the many ships built at BIW. At its christening and launch ceremony in 1976, the ship did not move immediately after a bottle of champagne was broken over its bow.

Film star John Wayne, who was a board member of one of the subcontractors that worked on the ship, attended the ceremony. Someone suggested that he give the vessel a shove. He stepped up and put his hands on the ship just as it began to move, making it look as though he had launched it using his own strength.

## August 17, 1997
## Phish Concert Draws 75,000 to Former Loring Air Force Base

The town of Limestone ends its two-day reign as Maine's largest community as the band Phish concludes The Great Went concert festival at the former Loring Air Force Base, where 75,000 fans were in attendance.

Many concertgoers spent the weekend nights sleeping in tents, campers and other vehicles that lined the entire length of the facility's 800-acre runway.

It was the top-grossing rock concert in the United States that summer.

The next year, on August 15 and 16, Phish performs at the Lemonwheel festival, also held at Loring, drawing more than 60,000 people.

## August 18, 1957
## Norwegian Coin Found in Brooklin

Amateur archaeologist Guy Mellgren, according to his own report, finds an eleventh-century Norwegian coin at the Goddard prehistoric archaeological site on Naskeag Point in Brooklin.

The coin, donated since then to the Maine State Museum, has given rise to theories that Norsemen from that period traveled to Maine, or that local tribes acquired the coin in trade from people who had contact with the Norsemen farther up the Atlantic coast.

Some researchers have raised the possibility that while the coin appears to be real, the claim of its discovery at the site might be a hoax, or the origin of its presence there is misinterpreted.

Archaeologist Bruce Bourque, author of *12,000 Years in Maine* and a lecturer in archaeology at Bates College, notes in a 1993 interview that trade among indigenous groups was common along the Atlantic coast before widescale European settlement began.

Local people in Labrador probably got the coin from Norse explorers, and it made its way through the trade network to Maine, just as stones that originated in Labrador did, Bourque says.

## August 19, 1692
## Wells Man Hanged in Salem for Witchcraft

George Burroughs, 42, of Wells, is hanged in Salem, Massachusetts, after being tried for and found guilty of witchcraft. The execution proceeds even though Burroughs' chief accuser, Margaret Jacobs, 17, recants her testimony, saying that she suffered "such horror of conscience that I could not sleep for fear the devil should carry me away for telling such horrid lies."

Famed Puritan minister and pamphleteer Cotton Mather (1663-1728) witnesses Burroughs' hanging, delivering a sermon about the devil's trickery even while Burroughs is dangling, still alive, from the noose.

Of the nineteen defendants executed as a result of the quickly discredited Salem witch trials, Burroughs is the only religious minister and the only Harvard College graduate to be put to death. Burroughs, who grew up in Roxbury, Massachusetts (now part of Boston), becomes known for reciting the Lord's Prayer during his execution, something it was believed a witch never could do. Burroughs lived in Falmouth (now Portland), but he moved to Wells after the Wabanaki Confederacy destroyed Falmouth in 1690. He was arrested April 30, 1692, after members of his congregation to whom he owed money accused him of witchcraft.

Eleven months after Burroughs' execution, his widow marries again, and Mather performs the wedding ceremony.

## August 19, 1974
## University of Maine Graduate Leaves Motorola, Helps Invent Revolutionary Microprocessor

Electrical engineer and University of Maine graduate Chuck Peddle (1937-2019) and six colleagues leave their jobs at Motorola after unsuccessfully trying to convince the company to focus on manufacturing small, cheaper microprocessors. The group goes to work for MOS Technologies in Valley Forge, Pennsylvania, where it invents the 6502 microprocessor, which paves the way for low-cost personal computers, revolutionizing the industry.

The chip is used in such early models as the Commodore II and the Apple II.

Born in Bangor and raised in Augusta, Peddle receives the University of Maine Alumni Association's Career Award in April 2019. However, his sister, Marty Peddle Furber, of Hallowell, says her brother did not seek accolades.

"Once he finished something, he just moved on to something else," she says. "He was an inventor and innovator and just moved on. He was very casual."

## August 20, 2010
### Federal Officials Arrest Forty-seven in Gang Sweep

Federal officials announce they have arrested forty-seven people—more than half of them known gang members—as part of a regional action against gangs. Twenty-four of the suspects were arrested in Maine.

The other arrests occurred in Connecticut, Rhode Island, and Massachusetts, according to US Immigration and Customs Enforcement.

The arrest pool includes twenty-eight known gang members and others who are associated with them, such as by purchasing illegal drugs from them, the office said.

The arrests in Maine included twenty-three in Portland and one in Westbrook. Nineteen occurred in June through the efforts of a gang task force. The rest occurred during the week leading up to the announcement.

The Maine suspects were identified as members of the Asian Boyz and two splinter groups of the Bloods or people affiliated with those gangs.

## August 21, 1942
### *Bambi* Released; Famous Deer Based on Captured Maine Fawns

Walt Disney releases the animated film *Bambi*, which benefited from various Maine influences.

Disney sent one of his employees, Damariscotta native Maurice "Jake" Day, a prolific artist, sculptor, photographer, and naturalist, back to Maine to paint and photograph the area around Mount Katahdin in various seasons during the production of *Bambi*. As a result, many of the scenes in the movie are inspired by the Baxter State Park area.

To aid the film's development further, the Maine Development Commission sent two orphaned fawns, Bambi and Faline, to Hollywood by train for animators to study.

Also, composer Frank Churchill (1901-1942), a Rumford native, receives two Oscar nominations in connection with the film, including one for the tune "Love is a Song."

## August 22, 1912
### Publishing Tycoon Presents Portland with Kotzschmar Organ

During a ceremony dedicating a new Portland City Hall, built to replace one that burned in 1908, publishing tycoon and Portland native Cyrus H.K. Curtis, publisher of the *Saturday Evening Post* magazine, presents the city with a gift—the Kotzschmar Organ, one of only two municipal organs in the United States.

Curtis commissioned the Austin Organ Co., of Hartford, Connecticut, to build the five-keyboard, 7,000-plus-pipe organ and install it in the City Hall auditorium. It is named for Hermann Kotzschmar, the city's most prominent musician, whom Curtis' father brought to Portland.

After a century of use, an artistic restoration of the organ is completed in 2015 at a cost of $2.6 million, more than half of which is financed through private fundraising.

## August 23, 1724
### New England Forces Attack Abenaki Village, Kill Dozens of Tribe Members

During a Colonial-era conflict known as Governor Dummer's War, about two hundred New Englanders under the command of Capt. Johnson Harmon and Capt. Jeremiah Moulton attack the Abenaki village at Norridgewock, killing dozens of Wabanaki Indians as well as Rev. Sébastien Râle, leader of the Catholic mission there.

The attackers are trying to open the Kennebec River valley to English settlement, while also curtailing Catholic missionaries' expansion of French influence in the region. Boston authorities pay the soldiers a reward for the scalps they turn in, including that of Râle.

A granite monument commemorating Râle is erected in 1833 in the town of Madison.

## August 23, 1780
### Damariscotta Area Man Hanged for Aiding British

The only military execution in Maine history occurs at Limestone Hill in Thomaston.

After a Tory raiding party killed an American Revolution

supporter and wounded his wife in what is now Waldoboro, Revolutionary War Brig. Gen. Peleg Wadsworth issued a proclamation that the next person caught aiding British forces or British supporters will be executed.

That threat was put to the test when Jeremiah Braun, of the Damariscotta area, was tried for guiding a British party into the backcountry.

Braun was convicted and sentenced to death by hanging. His execution shocks local patriots as much as it does the Tories, but Wadsworth, though agitated about it, expresses no regret.

"The Act of severity tho' painfull in the highest degree proved salutary," he writes decades later, in 1828, "for there was not found another instance of this kind. ... "

His assertion is false, however. Shortly after Braun's death, Wadsworth sentences another man, Nathaniel Palmer, to death for helping the enemy. Palmer evades Braun's fate by escaping from Wadsworth's barn while awaiting execution.

Wadsworth is the maternal grandfather of famed poet and Portland native Henry Wadsworth Longfellow.

In 1824, Limestone Hill becomes the longtime site of the Maine State Prison, where some civilian executions are carried out in the nineteenth century.

## August 23, 1879
### Young Theodore Roosevelt Climbs Mount Katahdin with Two Friends

Theodore Roosevelt, then 20, arrives in northern Maine for a month of camping, hiking and canoeing, during which, long before the development of marked trails, he climbs Mount Katahdin while carrying a forty-five-pound pack.

He reaches the peak with friends Wilmot Dow and Bill Sewall.

Afterward, the future president and Dow embark on a fifty-mile, six-day expedition up the Aroostook River in a dugout canoe, hacking their way through beaver dams and log drifts and spending up to ten hours a day in icy water up to their hips.

"But, oh how we slept at night" Roosevelt wrote in a September 14 letter to his sister Anna "Bamie" Roosevelt, his lifelong confidante. "And how we enjoyed the salt pork, hardtack and tea which constituted our food!"

Sandy Stream Pond and North Basin in the fall at Baxter State Park.

August 24, 1857

### Maine-born Painter Eastman Johnson Begins Two-month Visit in Minnesota Territory

Eastman Johnson (1824-1906), a prolific painter who was born in Lovell and raised in Augusta and Fryeburg, begins a two-month visit to Grand Portage, Minnesota Territory.

While there, according to Teresa A. Carbone and Patricia Hills' lavishly illustrated book *Eastman Johnson: Painting America*, he creates a series of portraits "that for several reasons have come to be regarded as perhaps the most sensitive midcentury likenesses of Native Americans."

Johnson, a co-founder of New York City's Metropolitan Museum of Art whose career spanned more than five decades, is known in his time as "the American Rembrandt."

## August 24, 2016
### Katahdin Woods and Waters National Monument Established

President Barack Obama proclaims the establishment of Katahdin Woods and Waters National Monument, which occupies 86,563 donated acres in northern Maine. The site includes a seventeen-mile loop road that offers clear views of Mount Katahdin, Maine's highest peak, to the west. It offers trails for hiking, mountain biking, and snowmobiling, as well as canoeing and kayaking in the East Branch of the Penobscot River.

The land is a gift of Burt's Bees consumer products magnate Roxanne Quimby, who hoped to turn the site into a national park. When faced with local opposition, she changed her focus to getting it accepted as a national monument. She and her foundation, Elliotsville Plantation, Inc., began buying land for the project as early as 2001.

## August 25, 1894
### Celia Thaxter Dies on Appledore Island

Renowned poet and author Celia Thaxter (1835-1894) dies on Maine's Appledore Island, in the Isles of Shoals, the inspiration for many of her poems. She is 59.

Although she was born on the mainland—in Portsmouth, New Hampshire—and spent many years away, she is associated most closely with the island, where she was the hostess at her father's hotel, the Appledore House.

Thaxter married at 17 and had two sons. Her family lived in Newtonville, Massachusetts, where she became familiar with many figures in Boston literary circles. However, she called her home a "household jail" and wrote a poem about it, "Landlocked." A friend submitted it to *The Atlantic Monthly* magazine, which published it and many other Thaxter poems.

Thaxter spent much more time on Appledore helping her family after her father died in 1866. Her literary fame drew well-known cultural figures such as Ralph Waldo Emerson, Henry Wadsworth Longfellow, John Greenleaf Whittier, Sarah Orne Jewett, and Childe Hassam to the island, where they spent vacations.

"I am busy every instant, so glad and thankful to be here. No tongue can tell it; just to be here, it is all I ask," she wrote, shortly before her death, in a letter to her friend Rose Lamb.

## August 26, 2005
### Portsmouth Naval Shipyard Spared from Closing

Workers at the Portsmouth Naval Shipyard in Kittery breathe a collective sigh of relief when they learn that a federal base-closing commission has left the shipyard off a list of military installations scheduled for closure.

Gov. John Baldacci and members of Maine's congressional delegation attend a celebratory rally in front of the shipyard after the news is announced.

Maine's elected officials thank the shipyard's supporters, their own staffs and the shipyard workers for their work in promoting the yard. They also praise their counterparts in New Hampshire for cooperating in the lobbying effort to keep the shipyard in business.

The teamwork marks a turnabout from a time several years earlier when Maine and New Hampshire tussled before the US Supreme Court about where the boundary line separating the two states is and which side of the line the shipyard is on. Maine won that battle.

The shipyard, established more than two centuries ago and run by the US Navy, remains open and operating in 2021.

## August 27, 1902
### Crowds Line Streets in Bangor to See President Theodore Roosevelt

A train hauling five special Pullman cars brings President Theodore Roosevelt and state and local dignitaries to Bangor, where it arrives at noon at the city's western train station to the hurrahs of hundreds of onlookers gathered on Railroad Street.

Rail yardmen rush up, remove their caps and stand several feet from the president. He acknowledges them, removing his silk hat, and bows. Everyone cheers.

Gussied-up carriages take Roosevelt and his party to the Bangor House, the city's best-known hotel, with crowds lining the streets thickly the whole way.

Then Roosevelt gets a tour of the city. He passes along flag-festooned, spectator-lined streets, past houses decorated for the occasion, past the flower-covered Children's Home, draped with bunting and ringed by a yard full of excited children.

The carriages stop. The children sing a song. A girl gives Roosevelt a bouquet. He signs the home's guest book.

By the time the entourage returns to the Bangor House, the crowd there has grown from hundreds to thousands. Roosevelt steps inside, walks through, and appears on a balcony overlooking the street, inspiring more cheers and waving of handkerchiefs. He speaks for five minutes, recalling the spirit that helped the North win the Civil War.

"There isn't any patent cure-all to get good government," he says. "Each man must do his duty and no more. Questions of birth and station mustn't be given place. When you who were in the Union army went into battle, you didn't bother about the antecedents of the men at your right and at your left. You wanted to be sure that they would stay put. We must strengthen the government by paying heed to the fundamental principles of American manhood."

Later, a gun salute heralds his arrival at the city's Maplewood Park, which teems with a swaying, swooning audience. He rises on a platform at 3:08 p.m. and, apparently mindful of Maine's rural character, launches into a paean to American farm life. He notes that farming, while still fostering cherished traditions, has progressed and become an "applied science."

"But after all this has been said," he notes, "it remains true that the countryman, the man on the farm, more than any other of our citizens today, is called upon continually to exercise the qualities which we would like to think of as typical of the United States throughout its history— the qualities of rugged independence, masterful resolution and individual energy and resourcefulness."

Then, after a homily about moral standards that might be mistaken for one given by a local parson, he and his party shake hands, squeeze through the crowd, provoke another gun salute, and return to the Bangor House.

They wait there until 4:15, when carriages take the president and his retinue back to the train station, where they depart for another engagement in Ellsworth.

So much activity in less than five hours, so much being jostled about, so much frenetic hustling here and there might have cowed a lesser being, but not Roosevelt, a former rancher, deputy sheriff, wilderness explorer, and police commissioner.

And he was, after all, a Rough Rider.

## August 28, 2006
### Chewonki Foundation Unveils First Hydrogen Fuel Cell in Maine

The Chewonki Foundation, a Wiscasset organization, unveils what it bills as the first hydrogen fuel cell of its kind in Maine. The new system is installed to provide backup power and heat in the foundation's educational center building.

It took three years for the foundation to complete the $250,000 project in cooperation with the nonprofit Hydrogen Energy Center in Portland and the Maine Energy Investment Corp. The Maine Technology Institute helps fund the effort with a grant.

At the fuel cell's Wiscasset introduction, Gov. John Baldacci signs an executive order permitting the formation of the Maine Energy Fuel Cell Partnership. That group's goal is to hasten the development of commercial-grade hydrogen production, storage, and distribution.

A hydrogen shed stands on the Chewonki grounds. In it, an electrolyzer unit, powered by rooftop solar panels, generates hydrogen by using electricity to split groundwater into hydrogen and oxygen. Compressed hydrogen is stored in eight high-pressure gas bottles.

If Chewonki should lose power in a storm, which sometimes happens, the hydrogen travels to the education center through an in-ground pipe. A fuel cell in the building combines hydrogen with oxygen to make electricity.

Chewonki, founded in 1915, teaches about the development of sustainable communities and stewardship of nature.

## August 29, 1786
### Shays' Rebellion in Massachusetts Helps Delay Maine Statehood

Protesters in Northampton, Massachusetts, angry about tax collections and property confiscations by the government, prevent the court there from holding a session. The protest grows into what becomes known as Shays' Rebellion, named for Daniel Shays, a Revolutionary War veteran who participated in it.

That and other protest actions severely dampen enthusiasm in Maine for a proposal to separate from Massachusetts.

The three delegates from Falmouth (now Portland) to a September convention on separation are instructed, according to the *Falmouth Gazette*, "not only to oppose every measure that might be taken to establish a new Government, but also to discount all attempts for obtaining redress of any grievances that we might labor under."

The instructions say Maine's separation movement would inflame further the chaos that the armed rebellion in western Massachusetts has caused.

Shays' Rebellion is one of many developments that delay Maine statehood until 1820.

## August 29, 1902
### Famed Prohibitionist Carrie Nation Visits Bangor, Targets Bangor House

The Bangor House, an imposing landmark on Bangor's Main Street, dodges calamity more than once in its 143 years in the hotel business.

It survives Bangor's Great Fire of 1911, standing just south of the zone of destruction. It also escapes the wrecking ball when a great—and some critics say misguided—wave of urban redevelopment sweeps over the city in the 1960s.

On this day in 1902, its staff quashes an uninvited confrontation, if a newspaper account of the event is to be believed, with a patron whose chief occupational tools are an acid tongue and a hatchet.

Carrie Nation (1846-1911), a militant prohibitionist who has become nationally famous for violently chopping up saloons with her hatchet, has come to call.

And she's not happy.

According to a *Bangor Daily News* story about her visit, Nation stops in Bangor briefly in the morning while traveling to Ellsworth to deliver a temperance speech. Afterward, returning to Bangor, she boards a carriage at the train station, directs the driver to the Bangor House and asks him whether he knows of anyplace where liquor is available.

Yes, the driver tells her, there are many such places—including the hotel where she is headed.

It's worth mentioning that in Maine, prohibition has been nominally in effect since the 1850s.

Nation prowls around the hotel lobby, looking for the bar. She fails to find it. She baits the hotel barber, asking him where she can get a drink. He offers her bay rum—an after-shave lotion—as a joke.

"What Mrs. Nation said to the barber," the *News* reports the next day, "would not look well in type, and it made him shrink two sizes."

A manager guides her to the dining room, where she summons

Joseph Owen

a waiter and demands a beer. Told that wasn't possible, she repeats the demand loudly, drawing co-proprietor Capt. H.C. Chapman's attention. He gently but doggedly tells her to leave, gets her to collect her belongings and escorts her to the street, where police officers are waiting to take her to City Hall.

That evening, at a speaking engagement in the city, Nation begins by unleashing a torrent of invective about the Bangor House and its mistreatment of her. Then for fifty minutes she presents "a rambling talk, incoherent and disjointed," the *News* says, about her saloon-smashing adventures and occasional imprisonment in Kansas. She lambastes Republicans and tobacco, noting that she often snatches cigarettes out of the mouths of men. She sells photos of herself and tiny souvenir hatchets to the crowd. She announces she will sue the Bangor House. Told that no hotel will take her in after her escapade that day, she accepts an invitation to stay at the home of a member of the audience.

On the following day, the *News* says, Nation plans to "make a tour of the city and, possibly, attempt to smash saloons."

More than a century later, one looks back and wonders whether the *News* reporter's disdain for this easy target reflects a clandestine fancy for liquor, a dislike of hatchet jobs other than his own, or the realization that he has less to gain from portraying Nation favorably than he does from burnishing the hotel management's image.

After all, he probably will need to deal with those folks again someday.

## August 29, 1968
### Muskie Accepts Nomination for Vice President on Ticket with Humphrey Amid Chaos in Chicago

US Sen. Edmund S. Muskie delivers a speech in acceptance of his nomination for vice president at the Democratic National Convention in Chicago, an event marred by a bloody police crackdown on unarmed anti-war protesters in the streets.

The Maine Democrat and the presidential nominee, Vice President Hubert Humphrey, later lose the November election to Republican presidential nominee Richard Nixon and Nixon's running mate, Maryland Gov. Spiro Agnew.

The Democratic ticket is burdened largely by the controversial Vietnam War legacy of President Lyndon Johnson, under whom Humphrey still serves as vice president while running for the top job.

Speaking to the convention attendees, Muskie, mindful of the chaos unfurling in Chicago's streets, speaks mostly about the conflict between freedom and responsibility.

"The practice of freedom has made possible tremendous advances in the lives of our people," he said. "Ironically, these very advances have highlighted our shortcomings, which have denied hope for improvement to too many Americans; which have concealed the reality of hunger, poverty and deprivation for many under an illusion of prosperity and equality for all."

Muskie is the third full-time Maine resident to become a major-party vice presidential nominee. The first was Hannibal Hamlin, of Hampden, who became the first Republican vice president when elected to the office in 1860 as Abraham Lincoln's running mate. The second was Democrat Arthur Sewall, of Bath, who ran unsuccessfully with William Jennings Bryan in 1896.

Maine also had one full-time resident who became a major-party presidential nominee—Augusta resident James G. Blaine, whom the Republicans nominated in 1884. He lost to New York Gov. Grover Cleveland.

## August 30, 1917
### First Submarine Built at Navy Shipyard Commissioned

The first submarine ever built at a US Navy shipyard, the USS *L-8*, is commissioned.

The Navy paid the Lake Torpedo Boat Co. $52,700 for the plans. The keel was laid down February 24, 1915, at Portsmouth Naval Shipyard in Kittery. The vessel was launched April 23, 1917, seventeen days after Congress declared war on Germany during World War I.

The 165-foot sub is equipped with four eighteen-inch torpedo tubes. During the waning days of the war, it takes part in patrols looking for German U-boats, using the strategy of accompanying a decoy fake merchant ship and waiting for a German submarine to surface and attack it with deck guns, then firing torpedoes at the Germans. There is no record that the *L-8* ever lured a German submarine into such a

Waiting room at Union Station (see page 282) in Portland around 1890.

trap, however.

The *L-8* is decommissioned in 1922 and sunk as a target in 1926 off Rhode Island in a torpedo test. A Rhode Island company begins to work amid the wreckage in the late 1980s and early 1990s. The company recovers a propeller, which it gives to the Naval War College.

High-resolution mapping of the wreck shows that it is largely intact at a depth of 110 feet.

August 31, 1954

### Hurricane Carol Makes Landfall in New York, Heads for Maine

Hurricane Carol makes landfall on New York's Long Island and proceeds to ravage much of New England and Atlantic Canada. It causes the most severe damage on the coasts of Connecticut and Rhode Island.

In Maine, falling trees damage houses, crush cars, cut power lines, and block highways. Wind speed of eighty mph is recorded in Augusta. The storm causes $1.7 million—$16.4 million in 2019 value—in damage to the state's apple crop.

Many remember it in connection with Hurricane Edna, which wallops Maine and New Hampshire only eleven days later with a ferocity they escaped under Carol.

## August 31, 1961
### Portland's Historic Union Station Razed, Replaced by Strip Mall

Portland's Union Station, which stood on St. John Street for seventy-three years, is torn down and later replaced by a strip mall that is still there.

The demolition of the mostly granite building, including its prominent clock tower, occurs about a year after most passenger train service was discontinued in southern Maine.

Several people who live in the neighborhood watch the station's destruction for weeks.

"It's too late to do anything about it now, but it's a crime to take down that building," says Joseph Murillo, a Valley Street resident and one of the many regulars who maintain an informal sidewalk vigil while the landmark slowly disappears.

Loss of the station becomes one of the reasons for the establishment, three years later, of Greater Portland Landmarks, an organization that seeks to preserve historic buildings in the area.

—30—

# SEPTEMBER

## September 1, 1998
### Gannett Family Sells *Portland Press Herald*, Other Maine Newspapers

Guy Gannett Communications agrees to sell the *Portland Press Herald* to The Seattle Times Co., ending the family's 110-year history of publishing newspapers and magazines in Maine.

At the time, the *Portland Press Herald* has a daily circulation of 74,500 and a Sunday circulation of 124,500.

The deal, for a reported $230 million, also includes the *Kennebec Journal* in Augusta, the *Morning Sentinel* in Waterville, and the weekly *Coastal Journal* in Bath.

The sale is expected to close in October and the company will be renamed Blethen Maine Newspapers.

The agreement ends a five-month search for a buyer during which more than one hundred companies expressed interest in buying the Guy Gannett-owned newspapers.

Following the sale to The Seattle Times Co., the newspaper chain will be sold three more times.

## September 1, 1814
### British Forces Occupy Castine, Establish Short-lived New Ireland

A British force occupies Castine during the War of 1812. The town becomes part of the short-lived second incarnation of the British crown colony of New Ireland.

When the British leave the following April, they take with them 10,750 pounds collected as tariff duties during their occupation. That money is used to fund the establishment of Dalhousie University in Halifax, Nova Scotia.

## September 1, 1846
### Thoreau, Famed Author of *Walden*, Departs Bangor for North Woods

Transcendentalist author Henry David Thoreau, later the writer of the 1854 book *Walden; or, Life in the Woods*, departs northward from Bangor on the first of his three wilderness expeditions into Maine's North Woods.

The second occurs in 1853 and the third, in 1857.

During those visits, Thoreau explores Moosehead Lake and climbs most of Mount Katahdin in an age when no clearly marked mountain trails exist and the nearest settlement is dozens of miles away.

## September 2, 1816
### Pro-Separation Backers Win 54 Percent of Vote

In a second referendum on Maine's proposed separation from Massachusetts to become a new US state, the pro-separation side wins again, with 54 percent of the vote.

While the margin of victory is smaller than the 62 percent win in a May 20 vote, the rate of voter participation is much greater, giving the result more credibility.

The referendum creates a firestorm of controversy, however, because of complicated arithmetic arising from the requirement of a five-ninths majority for passage, and how that majority is defined.

Historian Ronald Banks, in his book chronicling the plodding progress of the separation movement over thirty-five years, quotes the pro-separation *Portland Gazette's* reaction: "It is greatly to be feared that we shall be under the necessity of continuing our old vassalage to Massachusetts."

Maine's quest for statehood finally bears fruit in 1820.

## September 3, 1853
### Spool Factory, Other Businesses Burn in Augusta Fire

The Harnden & Brother spool factory on Augusta's west-side riverfront catches fire about two o'clock in the morning The fire eventually consumes a grist mill, machine shops, six sawmills, a boardinghouse, and other commercial enterprises.

When only the three-story, 160-by-60-foot spool mill is burning, a night watchman and a few people who come to his aid try to use a pump to put out the flames, but the fire's intensity drives them away. The fire soon spreads to the grist mill.

Firefighters using several engines are able to save several other nearby buildings from destruction. The blaze throws more than two hundred people out of work.

It is the community's worst fire to date, but it will be exceeded twelve years later by the Great Fire of 1865, which wipes out most of the downtown commercial district.

## September 3, 1902
### Sarah Orne Jewett Injured in Carriage Accident

On her 53rd birthday, South Berwick novelist, poet, and short story writer Sarah Orne Jewett (1849-1909) suffers an injury in a carriage accident that effectively ends her writing career.

It happens as Jewett is taking her sister Mary and two friends from South Berwick to Berwick, a trip she made many times before. As her horse descends a hill, it steps on some loose stones, loses its footing and falls, tipping the carriage over. One friend is bruised, and another friend and Jewett's sister are unharmed. Jewett, however, suffers blows to her head and her spine from which she never recovers fully.

A year later, she still is spending much of each day in bed. She can write letters and read lying down, but she cannot sit at a desk.

Her condition is a far cry from that of earlier years, when, for example, she traveled blissfully in 1882 to Europe with her friend and companion Annie Fields, making a six-month tour of Ireland, England, Norway, Holland, Germany, Switzerland, Italy, and France. She made three additional voyages to Europe after that.

Traveling—even traveling close to home—provided inspiration for her writing. She and Fields rented a cottage in Martinsville, a midcoast Maine village where Jewett began absorbing details of the landscape and people that she later would put to use in a novella, *The Country of the Pointed Firs*, her best-known work.

Her first publication, a story in *The Atlantic Monthly*, appeared in print when she was 19. *Pointed Firs* was published in 1896, when she was 47. The hallmark of her work is character development and the depth of local color, making the writing emblematic of the regionalist movement of the time.

After the accident, Jewett stays closer to home, although she does travel to Boston, Mount Desert Island, and other places within a conquerable distance from South Berwick.

On June 23, 1909, she suffers a cerebral hemorrhage—her second—and dies the next day.

Biographer Elizabeth Silverthorne provides what might have been the kernel of a fitting eulogy for a writer admired by both the public and her peers: "Sarah Orne Jewett explored the ethos of New England and preserved forever an important segment of its history along with the homely details of a vanished way of life, including patterns of speech, behavior, and thought. In her writing and in her life she exemplified qualities of simplicity, serenity, sincerity, and sympathy, along with a wise optimism. She was secure in her belief that after the long chill of winter, the warmth of spring will follow in the lives of men as in nature."

Jewett's home on Central Square in South Berwick is a National Historic Landmark. It is a house museum owned and operated by Historic New England, a nonprofit preservation group.

## September 4, 1969
### B-52 Crashes After Takeoff; Seven Die in Limestone

Six crew members and an Air Force observer die when a US Air Force long-range B-52 bomber crashes just moments after takeoff from Loring Air Force Base in Limestone.

The 158-foot-long plane, fully loaded with fuel as it begins a nighttime training exercise, crashes into a bog about three miles north of the base. Witnesses report having seen a ball of fire in the air before the crash.

It takes an Air Force rescue crew and state troopers three hours to bulldoze a path and wade waist-deep through a swamp to reach the crash site, guided by the glow of the burning wreckage; and it takes another three hours to find the first bodies.

The dead include six officers and a master sergeant, all from out of state.

The plane belongs to the 42nd Bombardment Wing at Loring, part of the 8th Air Force.

The base is named after Charles J. Loring Jr., a Portland native who died during the Korean War when he crashed his damaged plane into an enemy artillery installation, destroying it. No longer needed after the Cold War ends, Loring eventually closes in September 1994.

## September 5, 1813
### *Enterprise* Defeats *Boxer* in Battle off Monhegan

In a War of 1812 encounter, the US brigantine *Enterprise* intercepts the British brigantine *Boxer* as the *Boxer* chases and fires upon a merchant ship heading to port in Bath. Capt. Samuel Blyth, 29, the British commander, was trying to disrupt commerce along the New England coast, especially in Maine.

After a morning of drifting near Monhegan Island with no wind and being too far apart for battle, the two ships move closer to one another when the wind picks up in the afternoon.

In a fierce, closely fought engagement, the ships blast each other with cannon fire for a half-hour. The *Enterprise's* first volley kills Blyth immediately. Moments later, Lt. William Burrows, also 29, in charge of the *Enterprise*, is struck mortally in the thigh. He survives long enough to accept the *Boxer's* replacement commander's sword in surrender, then is taken below deck and dies eight hours later.

The victorious *Enterprise* arrives two days later in Portland with the *Boxer* in tow. The remains of both captains are buried together in the city's Eastern Cemetery.

## September 5, 1905
### Treaty of Portsmouth Ends Russo-Japanese War

Russia and Japan, after weeks of talks at Portsmouth Naval Shipyard in Kittery, sign the Treaty of Portsmouth, ending the 1904-05 Russo-Japanese War.

The war resulted from the two empires' competing ambitions to carve out spheres of influence in Manchuria and Korea. When negotiations failed, Japan struck the Russian Eastern Fleet in a surprise attack in Port Arthur, China.

The 1905 peace talks bogged down when Japan demanded that Russia pay the Japanese reparations. It the end, Russia agrees to pay nothing, and the two nations divide Sakhalin Island.

President Theodore Roosevelt's remote but personal management of the negotiations wins him the Nobel Peace Prize and accolades from other world leaders.

## September 5, 1960
### Maine Central Railroad cuts presage passenger trains' demise

Maine Central Railroad Co., which had been in business since 1862, operates its last passenger train. The railway once operated passenger trains throughout coastal, western, central, and parts of eastern Maine.

In January 1965, the Boston and Maine Railroad discontinues its Portland-to-Boston passenger trains. The end of the service essentially deprives the state of passenger trains until the Amtrak Downeaster train debuts in 2001. Maine Central remains in business as a company until its sale in 1981 to Guilford Transportation Industries.

## September 6, 1924
### Around-the-world Pilots Stop in Brunswick, Old Orchard Beach

Lt. Lowell H. Smith, Lt. Erik Nelson, and Lt. Leigh Wade, all of the US Army, take off in three Douglas cruiser planes, headed for Boston from Mere Point in Scarborough, needing only to cross the United States to complete the first around-the-world plane flights.

This is happening three years before Charles Lindbergh's celebrated nonstop New-York-to-Paris flight of 1927.

The three aviators arrived the previous day from Pictou, Nova Scotia, landing on Casco Bay near Brunswick's Mere Point. They had intended to fly to Old Orchard Beach, where thousands of spectators were awaiting their arrival; but they got lost in dense fog around Orr's Island, prompting them to land where they did. They spent the night there.

A formation of planes flying up from Boston to Old Orchard Beach to greet the globe circumnavigators had to turn back and go home, also because of fog.

Smith, Nelson, and Wade stop on September 7 in Old Orchard Beach on their way to Boston, still attracting an enormous crowd despite their tardiness.

They began the trip March 17 in Santa Monica, California, and would end it there September 28 after flying westward at intervals for more than six months.

September 7, 1943
## Former Maine Governor Part of Secret World War II Mission in Italy

In the midst of World War II's Italian campaign, a former Maine governor, William Tudor Gardiner, takes part in a secret mission to meet with Italian generals before the Italians strike an armistice with the United States.

Italian forces smuggle Gardiner, then a US Army colonel, and Army Brig. Gen. Maxwell Taylor, commander of the 82nd Airborne Division artillery, into Rome, making it appear to onlookers that they are ordinary prisoners of war. Taylor and Gardiner confer with Italian military leaders, who have lost control of much of their country to the Germans in the wake of dictator Benito Mussolini's fall from power in July.

The Italians' description of their inability to hold Rome if the Germans attack prompts the Americans to send a coded message by radio to their superiors, advising them to call off a US plan to drop 82nd Airborne Division troops on Rome to assist the Italians, given the Germans' overwhelming military presence around Rome. The flights carrying the 82nd Airborne troops are launched anyway, but they are called back in time to avert a military disaster.

The next day, in quick succession, the Italian government capitulates to the Americans, but the Germans occupy Rome, which they hold for nearly a year.

Gardiner returns from his secret mission unscathed. Ten years later, he dies when a plane he is flying over Pennsylvania explodes and crashes, killing him and two passengers.

## September 8, 1803
### *Eastern Argus* Newspaper Publishes First Issue

The Portland-based newspaper *Eastern Argus* publishes its first issue. The paper is the first one in Maine supporting President Thomas Jefferson's Democratic-Republican Party, the nemesis of the Federalist Party, which dominated the press. The Federalists, who tend to oppose the District of Maine's separation from Massachusetts, gradually are losing influence in Maine. In nineteenth-century Massachusetts gubernatorial elections, for example, Maine men cast a majority of the votes for the Federalist candidate in every election until 1804; after that, they always favor the Democratic-Republican candidate.

## September 8, 1809
### Surveyor Killed in 'Malta War'

Surveyor Paul Chadwick, 22, is shot fatally in a confrontation with a group of men, some dressed as Indians, in Malta—now called Windsor. Chadwick was carrying out a surveying assignment from Massachusetts officials who claimed to own the land; the men, probably squatters, challenged the officials' ownership.

Seven men are arrested September 15 and charged with murder in a case that becomes known as the Malta War. An armed mob approaches the Kennebec County jail in Augusta to try to free the suspects, but the militia keeps them at bay.

At the close of an eight-day trial in November, a jury finds the men not guilty.

## September 8, 1958
### Clauson Wins Last Gubernatorial Race Held in September

Waterville Mayor Clinton Clauson, a Democrat, wins the Maine gubernatorial election in his race against Republican Horace Hildreth.

It is the last statewide Maine election held in September; all future elections are to be held in November in conjunction with national voting. The September voting tradition engendered the saying, "As Maine goes, so goes the nation," suggesting Maine's role as a bellwether indicating likely national voting trends.

The 1958 election also is the first election in which a candidate is elected to a four-year term as governor. However, Clauson serves only eleven months and dies in December.

### September 9, 1957
### Maine Voters Approve Moving Election Day from September to November

Maine voters approve a change to the Maine Constitution that ends the 137-year-old practice of holding statewide elections on the second Monday in September.

Instead, that voting will occur on the first Tuesday after the first Monday in November, just as it does in every other state.

The September date was designated originally for the benefit of farmers. Elections occurred roughly between late-summer harvest and the early fall harvest.

Another approved constitutional change increases the length of gubernatorial terms from two years to four and limits to two the number of terms a governor can serve consecutively.

That change will be effective for the first time in the gubernatorial election of 1958. Voters adopt both changes by more than a three-to-two margin.

### September 9, 2014
### Hope Elephants Founder Apparently Killed by Retired Circus Elephant

James Laurita, 56, founder of Hope Elephants, is crushed to death at his property in the Knox County town of Hope, apparently accidentally by one of the two retired circus elephants for which he was caring.

Laurita and his brother had gotten into the circus business in the 1970s. He founded Hope Elephants in 2011 as a way to care for Rosie and Opal, which had performed in circuses for about forty years and were suffering from a variety of physical ailments.

Laurita's body is found inside a corral after he went in to feed the two elephants around seven o'clock in the morning.

A deputy sheriff says he thinks Laurita fell in the corral and hit his head on concrete.

The state medical examiner determines later that Laurita succumbed to asphyxiation and chest compression fractures, probably because one of the elephants stepped on him.

Laurita had handled the elephants back in his circus days. After leaving the circus, he earned a veterinary degree from Cornell University, then worked at the Bronx Zoo in New York City and Wildlife Safari in Oregon. He and his family moved in the mid-1990s to Maine, where he set up a veterinary practice.

In 2011, Laurita and his brother, Tom, after winning over town officials and neighbors to their proposal, founded the nonprofit Hope Elephants and brought their former charges to Hope.

Laurita cared for the elephants and provided therapy to them, and the brothers made them available for schoolchildren to visit so they could learn more about the endangered creatures.

Animal rights groups criticized the arrangement, saying the Hope property is unsafe and that Maine doesn't have the proper climate for elephants. The most recent annual US Department of Agriculture inspection of the premises, however, conducted in April, determined that Laurita's license was active and that Hope Elephants was complying with federal regulations.

September 10, 1917

## Constitutional Amendment Granting Women Right to Vote Defeated by 2-to-1 Ratio

Maine's men, contradicting earlier action by the Legislature, vote by a nearly two-to-one ratio to reject a proposed state constitutional amendment granting women the right to vote.

The House, with Percival Baxter, a future governor, leading the charge, had voted 113-35 to approve the measure; and women's suffrage had fared even better in the Senate, 35-0, under the prodding of Sen. Guy Gannett.

The anti-amendment side wins by a ratio of nearly two-to-one—a final tally of 36,713 to 19,428—although voter turnout is far lower than it was for a 1911 referendum on liquor prohibition.

The *Daily Eastern Argus* comes away from the referendum with egg on its face, having predicted the opposite outcome in its September 10 edition.

"With so many representative elements in the State avowedly in favor of the 'yes' side, and the 'no' advocates having failed to sustain their opposition with convincing argument, it seems reasonable to look for a suffrage victory," the newspaper opined in its Election Day edition.

Women eventually gain voting rights in 1920 with the passage of the 19th Amendment to the US Constitution, which, by that time, Maine supports.

The shifting social attitude reflected in the complicated record of voting on women's suffrage in Maine has striking parallels with state voting trends in the gay-rights and gay-marriage questions of the late twentieth and early twenty-first centuries.

## September 10, 2013
### Cross Insurance Center in Bangor Replaces Fabled Bangor Auditorium

The 5,800-seat Cross Insurance Center opens in Bangor, replacing the just-demolished Bangor Auditorium.

The new facility is used for sports events, concerts, conventions and other gatherings. For concerts, it can add another 2,700 seats.

Woodrow Cross, 96, from whom both a family-owned, New England-wide insurance company and the new Bangor events venue draw their names, cuts the ceremonial ribbon to open the site.

Cross tells the *Bangor Daily News* that he remembers when the Bangor Auditorium was built in the 1950s. It served the city well, but a change was needed, he says.

"I'd rather have my name on this one," Cross says.

## September 11, 1922
### Dora Pinkham Becomes First Woman Elected to Maine House

Dora Pinkham, a Republican schoolteacher and bookkeeper from Fort Kent, becomes the first woman elected to the Maine House of Representatives. Her election takes place a scant two years after the 19th Amendment to the US Constitution granted women the right to vote.

The Protestant candidate's victory seems all the more remarkable in light of the fact that she will represent a House district that is overwhelmingly Catholic and of French-Canadian origin, in an age rife with Ku Klux Klan agitation and other sectarian strife.

Pinkham loses a re-election bid in 1924, but in 1926 she and Katherine C. Allen, a farmer and Republican from Hampden, become the first women elected to the Maine Senate, where Pinkham serves two terms.

September 11, 2001

## 9/11 Terrorists Take Flight from Portland to Boston on Morning of Attacks

In Portland, Mohamed Atta, an Egyptian, and Abdulaziz al-Omari, from Saudi Arabia, take a 6 a.m. Colgan Air flight from Portland International Jetport to Boston, where they board American Airlines Flight 11 to New York, use box cutters to seize control of the plane with three other hijackers and crash it into the North Tower of the World Trade Center, collapsing it and causing the deaths of more than 1,600 people.

The hijacking is part of a larger plot involving three other hijacked passenger jets. One of those planes strikes and flattens the Trade Center's South Tower. One plows into the Pentagon in Virginia.

Passengers overcome the hijackers in the last plane, and it crashes in a field in Pennsylvania, killing everyone aboard.

The crashes kill 2,977 victims, inflict about 25,000 injuries, and cause about $10 billion worth of damage. They become the catalyst for America's longest war. The United States invades Afghanistan in the fall because that country sheltered the plot's organizer, Osama bin Laden, and his international guerrilla group, called al-Qaida. As of May 2021, more than nineteen years later, American forces still are there but are scheduled to withdraw that year.

Among the details that emerge from the massive investigation of what come to be known as the 9/11 attacks, the FBI and police learn that Atta and al-Omari spent the night at the Comfort Inn in South Portland before leaving for Boston.

Portland Police Chief Michael Chitwood says Portland International Jetport surveillance video clearly shows Atta's face there.

Atta had picked al-Omari up at the Milner Hotel in Boston on September 10. They drove in a rented car to South Portland, where they arrived at the motel at 5:43 p.m.

Financial records and bank video show that they made two ATM withdrawals in Portland, and witnesses saw them at a Walmart store and in a Pizza Hut parking lot.

What is less clear is why they went to the Portland area at all.

Investigators later consider several theories, including the hijackers trying to gauge whether they are being followed, keeping an appointment with another person involved in the plot, using Portland's airport because its security checks might be less stringent than those used in Boston, or using Portland to avoid getting stuck in morning traffic on the way to Boston's Logan International Airport.

A federal commission investigating the 9/11 attacks releases its report on July 22, 2004. Even by then, the commission professes not to know why two of the hijackers went to Portland before participating in the deadliest terrorist attack on American soil in history.

"Interrogation of detainees has produced no solid explanation for the trip," the report states.

## September 12, 1910
### Voters Reject Plan to Split York

Making their first use of a recently enacted authority to overturn laws passed by the Legislature, Maine voters stop a plan to split the town of York in two dead in its tracks.

The statewide vote is 31,772 against the plan and 19,692 for it.

In York, the proposal loses even more resoundingly, 436-90.

The issue started as a squabble between the town's wealthy York Harbor enclave and the working-class vacation resort of York Beach, on one side; and the inland portion of town, on the other.

York Harbor and York Beach residents often had disagreements, but on this they were agreed—the coastal part of town should split away and become the town of Gorges, which they said would be a tribute to Sir Ferdinando Gorges, the seventeenth-century Englishman who founded the colony of Maine remotely but never set foot in it.

The inland people objected. Among other reasons they gave was that if Gorges were to split away, according to York's Maine House of Representatives member, Josiah Chase, a Democrat, it would take two-thirds of the population and property valuation, three of the town's four schools and part of the fourth, all of the post offices, the whole hydrant system, and eight of the ten churches.

The remainder of York would be responsible for maintaining 105 miles of roads, while Gorges would need to take care of only thirty-five miles.

Nonetheless, for opaque reasons suspected to have been manufactured by lobbyists, the Senate voted 24-5 for the plan, and the House, spurning Chase's entreaties, voted 93-35, also passing it. Republican Gov. Bert Fernald signed it on April 1, 1910.

Then the York Referendum Association, led by Chase and Town Clerk George F. Plaisted, gathered thirteen thousand signatures, including sixty-four from the Portland jail, to place the referendum question on the September ballot.

Since then, the town's increasing number of year-round residents and tens of thousands of summer visitors have come to regard the seaside resort town as prosperous, relaxing, inspirational, and attractive; but they don't call it Gorges.

## September 12, 1954
### Hurricane Edna Follows Hurricane Carol into Maine, Kills Eight, Causes Widespread Destruction

Twelve days after the destruction of Hurricane Carol, Hurricane Edna slams into Maine, drowning eight people, delivering the state's heaviest rainfall in fifty-eight years and causing about $25 million (about $244 million in 2020) in damage, mostly from flooding.

It kills eight people in Maine and becomes the most expensive storm in the state's history. Gov. Burton Cross says the damage to highways and bridges alone will cost about $2 million—or about $19.2 million in 2020—to repair.

In Unity, with the water of Sandy Creek rising, rescuers working for seven hours during the height of the storm finally fetch a mother and five of her children from the roof of their nearly submerged car. Another of her children, 8-year-old Ruth Brockway, and a member of the rescue party, Alton McCormick, 47, drown in the creek.

The storm also causes damage in Massachusetts, New Hampshire, New Brunswick, and Nova Scotia. The highest rainfall total is 7.5 inches.

Hurricane-force wind reaches its highest speed, 120 mph, on Martha's Vineyard. Flooding along Maine's Androscoggin and Kennebec rivers washes out roads. The Kennebec is twenty feet above its normal level in Augusta. About 20 percent of the state loses electricity.

TV journalist Edward R. Murrow and a CBS news crew fly into

the storm to record a segment for Murrow's *See It Now* program, depicting hurricane research done in an Air Force Hurricane Hunter plane.

The US Weather Bureau's Bob Simpson, also on the flight, makes an on-air pitch for more funding for weather research.

On September 13, President Dwight Eisenhower declares parts of Maine a disaster area, making the state eligible for substantial federal assistance.

After the back-to-back hurricanes, Congress gives the bureau more money to set up the National Hurricane Research Project, which acquires its own fleet of research planes.

## September 12, 2002
### Van Plunges into Allagash, Killing 14 Migrant Workers in Maine's Deadliest Crash

A speeding van loaded with fifteen migrant forestry workers from Guatemala and Honduras careens off a bridge over the Allagash Wilderness Waterway in northern Maine and crashes into the water. Only one man escapes alive, by kicking out a rear window of the van and swimming up to the surface of the river.

In terms of the number of deaths, it is the worst traffic accident in Maine history.

The men were riding in the van to work at a logging camp. Police said the van probably was traveling about 75 mph on the dirt road, on which the speed limit was 45 mph. It reached the 260-foot, guardrail-free Johns Bridge about eight o'clock in the morning.

A state police spokesman said the van apparently hit curbing on the bridge, flipped and went into the water upside down.

"I don't know how it was possible for me to get out," survivor Edilberto Morales Luis, 24, from Guatemala, tells the *Portland Press Herald* through an interpreter the day after the crash. He adds that coworkers riding in the van urged the driver to slow down. Four of them were his relatives.

The men are about five miles from their job site when the accident occurs, but deep in the woods and ninety miles from the nearest town.

The loggers were among about twelve hundred migrants, mostly from Central America, who received special visas to accept jobs with Maine timber operations that year.

September 13, 1921

**Roosevelt Stricken with Polio at Campobello, Takes Painful Boat Ride to Eastport**

Future President Franklin D. Roosevelt, stricken with a paralytic illness believed to be polio while at his family's vacation home on the New Brunswick island of Campobello, is taken across the water in excruciating pain by motor launch to Eastport, Maine.

There he is loaded into a train from a special baggage cart, initially away from the prying eyes of news photographers.

The press is interested in him because, among other reasons, he was the unsuccessful Democratic vice-presidential nominee the previous year and showed political promise for the future. Roosevelt and his minders take great care over the coming years, while he is learning to cope with leg braces that he uses for public speaking engagements, to make sure he never is photographed in a wheelchair or portrayed in any other compromising pose that might convey an image of weakness.

Although Roosevelt has spent summers at Campobello since 1885, he shuns the family's summer home and the painful memory associated with it for the next twelve years.

September 13, 1948

**Margaret Chase Smith Wins Senate Seat, Becomes First Woman to Serve in Both Houses of Congress**

Margaret Chase Smith, of Skowhegan, wins election to the US Senate, becoming the first woman to serve in both houses of Congress and the second woman elected to the Senate.

Smith, running after eight and a half years of service in the US House of Representatives, collects 76 percent of the vote on Election Day, defeating Democrat Adrian H. Scolten, a Portland dermatologist.

Smith eventually serves four consecutive six-year Senate terms before being defeated in a re-election bid in 1972.

September 13, 1954

**Muskie Elected First Democratic Governor in 20 years**

In an election undoubtedly affected by the ravages of Hurricane Edna the previous day, Democrat Edmund Muskie, 39, defeats Republican Gov. Burton M. Cross in the gubernatorial election, becoming the first

Democrat elected to the Blaine House—the governor's mansion—in twenty years.

Cross (1902-1998), meanwhile, becomes the first incumbent governor to lose a re-election bid since 1920.

Muskie (1914-1996), a Rumford native and Waterville lawyer, later serves twenty-one years in the US Senate, is nominated for vice president in 1968, runs unsuccessfully for president in 1972, and is appointed secretary of state in 1980 during the administration of President Jimmy Carter.

## September 14, 1908
### Constitutional Amendment Establishes 'People's Veto'

Voters approve by a more than two-to-one margin an amendment to the Maine Constitution that establishes the right to a "people's veto" by referendum and an initiative by petition at general and special elections.

The amendment becomes effective January 6, 1909. Maine becomes the first Eastern state to embed into law the people's right to statewide initiatives and referendums.

According to the Initiative and Referendum Institute, Maine's amendment owes much of its existence to Ronald T. Patten, of Skowhegan, an editor of the *Somerset Reporter* newspaper. Patten had begun to advocate for the idea in the early 1890s. He succeeded in getting bills submitted in the Legislature. In 1907, with momentum on the issue building, legislators approved handily a bill on amending the Maine Constitution, despite opposition from banks, timberland owners, and railroads.

The amendment still was subject to passage by popular vote, however. Newspapers wrote editorials condemning the proposal, and five-term Republican US Sen. Eugene Hale sent voters a copy of a diatribe that his Senate colleague Henry Cabot Lodge, of Massachusetts, had written against it.

The voters ignored all that attempted persuasion, adopting the amendment 53,785-24,543.

"It is a change of far-reaching importance," the *Kennebec Journal* writes less than enthusiastically on its September 18 editorial page. "It remains to be seen how well it will work in actual practice."

## September 15, 1908
### Drought-Aided Fire Ravages Saco

A fire that starts in a pile of

wood shavings at George A. Crossman & Sons lumberyard in Saco consumes fifteen acres of lumberyards, more than twenty tenement buildings, several factories, and some railroad property in Saco and Biddeford.

The flames spread from the Crossman site to the roofs of nearby homes. When those begin to burn, they discharge embers that waft across the Saco River and set the Diamond Match Co. lumberyards ablaze. Those eventually are destroyed, despite the efforts of the Biddeford and Saco fire departments and a bucket brigade to put out the fire.

About forty families are left homeless. In all, the blaze consumes about one million board feet of lumber.

A persistent drought made the risk of fire greater than usual in the two cities, and wind fans the flames.

## September 16, 2019
### Explosion Kills Farmington Fire Captain

An explosion at the Farmington offices of LEAP, an agency that helps people with intellectual and developmental disabilities, kills Capt. Michael Bell, of the Farmington Fire Rescue

Department.

Six other firefighters and a building maintenance worker who went to the scene to investigate reports of a propane smell are injured when the blast occurs.

The explosion is so powerful that it throws a vehicle across a street and can be heard thirty miles away. It also destroys eleven nearby mobile homes.

The LEAP director says the casualty list could have been much longer if the maintenance worker, Larry Lord, 60, of Jay, hadn't taken the trouble to evacuate the building when the gas was detected. Lord suffers burns and a leg injury and is taken to a Boston hospital by medical helicopter.

On September 27, investigators say a leak in a propane line caused the explosion.

In January 2020, Maine's Office of State Fire Marshal concludes that a Manchester company, Techno Metal Posts, installing four ten-foot-long bollards, or posts, in the building's parking lot on September 10, accidentally cut the underground propane line, causing the leak and the explosion, according to a Department of Public Safety spokesman.

Seven feet of each bollard was underground. The propane line was buried 2.5 to 3 feet under the parking lot. Each bollard is about four inches thick, but its tip is a 10.5-inch-wide auger head that allows the bollard to be drilled into the ground. An auger head sliced into the propane line.

The investigators do not determine which of several possible sources caused the gas to ignite.

In a heavily redacted report that the Office of State Fire Marshal releases in mid-2020, firefighters said they noticed no propane smell outside the building when they arrived there, but their measuring devices detected increasingly dense levels of it as they entered the basement. The explosion happened just as a firefighter was moving to an electrical panel to cut off power to the building, according to the firefighters' accounts.

They also noticed that although it was a warm day, a layer of ice about a quarter-inch thick had built up under a propane storage tank outside the building.

The company later pays a $1,000 fine as part of a consent agreement with the Public Utilities Commission.

On March 17, 2020, Gov. Janet Mills signs into law a bill requiring that "dig safe" laws be changed to include regulation of underground liquid propane lines. Rep. Seth Berry, D-Bowdoinham, says he submitted the bill partly as a response to the Farmington blast.

## September 17, 1604
### French Explorer Champlain Visits Future Site of Bangor

French royal cartographer Samuel de Champlain (1567-1635), traveling by sea from the French colony on nearby St. Croix Island and using Indian guides, sails up the Penobscot River to Kenduskeag Stream at what is now Bangor.

## September 17, 1865
### Arsonist's Fire Destroys Most of Downtown Augusta

After several weeks of drought, a fire in the early morning starts in a trio of newly completed two-story buildings in downtown Augusta and spreads rapidly, consuming most of the city's downtown.

The downtown blocks between Winthrop and Bridge streets must be abandoned to the flames, but firefighters from Augusta and neighboring communities are able to save the buildings on the north end of downtown. A US Arsenal steamer pours water onto the

An artist's conception of French explorer Samuel de Champlain (1574-1635).

wooden bridge across the Kennebec River to keep it from burning, and people in a hillside house on Oak Street cover their roof with carpets and pass buckets of water to keep them wet, helping to prevent the fire's advance to the west.

The fire destroys every bank, clothing store, lawyer's office, and millinery store; two hotels; and the post office. The cost of the damage is estimated to be $500,000—the equivalent of about $8.6 million in 2020.

Historian James North, in his *History of Augusta*, published five years after the fire, concludes that the blaze was the work of an arsonist, George W. Jones, of China. Jones became incensed when soldiers stole some of the lobsters he was selling from a cart in the city, and when the police offered him what he considered to be insufficient assistance, he threatened vengeance. He returned to China but was seen in Augusta again the day of the fire.

Two days later, Jones sets a fire in Portland, again in connection with a grievance involving his lobster cart. Witnesses report that fire before it does any significant damage, however. Jones is arrested, convicted of arson and sentenced to a term in the state prison. Portland escapes from the incident unscathed, but ten months later it will endure a fire inflicting far greater devastation than the one in Augusta.

## September 18, 1918
### Future Maine Governor Becomes World War I Fighter Ace

US Army Flight Cmdr. Sumner Sewall, of Bath, Maine, serving with the 95th Aero Squadron, shoots down the last of five enemy fighter planes over which he achieved victory in less than four months in World War I, earning himself the status of fighter ace.

Writing home to his mother in July from France, Sewall (1897-1965) described his recent air combat experience.

"We were patrolling about over the lines in a big formation of ten planes when we sighted a formation of six Boche (German) machines about five kilometers inside their lines," he writes. "Well we dived on them and attacked. I wish you could have seen the mess that followed. Sixteen planes just rushing around upside down and on their ear some climbing and others diving. Black crosses"—a reference to the emblem on the Germans' planes—"would go swirling around. Really it was the darndest stew I have ever seen."

Sewall sometimes was on the receiving end of bullets. In late September, after the Saint-Mihiel offensive, fellow pilot Lance Holden writes a letter home, citing the high percentage of casualties among pilots. He mentions that Sewall was shot down with his gas tank on fire.

Sewall spends several years in the Maine Legislature in the 1930s, then later is elected Maine's governor, serving from 1941 to 1945.

## September 19, 1775
### Benedict Arnold Begins Expedition to Attack Quebec

With the Revolutionary War having begun the previous spring, Col. Benedict Arnold sets sail from Newburyport, Massachusetts, with his expeditionary force, bound for Quebec.

The Arnold Expedition has

been waiting for three days, delayed by unfavorable wind and then the accidental grounding of one of Arnold's ships in the channel to the sea.

Fishermen aboard two small vessels tell Arnold they have seen no trace of enemy British ships in the area, which comforts the commander somewhat. When they arrive the next morning at the mouth of the Kennebec River, only eight of the eleven ships in the fleet are still together.

The group sails up Maine's Kennebec River; acquires flat-bottomed bateaux, vessels that—fatefully—are constructed of unseasoned wood; then endures weeks of dragging its weapons, supplies, equipment, and the leaky, disintegrating bateaux though the Maine wilderness before attacking the British fortifications at Quebec unsuccessfully in December.

## September 20, 1883
### John Appleton, Longest-serving Chief Justice, Steps Down

John Appleton (1804-1891), of Bangor, chief justice of the Maine Supreme Judicial Court, retires after serving twenty years and eleven months in that role, longer than any other chief jus-

tice in Maine history.

A New Hampshire native, the Bowdoin College graduate was admitted to the bar in that state, then moved back to Maine to practice law in Dixmont, Sebec, and Bangor.

He was appointed as a Maine Supreme Judicial Court associate justice in 1852, then became chief justice in 1862.

Appleton influenced the development of Maine law greatly. His treatise *The Rules of Evidence, Stated and Discussed*, published in 1860, set a template on that subject that became a national model. He also was noted for his embrace of free-market capitalism and opposition to government loans or tax breaks for businesses.

In April 2020, Chief Justice Leigh Saufley, appointed by Gov. Angus King, resigns after serving eighteen years and four months in the post, the second-longest tenure in Maine history. She becomes dean of the University of Maine School of Law.

## September 20, 1993
### Youngest Female Pilot to Fly West Across United States Departs from Augusta

Victoria "Vicky" Van Meter, of Meadville, Pennsylvania, who

began flying airplanes at age 10, becomes at age 11 the youngest girl ever to fly across the United States from east to west when she pilots a Cessna 172 from Augusta to San Diego, California, taking five days to make the trip. Her record is broken later.

The following year, at age 12, Van Meter (1982-2008), becomes the youngest female pilot to make a transatlantic flight when she files a Cessna 210 from Augusta to Glasgow, Scotland.

Van Meter later graduates from Edinboro University in Pennsylvania with a bachelor's degree in criminal justice, then becomes a Peace Corps worker in Moldova, a former part of the Soviet Union. In 2008, having battled depression and resisted taking medication, she dies from a self-inflicted gunshot wound.

A statue of her in the Augusta State Airport's terminal building commemorates her 1993 transcontinental achievement.

## September 21, 1749
### Kennebeck Proprietors Meet in Boston, Plan Strategy for Kennebec River Valley

Nine members of the Kennebeck Proprietors, the legal heirs of Pilgrims who had obtained rights to land in the Kennebec River valley, meet at the Royal Exchange Tavern in Boston. The meeting results in the commissioning of land surveys and authorizes the initiation of lawsuits against squatters and competitors.

Friction between landowners and squatters, and occasional violence resulting from that friction, will become a catalyst affecting Maine politics well into the early nineteenth century.

## September 21, 1868
### First Students Enroll in What Later Becomes University of Maine

Having been established three years earlier as a land grant college under the Morrill Act, the Maine State College of Agriculture and the Mechanical Arts opens in Orono, admitting its first twelve students. In 1897 its name becomes the University of Maine.

Gov. Samuel Cony signed the bill creating the college in February 1865. In January 1867, the board of trustees received a report from nationally famed architect Frederick Law Olmsted that recommends setting up the campus like a village. White Hall, the campus's first building, was built in 1867-68.

The first students are expected

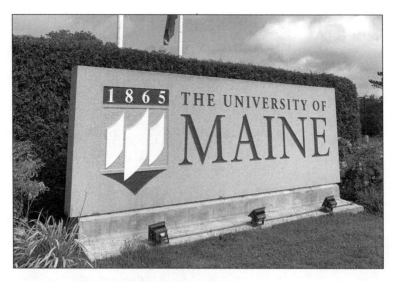

A sign welcomes visitors to the University of Maine campus in Orono.

to cover part of their expenses by working up to three hours per day on the college's farm. In 1868 the farm produces ninety tons of hay, eleven hundred bushels of potatoes, and eighty-five bushels of barley. Attendance at chapel is mandatory.

Six students receive degrees in the first graduation, which is held in 1872. Women are admitted to all curricula starting that year.

The first master's degree is awarded in 1881. Also that year, Maine residents are required to pay tuition charges for the first time. The number of new enrollees declines from fifty to seventeen.

In 1886, the school's entire cow herd is exterminated because of tuberculosis.

In 1902, Adelbert Sprague, a UMaine student, composes the music of the "Maine Stein Song." His roommate Lincoln Colcord writes the words. Singer Rudy Vallee, a former UMaine student, makes the song a national hit in 1929.

The Smith-Lever Act of 1914 mandates that the university provide service beyond its campus through farm extension, home demonstration, publication, lectures, and radio and television programs. The University of Maine Cooperative Extension still does that today.

The university's first doctoral degree is awarded in 1960.

## September 22, 1942
## Two B-25 Bombers Crash in Aroostook County; 14 Crew Members Killed

Two Army planes, both B-25C Mitchell medium bombers, crash in separate incidents in Aroostook County, killing a total of fourteen crew members.

Both planes were flying in poor visibility, according to air base headquarters in Presque Isle. One plane crashes in Perham, about fifteen miles west of Caribou; the other, about six miles northeast of downtown Presque Isle, off Fort Fairfield Road.

The Perham crash occurs on a remote tree-covered hillside. Residents who report the crash say it caused an explosion that could be heard miles away.

Soldiers from the air base in Presque Isle, twenty miles to the southeast, hike six miles, escorted by local guides through difficult forested terrain, to find the wreckage.

The flight crew consists of two officers and five enlisted soldiers, all of whom are dead. The Perham

guides help recover the bodies.

The plane's impact creates a crater about twenty-five feet in diameter, and the wreckage is scattered over an area about seventy-five yards across.

Meanwhile, in Presque Isle, civilian witnesses on the ground say they saw the other plane burst into flames before it crashed into woods next to a potato field.

The victims are, again, two officers and five enlisted crew members. Other soldiers go to the crash site and recover the bodies.

The Army appoints a board of inquiry September 23 to find out why the planes went down.

A report on the Perham crash later concludes that the pilot probably became disoriented and flew downward too steeply to recover altitude when the plane emerged from the clouds.

## September 23, 2010
## Bob Marley Sets Record for Longest Comedy Show

Bob Marley—the Maine comedian, not the deceased reggae singer—sets a Guinness World Record by completing a performance of the longest standup comedy show ever, forty hours, at the Comedy Connection in Portland.

Audience members paid $10 per

hour to see Marley, 43, ridicule Halloween, the Easter Bunny, and the length of his performance, thereby raising thousands of dollars for the Barbara Bush Children's Hospital at Maine Medical Center.

The previous record was thirty-eight hours and six minutes, which Lindsay Webb, of Australia, set in October 2009. When Marley reaches forty hours, at 11:02 p.m., he takes possession of his framed certificate from Guinness—and shortly after that, one might assume, a pillow and a mattress as well.

"I feel like Forrest Gump right now," he says, an apparent reference to the movie of the same name, in which the title character runs across the United States. "I think I'm going to go home."

Guinness regulations require that at least ten people be in the audience and awake at all times during his performance.

Oliver Keithly, the Comedy Connection's owner and Marley's manager, tells the *Portland Press Herald* that wasn't a problem. On the evening of the twenty-third, the admission waiting line grew so long that the end of it was outdoors, on the Custom House Wharf.

The rules allowed the Maine-themed entertainer to accrue five minutes of rest time for every hour of performing, so he took a twenty-five minute nap in the morning; other than that, it was wall-to-wall Bob, all the time.

## September 24, 2018
### Crab Island, Once Owned by Arctic Explorer Peary, Up for Sale

The *Portland Press Herald* reports that a small, private Casco Bay island once owned by Arctic explorer Robert Peary is up for sale.

Crab Island, the property in question, is about a ten-minute boat ride away from Freeport, just beyond the mouth of the Harraseeket River. It has two sandy beaches and a two-bedroom cottage with a large stone fireplace, two wells, and a septic system.

LandVest listed the one-acre property in August for $950,000. It had not been on the market for sixty-five years.

Peary (1856-1920), a Bowdoin College graduate who led an expedition to the North Pole in 1909, bought a string of small islands in the bay. He offered $800—the equivalent of about $22,500 in 2020—for Crab Island, although it's not clear that's what he paid for it.

The Peary family sold the island in the 1950s.

Another spot the Pearys owned, and one of far greater significance to them, is Eagle Island, just south of Harpswell. The Pearys' former summer home there is a National Historic Landmark. It is open for tours in the summer.

Peary was born in Pennsylvania, but his mother was from Maine. She moved back there with him when he was still a young boy, after Peary's father died.

Peary sailed on Casco Bay often when he was a teenager at Portland High School. He camped on Eagle Island then and made up his mind that it would belong to him someday.

About a decade later, long before his Arctic adventures, he bought it.

## September 25, 1827
### John Baker Arrested After Picking Capital of Self-proclaimed Republic of Madawaska

A New Brunswick sheriff and fourteen armed policemen arrest John Baker in Meruimticook, which Baker had designated as the capital of his self-proclaimed temporary Republic of Madawaska.

Baker, a continuous thorn in the side of British authorities in a region where the border between Maine and the future Canadian provinces of Quebec and New Brunswick was poorly defined, had petitioned the Maine Legislature for letters of ownership of the Madawaska territory.

Today the area is part of New Brunswick, but Baker's legacy survives in that both the village where he lived and the nearby brook, once called Meruimticook, are named Baker Brook after him.

The Baker unrest was a precursor to the so-called "Aroostook War," a more severe version of the border dispute that eventually was settled by the Webster-Ashburton Treaty of 1842.

## September 25, 1984
### St. Croix Island Achieves Historic Site Designation

Congress designates uninhabited St. Croix Island, near Eastport, as an international historic site, unique in the national park systems of both the United States and Canada. The island is where French colonists under the leadership of Pierre Dugua, Sieur de Mons, landed in June 1604, before the establishment of English colonies at Jamestown (1607) and Plymouth (1620), and spent a disastrous winter

Courtesy of By David E. Heath/Shutterstock.com

Historic Fort Western in Augusta

during which more than half of the colonists died.

The next year, François Gravé Du Port and royal cartographer Samuel de Champlain moved the colony across the Bay of Fundy to Port-Royal, in what is now the Canadian province of Nova Scotia.

From St. Croix Island, Champlain charted the Atlantic coast as far south as Cape Cod.

## September 26, 1775
### Col. Benedict Arnold Processes Murder Accusation at Fort Western on Kennebec River

Col. Benedict Arnold, about to leave Fort Western on the Kennebec River for his soon-to-be famous trek through the wilderness on the way to attack the British at Quebec, pauses to deal with a soldier convicted of murder after the soldier shot a man in the dark who was not his intended target.

The incident occurred on the night of September 23 when several of the men in the expedition were drunk, including Pvt. James McCormick, of North Yarmouth. It happened in what is now the city of Augusta but then was a remote wilderness outpost.

McCormick got into a violent quarrel with Capt. William Goodrich and, befogged by drink,

309

decided to kill him. He entered a room in a private home where several soldiers were sleeping and fired a musket in the darkness at a man he thought was Goodrich but instead was Sgt. Reuben Bishop, of Capt. Thomas Williams' company, who had been lying by the fire. Then McCormick fled.

It took Bishop twelve hours of severe agony to die from his abdominal wound. The next morning, a sergeant stopped McCormick across the river from the fort, in the area that is now downtown Augusta, and questioned him, thinking he might be a deserter. It became apparent that McCormick had been out all night, and his actions suggested he had done something terrible.

A court-martial was convened on September 25. The court quickly found McCormick guilty of the crime. He professed to be innocent, even as the gallows that would be used to hang him were built.

The next morning, Arnold takes the condemned man to the gallows, where McCormick confesses that he committed the crime but shot Bishop in a case of mistaken identity.

Arnold grants him a reprieve and sends him with an armed escort back to George Washington's headquarters in Cambridge, Massachusetts. In the face of a daunting military challenge, some headaches are best left to commanders in the rear.

As it turns out, Washington has no need to decide what to do about the matter. McCormick dies in prison while awaiting execution.

Arnold, mindful of the need to instill discipline in his unruly attack force, has another soldier given thirty-three lashes and discharged for stealing. Three others are whipped for stealing, and a fourth is punished for doing nothing to stop one of thieves. The next day, another thief gets thirty-three lashes.

Amid all this disorder, it must be hard for the men in the expedition to foresee that the injuries, cold, and starvation that await them in Maine's North Woods will be far worse.

## September 27, 1962
### Conservationist Rachel Carson's *Silent Spring* Published

The publisher Houghton Mifflin releases aquatic biologist, nature writer and conservationist Rachel Carson's seminal book *Silent Spring*.

Carson (1907-1964) was a

Rachel Carson, 1940, and the cover of her book, *Silent Spring*.

summer resident of Maine's Southport Island, where she owned a cottage overlooking Sheepscot Bay.

Born and raised in western Pennsylvania, she began writing as a child. Her academic career suffered because of her need to work during the Depression, and she eventually abandoned her doctoral studies at Johns Hopkins University. By 1962, however, she has written three previous nature-themed best-selling nonfiction books and has been nationally famous for more than a decade.

Copies of *Silent Spring* began circulating before its official publication date. The chemical industry was aghast about it because of its conclusion that pesticides, while necessary at some level, are harming the environment and endangering people.

The *New Yorker* published three long advance excerpts from the book in consecutive issues in June, raising public alarm and prompting the chemical companies to launch a campaign to discredit the book and destroy Carson. *Monsanto Magazine* even published a parody of the opening fable in Carson's book, calling it "The Desolate Year." It asks readers to imagine the horrors that might ensue if pesticides were not used.

Carson's new book gets extensive press coverage. Reviews are largely favorable, although *Sunday Book Review* science writer and editor Walter Sullivan describes it a one-sided effort to "scare the living daylights out of us" and calls it a "20th-century *Uncle Tom's Cabin*." Even he acknowledges its power, however.

With industry and government officials mounting a spirited defense of chemical use, Carson becomes a divisive figure. An episode of *CBS Reports*, "The Silent Spring of Rachel Carson," which airs April 3, 1963, does much to burnish her image, however. Her calm, measured responses to interview questions contrast mightily with the excited and sometimes self-contradictory tone of industry spokesmen and government bureaucrats.

Eleven years earlier, Carson bought land near West Southport while taking a leave of absence from her US Fish and Wildlife Service job. She arranged for her cottage to be built there, overlooking the bay and Georgetown Island, as a summer writing retreat. It was ready the next year. It was her refuge, and she became a good friend of the surprised neighbors.

By the time *Silent Spring* is out, however, Carson has been undergoing radiation treatment for breast cancer. A year after the CBS program airs, severely weakened, she suffers a fatal heart attack at her winter home in Silver Spring, Maryland.

In a 2012 biography of Carson, William Souder sums up the effect of Carson's career and her most famous book.

"Because the environmental movement survived the end of the Cold War, the context in which it was born, Carson can be credited not only with putting the movement into motion but for doing so in a way that would allow it to eventually stand on its own," Souder writes. "*Silent Spring* was many things—plea and polemic and prayer—but most important it was right. This was eventually conceded even by some early skeptics."

The Rachel Carson National Wildlife Refuge, named for the

writer, consists of eleven parcels of Maine seacoast land scattered from Kittery to Cape Elizabeth.

## September 28, 2017
### Bath Iron Works Wins Contract to Build More Arleigh Burke-class Destroyers

Bath Iron Works and Maine's congressional delegation announce that the Maine shipyard has won a contract to build two more Arleigh Burke-class destroyers for the US Navy.

The Navy does not release the contract price, saying it plans to issue more such contracts, and it wants to keep bidding competitive. BIW, owned by General Dynamics, competes with Ingalls Shipbuilding in Pascagoula, Mississippi.

The contract award is modified to include the installation of Flight III radar design upgrades on one of the destroyers, which are expected to make it easier for the ship's crew to detect and destroy ballistic missiles and other enemy targets.

At the time of the contract award, BIW is Maine's fifth-largest private employer. In Maine Department of Labor statistics for the second quarter of 2020, it is ranked fourth.

Courtesy of Maine Historical Society
Henry Wadsworth Longfellow, 1859

## September 29, 1888
### Henry Wadsworth Longfellow Monument Unveiled in Portland

The monument to poet and Portland native Henry Wadsworth Longfellow (1807-1882), which stands on Longfellow Square in Portland's West End, is unveiled.

A dedication ceremony is held beside the monument in what then is called State Street Square, now Longfellow Square. The event features a band performance, a succession of speakers, and one hundred schoolchildren singing Longfellow's 1838 poem "Psalm of Life." Several of the poet's relatives attend.

Sculptor Franklin Simmons, who grew up in Bath, designed and built the monument in his studio in Rome, Italy. Renowned local architect Francis H. Fassett designed the pedestal, and the Hawkes Brothers built it. Longfellow was born and raised in Portland. He lived in Cambridge, Massachusetts, for most of his adult life, but he visited Portland then and wrote his poem "My Lost Youth" as a tribute to the city.

## September 30, 1994
### Loring Air Force Base Closes

The last B-52 departed Loring in November 1993, and ceremonies were held in February 1994 to celebrate the end of the flying mission. The following month saw the last KC-135 depart and after forty-one years, Loring AFB officially closes on September 30.

## September 30, 2014
### Task Force Releases Report on Invasive Green Crab

A task force assembled by Gov. Paul LePage in response to complaints from shellfish harvesters releases a report concluding that the invasive European green crab is spreading rapidly along Maine's coast.

The report cites explosive growth of the crab population from 2012 to 2013 along the coast and in river estuaries, with no signs of abating. The voracious crabs threaten to gobble up large quantities of bivalve shellfish, marine worms, sea urchins, scallops, and lobsters.

The state Department of Marine Resources has cited efforts to develop uses for the crabs such as aquaculture feed, food additives, and pet food, but it emphasizes that its chief regulatory concern is finding ways to reduce the crab population.

—30—

# OCTOBER

October 1, 1955
**Bangor Auditorium Opens**

The 5,948-seat Bangor Auditorium opens in Bangor. More than four thousand people turn out to attend the dedication ceremony.

The facility, at 320 feet long and 146 feet wide, is one of the largest event venues in the Northeastern United States. Planning of the building began twenty-five years earlier.

"I have been all over the world and seen the seven wonders of the world," Bangor City Councilor Devreaux McCarthy tells the *Bangor Daily News*. "To me, honestly, this is the eighth."

The auditorium hosts sports contests, circus performances, political rallies, school graduations, trade shows, and other events before it is demolished in 2013.

The Cross Insurance Arena, currently still in use, replaces it later that year.

October 1, 2015
**SS *El Faro* Sinks off Bahamas; 33 Crew Members Die**

The American-flagged, 790-foot cargo ship SS *El Faro*, on its way from Jacksonville, Florida, to Puerto Rico, sinks off the Bahamas while attempting to travel through Hurricane Joaquin, a Category 3 storm.

The disaster kills all thirty-three crew members, including ship master Capt. Michael Davidson, of Windham, and three other Maine residents—Michael Holland, of Wilton; and Danielle Randolph and Dylan Meklin, both of Rockland.

The Puerto Rico run was supposed to be the ship's last before a major retrofitting. A 2014 Coast Guard inspection had noted a marked increase in safety concerns since 2013, and parts of the boilers were severely deteriorated. The ship also carried obsolete open-top lifeboats.

When the storm proves to be much more powerful than what was predicted in the twenty-one-hour-old weather reports the *El Faro* had received, the engines lose power, and the ship is adrift before sinking.

The loss of the *El Faro* and its crew is the worst disaster for a U.S.-flagged ship since 1983. It takes months to find the wreckage, which lies in pieces at a depth of fifteen thousand feet, A voyage data recorder is retrieved, but no bodies are recovered.

In addition to the victims' families, the loss is difficult for the Maine Maritime Academy. All four of the Mainers who died graduated from the school in Castine, as did another crew member, Mitchell Kuflik, of Brooklyn, New York.

During its review of the sinking, the National Transportation Safety Board issues several recommendations, including better tropical weather forecasts and faster and more efficient dissemination of those forecasts.

## October 2, 1897
### Neal Dow, Famed Anti-alcohol Crusader, Dies in Portland at 93

Former Portland Mayor Neal Dow, renowned for his lifelong crusade against alcohol consumption, dies in Portland at 93.

Dow served two terms in the Maine House of Representatives. He also was the Prohibition Party's candidate for president in 1880.

Portland's *Daily Eastern Argus* newspaper, whose political leanings in the nineteenth century often were opposed to Dow's,

Courtesy of Maine Historical Society

Neal Dow, 1874

lionizes him by saying that "the record of his life is a record of which his native city has good reason to be proud."

The newspaper calls particular attention to Dow's service in the Civil War.

"It is with pride that his fellow citizens recall how, on the outbreak of hostilities, although nearly 60 years of age—or fifteen years beyond the subsequent draft limit—he, as a volunteer, raised a regiment, took the field, was twice wounded in battle, was for nine months the victim of all the horrors of Libby Prison (a Confederate military prison in Richmond, Virginia), and became a brigadier general after having enlisted at a time ... when he was old enough to be the father of nearly every distinguished commander on the Union side."

Dow's former house at 714 Congress Street in Portland is the headquarters of the Maine Woman's Christian Temperance Union and is a museum showcasing Dow's life and career.

## October 3, 1851
### 'Yankee Gale' Kills More Than 160 Fishermen off Prince Edward Island

An unexpected storm begins and hammers the coast of Prince Edward Island for nearly two days, destroying more than seventy vessels and killing more than 160 American fishermen, including many from Maine.

Given the scope of the devastation, no accurate count of deaths was recorded, but modern accounts say the actual toll could have been as high as 110 vessels and 250 deaths. What is known is that bodies washed ashore for days, even weeks, and so overwhelmed the towns that many fishermen were buried in mass graves. Local families took in the hundreds of fishermen who survived.

The storm was named the "The Yankee Gale" because most of the fishermen who were killed came from New England. The storm came up quickly on the fleet, mostly schooners and pinkies jigging for mackerel close to the Prince Edward Island coastline.

The *Eastern Argus* of Portland reports on October 14, "The whole shore is strewed with the wrecks of vessels, and the bodies of their crews."

It remains the most deadly natural disaster in the history of Prince Edward Island.

## October 3, 2014
### Great Northern Paper Bankruptcy Case Moved from Delaware to Maine

A federal judge orders the bankruptcy case of Great Northern Paper Co. transferred from Delaware to Maine. A lawyer for the towns of Millinocket and East Millinocket, where GNP operated two mills, says at the hearing that the company owes the towns more than $3 million in back taxes.

GNP filed for bankruptcy September 22, foreshadowing the end of papermaking in the Millinocket area and casting a pall over the community's economic future.

The company, managed by New Hampshire-based private-equity firm Cate Street Capital, closed its East Millinocket mill in January and laid off two hundred workers a few weeks later.

The federal judge's ruling moves the case from a jurisdiction where GNP's parent company is located to a state where its major creditors are. When the company filed for bankruptcy, it listed more than $50 million in liabilities and almost one thousand creditors.

The company's Millinocket mill closed in 2008.

Maine's papermaking industry suffered another blow just two days before the federal judge's GNP ruling. Verso Paper announced that it was closing its paper mill in Bucksport, and that its 580 employees there all would be laid off.

The decision was expected to devastate the town of about five thousand people. Town officials said the company paid more than $4 million in property taxes each year, and losing that would force the town to cut back municipal services severely.

Verso's Bucksport mill is demolished soon after its closure. A demolition crew brings down its smokestack on October 29, 2019.

A salmon farm is expected to be built on the site.

October 4, 1992
## Portland Granted Eastern League Expansion Baseball Team

Portland is granted an Eastern League minor league baseball expansion team. The Portland Sea Dogs begin playing April 7, 1994, as a double-A affiliate of the Florida Marlins. They make the playoffs for the first time in 1995.

In 2003, the team becomes a Boston Red Sox affiliate. The team wins the Eastern League championship in 2006, defeating the Akron Aeros (now called the Akron RubberDucks). It is Maine's first professional baseball championship in ninety-one years, and it comes at the expense of the team that beat the Sea Dogs in the championship series in 2005.

The Sea Dogs play their home games at Hadlock Field in Portland.

October 4, 2009
## Dempsey Challenge Bike Ride Begins in Lewiston

The Dempsey Challenge, an annual bicycle ride held to support Lewiston's Patrick Dempsey Center for Cancer Hope and Healing, debuts at Simard-Payne Police Memorial Park in Lewiston. Participants ride ten, twenty-five, fifty, or one hundred miles,

Members of the Portland Sea Dogs walk onto the field from a wall of cornstalks as part of the "Field of Dreams" game at Hadlock Field.

or run or walk five kilometers (3.1 miles) to collect fundraising pledges for the center. The event roster is capped at thirty-five hundred participants, who raise more than one million dollars.

Actor Patrick Dempsey, who rides fifty miles that day, and his sister, Mary, founded the cancer center the previous year to help the community where they grew up. They did so in response to the experience of their mother, Amanda, who was diagnosed with cancer in 1997, was treated in Lewiston, and eventually dies from cancer in 2014.

## October 5, 1785
### First Gathering Held to Discuss Separation from Massachusetts

In response to a notice published in the Falmouth Gazette, about thirty men from Cumberland, Lincoln, and York counties gather at the meetinghouse of ministers Thomas Smith and Samuel Deane in Falmouth to discuss, for the first time in a formal setting, a proposal that Maine separate from Massachusetts to become a new US state. Opponents of the convention criticize it as being unconstitutional and insurrectionary.

The only result of the meeting is the appointment of a committee that would draft a letter to be circulated among all Maine residents, inviting them to a January 4, 1786, meeting to be held on the same subject.

Despite several more such meetings over the next few years, the proposed separation would not occur until nearly thirty-five years later.

## October 5, 1981
### Humorist Jud Strunk Suffers Heart Attack Flying Plane, Dies in Crash

Singer-songwriter and comedian Jud Strunk, 45, suffers a heart attack while flying a plane over Carrabassett Valley. The plane crashes, killing him and a passenger. Strunk was best known for his 1973 hit single "Daisy a Day."

Although a native of Jamestown, New York, Strunk, who played the tenor banjo and the piano, often sang about his adopted state of Maine. He moved to Farmington in 1960 and later to a farm in Eustis.

He also was an actor, performing on Broadway and in television shows, including regular appearances on *Rowan & Martin's Laugh-in*.

## October 6, 1869
### Bangor Children's Home Dedicated

The newly built location of the Bangor Children's Home is dedicated at 218 Ohio Street in Bangor.

A group of Bangor women established the home's predecessor organization, the Bangor Female Orphans Asylum, in 1836 on the city's Fourth Street. For many years, that institution took in girls and arranged for their adoption.

In 1866, its managers accepted a gift of $1,200 from Franklin W. Pitcher to build a more useful home for the asylum to replace the Fourth Street building.

Conditions attached to the gift included a requirement that the institution begin accepting boys as well as girls, and that it conduct a community fundraising drive to establish a $25,000 endowment.

Boston architect Henry W. Hartwell designed the three-story, brick-faced building, which has a dormer-laden mansard roof.

The building stands on a hill that offers a panoramic view of the city's center.

The Bangor Children's Home exemplifies the stick-style architecture that was becoming popular after the Civil War, as well as the social concerns of Americans of the mid-Victorian Era.

The building is added to the National Register of Historic Places on September 9, 1975. It now is the location of the Hilltop School, which is a preschool education and day care center.

## October 7, 1923
### First Section of Appalachian Trail Opens in Upstate New York

The first section of the Appalachian Trail opens in Bear Mountain and Harriman state parks in upstate New York, about forty miles north of New York City.

The brainchild of Benton MacKaye, the trail eventually grows to about 2,200 miles, with its northern terminus being Baxter Peak on Mount Katahdin, Maine's highest mountain.

Civilian Conservation Corps workers, whose Depression-era work is memorialized by a statue in front of the Maine State Cultural Building in Augusta, complete the trail's last link August 14, 1937, near Maine's Sugarloaf Mountain.

A plaque is installed on a nearby boulder to commemorate the achievement.

## October 7, 1947
### Forest Fires Ravage Much of Southern, Down East Maine

Woods fires are discovered in Bowdoin, Portland, and Wells after almost no rain has fallen in southern Maine since June 25.

Over the next few weeks, those and many other blazes that constitute the Great Fires of 1947 sweep through drought-ravaged York County and other coastal regions, essentially destroying the towns of Shapleigh and Waterboro and inflicting severe damage on the cities of Biddeford and Saco and several other towns in that area.

Sixteen deaths are attributed to the fires. Statewide damage is estimated at $30 million, equal to about $353 million in 2020.

The flames take an especially hard toll on summer colonies in Kennebunkport and Bar Harbor (see entry for October 21, 1947, about fires around the latter town). Nearly twenty thousand acres in the Jonesboro area, in eastern Maine, are consumed, as are about twenty-five hundred acres to the north in Madison and Norridgewock.

The fires also cause many long-term changes. The destruction of summer cottages in Goose Rocks

Beach is followed by construction of year-round homes there, changing the community greatly. Stands of white pine virtually disappear throughout southwestern Maine. Many people make a point of rebuilding away from trees to provide a fire break.

The disaster prompts the establishment in 1948 of many volunteer fire departments and more compliance with national training standards. The state and municipalities begin to upgrade their firefighting equipment. At the state level, officials strive for greater centralization and organization of firefighting capability and strategy.

"It is frankly admitted that there was no fire action plan to meet such a disaster," Austin Wilkins, a state forest firefighting supervisor, writes in his final report on the 1947 fires.

In 1949, the Legislature passes a variety of laws designed to enhance fire protection measures. One law authorizes the governor to enter agreements with other states about mutual aid in fighting fires. Another gives the state forest commissioner ultimate authority in fighting forest fires in the state's organized territory. Still others address the financ-

ing of forest fire suppression, the disposal of slash, and the legalization of wardens' lighting of backfires.

## October 8, 1829
### Gov. Enoch Lincoln Dies in Office

Gov. Enoch Lincoln, Maine's sixth governor, dies in Augusta at 40, becoming the state's first governor to die while in office.

Lincoln's chief claim to fame might be his role in helping determine that Augusta would become Maine's capital and that the State House would be built there on Weston's Hill, but he also is noted for the unexplained disappearance of his body. Lincoln's remains, buried with a few other Maine notables at a monument in Augusta's Capitol Park, are discovered to be missing in the twentieth century. Nobody has been able to explain their absence.

Lincoln, a Massachusetts native who moved in 1812 to Fryeburg and in 1817 to the town of Paris, was the son of one Bay State governor and the brother of another. He considered himself more poet than politician. He also railed against slavery and accurately predicted that its existence would bring about a civil war.

**October 9, 1866**

## Wiscasset Fire Destroys More than 50 Buildings, Including Customs House

A fire that ignited at about three o'clock in the morning burns until noon in Wiscasset, destroying more than fifty buildings, including the customs house, a hotel, a marble works, and hay warehouses, as well as two yachts at the wharf.

A strong northeast wind makes it impossible to stop the fire, and it races to the waterfront, according to Portland's *Daily Eastern Argus* newspaper.

Firefighters focus more on stopping the flames from spreading windward, to prevent the whole town from being incinerated.

More than forty families are left without a home. The total loss is valued at $200,000, the equivalent of about $3.6 million in 2020.

**October 10, 1980**

## President Carter Signs Maine Indian Claims Settlement Act

President Jimmy Carter signs the Maine Indian Claims Settlement Act, ending 1976 lawsuits by the Maliseet, Passamaquoddy, and Penobscot tribes, in which they claimed about 12.5 million acres of Maine, or two-thirds of the state's territory.

Under the new law, the tribes will receive a total of $81.5 million as compensation for land that was taken from them.

The tribes claimed the land was sold to non-Indians in violation of the 1790 Non-Intercourse Act, which forbids the transfer of Indians' property without congressional approval. As compensation, the government will give them a $27 million trust fund and another $54 million to buy 300,000 acres of forest from timber management companies.

Carter uses an eagle feather to sign the agreement, with US Secretary of State Edmund Muskie, a former Maine governor and senator, and Gov. Joseph Brennan in attendance. Andrew Akins, chairman of the Passamaquoddy and Penobscot negotiating committee, and other Indian representatives also witness the event.

"This was one of the most difficult issues I ever got involved in," the *Bangor Daily News* reports Carter as saying. "It aroused the animosity of just about everybody."

The president calls the resolution of the dispute "a reaffirmation that our system works. ... This should be a proud day for us all."

October 10, 2019
## Howard Hill Historical Park Dedicated in Augusta

The 164-acre Howard Hill Historical Park, which includes two cliffside scenic overlooks providing views of the State House complex, is dedicated in Augusta.

"From a wildlife perspective, Howard Hill has it all. With softwoods and hardwoods, it provides a home or stopping-off point for a whole host of wildlife species," Maine Inland Fisheries and Wildlife Commissioner Judy Camuso says at the ceremony.

The Kennebec Land Trust, using a mix of private and public money—but none from Augusta city funds—bought the land for about $925,000 from local lawyer Sumner Lipman and transferred the title to the city in 2017. The trust retains a conservation easement to the park.

The land trust initially expected to receive $337,500 from the Land for Maine's Future fund to help pay for the $1.2 million project. Five of the six Land for Maine's Future board members, however, all appointees or former employees of Gov. Paul LePage, voted to reduce that funding to $163,500, and they cast doubt on the reliability of the property's $1 million appraisal. The city assesses it for tax purposes at $171,000.

The land trust took out a loan from a local bank to plug the unexpected gap.

LePage, who left office in January 2019, criticized the project repeatedly, as well as Maine land conservation programs generally, and he delayed the sale of bonds to finance the Land for Maine's Future program.

Howard Hill is named for Capt. James Howard, an eighteenth-century settler who commanded Fort Western, a 1754 British fort that still stands on the east bank of the Kennebec River in Augusta.

Howard's descendant William Howard Gannett, a local publishing tycoon, owned and lived next to Ganneston Park, a large wooded estate that encompassed the Howard Hill site. The old park featured gardens, ponds, carriage roads, and trails that Gannett allowed the public to use.

Proposals to turn the hill into a park and include "Howard" in its name have its roots that reach back more than a century. The July 22, 1905, issue of the *Daily Kennebec Journal* includes a column proposing that the site be called "Betsey Howard Hill" to replace another, informal name incorporating a racial slur used to describe Black people.

Betsey Howard, the writer explained, was a daughter of Lt. Samuel Howard, Captain Howard's brother, who first lived at Fort Halifax, in what is now Winslow.

When the French and Indian War ended, he and his family moved to Augusta and acquired the Howard Hill area. After Samuel Howard and his wife died, Betsey Howard continued living on the property until her own death, the writer said.

James North's 1870 *History of Augusta* confirms most of these details and does not contradict the rest.

The 1905 writer says a Black family moved onto the hill later, resulting in the informal name saddled with a slur, "a designation not at all pleasing or applicable to the place, and one which the colored residents of our city have a right to resent."

Praising the landscape there, the writer added, "Whether this is ever used for a park or not, it is certainly to be hoped that the magnificent forests which clothe it may be preserved."

October 11, 1983
## America's Last Hand-cranked, Operator-assisted Telephone Service Ends in Bryant Pond

Residents of the Oxford County village of Bryant Pond lose the last hand-cranked, operator-assisted telephone service in the United States when the phone company's new owner converts its equipment to dial-it-yourself technology.

The changes engender local opposition from a group that protests against it by using the slogan "Don't yank the crank."

The Oxford County Telephone and Telegraph Co. bought the system earlier in the year from sole owner Elden Hathaway for $50,000, and now the company is putting a modern dial system in place.

The phone company's Robert Jamison makes the last call on the old magneto system to employee Corey Snowden at a hospital in Portland. Then Jamison and Art Fisher pull a heat coil from the switchboard in Hathaway's living room amid flying sparks and photographers' camera flashes, and the system goes dead.

For some in town, the mood is somber. Others are outraged.

"It'll be a sorry day in hell before I buy one of these (dial) phones,"

Ashley Wing tells the *Portland Press Herald.* "I think it stinks. It was a screwed-up deal and the PUC shouldn't have let it happen. The people never had a choice."

Paul Hillquist is on the other end of the reaction spectrum.

"I'm very happy with the changeover," he says. "It appears everyone will adapt well to the new system."

"To tell the truth, I'll probably be for it eventually," lifelong Bryant Pond resident Alice Hoyt says. "The change really didn't make that much difference to me, but I'm going to miss (the crank). It's like losing a member of the family."

If any reporter approaches them all years later to inquire what they think about cellphones, there is no evidence to that effect.

## October 11, 2002
### Lewiston Mayor Meets with Local Somali Leaders Following Controversial Letter

Lewiston Mayor Larry Raymond meets with local Somali leaders in the wake of an open letter he released, in which he asked that they slow the rate of Somali migrants coming to the city because it doesn't have the ability to absorb a large number of new arrivals coming about the same time.

The letter drew national attention, with some critics calling the letter racist and others saying the mayor's concern about the logistics of caring for the new arrivals is justified.

Supporters of the Somalis held a rally in their defense.

Raymond, saying he has two adopted Black grandchildren, denied allegations of racism. He refused to apologize and said his purpose had been misinterpreted.

## October 12, 1865
### Belfast Fire Destroys 125 Buildings, Including Much of Waterfront

A mere twenty-five days after the worst fire in Augusta's history devastates the city's downtown, a blaze starts accidentally in a boat shop at the foot of Main Street in Belfast. Aggravated by the wind, the fire destroys 125 buildings in a twenty-two-acre area, including much of the city's business district and its waterfront on Penobscot Bay.

During the eight-hour effort to contain the flames, firefighters explode or demolish buildings on several streets to create fire breaks and prevent the destruction of the entire city core.

Members of the Brady Gang lie dead on Central Street in Bangor following a shootout with the FBI.

---

**October 12, 1937**

## Gangster Al Brady Killed Outside Dakin's Sporting Goods Store in Bangor

Bank robber Al Brady, 26, and an accomplice, Clarence Lee Shaffer Jr., 20, are killed in an FBI ambush outside Dakin's Sporting Goods Store in downtown Bangor.

The criminal gang, the target of a yearlong manhunt and prone to boasting about their exploits, had been convicted or implicated in several robberies and slayings in their native Indiana. They visited Dakin's twice before to buy guns and ammunition for use in committing more robberies.

Arriving in a black Buick sedan with Ohio license plates, they also inquired about the availability of tommy guns.

When the store manager said he wasn't allowed to stock those, the robbers asked if he could get some anyway and said they would return later. The manager tipped off the police, triggering the FBI ambush.

327

The robbers return on October 12.

When one gang member, James Dalhover, 30, enters the store, an agent planted inside pulls on a string attached to a piece of cardboard in the store window as a signal that the ambush could begin. Brady and Shaffer, caught by surprise, fire off some shots but are gunned down immediately, with bullets flying everywhere.

"Brady and his gang were supposed to be masters of crime," the *Bangor Daily News* comments. "But in their tragic adventure here they acted, from first to last, with almost incredible stupidity."

The body of Brady, the gang leader, who is on the FBI's "public enemies" list, is buried in an unmarked grave in Bangor's Mount Hope Cemetery. A stone is placed there in 2007, when a re-enactment of the shootout is staged downtown.

## October 12, 2019
### Biddeford's *Journal Tribune* Publishes Final Issue

Biddeford's *Journal-Tribune* daily newspaper publishes its final issue, leaving Maine with six dailies.

The paper took its most recent

form on May 2, 1977, when the *Biddeford-Saco Journal* merged with the semi-weekly *Sanford Tribune*.

Its roots, however, date to February 7, 1845, with the debut of the Saco-based *Union*, a weekly newspaper. Mergers and name changes resulted in that paper later becoming part of the *Biddeford-Saco Journal*.

## October 13, 1950
### 'But Mother—She Loves Lobsters'

Twentieth Century Fox releases the film drama *All About Eve*, starring Bette Davis (1908-1989) and a cast including Gary Merrill (1915-1990), actors with strong Maine connections.

The movie wins six Academy Awards.

Davis and Merrill married each other while the film was in production; they divorce ten years later after adopting two children. Merrill later has a four-year affair with actress Rita Hayworth. His autobiography, *Bette, Rita, and the Rest of My Life*, is published in 1989, shortly before he dies of lung cancer.

Merrill writes in his book that he and Davis "discovered that we had both spent our childhood summers in Maine—I at Prout's

Neck, she at Ocean Park, a summer community quite close by. Because of her early introduction to the coast of Maine, we found that our love for it was similar—a happy discovery, common ground."

Davis, in her 1962 book *The Lonely Life: An Autobiography,* recalls that Merrill's mother was a major hurdle she had to overcome.

She records this exchange between Merrill and his mother:

"'Have you gone crazy, Gary? Marrying a middle-aged woman who will throw all your antiques into the ocean?'

"Merrill's defense of me was heroic.

"'But mother—she loves lobsters.'"

Davis' father was from Augusta and is buried there. Merrill, a Bowdoin College graduate, dies in Falmouth, where he moved in 1965.

## October 13, 2015
### Sherman's Books Buys
### Maine Coast Book Shop

Sherman's Books & Stationery, which already operates five bookstores in Maine, announces it will acquire Maine Coast Book Shop & Cafe in Damariscotta.

Sherman's, which traces its roots to 1886, when William Sherman opened a store in Bar Harbor, said it will reflag all six stores under the name "Sherman's Maine Coast Book Shops."

In May, owners Susan and Barnaby Porter announced they plan to sell the fifty-year-old store located in the historic Lincoln Hall.

With the acquisition of the Maine Coast Book Shop, Sherman's will operate the largest bookstore chain in Maine, stretching from Bar Harbor to Portland.

## October 14, 1854
### Mob Tars, Feathers
### Jesuit Priest in Ellsworth

Reflecting the hostility of many of Maine's Protestants to an influx of Roman Catholics, a mob of Know Nothings in Ellsworth tars and feathers a Jesuit priest from Switzerland, Johannes Bapst, and tries unsuccessfully to set fire to him. The local sheriff disperses the mob at gunpoint.

Earlier in the year, Know Nothings blew up a Catholic school Bapst had founded in Ellsworth and tried to burn his church.

Bapst later becomes the first president of Boston College. John Bapst High School, a Catholic school in Bangor, is named after him.

### October 14, 2015
### Workers Find Remains of Female Tennessee Hiker Missing for Two Years

Workers employed by a Navy contractor in western Maine's Redington Township find the skeletal remains of Appalachian Trail hiker Geraldine Largay, of Brentwood, Tennessee, who was reported missing in July 2013.

Largay, hiking alone and using the trail name "Inchworm," died at least twenty-six days after she got lost. The state medical examiner determines that she succumbed to starvation and exposure. Her ordeal is described in the book *When You Find My Body*, the title of which comes from a note that Largay wrote to her husband while awaiting a rescue that never came.

### October 15, 1952
### E.B. White's *Charlotte's Web*, Set in Maine, Appears in Print

Harper & Bros. publishes the children's novel *Charlotte's Web*, by Pulitzer Prize-winning essayist and novelist E.B. White (1899-1985), who, with his author and editor wife, Katharine (1892-

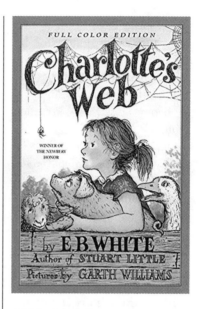

1977), lived for many years in a farmhouse in the Hancock County town of Brooklin.

Elwyn Brooks White, a New York state native, wrote for six decades for the *New Yorker* magazine and was a several-time editor and reviser of *The Elements of Style*, a standard writing guide written by William Strunk Jr. in 1918. He also wrote the 1945 children's classic *Stuart Little*.

A fierce defender of his privacy, White was known to slip out of his office via fire escape when visitors he didn't know were announced, according to fellow *New Yorker* writer James Thurber. This behavior contrasted sharply with his wife's character, according to the Whites' personal secretary, Isabel Russell.

"EB's voice was low, his gestures slight, his temper moderate. His presence in any locale was unobtrusive, quiet; K's was volcanic. If, at any given moment, she was not the focus of attention in a room, she was so violently busy with her individual concerns that she could not be ignored for long," Russell wrote in her book about the couple.

In the foreword to *Charlotte's Web*, Kate DiCamillo quotes White as saying, "All that I hope to say in books, all that I ever hope to say, is that I love the world."

## October 16, 2012
### Earthquake in Waterboro Felt Across New England

A magnitude-4.5 earthquake in the York County town of Waterboro is felt across New England. It is detected even in central New York state and northern New Jersey.

The epicenter originally is reported to be two miles northeast of East Waterboro and three miles west of Hollis Center, but a review of data prompts the conclusion that the very center of Waterboro is the epicenter's location.

The Waterboro selectmen probably don't need to be convinced of that. A video camera operating during one of their meetings records a loud boom in the meeting room and the camera shakes from the impact. The board members and all other people in the room immediately leave the building.

While most people in Maine don't feel them, earthquakes often are detected in the state. The Maine Geological Survey records 106 earthquakes in the period from April 1997 to January 2019 in various places around the state, including some temblors whose epicenters are outside the state.

Of all those, the Waterboro quake is the strongest one with an epicenter located in Maine.

## October 17, 1793
### Maine's Effort to Separate from Massachusetts Remains Stalled

After eight years of failed efforts to separate Maine from Massachusetts, a meeting called by separation proponents occurs at the courthouse in Portland. They hope that a provision in the 1780 Massachusetts Constitution calling for a people's review of that document might provide impetus for the District of Maine's separation and that it could occur in 1795. They call for a districtwide convention on December 31 in Portland.

The flurry of activity fails to generate sustained enthusiasm for the movement, however. Maine does not achieve statehood until 1820.

## October 18, 1775
### British Naval Attack Destroys Maine's Largest Seaport

In the opening phase of the Revolutionary War, a British fleet under the command of Lt. Henry Mowatt, aboard the HMS *Canceaux*, attacks the part of Falmouth that now is downtown Portland with incendiary cannonballs and, later, militia units lighting fires. More than four hundred homes are destroyed or damaged.

The incident traumatizes and scatters the local population, and it emblazons Mowatt's name on their collective memory as a synonym for the devil.

Mowatt (1734-1798), whose name in some records is spelled "Mowat," was a native of Scotland's Orkney Islands.

His long British navy career included, before America's Revolutionary War, many surveying voyages along Maine's coast and around the Gulf of Saint Lawrence. He also acted as a maritime policeman by intercepting smugglers and confiscating their cargo.

By the time of his attack on Falmouth, he already has been in the British navy for twenty years. His service includes sea warfare against the French during the Seven Years' War, which is known as the French and Indian War in North America.

Those who later condemn Mowatt for his destruction of Falmouth often regard the attack as a personal vendetta inspired by a tense standoff the previous May with local revolutionaries, who briefly held Mowatt captive in Falmouth and forced the *Canceaux* to leave the harbor. However, biographer Harry Gratwick, in a 2015 book about Mowatt, describes the bombardment as a case of a sea captain carrying out explicit orders that British officials later find inconvenient to acknowledge. When the attack unexpectedly galvanizes the American resistance to British rule, Mowatt's reputation at home suffers, as does his naval career.

Prominent nineteenth-century Maine historian William D. Williamson also blames Mowatt for the April 1775 removal of Fort Pownal, at the mouth of the Penobscot River.

Maine residents complained at the time that the fort's removal deprived them of trading opportunities and left them exposed to Indian attacks.

Gratwick concludes Mowatt wasn't involved, however, citing the *Canceaux's* log, in which Mowatt writes that his ship was far away, in Falmouth's harbor, on the day Fort Pownal is disassembled. Instead, British navy Lt. Thomas Graves, arriving on the armed schooner HMS *Diana*, accompanied by the schooner HMS *Neptune*, and acting on orders of the Massachusetts governor, Gen. Thomas Gage, is responsible for the fort's removal. The *Diana's* log is lost later, but a British soldier's written account of Graves' action survives, Gratwick writes.

Mowatt participates in another key event of the American Revolution in Maine—the British destruction in 1779 of the Americans' Penobscot Expedition, which is launched in an unsuccessful effort to dislodge the British garrison at Fort George, in what is now Castine. Mowatt is commanding

HMS *Albany* at Fort George when the Americans attack.

Together with land-based troops, Mowatt's three-ship fleet holds off the Americans for three weeks. Then a British relief fleet arrives, chases the American ships up the mouth of the Penobscot River and destroys them. It is America's worst naval disaster until the Japanese bomb Pearl Harbor in 1941.

After the Americans defeat the British, Mowatt returns home to England in 1782. He seeks another sea command and finally gets it in 1795. He suffers a fatal stroke aboard his ship, HMS *Assistance*, in 1798 while off the coast of Virginia. He is buried in Hampton, Virginia, in a nation whose birth he fought hard to prevent.

## October 18, 2019
### Caribou Native Part of First All-Female Spacewalk Team

Astronaut and Caribou native Jessica Meir, 42, becomes one of two participants in the first all-female spacewalking team, conducted to install lithium-ion batteries on the outside of the International Space Station.

Together with fellow spacewalker Christina Koch, Meir

*Courtesy of NASA*

US astronaut Jessica Meir, of Caribou, in 2019.

exits the station at half past seven in the morning Eastern time and stays outside for seven hours and seventeen minutes while the Earth passes beneath their feet. It is Meir's first spacewalk and Koch's fourth. The astronauts receive a call from President Donald Trump, who tells them, "The job you do is incredible."

"We've been training for six years, so it's coming up here and doing our job," says Meir, who holds a doctorate in marine biology and was picked for the astronaut corps in 2013. "At the same time, we recognize that it is a historic achievement and we want to give credit to the women who came before us. We have followed in their footsteps to get where we are today."

The same two astronauts conduct a second all-female spacewalk together on January 15, 2020, outside the station.

The first spacewalking woman was Russian cosmonaut Svetlana Savitskaya, who carried out her assignment in 1984. NASA astronaut Kathy Sullivan followed suit soon afterward, and fourteen other American women have done so since then.

In December 2020, NASA announces that Meir is part of a team of 18 astronauts who will be training for a 2024 moon landing, the first such landing since 1972.

## October 19, 1814
**Maine's Pleas for Help Driving British from Eastern Maine Ignored**

In an era when Maine remains part of Massachusetts, three men representing Maine counties in the Massachusetts Senate ask the Massachusetts General Court (the state legislature) to appoint a committee to consider raising a force to drive British troops out of eastern Maine, which those troops recently attacked and occupied.

The General Court does nothing in response to that appeal or to one submitted a month later.

## October 19, 2002
**Last Major Shirt Manufacturer in US Closes in Waterville; 235 Left Jobless**

The C.F. Hathaway shirt factory, the last major manufacturer of shirts in the United States, closes in Waterville, putting 235 people out of work.

The closure is part of a larger pattern of clothing makers going out of business around the same time in Maine, falling prey to cheaper competition from overseas.

Charles F. Hathaway founded his shirt-making company in the mid-nineteenth century on Appleton street in Waterville. By the mid-1950s, the company had prospered and was known for the quality of its shirts as well as its "man with the eyepatch" advertising.

The company moved in 1956 to the site of the former Lockwood Mill, which had closed the previous year, laying off seven hundred workers.

Shirt manufacturing continued at the old mill building next to the Kennebec River under the Hathaway company and its successor, Warnaco, for forty-six years before the closure.

Private developer Paul Boghossian's purchase of the mill build-

People enter the Hathaway Creative Center, formerly the C. F. Hathaway shirt factory, in 2016.

ing and other former Lockwood property occurs in 2006. They now house health care offices, retail shops, apartments, and recreational spaces.

## October 20, 1860
### Future King Edward VII Dines in Portland

Spectators gather at Portland Harbor to watch the Prince of Wales—Britain's future King Edward VII (1841-1910)—depart for England aboard his ship, HMS *Hero*.

The 18-year-old prince, who arrived by special train that afternoon from Boston and was treated to lunch at the city's Preble House, is returning home to England after touring Canada and the United States.

He spent three days in the White House as a guest of President James Buchanan, and he toured George Washington's Mount Vernon estate in Virginia with the president.

Organizers of the trip originally thought about having the prince return to England from New York, but they worried that too many British sailors might try to jump ship in that busy port. As it was, 140 sailors reportedly deserted during the tour.

October 20, 1873
**First Local Grange
in Maine Organized**

Amasa K. Walker and Allen Carter, with help from others, organize the first local Grange in Maine, Eastern Star No. 1 of Hampden, to help farmers during the Panic of 1873. Oliver Hudson Kelly founded the national organization in 1867 after witnessing the widespread devastation in the South after the Civil War, which ended in 1865.

"To improve the situation, he conceived of a secret society of farmers, which would assist in binding up the nation's wounds by emphasizing fraternal and brotherly love," writes Maine Grange chronicler Stanley Russell Howe.

The Maine State Grange is established in 1874.

October 20, 1977
**German Tourist Mistakes Bangor for San Francisco, Becomes Local Celebrity**

The *Bangor Daily News* publishes a story about Erwin Kreuz, 49, a German brewery worker making his first visit to the United States.

He was bound for San Francisco when his flight stopped in Bangor for refueling and customs clearance. Kreuz, who could not speak English, disembarked and stayed on the ground, thinking he already had arrived in California.

He spent four days in mid-October wandering around the Bangor area, looking in vain for the Golden Gate Bridge and other famous San Francisco landmarks, before meeting Gertrude Romine, the German-speaking owner of a restaurant in Old Town. She told him where he actually was.

News reports of the incident draw nationwide attention and make Kreuz a local celebrity. A Chamber of Commerce-sponsored Oktoberfest event makes him the guest of honor, he is made an honorary member of the Penobscot Indian Tribe, and he is flown to Augusta to meet Gov. James B. Longley.

Kreuz makes two more trips to Bangor—in 1978 and 1979, respectively—and is the celebrity guest at the dedication of the Bangor Mall in 1978.

He also eventually travels to San Francisco after his 1977 visit to Bangor. When he returns home, he says he likes Bangor better.

## October 21, 1947
### Wind-whipped Fire Destroys Huge Swath of Bar Harbor

Strong wind fans the flames of fires already burning for three days on Mount Desert Island, boosting the area burned from about 169 acres to more than 2,000. On the afternoon of the next day, the wind changes and pushes the fire directly toward Bar Harbor. It travels six miles in less than three hours, destroying sixty-seven majestic summer cottages on Millionaires Row; they never are replaced. Five hotels and 170 permanent homes also are destroyed.

Heading in other directions, the fire also destroys the Jackson Laboratory. About four hundred people flee on boats before the roads, blocked by fire, can be opened again. When the fire is declared under control on October 27, the total area burned on the island comprises 17,188 acres, including more than 10,000 in Acadia National Park. Property damage exceeds $23 million—equal to about in $271 million in 2020.

The island's blazes are part of the wave of fires that sweep over southern and eastern Maine in 1947, "the year Maine burned."

Among other results, the fires change the composition of the forest on Mount Desert Island. It eradicates mature stands of spruce and fir. Birch, aspen, and oak trees take their place, giving Acadia National Park a palette of fall foliage colors that it did not display earlier.

Motels and other businesses catering to short-term tourists replace the summer cottages of the wealthy, but probably the latter would have disappeared even without the fire. That aspect of Bar Harbor life had been in decline since the 1890s, and many of the grand homes that once had stood there were demolished before the fire struck.

## October 22, 1886
### Fire Rips through Farmington, Destroying Buildings, Igniting Panic

Amid wildly blowing wind, a fire destroys thirty-three houses, nineteen stores, three churches, two hotels, a bank, the county jail, and the post office in Farmington.

The fire begins in a Front Street barn owned by John A. Storyell, where about forty-five tons of hay are stored. The wind carries cinders in all directions, so that at one time, eight buildings are in flames, including two that are a half-mile away.

The blaze seems to be dying down until the wind becomes active again. The fire then barrels down Main Street, reducing buildings on both side to ruins.

Among the destroyed buildings is the Town House, the oldest structure in town, having been built eighty-five years earlier.

Firefighters' efforts are of little avail because of the conflagration's speed and the fact that the town's firefighting equipment is not up to the task. The fire is fully extinguished by the evening of October 23.

Officials think at first that sparks thrown off by a Sandy River Railroad locomotive caused the barn to burn, but then rumors about arsonists begin to spread.

Portland's *Daily Eastern Argus* reports that watchmen in West Farmington interrupted a male person trying to set a storage building behind a retail store alight, but the person ran off with a friend. A maid in the Elm House hotel finds packs of partially used matches near a woodpile.

Night watchmen begin carrying guns instead of ax handles, according to the paper.

October 23, 1651
### Massachusetts Bay Colony Asserts Authority over Southwestern Maine

The Massachusetts Bay Colony's General Court sends a letter to authorities in southwestern Maine, the part of Maine that retains the name after a division of that colony into four parts, saying that the area is under Massachusetts' jurisdiction. No response is given.

In November 1652, four Massachusetts commissioners arrive in Kittery with a marshal and armed deputies. Kittery submits that day to Massachusetts' authority, and York does so six days later. In 1653, Wells also falls into the Massachusetts orbit. Thus begins Boston's domination of Maine, which will last until Maine achieves statehood in 1820.

October 23, 1864
### Fifty Businesses Burn in Eastport; Authorities Suggest Confederate Sympathizers May Be Responsible

A seven-hour fire consumes about fifty businesses in downtown Eastport, then a community of nearly four thousand people, or more than three times its population today.

The fire breaks out on Union Wharf and wipes out the entire

business district.

The loss is estimated at $500,000, or $8.4 million in 2020 value.

Its wreckage includes all the homes on Boynton Hill and the schooner *Camilia*, with nearly all its cargo.

Because the blaze occurs during the Civil War and so close to the US border with Canada, authorities speculate that Confederate sympathizers might have started the fire, just as they had launched a raid from Canada into St. Albans, Vermont, four days earlier.

## October 24, 2007
### Navy Requests Upgrades to Arleigh Burke-class Destroyers

The Navy says its Arleigh Burke class of destroyers, some of which were built at Bath Iron Works in Maine, need about $59.8 million worth of upgrades to their bows because they tend to sustain structural damage when fully loaded and traveling in rough seas.

A Navy spokesman says defense industry reports of "serious structural defects" appear to be exaggerated, however.

The ships are fully capable of carrying out their missions, he says, and the repairs should assure the Navy that it will get the full

thirty-five years of life expectancy out of them.

The bows on ships under construction are being strengthened, and those recently delivered are being upgraded after shakedown cruises.

The rest of the fleet will be retrofitted during docking opportunities, the spokesman says.

BIW built the first Arleigh Burke-class destroyer. The shipyard was unaware of the defect until 2003, a shipyard spokesman says.

The ships were built to Navy specifications, but the standards don't match the force of actual sea conditions, he says.

## October 25, 1836
### Circus Ship *Royal Tar* Burns, Sinks in Penobscot Bay; 32 People, Many Circus Animals Die

The passenger steamship *Royal Tar*, heading from Saint John, New Brunswick, to Portland, burns and sinks in Penobscot Bay while carrying a variety of circus animals, as well as seventy-two passengers and twenty-one crew members.

Thirty-two people and most of the animals die in the sinking. Two of the ship's four lifeboats were removed to make room for

Illustration of the burning and sinking of the *Royal Tar* ship from *The Tragedy Of The Seas; Or, Sorrow On The Ocean, Lake, And River, From Shipwreck, Plague, Fire And Famine* by Charles Ellms.

the animals.

The 164-foot-long *Royal Tar* was built in Saint John and was completed earlier that year. It departed Saint John on October 21 carrying an elephant named Mogul, a Bengal tiger, two lions, two camels, six Arabian horses, some monkeys, and a variety of other exotic animals. The menagerie comprises a traveling circus bearing the ungainly name of Dexter's Locomotive Museum and Burger's Collection of Serpents and Birds.

Also traveling on the ship are a brass band; a large collection of waxworks; a two-ton show wagon, called an omnibus; several other wagons; and other horses.

The circus had been touring New Brunswick and Nova Scotia. Windy weather prompted the *Royal Tar* to dock at Eastport, then twice more. It departed from Machias on October 25, heading southwest.

When the ship is near the island of Vinalhaven, a fire breaks out below deck. Dense smoke prevents access to the pumps, which also are below deck.

The first engineer and fifteen other men jump into one of the two remaining boats, a longboat, and row away, finally reaching Isle au Haut, seven miles distant.

The captain and two other men lower the other boat—a jolly boat, a small vessel meant to ferry passengers back and forth between a larger ship and land—into the water to prevent it from burning. By this time, the middle of the *Royal Tar* is engulfed in flames.

One passenger ties a stocking loaded with silver dollars around his waist and lowers himself into the water. He immediately sinks out of sight.

The pilot from the nearby US revenue cutter *Veto* approaches in a rowboat, then panics at the sight of the chaos on the *Royal Tar* and rows back. The *Veto* draws nearer and rescues forty people, costing its captain severe wounds and burns. The *Veto* itself also catches fire twice.

Eventually, Mogul the elephant, standing on deck throughout the fire, crashes through the ship's rail and falls to the water, taking some unfortunate passengers with him. Of all the fatalities, thirty-one people drown and one is burned to death.

The name of the *Royal Tar* is a nickname of Britain's King William IV (1765-1837). The nickname is a reference to William's extensive service in the British navy.

## October 25, 1866
## William Patten, Prolific Novelist, Born in Corinna

William George Patten, a prolific, nationally-known writer of dime novels who uses a robust collection of widely varying pseudonyms, is born in the Penobscot County town of Corinna.

Later known as Gilbert Patten, he writes the vast majority of a seventeen-year-long weekly series of stories about the fictional character Frank Merriwell, a Yale University star athlete who solves crimes in his spare time. Patten uses the pen name Burt L. Standish when he writes the Merriwell books, but he also writes other fiction under the names Herbert Bellwood, William West Wilder, Harry Dangerfield, Gordon MacLaren, and Julian St. Dare.

Patten sells his first two stories for $6 to the Banner Weekly Publication in the early 1880s while he is a student at Corinna Union Academy.

He works as a newspaper reporter at the *Dexter Eastern State* and the *Pittsfield Advertiser*, then founds his own short-lived paper, the *Corinna Owl*. All through that period, he continues to write and sell fiction to magazines. The first Merriwell story, published by

Street & Smith, appears in 1896. He also writes several other series of books for boys.

Patten lives most of his life in Camden, but he moves in 1941 to California.

He dies in 1945 in Vista, a suburb of San Diego.

The Maine State Library in Augusta maintains a group of letters and other correspondence by or about Patten in its special collections.

## October 26, 1775
### Arnold Expedition Conducts Ten-Mile Portage of Heavy Boats, Supplies in Maine Wilderness

Benedict Arnold's northbound wilderness expedition to Quebec conducts a ten-mile portage of heavy boats and supplies connecting a series of Maine ponds to reach the Height of Land, from which his men can descend to waterways flowing toward the St. Lawrence River and the British fortress they intend to attack.

"We advanced on the Portage about 3 miles this evening (at Dusk) much fatigued," Arnold writes in his journal. "The whole of our baggage did not arrive until very late, & we made it near midnight before we could pitch our tents; the whole dis-

Courtesy of Everett Collection/Shutterstock.com
Benedict Arnold (1741-1801)

tance today abt 10 miles."

A few days later, the undertaking becomes even more miserable when about four inches of snow fall and Arnold's men become lost and disoriented while trying to walk around the swampy edges of Spider Lake, which is named that because its many streams and extensions are reminiscent of a spider's legs.

Having lost many of their supplies, the men are starving. Two officers approach a fire with about a dozen men sitting around it, and they realize the men are devouring another officer's Newfoundland dog.

## Oct. 27, 1775
### Arnold Reports Many Boats Lost; Continues March to Quebec

Col. Benedict Arnold, continuing his seven-week march to Quebec at the start of the American Revolution, writes a letter to Gen. George Washington to report that his Army expedition has lost many of the boats that it used to ascend the Kennebec River from Fort Western (now Augusta), and that he has sent soldiers who have become sick and enfeebled back down the river.

Arnold is writing from Chaudière Pond, today called Lake Mégantic, just as his troops are massing to head downstream on the Chaudière River toward the British-controlled fortress at what is now Quebec City.

"Our bill of fare for last night and this morning consisted of the jawbone of a swine destitute of any covering," 20-year-old Rhode Island native Dr. Isaac Senter, the expedition's surgeon, writes in his journal that evening. "This we boiled in a quantity of water, that with a little thickening constituted our sumptuous eating." After the expedition's long march that day across the hilly, snow-covered Height of Land (in today's Coburn Gore),

however, the men perked up when they found a stream filled with trout.

Capt. Henry Dearborn, who after the revolution would settle in Gardiner and become secretary of war under President Thomas Jefferson, writes in his journal on the same evening that the men still moving forward became dispirited when they learned that Col. Roger Enos had succumbed to his officers' entreaties to quit the expedition, then led his division back to Fort Western with far more provisions than he needed to make the trip.

"Our men made a General Prayer, that Col.: Enos and all his men, might die by the way, or meet with some disaster, Equal to the Cowardly dastardly and unfriendly Spirit they discover'd in returning Back without orders, in such a manner as they had done, And then we proceeded forward," Dearborn wrote.

Enos later will be court-martialed for his action. The court will acquit him, but he will spend much of the next few years furiously fending off attacks on his reputation in connection with his role in the Arnold Expedition, which, desperately short of men and supplies, ends in failure when the British repulse its December 31 attack on Quebec.

## October 27, 1984
### Auburn Man Burns Girlfriend's Child to Death in Oven

Auburn resident John Lane, 36, forces the screaming 4-year-old daughter of his girlfriend, Angela Palmer, 29, into an oven and burns her to death, claiming he is "cooking Lucifer."

The smell of smoke and neighbors' complaints about the sound of loud religious music blaring from the couple's apartment draw firefighters and police to the scene, where they remove a chair holding the oven door shut and discover the girl's remains.

A month later, the responding police officer quits his job because of the stress caused by what he saw in the apartment.

Lane is convicted in Bangor and sentenced in November 1985 to life in prison. In 1987, the Maine Supreme Judicial Court upholds the conviction.

Palmer, also charged with murder, is acquitted of a manslaughter charge.

With clearance from a judge to do so, Lane seeks a new trial in 2015, claiming poor legal representation in the 1985 trial. He says his lawyer should have entered his mental health records into evidence, and that when a psychiatrist stated that Lane knew his actions were wrong, the lawyer should have challenged that.

As of 2021, he is still listed as a prisoner at the Maine State Prison in Warren, serving a life sentence.

The case becomes the subject of a book by lawyer Elliot Epstein titled *Lucifer's Child*.

## October 28, 1787
### *Kennebec Journal* Co-founder Luther Severance Born in Massachusetts

*Kennebec Journal* co-founder and editor Luther Severance is born in Montague, Massachusetts.

Severance, who later serves as a two-term Whig Party member of the US House of Representatives from Maine's Third Congressional District, also becomes US commissioner—equivalent to ambassador—to the kingdom of Hawaii from 1850 to 1853.

James G. Blaine, later a US House speaker and presidential candidate, is the newspaper's co-owner and editor at the time of Severance's death in 1855. He writes a memorial tribute to Severance and summarizes the stay in Hawaii, then known as the Sandwich Islands.

"It was during Mr. Severance's Commissionership that the subject of annexation of the Sandwich Islands to this government was first prominently agitated," Blaine writes.

"In response to a communication from the State Department at Washington, Mr. Severance prepared a paper on this subject, which was extraordinarily minute and accurate in regard to the resources and capabilities of the islands in a commercial point of view. ..."

The United States annexes Hawaii in 1898, thirty-three years after Severance's death and five years after Blaine's.

Before going to Congress, Severance also is a member of the Maine House of Representatives and the Maine Senate.

His gravesite is in Augusta's Forest Grove Cemetery, literally a stone's throw from that of Russell Eaton, with whom Severance founded the *Kennebec Journal* in 1825.

Several other former owners of the newspaper are buried in the same cemetery—or, in the case of Blaine, at a park next to it.

## October 29, 2006
### 165-foot-tall Construction Crane Topples onto Residential Buildings

Heavy wind topples a 165-foot-tall construction crane being used at a Maine Medical Center construction site in Portland onto three nearby residential buildings, damaging all of them.

The incident displaces about a dozen people, but nobody is injured.

The collapse, reported about 9:56 a.m., prompts authorities to close off affected streets and to reroute traffic elsewhere.

The crane collapse is just a sample of the damage inflicted by the stormy weather, which features gusts of more than 70 mph. Fallen power lines and tree limbs abound throughout the region.

The same day the crane is blown over, a falling tree lands on a moving car on Westbrook Street in South Portland, injuring five people, according to a police dispatcher. The wind also rips the roof off the Cookie Jar Bakery in Cape Elizabeth.

## October 30, 1991
### 'Perfect Storm' Ravages Atlantic Coast

A hurricane later commemorated in Sebastian Junger's best-selling book *The Perfect Storm* and a film of the same name reaches peak intensity off Canada's Atlantic coast.

The then-unnamed storm began to grow October 28, when it sank the Gloucester, Massachusetts-based fishing boat *Andrea Gail*, killing its six crew members.

Also known as "the Halloween storm," the multi-day event batters Maine and the rest of the Eastern Seaboard—especially Massachusetts, where one hundred homes are destroyed or severely damaged. Damage is reported as far south as Jamaica and as far north as Newfoundland.

At its October 30 peak, the storm generates ocean waves ranging in height from forty to eighty feet.

In Maine, hundreds of homes are affected, most prominently the summer residence of then-President George H.W. Bush on Walker's Point in Kennebunkport. The famous vacation residence, visited by several world leaders, sustains extensive damage when the wind and water knock out windows and flood the interior.

Twenty-five-foot waves plow ashore and smash into houses at Camp Ellis, part of Saco, and twenty families are evacuated. In Kennebunkport, water three feet deep covers 1.5 miles of Beach Avenue and penetrates about forty homes across the street. Police report high water reaching the first floor of about one hundred homes in Wells. Twelve vulnerable houses in Cape Elizabeth are evacuated.

The tidal surge, propelled by 50-mph wind, is one of the ten most severe in Maine's history at the time.

### October 31, 1879
### Jacob Abbott, Author of 180 Books, Dies in Farmington

Prolific Maine author Jacob Abbott dies at 75 in Farmington, where he resided. Abbott's writing career produced 180 books, consisting of works of juvenile fiction, history, biography, religion, and science. Many of them were translated into other languages.

The Hallowell native, Bowdoin College graduate, and ordained minister taught mathematics and natural philosophy for four years at Amherst College, then directed the Mount Vernon Female School in Boston. He organized a Congregational church in 1834 in Roxbury, Massachusetts, then left it in the care of his brother John Abbott.

While still a young man, he moved to Farmington, where his brother Samuel Abbott had founded the Abbott Family School for Boys at Little Blue. Samuel Abbott died a few years later, so Jacob Abbott took over its management briefly with his sisters.

They sold it and moved across the road to Few Acres, which remained their home after that, although Abbott spent winters in New York.

Abbott's brothers John Abbott and Gorham Dummer Abbott also were authors, as were his sons, Benjamin, Austin, Lyman, and Edward.

—30—

# NOVEMBER

**November 1, 1949**
**Flagstaff Post Office Closes;**
**Town Soon to be Underwater**

The US Post Office that served the town of Flagstaff for fifty years officially closes in advance of a man-made flood that will soon engulf the town as well as neighboring Dead River Plantation.

The communities will be evacuated and flooded to create Flagstaff Lake as part of a hydroelectric project for Central Maine Power.

Postmaster Evan Leavitt tells The Associated Press the twenty or so families that remain in the town will get their mail by rural carrier from New Portland until they leave.

By March 1950, spring runoff from the Dead River is inundating the town as the water begins to build behind the new dam at Long Falls. The last people to leave the town are Roy Parsons and his son Everett, who wait until the river backs to within fifty rods of their farm and decide if they are going to get out over roads, it has to be then. Parsons' house is simply flooded, while his sister's house was burned during clearing.

Flagstaff got its name because Benedict Arnold and his soldiers planted a flag there during their march to Quebec in 1775.

**November 1, 1972**
**Piscataqua River Bridge Opens,**
**Connects Maine, New Hampshire**
**Via Interstate Highway**

The Piscataqua River Bridge opens. The six-lane, fifteen-hundred-foot span becomes the third bridge linking Kittery, Maine, and Portsmouth, New Hampshire. As a newly opened portion of Interstate 95, it also quickly becomes the most frequently used route into and out of Maine.

The new bridge enables travelers to avoid the Portsmouth traffic circle, which often is clogged with traffic in the summer.

The $21 million bridge opens officially when Maine Transportation Commissioner David H. Stevens cuts a red, white, and blue ribbon hanging across the center of it.

The entire project, including approach roads, cost about $35 million—about $220 million in 2020 value.

## November 1, 2014
### Apartment Fire Kills Six, Leads to Jail Term for Owner

An apartment house fire on Noyes Street in Portland, near the University of Southern Maine campus, kills six people, all in their twenties. It is Maine's deadliest house fire in thirty years.

Firefighters and investigators recover five bodies at the scene. One severely burned man who escapes from the three-story building is taken to a Boston hospital, where he is listed in critical condition. He dies days later from his injuries.

The fire at the two-unit apartment house breaks out around seven in the morning. Witnesses say the fire appeared to start on the front porch. Seven people escape from the house uninjured.

Investigators later conclude the fire is an accident caused by improper disposal of smoking materials. That action ignited a chair and a couch on the porch, and the flames entered the building through an open door. The building has no smoke detectors, they say, and furniture was blocking a rear stairwell. One of the apartments did not comply with the fire code, they determine.

Building owner Gregory Nis-bet, opting for a trial by a judge, later is acquitted of manslaughter charges but is sentenced to three months in jail after conviction for a misdemeanor building code violation. He is released October 31, 2018, the day before the fourth anniversary of the fire.

The great loss of life prompts the city to institute policy changes. It imposes a citywide rental-unit registration fee designed to fund a building fire safety inspection program to focus on code violations and other problems.

In 2019, a memorial consisting of a granite stone with a plaque affixed to it is erected in nearby Longfellow Park to honor the six people who died.

## November 2, 1789
### President George Washington Visits Maine, Catches Two Cod

President George Washington, on his only visit to Maine, fishes for cod off the coast at Kittery, catching two of them. He also visits the site of what will become the Portsmouth Naval Shipyard.

## November 2, 1860
### Muscongus Island Rejects Lincoln, Declares Independence from US

The town of Bristol, like most of Maine, throws its support

in the presidential election to Republican candidate Abraham Lincoln, whose running mate is Maine's US Sen. Hannibal Hamlin. However, the residents of Muscongus Island—now called Louds Island—vote mostly for his Democratic opponent.

The island was paying taxes to Bristol for years even though it had been omitted from surveying maps and was not technically part of any town. Outraged by the election result, the islanders declare their independence from the United States and proclaim the Republic of Muscongus. When military officials go to the island in 1863, in the middle of the Civil War, to enforce the Union's draft law by registering nine eligible men there, islanders meet them with weapons and force them to return to the mainland.

One officer returns later, looking for one of the men, and the prospective draftee's wife pelts the officer with potatoes, driving him away. The draft targets eventually agree to pay money to hire military substitutes, which is legal at the time.

The Republic of Muscongus petitions the US government for readmission to the United States in 1934. The musical group Cas-

tlebay later records a song about this odd historical sideshow, called "The Independent Republic of Muscongus."

## November 2, 1971
### Bid to Abolish Maine Income Tax Defeated

In a statewide referendum initiated by business interests opposed to a state income tax, voters reject a proposal to abolish the income tax by a three-to-one margin. It was the first initiative placed on the ballot in twenty-four years.

A Republican-controlled Legislature passed the income tax law in 1969, and Democratic Gov. Kenneth Curtis signed the bill.

## November 3, 2009
### Voters Repeal Newly Enacted Law Allowing Gay Marriage

Maine voters overturn by referendum a law passed by the Legislature and signed by Gov. John E. Baldacci that allows marriages of same-sex partners.

The repeal question passes about 53 percent to 47 percent in an off-year election. Closer analysis reveals stark regional differences. A majority of voters in Cumberland, Hancock, Knox and Sagadahoc counties opts to keep the law in place; the repeal side wins majori-

Courtesy of Library of Congress
James G. Blaine, one of the most powerful political figures in Maine history.

ties in the other 12 counties, with the greatest proportion of "yes" votes coming in Aroostook (73 percent), Piscataquis (67 percent) and Somerset (65 percent) coun-

ties. The overturned law passed by comfortable majorities in Maine's Senate, 23-13, and the House of Representatives, 89-57.

"We prevailed because the people of Maine, the silent majority, the folks back home spoke with their vote tonight," says Mark Mutty, campaign manager of Stand for Marriage Maine, which advocated overturning the law.

Three years later, in a presidential election year, voters reverse course, authorizing same-sex marriages by referendum. That vote also produces a 53 percent to 47 percent result.

## November 4, 1884
### James G. Blaine Defeated by Grover Cleveland in Bid for Presidency

James G. Blaine (1830-1893), a Republican former US House Speaker and former US secretary of state from Augusta, loses the US presidential election to the Democratic nominee, New York Gov. Grover Cleveland, after one of the dirtiest presidential campaigns in US history.

During the campaign, Cleveland, a bachelor, answered accusations that he had fathered an illegitimate child by a woman in Buffalo, New York, by taking responsibility for the child. A Democratic-leaning Indianapolis newspaper noted that Blaine's first child had been born only three months after his marriage to Augusta native Harriet Stanwood in 1851 in Pitts-

burgh. Blaine defended himself by claiming that he and his wife also had been married in 1850 in Kentucky, but that marriage never was recorded. He filed a libel lawsuit against the newspaper.

Long-festering, complicated scandals in which Blaine was accused of taking bribes from railroad companies probably did more to damage his reputation, however.

With the November 4 election result uncertain initially, the Republican-aligned *Kennebec Journal* announces a Blaine victory with a front-page headline saying: "The Victory Won! A Glorious Result! Blaine and (vice presidential candidate and US Sen. John A.) Logan the People's Choice." By November 18, however, it is clear that Blaine has lost to Cleveland.

Political analysts later attribute his loss partly to Blaine's failure to repudiate a Protestant minister's last-minute public labeling of the Democrats as the party of "rum, Romanism and rebellion." "Romanism" is a reference to Roman Catholics, and "rebellion" means the South, which lost the Civil War nineteen years earlier.

Blaine later would serve as secretary of state again in the administration of President Benjamin Harrison.

## November 4, 2003
### Maine Legalizes Slot Machines at Racetracks

Maine voters approve a proposal to allow gambling in the form of slot machines at racetracks. The decision leads to the opening of what now is called the Hollywood Casino Hotel & Raceway in Bangor.

At the same time, they reject a proposal to authorize the Passamaquoddy Tribe and the Penobscot Nation, Maine's two major American Indian groups, to operate a casino.

## November 5, 1919
### Maine Ratifies 19th Amendment, Which Gives Women Right to Vote

Maine becomes the nineteenth state to ratify the 19th Amendment to the US Constitution, which eventually gives women the right to vote.

The decision reflects an about-face from the result of a statewide referendum only two years earlier, on September 10, 1917, when Maine men voted by a two-to-one ratio to deny women that right.

The amendment takes effect August 18, 1920, when Tennessee becomes the thirty-sixth state to ratify it, providing the requisite three-quarters of the forty-eight then-existing states needed for full ratification.

The timing of ratification creates a problem for election organizers in Maine, which then is the only state to hold its statewide elections in September rather than November. Municipal clerks throughout the state must contend with a concentrated rush of women registering to vote so they can participate in the election.

Eight Southern and Mid-Atlantic states—Alabama, Delaware, Georgia, Louisiana, Maryland, Mississippi, South Carolina, and Virginia—explicitly reject ratification before that date. Starting in 1923 with Delaware, however, they later change their minds and vote for ratification. The last of the eight states to do so is Mississippi, in 1984.

## November 5, 1974
### Longley Elected as State's First Independent Governor

James B. Longley (1924-1980), an independent candidate, wins a three-way race for Maine governor with 40 percent of the vote. Longley, who had been a Democrat before the campaign began, becomes Maine's first independent governor.

Calling himself "liberal on

Poster from the election featuring 1860 Abraham Lincoln and Hannibal Hamlin.

people and a conservative on fiscal responsibility," the Bowdoin College and University of Maine School of Law graduate defeats George Mitchell, a Democrat who later will serve as a US senator; and James Erwin, a Republican. Longley serves only one term as governor, as he pledged to do.

Although the Lewiston businessman is the first independent governor to occupy the Blaine House, he is not the first Longley there. Maude Longley was a housekeeper for Gov. Sumner Sewall and his family in the 1940s. Her diaries provide insight into what life in the mansion was like in the 1940s.

## November 6, 1860
## Maine's Hannibal Hamlin Elected US Vice President

Hannibal Hamlin, a Republican from Bangor, is elected US vice president, having run with Republican President Abraham Lincoln.

Hamlin, a former Democrat who bolted from the party over its pro-slavery stance, was selected for the Republican ticket to provide a regional and partisan balance with Lincoln, who is from

Illinois. He serves one term, until March 4, 1865, when the Civil War is nearly over.

About six weeks later, his replacement, Andrew Johnson, becomes president when Lincoln is assassinated.

## November 6, 1962
### Reed Re-elected Maine Governor

Incumbent Gov. John H. Reed (1921-2012), a Republican, is elected to a four-year term as Maine governor. It is the last time a Republican gubernatorial candidate in Maine wins more than 50 percent of the vote.

Reed, a potato farmer from Fort Fairfield, first became governor on December 30, 1959, when Gov. Clinton Clauson died. As president of the Maine Senate, Reed was first in line to succeed Clauson. Reed then won a special election in 1960 to finish Clauson's term.

## November 6, 2012
### Maine Referendum Voters Legalize Same-Sex Marriage

Maine, Maryland, and Washington become the first states to legalize same-sex marriages by referendum. The "yes" side gets 53 percent of the vote in Maine. The law in Maine takes effect December 29.

The vote reverses the outcome of a referendum held only three years earlier, in 2009, when Maine residents overturned a law passed by the Legislature affirming homosexuals' right to marry each other.

## November 6, 2018
### Maine Begins Using Controversial Ranked-choice Voting Method

Maine uses ranked-choice voting for the first time in a general election of candidates for the US House of Representatives.

Rep. Chellie Pingree, a Democrat from the First District, wins re-election to her seat with more than 50 percent of the vote in the initial tally, so ranked choices play no role in her victory. In the Second Congressional District, however, incumbent US Rep. Bruce Poliquin, running for re-election against three challengers, achieves only a 46.3 percent plurality in the first tally. When votes received by the two candidates who drew the fewest votes are redistributed to the voters' second and third choices, Democrat Jared Golden comes out on top. Golden becomes the first challenger to defeat an incumbent in the district since 1916.

Poliquin files a lawsuit in federal court, claiming he was the winner; but a judge rejects his claim, as does the US Court of

Appeals for the First Circuit when Poliquin files an appeal.

With Golden's election, Republicans are shut out of US House seats everywhere in New England for the 116th Congress.

## November 7, 1837
### Illinois Pro-slavery Mob Shoots, Kills Maine-born Abolitionist Editor

Journalist and slavery opponent Elijah Parish Lovejoy, 34, an Albion native who graduated at the top of his class from what is now Colby College in Waterville, is shot to death in Alton, Illinois, by a mob that has come to destroy his printing press.

Lovejoy started his career in education, becoming principal of China Academy in Maine, which he had attended as a student. He moved to St. Louis, where he became editor of the First Presbyterian Church's weekly newspaper, the *St. Louis Observer*.

Church officials soon told Lovejoy to stop writing about slavery. He refused. When in the spring of 1836 he condemned the public lynching of a free Negro and the acquittal of the killers, thugs came at night and destroyed his press. He moved across the river to Alton, in the free state of Illinois, but he encountered the same violent resistance. His first press there was pushed into the river before it could be delivered. Locals said his anti-slavery harangues were hurting the cotton shipping business, and they begged him to stop.

"If I have been guilty of no violation of law, why am I hunted up and down continually like a partridge in the mountains?" he wrote.

A month after he printed a July Fourth screed inviting people to form a chapter of the American Anti-Slavery Society, his print shop was wrecked again. When a replacement press arrived and was installed, a drunken mob began hurling stones at Lovejoy's print shop and set the roof on fire. Lovejoy stepped outside and was hit fatally by three musket balls.

In 1952, Colby College establishes the Elijah Parish Lovejoy Award to honor journalists who sacrifice their lives "to shed light on some of the most important issues of our times." The award is presented annually.

## November 7, 1972
### Gerald Talbot Wins Election, Becomes First Black Member of Maine House of Representatives

Newspaper compositor and civil rights advocate Gerald Tal-

*Photo by Kelley Bouchard; courtesy of Portland Press Herald*
Gerald Talbot, left, with University of Southern Maine President Glenn Cummings.

bot, a Democrat from Portland, wins election as the first Black member of the Maine House of Representatives.

Talbot, a Bangor native, attended the 1963 March on Washington and heard Rev. Martin Luther King Jr. deliver his "I Have a Dream" speech. Gov. Kenneth Curtis appointed Talbot to a state Human Rights Task Force in 1968. He also was the first president of Portland's NAACP chapter.

Talbot's House victory occurs in the same election in which President Richard Nixon, a Republican, wins re-election in a landslide that gives him a majority in forty-nine states, including Maine; and in which Maine's four-term US Senator Margaret Chase Smith, a Republican, loses her bid for re-election to Democrat William Hathaway.

During his three two-year House terms, Talbot champions migrant workers' rights, Indian tribal sovereignty, fair housing, and creating a holiday to honor King.

On September 10, 2019, the University of Southern Maine honors Talbot by creating a teaching fellowship bearing his name. The accompanying ceremony occurs on USM's Portland campus in the Glickman Library, the same place where Talbot worked as a janitor years earlier when it was an industrial building.

## November 7, 1973
### Augusta's Fort Western Designated National Historic Landmark

Augusta's Fort Western, built by the British in 1754 at the start of the French and Indian War, is designated a National Historic Landmark.

Col. Benedict Arnold's men stopped at the fort in 1775 during their ill-fated expedition to attack Quebec at the start of the American Revolution.

The fort's main building, surrounding by a reconstruction of its original palisade and blockhouses, is now the oldest log fort in the United States and a well-preserved example of an eighteenth-century trading post. It is owned by the city of Augusta and operated as a museum during the warmer months.

## November 8, 1836
### Board Game Pioneer Milton Bradley Born in Vienna

Milton Bradley, future business manager and board game pioneer, is born in the Kennebec County town of Vienna.

Bradley's family moves to Lowell, Massachusetts, in 1847. He becomes a mechanical engineer and patent solicitor in Springfield, Massachusetts, then develops a board game, The Checkered Game of Life, which includes such punishments as being sent to a whipping post for failure to observe the Sabbath properly. The game continues to be sold today under the title The Game of Life, with less onerous punishments and more rewards for good behavior.

In 1875, Bradley founds the Milton Bradley Co., which manufactures board games, school materials, books, and early animations. The company's later games include Candy Land, Operation, Battleship, and Chutes and Ladders.

## November 8, 1966
### Curtis Defeats Incumbent, Becomes Nation's Youngest Governor

Maine Secretary of State Kenneth M. Curtis, 35, a Democrat, defeats Gov. John H. Reed, 45, a Republican, in Maine's gubernatorial election. It is the most recent instance in which a sitting Maine governor has run for re-election unsuccessfully.

Curtis takes office in 1967 as the nation's youngest governor. He serves two four-year terms and later becomes US ambassador to Canada.

Reed also becomes a US ambassador, serving in Sri Lanka.

## November 8, 1976
### Wild Snapdragon Thought to be Extinct Found in Northern Maine

The revelation that the Furbush's lousewort, a wild snapdragon previously thought to be extinct in Maine, has been found in the northern Maine area expected to be flooded by the proposed Dickey-Lincoln hydroelectric dam project adds a crucial element to the political momentum against the project.

The dam proposal, discussed publicly since at least 1963, is never built.

## November 9, 2017
### Secretary of State Dunlap Files Federal Lawsuit Against Voter-fraud Commission

Maine Secretary of State Matthew Dunlap files a federal lawsuit against President Donald Trump's voter-fraud commission, of which Dunlap is a member, in an effort to get information about the panel's correspondence and its work.

One of four Democrats on the eleven-member Presidential Advisory Committee for Election Integrity, Dunlap says he requested the information three weeks earlier and never received it. The committee doesn't tell him what it is doing, he says. As a result, he files the suit in the US District Court for the District of Columbia.

The suit claims Vice President Mike Pence, the committee chairman, and Kansas Secretary of State Kris Kobach, the vice chairman, are violating the Federal Advisory Committee Act, because that law forbids keeping members of such a committee in the dark about the committee's actions.

David Becker, former director of the elections program at the Pew Charitable Trusts and executive director of the Center for Election Innovation and Research in Washington, D.C., says the situation is highly unusual.

"I can't recall a single instance of a presidential advisory commission being sued by one of its members," he tells the *Portland Press Herald*.

Trump set up the panel to investigate his claims that illegal voting cost him the popular vote in the 2016 presidential election, although he offered no proof of that. Other attempts to ferret out voter fraud, including one in Maine, found cases of it to be rare or non-existent.

The committee is shut down in January 2018, less than eight months after it was formed. On

June 27, a US District Court judge orders that all committee correspondence be provided to Dunlap by July 18. The Trump administration complies.

On August 3, Dunlap makes more than one thousand pages of commission files public, saying that the panel found no evidence of widespread voter fraud.

## November 10, 1866
### First Veteran Admitted to Togus Hospital

Nineteen months after the Civil War's end, the first patient is admitted to the National Asylum for Disabled Volunteer Soldiers, Eastern Branch, at the former Togus Springs summer resort near Augusta, the first such facility in the nation.

The hospital complex accommodates fewer than four hundred patients at first, but an aggressive building program in the late 1860s eventually provides services for nearly three thousand veterans.

Growth through the rest of the century leads to construction of a narrow-gauge railway from the Kennebec River in Randolph, to transport both passengers and coal. Togus offers band concerts, a zoo, a hotel, and a theater for Broadway shows, making it a popular spot for Sunday picnics.

Another building program in the 1930s, featuring mostly brick construction, changes the campus appearance significantly, giving it a look that persists to this day. The facility now is known as the VA Maine Health Care System, Togus Campus.

The full VA Maine Health Care System, including outlying clinics, employs about fourteen hundred people.

## November 11, 1825
### Portland Whorehouse Riots Continue

Portland's *Eastern Argus* reports that the third riot within a year has occurred in reaction to the presence of bordellos in the city.

The first round of the so-called Portland Whorehouse Riots took place in 1824, when a group of men and boys ejected the bordellos' tenants and tore down the buildings as a crowd of witnesses stood by silently. About two o'clock on a spring morning in 1825, another mob tore down houses where the prostitutes had moved, setting one house on fire when its occupants resisted the rioters' efforts to demolish it. Several people were arrested, but nobody was convicted.

In the third, more violent confrontation, when a new mob tried to attack the latest set of buildings where the prostitutes had moved, a shootout erupted, killing one man and wounding several others.

The violence was not unique to Maine. The same year, when police tried to intervene as rioters in Boston were tearing down bordellos, the rioters beat them up.

## November 12, 1932
### Statue of Civil War Commander Howard Unveiled at Gettysburg

An equestrian statue of Oliver Otis Howard, a native of Leeds, is unveiled at the site of the Civil War's Battle of Gettysburg, in which Howard fought as commander of XI Army Corps.

Pennsylvania Gov. Gifford Pinchot and Maine Gov. William Tudor Gardiner, who will become a wartime Army officer himself a decade later in Italy, both speak at the unveiling ceremony. They are accompanied by delegations from each state.

The statue depicts Howard accurately without his right arm, which was amputated because of the wounds he suffered in 1862 during the Peninsular Cam-

paign. While he was recuperating, Brig. Gen. Philip Kearny, who had lost his left arm, joked that the two of them should shop for gloves together from then on.

At Gettysburg, Gardiner presents the statue of Howard. Bowdoin College President Kenneth Sills also speaks, reflecting on of the fact that Howard graduated from Bowdoin in 1850 at the age of 19.

"This statue is a symbol that this man saw his duty to his country both in military and civil service and performed his duty well," Sills says. "To say that is sufficient praise for any man."

## November 13, 2000
### Wild Atlantic Salmon Listed as Endangered Species

The federal government lists the wild Atlantic salmon as an endangered species in Maine. The decision, made by the US Fish and Wildlife Service and the National Marine Fisheries Service, grants federal protection for the species, which at the time is believed to have dwindled to fewer than 150 fish.

Gov. Angus King, an independent, and Maine's two Republican US senators, Olympia Snowe and Susan Collins, criticize the decision, having questioned the science behind the listing and the new rules' potential economic effect.

Conservation groups in Maine and Canada praise the listing.

The listing applies on eight rivers—the Sheepscot and the Ducktrap in midcoast Maine; the Narraguagus, Pleasant, East Machias, Machias, and Dennys in Washington County; and Cove Brook, which flows into the lower Penobscot River.

In 2005, the federal agencies finalize an Atlantic salmon recovery plan with the state of Maine. Four years later, they add the Androscoggin, Kennebec, and Penobscot rivers and their tributaries to the list of Maine rivers where the species is protected.

The National Marine Fisheries Service announces in 2015 a five-year action plan that will take measures to protect eight species that might be in danger of extinction, focusing particularly on the wild Atlantic salmon.

November 14, 1899
## Oakland Electric Light Co. Begins Operating, Becomes CMP in 1910

Walter Wyman, who studied engineering, and Harvey Eaton, a lawyer, begin operating the Oak-

land Electric Light Co., which they bought for $4,500 seven days earlier. The company eventually buys up other electric companies and becomes the Central Maine Power Co., Maine's largest electrical utility.

Dam construction began in the 1790s in Oakland because much of the water power potential on Messalonskee Stream, which drops 210 feet between its source in the Belgrade Lakes and the Kennebec River, is concentrated there.

At an 1850 dam near School Street, a technology was introduced that surpassed that of the shafts used to power belt-driven machinery elsewhere in the town. The dam's owner, Oakland Electric Light, founded in 1887, installed a 22.5-kilovolt electric generator there. It supplied electricity to about one hundred customers.

On December 26, 1899, Wyman and Eaton reorganize the company as the Oakland Electric Co. with Eaton as president and Wyman as general manager.

They dream up the Messalonskee Electric Co. to be able to submit a bid for the contract to supply electricity for next-door Waterville's electric streetlights beginning in 1901. They win the contract, even though they have no power plant to serve Waterville then.

The new company swiftly builds one and begins operations in 1901. Its charter expands and it absorbs Oakland Electric Light in 1905.

In 1910, it changes its name to Central Maine Power Co. Much of its revenue in those early years is derived from supplying power to local trolley systems.

A century after Wyman and Eaton bought the business in Oakland, CMP grows its customer base to more than six hundred thousand. Today the company, a subsidiary of Connecticut-based Avangrid, has its headquarters in Augusta and maintains 280 substations and about twenty-five thousand miles of power lines.

### November 15, 1888
### Bath Iron Works Wins Contract to Build First Ship

The Maine Steamship Company accepts a $160,000 bid from Bath Iron Works for the construction of the steamship *Cottage City*.

It is the four-year-old Bath shipyard's first shipbuilding project.

The vessel is delivered to the owners in May 1890. It carries passengers between Portland and New York for more than seven years without incident, then is sold to a ferry service in Seattle, where it carries prospectors bound for the Klondike gold fields and freight headed to Alaska.

The steamer finally breaks up on the rocks at Cape Mudge, British Columbia, after twenty-one years of service.

### November 16, 1975
### Final Log Drive Comes Down Kennebec River, Ending Era

Television crews and reporters converge on the Kennebec River in central Maine to record the last major log drive in the contiguous forty-eight US states.

The Maine Legislature passed a law in 1971 banning log drives after October 1, 1976, but in 1975 the practice already is dying out for economic reasons, given that it is cheaper to transport logs by truck.

The Legislature acted partly in response to pressure from a protest group headed by University of Maine graduate student Howard Trotzky.

He began a campaign in 1970 to get logs out of the Kennebec River by filing suit against the Kennebec Log Driving Co.; Hudson Pulp and Paper, of Augusta; Kennebec Pulp and Paper, of Madison; Scott Paper; and Central Maine Power Co. He sought a court order that the log drives be controlled to enable people to use the waterways for recreational purposes.

Trotzky acknowledged later that his real motivation was ecological.

"The Kennebec water was and still is a suspension of fibers and bark from top to bottom," he tells *Down East* magazine in a story it published in 1976. "You can sit out there in a canoe and look down and see it. In Wyman Lake, the bark that falls off the logs gets deposited on the bottom and covered up by sand. When the bark decays under there, it sends up bubbles of gas. The water is slimy, and there isn't enough oxygen in it for the fish."

The final log drive of any kind takes place in the spring of 1976, when a smaller cluster of logs moves downstream from the Moosehead Lake region to the Scott Paper Co. mill in Winslow.

Kimberly-Clark acquires Scott Paper in 1995. In November 1997, it notifies its 260 workers in Winslow that it will close the mill within two months because of excess capacity.

## November 17, 2018
### Thornton Academy Football Team Wins State Championship, Never Trails in 11 Games

Thornton Academy's football team completes its first unbeaten season since 1986 with a lopsided 49-14 win against Portland High School in Maine's Class A state championship game.

The 11-0 string of the Trojans' victories is all the more impressive because opposing teams never achieved even a temporary lead over Thornton in any game of the season.

In the championship game, team member and high school senior Anthony Bracamonte scores four touchdowns, including one on a punt return and another after catching a sixty-one-yard pass from quarterback Kobe Gaudette.

"We started this on August 13 and we had this day marked on the calendar the whole season," Bracamonte tells the *Portland Press Herald* after the game. "We practiced hard through the cold, through the rain. We worked hard every single second of it, so we deserve this."

Thornton Academy is a private high school in the coastal city of Saco.

## November 18, 1833
### Hallowell Anti-slavery Society Becomes Maine's First Abolitionist Group

Ebenezer Dole, his brother Daniel Dole, and others meet in Hallowell to form Maine's first anti-slavery group, called the Hallowell Anti-slavery Society.

The society's debut occurs about a year after William Lloyd Garrison, one of the more prominent American orators calling for the abolition of slavery, conducted a speaking tour across the state.

## November 18, 1920
### 17 Woodsmen Drown After Boat Explodes on Chesuncook Lake

An engine backfires on a motorboat crossing remote Chesuncook Lake in Piscataquis County with about thirty-four woodsmen aboard, causing two barrels of gasoline to explode and set the boat on fire.

The blast knocks Nelson Smith, of Orono, the company clerk, through a cabin window and inflicts burns on him, but he survives. Many other men jump into the water to escape the flames. Some of them succeed in swimming to shore, but seventeen others drown.

The drowning victims, all foreigners, work for Great Northern Employment Agency and are on their way to a Great Northern Paper Co. lumbering site at Cuxabexis Stream, only another mile or so away from where the disaster occurs.

Some men who jump into the lake cling to the sides of the burning forty-foot boat. The wreck finally drifts ashore, and they survive.

One man from the country of Poland jumps into the water with his pack on his back and matches in his hat. He makes it to shore safely, collects dry driftwood, and starts a bonfire to warm others coming out of the lake.

People in other lumbering camps notice the flaming wreck while it still is on the lake, and they rush to help those who come ashore and search for the bodies of the missing.

The steamship *Madeleine* takes the bodies to Chesuncook Dam. From there they go to Greenville by truck. Most of them are expected to be buried in that town.

The survivors are taken to the Cuxabexis Stream camps, and doctors are heading there to treat them.

## November 19, 1819
### Thomas Jefferson Reviews Draft of Maine Constitution Sent by William King

Former President Thomas Jefferson writes a letter to William King, a leading Maine statehood advocate, thanking him for sending Jefferson a draft of the proposed Maine constitution, being prepared in conjunction with Maine's anticipated admission to statehood in 1820.

While praising most of the document, Jefferson faults its terms on representation. "Equal representation is so fundamental a principle in a true republic that no prejudices can justify its violation because the prejudices themselves cannot be justified," Jefferson writes.

The two men already were acquainted with one another. King visited Jefferson the previous winter at his home in Virginia, where King solicited the former president's ideas on what to include in Maine's constitution.

Jefferson's letter to King is now part of the Maine Historical Society's collections.

Jefferson was the principal author of the Declaration of Independence and a mentor of James Madison, his presidential successor, who was a driving force behind the US Constitution.

## November 20, 1652
### Massachusetts Bay Colony Seizes Control of Kittery

Stamping out a three-year-old effort to form an independent English province of Maine, Massachusetts Bay Colony authorities convince forty-one residents of Kittery to submit unconditionally to Massachussetts. A few days later, they exact a similar pledge of loyalty from residents of nearby Agamenticus—now the town of York.

In doing so, the colony of Massachusetts is taking advantage of a period of relative chaos in England, when the monarchy has been overthrown and Oliver Cromwell is ruling as head of the Protectorate.

Massachusetts quickly takes over the southwestern part of Maine and incorporates York County. The county eventually comprises all of Maine until Cumberland and Lincoln counties are created in 1760.

The Blaine House in Augusta has been the home of most Maine governors since 1920.

November 20, 1862

## James G. Blaine Buys House for Wife; It Later Becomes Governor's Mansion

J. Rufus Child sells his home, at the northwest corner of State and Capitol streets in Augusta, to US Rep.-elect James G. Blaine (1830-1893) for $5,000. Blaine presents the house to his wife, Augusta native Harriet (Stanwood) Blaine, as a birthday present. The Blaine family owns the house for more than a half-century and makes extensive renovations to it.

James Blaine also has a mansion on Dupont Circle in Washington and a "cottage" in Bar Harbor, but he considers Augusta to be home.

In his book *The Blaine House: Home of Maine's Governors*, H. Draper Hunt writes, " 'Augusta stood for freedom,' Blaine's daughter recalled. 'for a large old yard of apple trees and a butternut tree in the corner, and a vegetable garden at the back. It stood for a stable with horses and a pony; it stood for the kindest neighbors in the world, whose front doors were never locked and whose cookie jars were never empty; and for a household of aunts who were only waiting to welcome and spoil us.' "

Long after James Blaine's death, his family donates the house in Augusta to the state of Maine for use as a governor's mansion in memory of James and Harriet Blaine's grandson Army 1st Lt. Walker Blaine Beale, who is killed in World War I combat in 1918 in France.

## November 20, 1885
### Daniel Wilkinson Hanged in Maine's Last Execution Before Death Penalty's Abolition

Knowing he is about to die, Daniel Wilkinson arises about four thirty in the morning in his Maine State Prison cell in Thomaston. He has his usual breakfast of bread, coffee and milk. He smokes a cigar.

When Deputy Warden Hinkley visits him, Wilkinson says he feels first-rate. The prison chaplain stops by to discuss Wilkinson's religious beliefs. Wilkinson, age 40, says he was raised Episcopalian but abandoned his religious convictions.

"If you had it in your power, the men who you claimed have wronged you, would you injure them?" the chaplain asks, apparently referring to witnesses who testified against Wilkinson at his murder trial. If the chaplain is hoping for contrition, he doesn't get it. "Yes, I would take my revenge," Wilkinson replies.

A prison teacher asks him to divulge his real name; prison officials assume "Wilkinson" is an alias. Wilkinson refuses to reveal it, saying it's best that it not be known.

He says he is dismayed about having killed a constable, William Lawrence, after escaping from prison. "I learned the facts from the papers and was horror-stricken at the thought ... of having killed a man, though unintentionally," he says.

Bette Knowles, a woman who took an interest in his welfare, arrives at the prison with her small daughter, having taken the train from Augusta. She and Wilkinson talk for about five minutes. She is crying. "Put your trust in God," Knowles says. "I wish I could," Wilkinson replies, and gives each of them a book of Scripture allegories with their names inscribed in them. He bids them goodbye.

Sheriff Wilder Irish and other officers come to collect Wilkinson shortly before noon. They lead him through the sunlit prison yard and into the carriage shop, where a scaffold awaits. A prison official ties his legs together and places a noose around his neck. The chaplain prays aloud. Irish asks the condemned man whether he has anything to say. He doesn't. A black hood is pulled over his head.

Irish puts his foot on a spring lever and says, "By authority of the power vested in me, I now hang you by the neck until you are dead, dead, dead, and may God have mercy on your soul."

At 11:59 a.m., before dozens of witnesses, Wilkinson becomes the last person in Maine to be executed by the state's criminal justice system. The sheriff triggers the spring. The trap falls. Wilkinson drops eight feet, then recoils a bit. The body sways, then is still. Four physicians repeatedly measure Wilkinson's vital signs. For the first minute, his muscles twitch involuntarily. Sometime after ten and a half minutes, the pulse vanishes; the heart has stopped beating at fifteen. After seventeen minutes, the body is cut down and placed in a coffin. The lid is screwed onto it. A bell rings. Inmates return to the prison shops, according to one newspaper account, "as if a life had not been blotted out."

Detailed newspaper descriptions of the hanging, and two similar ones earlier that year, energize death penalty opponents, who agitate feverishly for their cause at the Legislature. In 1887, legislators approve a bill abolishing the state's death penalty. The governor signs it.

### November 21, 1921
### Merger of *Portland Herald*, *Portland Daily Press* Creates *Portland Press Herald*

The first edition of the *Portland Press Herald* is published. It is a merger of the former *Portland Herald* and the *Portland Daily Press*, which was founded in 1862.

Guy Gannett, an Augusta businessman, after being approached variously by owners of several papers in a cutthroat environment of declining revenue, eventually bought the *Press*, the *Herald*, the *Portland Sunday Telegram*, the *Evening Express,* and the *Waterville Morning Sentinel,* all in 1921. He merged the *Press* and the *Herald.* In 1929, he adds

Augusta's *Kennebec Journal* to his stable of investments.

If two daily newspapers were to merge today, the company responsible for doing it probably would coat the process with a thick, sweet gauze of public relations initiatives, offering special discounts, publishing self-congratulatory advertisements in the paper, and composing soothing editorials to assure the public, or at least the advertisers, that everything is in order behind the scenes.

The *Press Herald* appears to have done little of that in 1921. In its first issue, there is no mention of the merger. The only hint at an effort to engage with its readers is a box in the lower left corner of the front page that asks married women, competing for the prize of free theater tickets, to send in comments about their husbands in answer to questions such as, "Are YOU one of the million women whose lives are wasted?" and "How much deception should a wife tolerate on the part of her husband?"

That premier issue also features a number of unintentionally amusing headlines, such as, "DEATH YARMOUTH'S OLDEST WOMAN; WAS HUNDRED AND TWO."

Apparently death was a woman, and she lived in Yarmouth.

The *Press Herald*, usually demonstrating a more professional tone and presentation, quickly becomes the flagship paper of the Gannett empire.

Gannett, and later his descendants, own the papers until 1998, when the company is sold—except the *Evening Express*, which closes in 1991—to the Blethen family, which owns *The Seattle Times*. The papers have had several owners since then.

## November 22, 1963
### Five Weeks After Maine Visit President Kennedy Assassinated

President John F. Kennedy, who gave a foreign policy speech at the University of Maine only a month earlier, is assassinated in Dallas, Texas.

Kennedy originally is buried in a thirty-by-twenty-foot plot surrounded by a white picket fence in Arlington National Cemetery in Arlington, Virginia. About sixteen million people visit it during the first three years after his death.

Because of the large crowds, cemetery officials and the Kennedy family decide to transfer his grave to a more appropriate setting. The new site, which opens in 1967, includes a gravestone that comes from Monson, Maine, a town noted for its production of slate. The inscription also is engraved there.

Just thirty-four days before his assassination, Kennedy delivered a foreign policy address at the University of Maine, in Orono.

In his speech, the president thanked the university for the honorary degree it was giving him, called the American college and university system a national asset, and looked forward to a peaceful end to the Cold War.

He also reflected soberly on the outcome a year earlier of the Cuban Missile Crisis, in which the United States and the Soviet Union, mobilizing their forces and employing a high-stakes form of cat-and-mouse diplomacy, barely had avoided a nuclear conflict.

"Some hail it as the West's greatest victory; others, as a bitter defeat," Kennedy told his UMaine audience. "Some mark it as a turning point in the Cold War; others, as proof of its permanence. The fact of the matter is, of course, that neither view is correct."

US Sen. Margaret Chase Smith and other Maine dignitaries joined the president on stage.

## November 23, 2018
### Future of Portland-to-Nova Scotia Ferry in Doubt

The *Portland Press Herald* reports that although nearly 50,200 people used the direct high-speed ferry service between Portland and Yarmouth, Nova Scotia, during the year—the busiest season ever—the ferry probably will not be returning.

Bay Ferries, the vessel's operator, plans to move its service to Bar Harbor. The Bar Harbor Town Council voted in October to lease a town-owned ferry terminal to Bay Ferries.

The company said it intends to invest $3 million to improve the terminal and to re-launch service there in 2019.

The following year, it carries out its plan for Bar Harbor-to-Yarmouth service.

The city of Portland received almost $153,000 in passenger and vehicle fees from the ferry traffic in 2018, about $34,000 more than in the previous year.

The ferry company cancels its service from Bar Harbor for all of 2020 because of the coronavirus pandemic. In February 2021, it announces that the service would not occur that year as well, also because of the pandemic.

November 24, 1916
## Sir Hiram Maxim, Inventor of Machine Gun, Dies in London

Sir Hiram Stevens Maxim, a native of the Piscataquis County town of Sangerville and the inventor of the machine gun, dies at 76 in London while the armies of World War I, underway just across the English Channel, are making prolific use of his weapon on the battlefield.

Maxim's innovation was making the gun's recoil supply the power to reload it. He moved to England in 1881 and remained there. Queen Victoria knighted him in 1901.

As a youth, Maxim worked with a carriage maker in the village of Abbott before moving to upstate New York and working in a threshing factory. He went to Canada and became a prizefighter, bartender, and painter of decorations.

Moving on to Massachusetts and back to New York, he patented a variety of inventions, including his first patent, for an improved curling iron, in 1866. He moved permanently to England in 1881.

Maxim experimented for more than twenty years in aeronautics and invented types of airplanes. In the first decade of the twenti-

eth century, he took the British to task for what he considered their indifference to mechanical flight, noting, when airplanes were in their infancy, that Britain was in danger of bombardment if a war were to occur. When World War I broke out in 1914, Germany used dirigibles to bomb Britain.

At the age of 70 he helped organize the British air force, and he lived to experience the age of aerial combat amply fulfilling his prediction.

Maxim's many electrical inventions include incandescent lamps, self-regulating current machines, several pieces of ordnance, and smokeless powder. British Prime Minister David Lloyd George appointed him in 1915 to the inventions board of the British munitions department.

Maxim's son, Hiram Percy Maxim, becomes a well-known inventor in the United States who devised the Maxim silencer.

November 25, 1997
## Federal Officials Order Dismantling of Edwards Dam in Augusta over Objections of Owner

For the first time, the Federal Energy Regulatory Commission orders the dismantling of a working hydroelectric facility—in this case, the Edwards Dam in Augusta—over the objection of its owner.

FERC denies the Edwards Manufacturing Co.'s application for a renewal of its license to operate the dam.

The commissioners also tell the company to work with the US departments of the Interior and Commerce in determining how to carry out the order, which is meant to restore unimpeded access to the lower Kennebec River and its tributaries by migrating fish.

Proponents of the decision include Maine state government and a coalition consisting of the Natural Resources Council of Maine, American Rivers, Trout Unlimited, and the Atlantic Salmon Federation.

The dam's owners and the city of Augusta promise that they will appeal the FERC decision, but the Edwards Dam is demolished in 1999.

November 26, 1861
## Humorist Artemus Ward, Famed Alter Ego of Charles Farrar Browne, Debuts in Connecticut

Humorist Artemus Ward (1834-1867) makes his debut

as what today would be called a stand-up comedian in New London, Connecticut.

Ward, whose real name is Charles Farrar Browne and who was born in Waterford, Maine, used Yankee speech mannerisms and deliberately misspelled words in his columns published under the "Artemus Ward" name starting in 1858. He became a key figure among America's Bohemian writers and entertainers and a close friend of Mark Twain, whose name also is an alias.

Abraham Lincoln regales his Cabinet with a humorous story from a published Ward anthology in 1862, reminding the Cabinet members afterward of the restorative powers of humor. Then, changing the subject, he immediately announces his intention to issue the Emancipation Proclamation. Reports of what happened in the meeting assure Ward's fame.

His career is short, however. He goes on the lecture circuit in England, where he dies in 1867 of tuberculosis.

November 27, 1898
## Steamship *Portland* Sinks in Portland Gale; Up to 245 Drown

The steamship *Portland* sinks in a severe weather event known

Courtesy of Maine Historical Society

Passenger steamer SS *Portland* around 1885.

as the Portland Gale, resulting in the deaths of 193 to 245 people, including sixty-three crew members. The ship is bound from Boston to Portland when the storm strikes it off Cape Ann in Massachusetts.

The exact number of victims is uncertain because the passenger list goes down with the vessel. In any case, in terms of loss of life, it is New England's worst maritime disaster of the nineteenth century.

When the storm strikes, it drives many ships to shore, wrecking them in Boston Harbor. In Portland, the *Daily Eastern Argus* newspaper mistakenly reports that the steamer *Portland* has not ventured into the storm

and is still at its dock. By November 29, the news that it sank emerges. Bodies of the victims begin washing ashore in Provincetown, Massachusetts, at the tip of Cape Cod.

The *Argus* reports that the *Portland* was a relatively flat-bottomed coastal vessel, not built for ocean voyages and too top-heavy for especially turbulent weather. In Portland, the steamship company's general manager pins the blame on the ship's captain, saying that because of predictions of a severe storm, he instructed the captain not to leave the dock until he received weather reports about the danger subsiding.

The precise site of the wreck is

discovered in 1989, confirmed in 2002, added to the National Register of Historic Places in 2005, and visited by divers in 2008.

## November 28, 1981
### UFO Sighting Reported in Starks

Longtime Somerset County Deputy Sheriff Bud Hendsbee and his wife, Helen, a Madison selectwoman, leave home in Madison in their pickup truck, headed for Farmington, where they plan to have dinner at a new restaurant.

According to an account given later by Bud Hendsbee, as they pass through the tiny town of Starks on Route 43 in the dark, a group of people in a car coming in the opposite direction stop to fetch an escaped dog. When he asks whether he can help them, one of the people, Kenos Henry, advises him not to go over the hill because a menacing unidentified flying object is on the other side of it.

The Hendsbees head in that direction anyway. They notice a far-off light sweeping from side to side, but it disappears, so they go to Farmington and enjoy dinner. On the way back, a hovering light confronts them suddenly in Starks, so bright that Bud Hendsbee is nearly blinded and unable to drive. The object changes position a few times, then hovers about sixty feet in the air directly in front of them in absolute silence. The Hendsbees turn around and take a different route home.

The next day, Bud Hendsbee calls the *Morning Sentinel* to report what happened. A story that appears in the paper spreads to radio and TV news broadcasts and prompts a barrage of phone calls to the Hendsbees, including one from researchers in Florida who say they are ready to fly up to Maine to hypnotize witnesses.

The Hendsbees refuse to take part in additional interviews after that.

## November 29, 1882
### James Shepherd Pike, Crusading Columnist from Calais, Dies

Calais native James Shepherd Pike dies at 71 after a journalism career that brought him fame first for his ardent anti-slavery, anti-Confederacy views; and later for his sensationalistic criticism of corruption that thrived under President Ulysses Grant's administration as well as what Pike portrayed as the abominable misrule by freed Blacks in the South during the Reconstruction period.

Pike's 1874 book *The Prostrate State: South Carolina under Negro*

*Government* was read widely and regarded by many as unbiased history at the time, but later scholars' research on Pike's writing and habit of reporting only details that support his own preconceived conclusions show his writing on South Carolina to have been infected from a personal racism that spanned and undermined his entire career.

"Pike was hardly a model of objectivity—he had long held racist views, and had incorporated essentially the same critique in articles written before ever visiting the state," Columbia University history professor Eric Foner writes in a book about the Reconstruction period, which followed the Civil War. "Moreover, he acquired much of his information from interviews with white Democratic leaders and seems to have spoken with only one black Carolinian."

Pike first gained a large readership when, in 1850, he became a Washington correspondent and editorial writer for the *New York Tribune*. He took a hiatus from journalism in 1861 when President Abraham Lincoln appointed him US ambassador to the Netherlands, a post in which he served a few years.

Afterward, he returned to the town of Robbinston, next to Calais, where he resided for the rest of his life.

Pike later was an active supporter of *New York Tribune* founder and editor Horace Greeley's campaign for president as the Democratic Party nominee in 1872. After Greeley lost the election and died, Greeley's newspaper sent Pike to South Carolina in 1873 to describe the political situation there.

His death occurs unexpectedly in Maine as he and his wife are preparing to leave for Philadelphia by train to spend the winter in a place warmer than eastern Maine, as they usually did.

## November 29, 1944
### German Spies Land on Maine Coast; Authorities Arrest Them

Erich Gimpel and William Colepaugh, two spies for Germany's Nazi government, disembark from a German submarine during World War II and land on Maine's coast at Hancock Point, southeast of Ellsworth. Their mission is to steal military and industrial secrets, including information about nuclear weapons research.

Gimpel, 34, was a radio engineer in Germany, then worked in Peru before German military intelligence recruited him. Colepaugh, 26, was a Connecticut native with a German mother. He defected to Germany after he failed to get a Navy commission and the US Navy Reserve discharged him. Gimpel met Colepaugh in The Hague, Netherlands. They both underwent training in Germany, then boarded the submarine in Kiel, Germany.

Once at the north end of Frenchman's Bay in Maine, the submarine, U-1230, dispatches an inflatable rubber boat to take the spies to shore. They land at 11:02 p.m. carrying two satchels containing sixty thousand dollars in cash, a hundred thousand dollars' worth of diamonds, some radio parts, automatic pistols, photographic apparatus, and invisible ink, all hidden in secret compartments under their clothes. They claw their way through the underbrush in a light snowstorm and begin walking along a road that leads to US Route 1.

A teenage boy on a bicycle sees them near Hancock Point. A local woman notices them later. Both witnesses report their observation of the strangers, who look out of place, and the FBI takes notice.

An off-duty taxi driver picks up the men on the road and takes them to Bangor, where they board a train for Portland. They eventually make their way to Boston, and then New York, where Colepaugh disappears, parties his way through of the money, then gets picked up by the FBI after a drunken night on the town. He tells the agents all about Gimpel. Gimpel is arrested on Dec. 31.

The Army puts both men on trial by court-martial in February at Fort Jay, in New York City. They are convicted of conspiracy and sentenced to hang. A few days before the date scheduled for their executions, however, President Franklin Roosevelt dies, and all executions are suspended.

In September, President Harry Truman commutes the men's sentences to life imprisonment. The sentences are reduced later. Gimpel is released on parole in 1955 and returns to Germany; Colepaugh is freed in 1960.

Gimpel's autobiography, *Spion für Deutschland (Spy for Germany)*, is published in 1956 in Germany.

"There is not, there was not, and there never will be any glamour in the métier of spy," he writes in closing his memoir. "The silent

Nazi spies who landed under cover of darkness in Hancock during World War II were eventually arrested in New York City.

battle the secret agent fights is a dirty battle, merciless and cold. It is the dirtiest side of war."

A German-language movie about Gimpel's wartime exploits is released that year. An English-language translation of the book is released in 1957 in the United Kingdom, and in 2003 in the United States.

November 30, 1989

## Fire Destroys Edwards Mill Complex in Augusta; Flames Visible for Twenty Miles

A massive fire destroys most of the long-vacant former Edwards Manufacturing Co. mill complex in Augusta at the base of Sand Hill.

The fire, which could be seen up to twenty miles away, began inside an elevator in the north end of the building, according to some workers there. Reported at 3 p.m., it makes fast work of the 150-year-old complex. Bales of cotton and oil-soaked wooden floors contribute to the fire's intensity.

Knowing they can't save the mill buildings, firefighters douse the southern and western ends of them, which are not burning yet, to prevent flames from spreading to the many old wood-frame homes and apartment buildings across the street, lining the bottom of Northern Avenue.

Several workers who were removing machinery and cotton bales from the building are able to escape without injury.

Before the mill ceased manufacturing cotton and wool products and closed in the early 1980s, it employed thousands of people over the decades. Many of them lived just up the avenue in the traditionally French Canadian neighborhood called Sand Hill. Others lived in homes and apartments along the streets at the bottom of the hill.

Two days later, on December 2, firefighters are sent back to the mill site to put out a fire that springs up from the embers of the November 30 blaze.

—30—

# DECEMBER

December 1, 1888
**Bowdoin Student MacDonald,
Founder of Maine Seacoast
Mission, Arrives on Frenchboro**

Alexander P. MacDonald, a
sophomore at Bowdoin College,
is sent to the remote island village of Frenchboro by Rev. Jonathan Edwards Adams, secretary
of the Maine Missionary Society,
in hopes MacDonald will spur a
religious revival.

MacDonald officially organizes
a new church and builds a chapel,
work which serves as a harbinger of his future. Inspired by the
islands of Maine and recognizing
the needs there, in 1905 he officially organizes the Maine Sea
Coast Missionary Society to serve
those remote islands, including
the lighthouse keepers. Today,
the Seacoast Mission continues to
serve the islands of Maine via its
boat *Sunbeam* and has expanded
its work to rural communities in
Washington County.

December 1, 1994
**Mitchell Appointed Special
Adviser on Ireland**

President Bill Clinton appoints

Courtesy of Dean Lunt
Alexander P. MacDonald

Maine's retiring US Sen. George
Mitchell to be his special adviser
on economic initiatives in Ireland.

Mitchell, 60, served in the Senate for fifteen years and was the
Senate majority leader for the
last six of those years. His new
appointment is preparation for
a much more demanding task—
joining the Northern Ireland
peace negotiations in 1995 as US
special envoy for Northern Ire-

land, also under Clinton's watch.

As chairman of all-party peace negotiations, Mitchell guides the participants to an ultimately successful conclusion—the 1998 Belfast Peace Agreement, also known as the Good Friday Agreement because that is the day on which the deal is struck. He receives the Presidential Medal of Freedom.

Mitchell later is appointed US special envoy for the Middle East under President Barack Obama. He serves in that post from 2009 to 2011.

### December 2, 1895
### US Rep. Thomas Brackett Reed, of Portland, Becomes Speaker of the House

US Rep. Thomas Brackett Reed (1839-1902), a Republican from Portland, becomes speaker of the US House of Representatives. He serves in that office until March 1899, a period that encompasses the sinking of the USS *Maine* in Havana harbor, and the Spanish-American War, which is a direct result of that sinking.

Reed unsuccessfully seeks the 1896 Republican presidential nomination. During the campaign, when asked to predict whether party delegates would nominate him, he says, "They could do worse, and they probably will."

### December 3, 1987
### Haskell, One of Four Governors in 1959, Served Less than Week

Former Gov. Robert N. Haskell dies in Bangor at 85. Haskell served five and a half days as governor in January 1959.

Haskell, an electrical engineer who was promoted to president of the Bangor Hydro-Electric Co. in 1958, became governor because Gov. Edmund S. Muskie resigned effective January 2 to take his seat early as a newly elected US senator. Haskell, as the Maine Senate president, was next in line to succeed him until the newly elected governor, Clinton Clauson, was sworn in on January 7. Clauson then died unexpectedly on December 30 and was succeeded by Maine Senate President John Reed.

That made 1959 the year in which Maine had four governors.

### December 3, 2004
### Tyson Foods to Close Jordan's Meat Plant in Downtown Portland

Arkansas-based Tyson Foods, Inc. says it will close the Jordan's Meats plant in downtown Portland, shuttering a fixture that has been in Portland for seventy-seven years.

The plant closing, planned for early February, and the closing of a distribution center in South Portland will leave about 285 people jobless.

Tyson says the plant's age, layout, distance from raw materials, and downtown location make it uneconomical for reinvestment. Earlier in the year, Tyson also closed its Augusta plant, laying off 170 people.

The announcement hits many longtime workers hard. One employee tells the *Portland Press Herald*, "Some people are crying; my supervisor is crying."

And some workers are just upset. "When Chet Jordan owned it, he was for the employees 100 percent. When Tyson took over, things started disappearing. Tyson's all about money," one says.

## December 4, 1899
### House Speaker Reed, Opposed to War with Spain, Quits Congress

US House Speaker Thomas Brackett Reed (1839-1902), of Portland, resigns from Congress after eleven terms in the House.

Reed and President William McKinley initially opposed a war with Spain in 1898. When McKinley switches his position and favors the war, Reed, an ardent anti-imperialist serving in an age when the American empire is expanding, refuses to back his fellow Republican. He leaves office instead.

## December 5, 1933
### Prohibition Ends in US, Capping Experiment Begun in Maine

The US Constitution's fourteen-year prohibition of alcohol consumption, an outgrowth of the Maine Law of the 1850s, comes to an end when Utah becomes the thirty-sixth state to ratify the 21st Amendment.

The Constitution requires that for an amendment to take effect, it must be passed by a two-thirds majority in both houses of Congress and ratified by three-quarters of the states. At the time of Utah's vote, the country has forty-eight states.

Reacting to the news, Rev. Frederick W. Smith, of Waterville, superintendent of the Christian Civic League, says the days of the drunkard are returning to the Pine Tree State.

Sale of beer containing up to 3.2 percent alcohol was authorized the previous July, and Smith notes that 1,214 arrests for intoxication occurred in July, August, and September, a 33 percent increase from the 903 recorded in the same period in 1932.

Apparently paying Smith no heed, Maine ratifies the amendment the next day. Having been the state that originated the social experiment known as Prohibition, it is the first state to cast aside the national ban on alcohol when such a decision no longer has any influence on whether the constitutional amendment becomes effective.

## December 6, 1819
### Voters Overwhelmingly Approve Draft of Maine Constitution

Voters approve a draft of the forthcoming state of Maine's new constitution. The "yes" side gets more than 90 percent of the vote.

## December 6, 1931
### Famed Botanist Kate Furbish Dies in Hometown, Brunswick, at Age 97

Botanist Kate Furbish, 97, dies in her hometown, Brunswick, after a six-decade career in which she walked all over the state to describe, depict, and catalogue the state's flora.

Merritt Lyndon Fernald, one of America's most accomplished academic botanists, met Furbish when he was 6 years old and growing up in Orono. When he began publishing books on the flora of Maine, he credited Furbish with being one of his major influences.

Furbish spent a few years as the chief botanist at the Poland Spring House, a resort that featured a massive hotel and greenhouses.

Her duties included cataloging all the flora of the outlying area, and she frequently sent specimens to and received them from other researchers who were doing the same thing elsewhere.

As she grew older, she became more focused on collecting and painting images of wild plants, despite the daily pain of neuralgia that afflicted her hands and feet.

One plant named for her, the Furbish's lousewort, is so rare that the rediscovery of it in 1976 influences the cancellation of a planned $1.3 billion hydroelectric dam project on the St. John River.

## December 6, 2001
### Leigh Saufley Sworn in as First Female Chief Justice of Maine Supreme Judicial Court

Gov. Angus King swears in Leigh Saufley, 47, as the first

female chief justice of the Maine Supreme Judicial Court, and the youngest.

Saufley, a University of Maine School of Law graduate, was one of the first female deputies in the Office of the Maine Attorney General, where she worked for ten years.

Gov. John McKernan appointed her to the District Court bench in 1990 and to Superior Court in 1993.

Saufley serves eighteen years and four months, longer than any other Maine chief justice except John Appleton, who held the job nearly twenty-one years, from 1862 to 1883. She steps down in April 2020 and becomes dean of the University of Maine School of Law.

During her tenure, Saufley advocates for increased funding for court staffing and infrastructure, especially to provide more courthouse security to protect crime victims and witnesses. Many courthouse security improvements are made during her tenure.

She also calls for additional funding for investment in mental health and addiction treatment.

At a February 26, 2019, news conference, Saufley says: "In many instances, folks who are dealing with addiction and are engaging in inappropriate activity can and should be diverted from the criminal justice system into rehabilitation and back to health."

## December 7, 1851
### Wharves, Businesses Along Portland Waterfront Destroyed by Massive Fire

A massive fire breaks out around five in the morning in the Larrabee & Jordan grocery store in Portland, on the eastern side of Commercial Wharf, destroying many wharves and commercial buildings along the city's waterfront. Twenty-seven stores and nine vessels burn.

The city's *Eastern Argus* newspaper gauges it to be the worst Portland fire in a half-century.

Because it was a Sunday morning, the fire probably went undetected until it was fully underway, roaring through the area's multitude of combustible material.

The lost businesses include several grocery stores and a pair of fish markets, as well as many other buildings.

One businessman loses six buildings, none of which was insured. The loss of goods includes vast quantities of mackerel, corn, molasses, and ship's sails.

The fire strikes during low tide, and ships are aground and dried out. Many are destroyed or sustain severe damage.

The flames hem in five or six firefighters on Commercial Wharf, giving them burns.

Police arrest people who are looting the shops during the blaze.

## December 8. 1819
### Petitions Submitted in Congress to Admit Maine as 23rd State

US Rep. John Holmes, Democrat-Republican from Maine, submits a petition to the House advocating the admission of Maine as the twenty-third US state. US Sen. Prentiss Mellen, a Massachusetts native residing in Portland, does likewise in the Senate.

Holmes later becomes one of Maine's first two US senators. Mellen is appointed Maine's first supreme court chief justice.

## December 8, 1820
### *Maine Gazette* Begins Publication

A four-page weekly newspaper, the *Maine Gazette*, begins publication.

The newspaper, which aligns itself with Whig Party policies, is the earliest lineal antecedent of today's Brunswick-based *Times Record*, a daily newspaper.

## December 9, 1814
### Delegates to President Madison: Save Maine from 'Treacherous' Massachusetts Policies

Near the end of the War of 1812, participants in a two-day meeting held at the Portland customs house conclude that they should appeal to President James Madison to save them from "treacherous" policies implemented by Massachusetts, of which the District of Maine is still a part.

The delegates are particularly incensed by the ongoing British occupation of eastern Maine. "Three months have now transpired since the belligerent power with whom we are contending has had undisturbed possession of one third of our territory," writes the committee that drafts the appeal.

The British occupation reinvigorates the decades-old movement to separate Maine from Massachusetts, a goal that finally is achieved in 1820.

## December 10, 2010
### Bushmaster Plant Closes, Reopens under Old Owner, New Name

Bushmaster Firearms International announces it plans to close its assembly plant in Windham, effective the following March 31.

Founded in 1973, the company employs seventy-three workers in Maine at the time of the announcement.

Bushmaster's parent company, North Carolina-based Freedom Group, Inc., says in a news release that the Windham staff will get comprehensive severance packages and help in finding new jobs. The parent organization will keep the Bushmaster name and transfer manufacturing to plants elsewhere.

The following June, former Bushmaster owner Richard Dyke and other investors announce a plan to reopen the Windham site and manufacture rifles there under the name Windham Weaponry. Their enterprise expects to hire back about half of the people who lost their jobs in the closure.

The New York City private equity firm Cerberus Capital Management acquired Bushmaster from Dyke in 2006 for $70 million. Bushmaster and three other weapons makers were placed under Freedom Group, which Cerberus owns.

On December 14, 2012, a man armed with a .223 AR-15 rifle uses the gun to kill six adults and twenty small children at Sandy Hook Elementary School in Newtown, Connecticut. The following week, Cerberus puts the Freedom Group up for sale.

In 2014, the families of nine of the twenty-six Newtown shooting victims file a lawsuit against the manufacturer, Bushmaster; the distributor, Camfour; and Riverview Gun Sales, the East Windsor, Connecticut, seller of the rifle, contending that the guns are for military use and are not designed for hunting or home defense. After court challenges, the US Supreme Court rules in November 2019 that the Newtown families' lawsuit may proceed.

By that time, Bushmaster is owned by Remington Arms. With adjudication of the parents' lawsuit pending, that company files for bankruptcy protection in mid-2020, and a sale of its assets is scheduled. The lawsuit remains unresolved in early 2021.

### December 11, 1957
### Film *Peyton Place* Premieres in Camden

The iconic film *Peyton Place*, whose title entered the English language as a synonym for a community full of tawdry secrets, holds its premiere in Camden, where much of it was filmed.

The Camden Theater hosts a

capacity crowd of 610, including celebrities chased by searchlights, for two showings of the movie, which is based on the best-selling novel by New Hampshire native Grace Metalious.

Husband-and-wife actors Gary Merrill and Bette Davis, who do not appear in the movie but who are both Maine residents, introduce the celebrities, including Camden doughnut queen Ellen Cooper.

The movie stars Lana Turner, Diane Varsi, Lee Miller, Hope Lange, Lloyd Nolan, and Arthur Kennedy. Twentieth Century Fox, which is distributing the movie, granted the premiere as a fundraiser benefiting the Camden Community Hospital.

The movie was shot in Belfast, Camden, Rockland, and Rockport. Locals who attend the premiere to see the movie say they are less awe-struck by movie stars in the audience than they are amused by the juxtaposition of places in the movie that in reality are far apart from one another. For example, one scene shows characters walking from what the audience recognizes as Main Street in Camden to the front door of Belfast High School in a matter of minutes.

After the first showing, Merrill presides over a charity auction at the high school gymnasium, where the *Peyton Place* script used in Camden and director Mark Robson's chair go on the block. A Rockland woman, Adelaide Adlmann, puts in a winning $41 bid for the chair. George Pew, of Falmouth Foreside, wins the script with a $195 bid and announces that he will donate the artifact to the Camden Public Library.

According to the *Portland Press Herald*, Merrill says he hopes that the "Peyton Place" filming experience will "convince Hollywood and television that Maine is a great place for picture-making. It would save me 3,000 miles of traveling every time I have to go to work."

## December 12, 2015
### Fishing Boat Captain Rescued by Guided-missile Destroyer

Dale Sparrow, 46, a fishing boat captain, experiences chest pains at about three in the morning while aboard the fishing vessel *Danny Boy* about forty nautical miles southeast of Portland. He alerts the Coast Guard. A $4.3 billion Navy ship comes to his rescue. You just never know who's going to be in the neighborhood.

The emergency affords the crew of the future USS *Zumwalt*, a stealth guided-missile destroyer, a chance to work in a real life-or-death situation.

Because of the *Danny Boy's* deck configuration, the Coast Guard concludes it's too dangerous to try to use a helicopter to hoist Sparrow off his boat. So it radios for help. The six-hundred-foot-long *Zumwalt* heads toward the fishing boat.

The crew launches a thirty-three-foot, rigid-hull inflatable boat, a type used by special forces, to bring Sparrow aboard the destroyer. Then the Coast Guard airlifts him from there to a hospital.

The Navy's most technologically advanced destroyer, built at Bath Iron Works, is at sea at the time because it is undergoing sea trials to test various systems on the ship. The ship slipped unexpectedly into Portland Harbor on December 10, surprising people on shore who saw it appear there.

### December 13, 1947
### Maine Turnpike Opens, Links Kittery to Portland

After five years of planning and two years of construction, the first forty-five-mile, four-lane section of the Maine Turnpike opens, linking Kittery to Portland. The *Portland Press Herald* dubs it the "Mile-a-Minute Highway."

It is the nation's second toll expressway, the first being the Pennsylvania Turnpike, which opened in 1940.

### December 13, 1955
### Maine Turnpike Extended to Augusta

The Maine Turnpike, having opened to the public in 1947, inaugurates an extension from Portland to Augusta that increases the toll road's length to what it is today.

The sixty-six-mile extension, including a spur to US Route 1 in Falmouth, is the largest highway construction project in Maine history at the time. It opens eight years to the day after the initial phase of the turnpike became operational.

The entire turnpike also is designated as Interstate 95.

### December 14, 1897
### Schooner Wrecks off Cushings Island; Six Sailors Drown

Six sailors drown when the schooner *Susan P. Thurlow*, built in the Washington County coastal town of Harrington, strikes a reef on a wretchedly stormy night off Cushings Island, near Portland.

The ship and its cargo are torn to pieces within an hour. One crew member, Charles Reimann, a German, survives the wreck by clinging to a broken spar and reaching safety on an island beach. Bodies of other crewmates are washed up on the same island during the night.

The next morning, Reimann rows a dory to Cape Elizabeth, where wreckage from the schooner litters the beach for a mile, and he takes a trolley into Portland to report the disaster. He tells the mayor, who asks the city manager to take the soggy, battered Reimann to a store for a new set of clothes.

A recovery crew sent to the island is able to find the bodies of five of the drowned crew members, and they are taken to a Portland mortician.

The ship is traveling from Hillsboro, New Brunswick, to New York when the sinking occurs.

## December 15, 1885
### *Red Jacket* Wrecked in Storm; Pieces Used to Build Home, Furniture

Lloyd's of London receives word that *Red Jacket*, the Rock-

land-built clipper ship that set an unbeaten record by crossing the Atlantic Ocean from New York to Liverpool in slightly more than thirteen days in 1854 during its maiden voyage, has come ashore onto the rocks and broken apart in a storm while moored in Funchal Harbor on the Portuguese island of Madeira. Two hundred tons of coal were on board at the time.

The wreckage is sold for 112 British pounds to Blandy Bros. & Co., Ltd., which uses the lumber from the ship in the construction of the home of the family that owned the company, as well as for furniture in the company's offices.

Some of the *Red Jacket's* wood eventually is returned to Maine and given to the Shore Museum in Rockland and the Penobscot Marine Museum in Searsport.

## December 15, 2001
### Amtrak Begins Downeaster Service Linking Portland, Boston

At 6:05 a.m., Amtrak's Downeaster passenger train begins its first run between Portland and Boston, reviving passenger service along that route for the first time in nearly thirty-seven years.

The project cost more than $50 million in public funds and took longer to accomplish—

eleven years—than construction of the Transcontinental Railroad, according to The Associated Press.

The train stops in Saco and Wells, Maine; then Dover, Durham and Exeter, New Hampshire; and, finally, Haverhill, Massachusetts, before arriving at North Station in Boston at the end of a two-and-a-half-hour trip.

The service begins with four daily runs each way on the 114-mile trip. Stops in Old Orchard Beach are added for summer travelers, and Woburn, Massachusetts, is added to the list of year-round stops.

The Northern New England Passenger Rail Authority estimates that 320,000 passengers would use the train during its first year of operation. The actual ridership proves to be far short of that figure during the train's first seven years of operation, but in 2008 it jumps to 388,352.

In 2019, the train achieves an all-time high number of riders—574,404—an 8 percent increase from the 2018 figure.

Regular train service is expanded in November 2012 up the coast to Freeport and Brunswick, making the total distance of each full Downeaster run 143 miles.

## December 16, 2007
### Singer Dan Fogelberg Dies at Home in Deer Isle

Singer-songwriter Dan Fogelberg, 56, dies of prostate cancer at home in Deer Isle, where he has lived for twenty-five years.

Fogelberg, a native of Peoria, Illinois, also lived many years in Colorado and recorded his music there. Achieving his greatest success in the 1970s and 1980s, he was known best for songs such as "Same Auld Lang Syne" (1980) and "Leader of the Band" (1982). His song "The Reach" (1981) is about fishing in Maine.

## December 16, 2011
### Toddler Ayla Reynolds Reported Missing; Largest Missing-person Search in Maine History Ensues

Twenty-month-old Ayla Reynolds disappears from her father's home in Waterville. She is reported missing from her bed the next morning, leading to the largest search for a missing person in Maine history.

State police discover some of Ayla's blood at the home, and they say they believe her father, Justin DiPietro, has not told them everything he knows about the incident; but DiPietro never is charged.

On January 11, 2012, dive

teams search the Kennebec River and Messalonskee Stream in Waterville for traces of Ayla. The divers' efforts produce no results.

In 2017, the state declares Ayla dead. On December 17, 2018, Ayla's mother, Trista Reynolds, who did not live with the girl, files a wrongful-death lawsuit against DiPietro, alleging that he caused Ayla's death through "intentional wrongful actions," but lawyers are unable to find him to serve him with a court summons.

In 2021, Ayla is still missing and police have received no recent leads to assist them in what remains an open investigation.

## December 17, 1970
### Nor'easter Dumps 22.8 Inches of Snow on Portland in Just 24 Hours

A nor'easter sweeps over all of Maine, leaving typical amounts of snow in much of the state, but the most copious quantity in the one place that has the least room to dispose of it—Portland.

In what turns out to be the city's heaviest accumulation of snow in a single twenty-four-hour period, the sky unleashes up to 22.8 inches of snow there, accompanied by 35 mph wind, according to the National Weather Service. Abandoned vehicles litter the Maine Turnpike in the Portland area. Most local schools are closed for two consecutive days.

Another coastal community, Brunswick, gets twenty-one inches. Inland cities and towns receive far less, the reverse of what often happens.

Little do the Port City denizens know that they are slogging though merely the opening act of what the *Maine Sunday Telegram* later calls a "1-2-3 walloping."

Another near-blizzard strikes on Christmas Eve, forcing plow drivers to work thirty-hour shifts. The storm closes the turnpike, causes many accidents resulting in injuries, strands hundreds of travelers, and costs businesses thousands of dollars that usually would have been spent on last-minute Christmas shopping.

In Biddeford, about one hundred sidelined travelers spend the night of the twenty-fourth in strangers' private homes, churches, and Biddeford Junior High School.

Late on the twenty-fifth, everything is open again. After a two-inch dusting on Saturday, the weather service calculates Portland's total snowfall for the month at fifty-four inches, and Brunswick's at seventy inches.

**December 18, 2019**

## Rep. Jared Golden Splits Vote on Articles of Impeachment

US Rep. Jared Golden becomes the only member of the US House of Representatives to split his vote on the two articles of impeachment of President Donald Trump. The Democrat from Maine's Second Congressional District votes to impeach Trump, a Republican, for abuse of power but against impeachment for obstruction of Congress. Both articles pass largely on party lines in the Democratic-controlled House.

Golden's split vote is, in a way, an echo of split results in the general elections of 2016 and 2018. Trump, running for president, won Golden's future congressional district in 2016, collecting a single electoral vote there under a state law that allows Maine's Electoral College vote to be split. It was the only Electoral College vote Trump received in New England.

In the 2018 election, Golden became the first person whose election to the US House was made possible by Maine's new ranked-choice voting law. Golden failed to obtain even a plurality of votes, but when the votes of third- and fourth-place finishers in the four-way race were redistributed based on voters' preferences, Golden achieved a majority.

The House impeaches Trump a second time, on January 13, 2021, a week before his presidential term of office ends. This time Trump faces only a single charge, one that alleges he incited a crowd of his supporters to conduct a deadly January 6, 2021, attack on the U.S. Capitol. Golden votes for impeachment, like all other House members from New England, all of whom are Democrats.

**December 19, 2011**

## Police Seize Father's Vehicle as Part of Ayla Reynolds Investigation

As part of the continuing investigation into the disappearance of Waterville tot Ayla Reynolds, age 20 months, police seize her father's sport utility vehicle and a Portland woman's car from the driveway at the man's Violette Avenue home.

Also, searchers use an airboat to look along Messalonskee Stream for signs of the girl, and dozens of police officers search for the girl in the area around the house where she lives with her father, Justin DiPietro, 24. They find nothing that helps them in the investigation.

DiPietro said Ayla, wearing a

soft cast on a broken arm, was put to bed on the night of the sixteenth. She was reported missing the next morning. Police have established that several adults were in the house at the time. They say it's possible the child was abducted.

As of early 2021, when she would be 11 years old, she remains missing and presumed dead.

## December 20, 2018
### Maine Launches Plan to Set Up Electric Vehicle Charging Stations

The *Portland Press Herald* reports that Efficiency Maine, a state agency whose mission is to help Maine residents use energy more efficiently, has contracted with a California company for the installation of seven electric-vehicle charging stations along Maine highways from the southern part of the state to the Quebec border.

The company, ChargePoint, is expected to install the stations in 2019. They also are expected to be the start of a three-phase plan to establish fast chargers on important highways statewide for Maine residents and tourists alike.

Locations of the initial seven stations are on either side of the Maine Turnpike at the turnpike's Kennebunk service areas, at the

West Gardiner turnpike service area, on US Route 202 in the North Windham area, in Farmington near the intersection of US Route 2 and Route 27, in Jackman, and at another site along US Route 201.

The agency's executive director, Michael Stoddard, says completion of the first two phases should result in charging stations no more than fifty miles apart on major thoroughfares.

A year later, the second phase of the plan begins with the awarding of grants to twenty-three Maine communities to help them install Level 2 charging stations, where drivers can recharge their electric vehicles in three to four hours.

By March 2021, the agency has awarded contracts for 136 level-2 plugs at 47 locations in Maine, and 60 of the plugs are operational. The rest are expected to be installed and functioning by the end of 2021, according to Anastasia Hediger, an Efficiency Maine program manager.

The project's third phase consists of another round of fast chargers along U.S. Route 1 from Rockland to Ellsworth, along the Interstate 95 corridor from Auburn to Lewiston and from Waterville to the Bangor-Brewer area, and in five undesignated other sites. Bid proposals for that phase are due in April 2021 and the agency hopes to award contracts in May.

Efficiency Maine also plans to issue a request for proposals for the installation of level-2 chargers in northern Aroostook County.

The state plan is intended to reduce the $5 billion per year that Maine drivers spend on automotive fuel, all of which comes from out of state and to reduce the amount of carbon monoxide fumes in the atmosphere.

Funding for the three-phase project comes from the $21 million Maine received as part of the federal government's settlement of a case involving German car manufacturer Volkswagen. Courts found that Volkswagen had violated the US Clean Air Act by secretly installing devices on some of its diesel vehicles that were meant to flout the law's requirements on vehicle emissions.

## December 21, 2005
### New Toll Plaza Planned For York

Maine Turnpike Authority Director Paul Violette announces that his agency is planning to replace the turnpike's toll plaza at York, which was meant to be temporary but has been functioning for thirty-five years.

Violette said the toll plaza, which is seven miles northeast of the New Hampshire state line on Interstate 95, is in an unsuitable location and has lasted more than twice as long as was originally intended.

The new toll gates would be built farther into Maine, within four miles of the old toll gates. The design has not been determined, and the agency also hasn't made up its mind about highway-speed, or open-road, tolling.

Fifteen years later, in 2020, a new $38.5 million toll plaza—delayed by controversy about the chosen site and other problems—finally is under construction at mile 8.8 on the highway. It will include three highway-speed E-ZPass tolling lanes in each direction, as well as nine cash lanes—four northbound and five southbound—according to the agency's website.

Reed & Reed, Inc., is the contractor for the project, which is scheduled to be finished in June 2021.

When the new toll collection point is up and running, the existing seventeen-lane toll gate, which now is about a half-century old, will be demolished.

Highway-speed tolling begins at the mile 44/Interstate 295 exit in Scarborough in June 2019. Construction of a $30 million open-road tolling station begins around the same time in West Gardiner, where the turnpike meets the northern end of I-295. That plaza also is expected to go into service in 2021. Another open-road toll plaza in West Gardiner is completed, as are one on the Falmouth spur and one in New Gloucester.

## December 22, 1807
### Embargo Act's Approval Hobbles Economy of Maine Seaports

President Thomas Jefferson signs the Embargo Act in response to British seizure of American cargo and impressment of American seamen during the Napoleonic Wars.

The law, which forbids trade with other nations, hobbles Maine seaports' economy, which was thriving until then.

The law is repealed two years later, but continued agitation from the British eventually leads to the War of 1812.

For several reasons, these events all influence the ultimately successful effort to separate Maine from Massachusetts in 1820.

## December 23, 1831
### The Age Newspaper Begins Publication in Augusta

The first publication of the Augusta newspaper *The Age* occurs, appearing in time to capitalize on the impending arrival of state government in the capital city and the printing contracts it is likely to offer.

In the 1850s, a part-owner of the newspaper is Melville Weston Fuller (1833-1910). *The Age* competes for several decades with the *Kennebec Journal*, which began publication in 1825. For a few years, Fuller is employed at *The Age* at the same time future US house speaker James G. Blaine is in a partnership that owns the *Kennebec Journal*.

"*The Age* and the *Kennebec Journal* were not respectful to each other in their columns," writes Willard King, Fuller's biographer, referring to that period when the two men's careers overlapped in Augusta. "In fact, neither Fuller nor Blaine gave promise of their future eminence in the pages of those papers."

More than thirty years later, Fuller is chief justice of the US Supreme Court in Washington at the same time when Blaine is serving there as US secretary of state.

## December 24, 2018
### Poliquin Drops Federal Lawsuit Disputing Results of Election

Incumbent US Rep. Bruce Poliquin, a Republican representing Maine's Second Congressional District, drops his federal lawsuit claiming that he, not Democrat Jared Golden, should have won the November 6 election for his seat.

Golden was declared the winner under Maine's new ranked-choice voting system.

Running for re-election against three challengers, Poliquin achieved a plurality but less than a majority of votes in the first tally. When votes received by the two candidates who drew the fewest votes were redistributed to the voters' second and third choices, in accordance with the new law, Golden came out on top.

Poliquin became the first incumbent since 1916 to lose a bid for re-election to the seat.

He says his opinion about the system has not changed, but he believes dropping the lawsuit is in Maine residents' best interests.

So far, that election is the only one in Maine in which the ultimate winner does not get a plurality of first-choice votes.

## December 25, 1870
### Livermore's Elihu Washburne Describes Events in Paris During Franco-Prussian War

"Never has a sadder Christmas dawned on any city," Livermore native Elihu Washburne writes in Paris while serving as the US minister to France. "The sufferings exceed by far anything we have seen."

On the ninety-ninth day of the Prussian army's siege of the city during the Franco-Prussian War, Washburne, one of the few Americans and few foreign diplomats remaining in the French capital, manages to put on a holiday feast, consisting of two hens and canned goods, for his son and some American friends trapped in the city. He has arranged the safe evacuation of thousands of his countrymen, provided food and shelter for a large group of German refugee women, helped set up a field hospital to treat wounded French soldiers, and kept his superiors in Washington—as well as his relatives, including brother Israel, a former Maine governor—updated on conditions in Paris, where the starving, freezing population is reduced to cutting down trees in public parks for firewood and eating horses, dogs, cats, and rats to stay alive.

After the French surrender on the following January 27 and the Prussian troops' two-day occupation of the city, the French turn on each other, with the republic's national government in Versailles combatting the forces of the upstart Paris Commune.

At the end of months of purges, gunbattles, and fires destroying priceless architectural treasures, during which Washburne tries repeatedly and unsuccessfully to dissuade Commune officials from executing the Paris archbishop, the regular army is estimated to have killed 20,000 to 25,000 people, a worse death toll than even that of the 1790s Reign of Terror that followed the French Revolution.

"What no one could yet appreciate, other than perhaps Washburne himself," writes historian David McCullough in his 2011 book *The Greater Journey: Americans in Paris*, "was the additional, immeasurable value of the diary he had kept day after day through the entire ordeal, recording so much that he had witnessed and taken part in, writing at great length at the end of an exhausting, horrible day, aware constantly of the self-imposed duty he felt to keep such an account."

## December 26, 1888
### Central Maine General Hospital Incorporated in Lewiston

The Central Maine General Hospital—known today as Central Maine Medical Center—is incorporated in Lewiston. D.J. Callahan is sworn in at an afternoon meeting as secretary of the board of corporators.

The institution is qualified under the law to hold property of a value up to $100,000—equal to about $2.9 million in 2019.

Six men are appointed to a committee that will recommend a site for the new hospital. A five-member committee is appointed to draft bylaws for the organization.

## December 27, 2005
### Nature Conservancy Buys 10,000 Acres in Hancock County

The Nature Conservancy announces it has bought nearly ten thousand acres of forested land in Hancock County for $2.2 million and that it plans to preserve the property.

The purchase is emblematic of many other land preservation steps taken by various organizations in this period.

The Nature Conservancy land, called the Spring River block, is next to state-owned conservation property northeast of Ellsworth.

"We plan to manage a great deal of it as though it is an ecological reserve," Nature Conservancy spokesman Bruce Kidman tells the *Portland Press Herald*.

Former owner H.C. Haynes Inc. gave the conservation group a two-year purchase option and reduced, and in some cases eliminated, its tree-cutting plans.

The agency completed several smaller land deals earlier during the same year, including a 1,400-acre conservation easement on Pleasant Mountain in Bridgton and smaller parcels in York's Mount Agamenticus area.

### December 28, 1972
### $231 Million Maine Yankee Nuclear Power Plant Commissioned

The Maine Yankee Nuclear Power Plant is commissioned, having taken four years to complete at a cost of $231 million on an 820-acre site on the shore of the Back River on Wiscasset's Bailey Peninsula.

The plant was built despite opposition from conservation groups and Gov. Kenneth M. Curtis, but that opposition's petition to federal authorities persuaded the Nuclear Regulatory Commission to impose stricter environ-

mental standards and monitoring.

During its twenty-four years of operation, the plant produces about 1.2 billion kilowatts of power, providing about a quarter of Maine's electricity needs and some of other states as well.

Bedeviled by infrastructure and equipment problems that become too expensive to solve, the plant closes in 1996.

### December 28, 2018
### Bluegrass, Country Music Pioneer Al Hawkes Dies at 88

Westbrook bluegrass and country music pioneer Al Hawkes dies at 88.

Skilled at the guitar and the mandolin, the singer-songwriter was a regular on the Maine music circuit and elsewhere. He was a member of both the Maine Country Music Hall of Fame and America's Old-Time Country Music Hall of Fame. The International Bluegrass Museum in Kentucky honored him for his work.

Hawkes also devoted himself to producing and engineering high-quality recordings, even giving renowned guitarist Chet Atkins advice on that subject. He founded his own record label, Event Records, in 1956.

MAINE YANKEE - THE WISCASSET EXPERIENCE

*Courtesy of Maine Historical Society*

Maine Yankee brochure, 1975. Maine Yankee, located in Wiscasset, went into commercial operation in 1972 (see page 399).

Several regional country and bluegrass acts, including Maine country singer Dick Curless, recorded music there. The company went out of business after a fire in the 1960s.

Part of Hawkes' legacy is a song he composed about his hometown: "The Song of Westbrook." Its simple lyrics include these lines: "I love Westbrook, and I always will. I may roam, but my heart (Hawkes pronounces it 'haht') is there still."

December 29, 2012
## First Same-sex Couples Obtain Marriage Licenses in Bangor

Three couples get married and a fourth obtains a marriage license early on a Saturday morning at Bangor City Hall, amid a crowd of about fifty well-wishers.

Normally city offices aren't open on Saturdays, but this is an exception. Special business hours were scheduled because this is the first day on which marriages of same-sex partners are legal in Maine, as a result of the outcome of a November 6 referendum.

In Portland, Steven Bridges and Michael Snell, both residents of the city, take part in Maine's first marriage of a gay couple when they exchange vows at 12:25 a.m. Other couples get married or obtain licenses to do so in Brewer, Brunswick, Orono, and South Portland. On Election Day, Maine, Maryland, and Washington became the first three US states to authorize gay marriage in statewide referendums.

Maine had appeared poised to become the first state to legalize gay marriage by legislative action in 2009 when the Legislature passed and Gov. John E. Baldacci signed such a bill, but voters overturned that law in a November 3 "people's veto" referendum that year.

December 30, 2006
## Penobscot Narrows Bridge Opens to Vehicles

The $85 million Penobscot Narrows Bridge, which carries US Route 1 across the Penobscot River and links the towns of Prospect and Verona Island, opens to vehicular traffic for the first time.

The cable-stayed 2,120-foot bridge features two 430-foot-high towers, the western one of which contains the world's tallest public bridge observation desk.

Dave Milan, the economic development director for nearby Bucksport, tells the *Bangor Daily News* that in addition to being a means to cross the river, the bridge should attract tourists, because the enclosed observation deck is the only one of its kind in the Western Hemisphere.

Cianbro Corp., of Pittsfield, and Reed & Reed, of Woolwich, built the bridge in forty-two months.

After a 1 p.m. ceremonial ribbon-cutting, emergency vehicles cross each side of the snow-laden span, using lights and sirens each way.

The structure replaces the seventy-five-year-old Waldo-Hancock Bridge, which is demolished later.

## December 31, 1775
### Army Forces Under Benedict Arnold, Richard Montgomery, Fail to Take Quebec City

As the first year of the American Revolution draws to a close, American Revolutionary forces led by Col. Benedict Arnold and Maj. Gen. Richard Montgomery attack the British fortress at Quebec City while a snowstorm rages. The assault fails.

Arnold, who led his men on an epic, hardship-filled journey up Maine's Kennebec River and through the wilderness of northwestern Maine and the countryside of what is now southeastern Quebec to reach the fortress, is wounded. Montgomery, whose forces descended the St. Lawrence River valley to join Arnold after having occupied Montreal, is killed in combat.

## December 31, 1970
### Muskie Shepherds Clean Air Act Through Congress; President Nixon Signs It into Law

President Richard Nixon signs the Clean Air Act, a compromise billion-dollar air-quality law that was shepherded through Congress by US Sen. Edmund Muskie, a Democrat from Maine. The Environmental Protection Agency estimates that the law's requirements prevent more that 200,000 premature deaths and 700,000 cases of chronic bronchitis in the twenty years after its passage. From 1990 to 2010, according to the agency, total emission of the six main air pollutants decreases more than 41 percent, even while the Gross Domestic Product increases 64 percent.

Muskie, who was a Waterville lawyer before entering politics, already had been instrumental in obtaining passage of the Water Quality Act of 1965 when he took on the 1970 challenge, establishing his credentials as a protector of the environment.

The 1970 law—along with its subsequent amendments—is far more transformative, however. While focusing on reducing pollutants emitted by automobiles, it also deals with the entire spectrum of air pollution. The law requires the establishment of EPA pollution standards; mandates that states set up their own implementation plans, which may be more stringent than the federal minimums; and sets the requirements for all new factories and federal facilities to control pollution.

—30—

# ACKNOWLEDGMENTS

"There's an old saying that victory has a thousand fathers but defeat is an orphan," President John Kennedy said at a 1961 news conference after the failed Bay of Pigs invasion of Cuba.

If that's true, then I'm going to count this book as a victory, and this is the part where I tell you who some of the other fathers and mothers are, in roughly chronological order.

Scott Monroe, managing editor of the *Kennebec Journal* and the *Morning Sentinel* newspapers, of Augusta and Waterville, Maine, respectively, asked me in mid-2019 to be on a committee that would make recommendations about how our newspaper chain—which also includes the (Brunswick) *Times Record*, the (Lewiston) *Sun Journal,* and the *Portland Press Herald*—would commemorate the 2020 bicentennial of Maine's statehood. Much of that commemoration wound up being the daily newspaper and online column on which this book is based.

Lisa DeSisto, chief executive officer of Masthead Maine, the newspapers' parent organization, heartily endorsed my proposal that we arrange for the publication of the columns in book form and took immediate steps to make that happen.

My research efforts would have been far less productive without guidance, fact-checking, assistance, and suggestions from the following people and organizations: *Portland Press Herald* metro editor John Richardson and his colleagues Julia C. McCue, Pat Horne, Steve Ericson, Brian Robitaille, and Tim Allen; *Kennebec Journal* and *Morning Sentinel* copy desk staff members Sarah Lane and Daryl Madore; Earle G. Shettleworth Jr., Maine's state historian; my former colleague David Cheever, the Maine secretary of state's special assistant for outreach and citizen engagement, vice chairman of the Maine200 Bicentennial Commission and a former Maine state archivist; another former colleague, John Hale, who has worked as a reporter at several Maine newspapers; and Isabel Turk, a Maine Historical Society library assistant.

My thanks go to the Maine State Library, which, aside from employing a staff—including longtime friend Anne Cough—that offers professional and courteous research assistance, affords the convenience of being only eight blocks away from my house. I spent so much time there that I almost pitched a tent in front of the microfilm readers.

Other institutions that helped boost this book's credibility include the Kennebec Historical Society, which was of great help in finding information about central Maine; and the Law and Legislative Reference Library, located at the Maine State House, where my former colleague Elaine Apostola and librarians Alex Burnett and Jessica Lundgren helped me track down dusty old laws that were integral to my research.

Dean Lunt, the publisher at Islandport Press, added much value to my first draft of this book, including items about a few dozen historical events of which I had been unaware or had overlooked. He also made many useful suggestions about expanding or shortening the items I contributed.

I am grateful to Dr. Thomas Keating, of Portland, for calling my attention to his *Maine History* article about the Medical School of Maine, which lasted about a century and closed about a century ago.

Finally, my wife, Mary, provided an additional set of proofreading eyes by checking almost all of the printed first draft. What a team player.

I take full responsibility for whatever errors might be found here. Probably when I made them, the phone had just started ringing, and a telemarketer was trying to sell me an extended warranty on our 14-year-old minivan. That happens a lot at our house.

# SELECT BIBLIOGRAPHY

## Newspapers

*Bangor Daily News*
*Kennebec Journal*
(Lewiston) *Sun Journal*
*Maine Sunday Telegram*
*The New York Times*
*Portland Press Herald*
(Waterville) *Morning Sentinel*

## Books

Ahlin, John Howard. *Maine Rubicon: Downeast Settlers during the American Revolution*, second printing. Calais, Maine: Calais Advertiser Press, 1967.

Arlen, Alice. *She Took to the Woods: Louise Dickinson Rich, a Biography*. Camden, Maine: Down East Books, 2000.

Atwood, Stanley Bearce. *The Length and Breadth of Maine*. Orono, Maine: University of Maine Press, 1974 (paperback republication).

Banks, Ronald F. *Maine Becomes a State: The Movement to Separate Maine from Massachusetts, 1785-1820*. Somersworth, New Hampshire: New Hampshire Publishing Co., 1973 (republication in paperback of 1970 hard-cover edition).

Barry, William David. *Maine: The Wilder Half of New England*. Gardiner, Maine: Tilbury House, Publishers, 2012.

Brunelle, Jim. *Maine Almanac*, second edition. Augusta, Maine: Guy Gannet Publishing Co., 1978-1979.

Butler, Joyce. *Wildfire Loose: The Week Maine Burned*. Camden, Maine: Down East Books, 1997, third edition.

Byrne, William, and William Augustine Leahy. *History of the Catholic Church in the New England States*. Boston: The Hurd & Everts Co., 1899.

Campbell, W.E. *The Aroostook War of 1839*. Fredericton, New Brunswick: Goose Lane Editions, 2013.

Carbone, Teresa A., and Patricia Hills. *Eastman Johnson: Painting America*. Rizzoli International Publications, Inc., 1999.

Chartrand, René. *Raiders from New France: North American Forest Warfare Tactics, 17th-18th Centuries*. Oxford, United Kingdom: Osprey Publishing, 2019.

Chase, Mary Ellen. *Jonathan Fisher: Maine Parson, 1768-1847*. New York: The Macmillan Co., 1948.

Church, Thomas. *The Entertaining History of King Philip's War*, second edition. Boston: no publisher given, 1712 (reprinted 1772).

Clark, Charles E., James S. Leamon, and Karen Bowden, editors. *Maine in the Early Republic*. Hanover, New Hampshire: University Press of New England, 1988.

Davis, Bette. *The Lonely Life: An Autobiography*. New York: G.P. Putnam's Sons, 1962.

Day, Clarence A. *Ezekiel Holmes, Father of Maine Agriculture*. Orono, Maine: University of Maine Press, 1968. University of Maine Studies, Series 2, No. 86.

D'Entremont, Jeremy. *Great Shipwrecks of the Maine Coast*. Beverly, Massachusetts: Commonwealth Editions, 2010.

Desjardin, Thomas A. *Through a Howling Wilderness: Benedict Arnold's March to Quebec, 1775*. New York: St. Martin's Press, 2006.

Donaldson, Scott. *Edwin Arlington Robinson: A Poet's Life*. New York: Columbia University Press, 2007.

Dorr, George Bucknam. *The Story of Acadia National Park*. Bar Harbor, Maine: Acadia Publishing Co., 1985.

Drisko, George W. *Narrative of the Town of Machias: The Old and the New, the Early and the Late*. Machias, Maine: Press of the Republican, 1904.

Emery, Edwin. *The History of Sanford, Maine, 1661-1900*. Fall River, Massachusetts: William Morrill Emery, 1901.

Epp, Ronald H. *Creating Acadia National Park: The Biography of George Bucknam Dorr*. Bar Harbor, Maine: Friends of Acadia, 2016.

Farnham, Mary Frances, compiler. *Documentary History of the State of Maine, Vol. 8*. Portland: Maine Historical Society, 1902.

Gimpel, Erich. *Agent 146: The True Story of a Nazi Spy in America.* New York: Martin Dunne Books, 2003. (First published in Germany in 1956 as *Spion für Deutschland.*)

Graham, Ada, and Frank Graham Jr. *Kate Furbish and the Flora of Maine.* Gardiner, Maine: Tilbury House, Publishers, 1995.

Gratwick, Harry. *Mainers in the Civil War.* Charleston, South Carolina: Arcadia Publishing, 2011.

Gratwick, Harry. *The Maritime Marauder of Revolutionary Maine: Captain Henry Mowat.* Charleston, South Carolina: The History Press, 2015.

Greenlaw, Linda. *The Hungry Ocean: A Swordboat Captain's Journey.* New York: Hyperion, 1999.

Griffin, Nancy. *How Maine Changed the World: A History in 50 People, Places, and Objects.* Camden, Maine: Downeast Books, 2017.

Hopkins, Stephen D. *Red Jacket: The Life and Times of a Maine Clipper Ship.* Rockland, Maine: Rockland Historical Society, 2016

Howe, Stanley Russell. *A Fair Field and No Favor: A Concise History of the Maine State Grange.* Augusta, Maine: Maine State Grange, 1994.

Hunt, H. Draper. *The Blaine House: Home of Maine's Governors.* Augusta, Maine: Friends of the Blaine House, 1994, second edition.

Hunter, Julia, and Earle G. Shettleworth Jr. *Fly Rod Crosby: The Woman Who Marketed Maine.* Gardiner, Maine: Tilbury House, Publishers, 2000.

Irwin, Clark T., Jr. *The Light from the River: Central Maine Power's First Century of Service.* Augusta, Maine: Central Maine Power Co., 1999.

Jordan, Anne Devereaux. *The Seventh-day Adventists: A History.* New York: Hippocrene Books, 1988.

Judd, Richard W., Edwin A. Churchill, and Joel W. Eastman, editors. *Maine: The Pine Tree State from Prehistory to the Present.* Orono, Maine: University of Maine Press, 1995.

Kennedy, Kate. *More Than Petticoats: Remarkable Maine Women.* Guilford, Connecticut: Globe Pequot Press, 2005.

Kershaw, Gordon E. *The Kennebeck Proprietors, 1749-1775.* Somersworth, New Hampshire: New Hampshire Publishing Co., 1975.

Kilby, William Henry, compiler. *Eastport and Passamaquoddy: A Col-*

*lection of Historical and Biographical Sketches*. Eastport, Maine: Border Historical Society, 2003. Reprint of 1888 edition.

King, Willard L. *Melville Weston Fuller, Chief Justice of the United States 1888-1910*. Chicago: University of Chicago Press, 1950 (1967 paperback edition).

LaFantasie, Glenn W. *Twilight at Little Round Top: July 2, 1863–The Tide Turns at Gettysburg*. Hoboken, New Jersey: John Wiley & Sons, Inc., 2005.

Lemke, William. *The Wild, Wild East: Unusual Tales of Maine History*. Camden, Maine: Yankee Books, 1990.

Lunt, Dean Lawrence. *Here for Generations: The Story of a Maine Bank and Its City*, revised edition. Yarmouth, Maine: Islandport Press, 2017.

Lunt, Dean Lawrence. *Hauling By Hand: The Life and Times of a Maine Island*. Yarmouth, Maine: Islandport Press, 2000.

McBride, Bunny. *Molly Spotted Elk: A Penobscot in Paris*. Norman, Oklahoma: University of Oklahoma Press, 1995.

McBride, Joseph. *Searching for John Ford: A Life*. New York: St. Martin's Press, 2001.

McCullough, David. *The Greater Journey: Americans in Paris*. New York: Simon & Schuster, 2011.

Milford, Nancy. *Savage Beauty: The Life of Edna St. Vincent Millay*. New York: Random House Trade Paperbacks, 2002.

Miller, Alan Robert. *The History of Current Maine Newspapers*. Lisbon Falls, Maine: Eastland Press, Inc., 1978.

Merrill, Gary. *Bette, Rita, and the Rest of My Life*. Augusta, Maine: Lance Tapley, Publisher, 1988.

Mosley, Leonard. *Lindbergh: A Biography*. New York: Doubleday & Co., Inc, 1976.

Moulton, Augustus F. *Portland by the Sea*. Augusta, Maine: Katahdin Publishing Co., 1926.

Mundy, James H. *Hard Times, Hard Men: Maine and the Irish, 1830-1860*. Scarborough, Maine: Harp Publications, 1990.

Murphy, Andrea, and Joyce Ray, et al. *Women of the Pine Tree State: 25 Maine Women You Should Know*. Amherst, New Hampshire: Apprentice Shop Books, LLC, 2014.

Nash, Charles Elventon. *The History of Augusta: First Settlements and Early Days as a Town, Including the Diary of Mrs. Martha Moore Ballard (1785 to 1812)*. Augusta, Maine: Charles E. Nash & Son, 1904 (released in book form in 1961).

Neff, John W. *Katahdin, an Historic Journey: Legends, Explorations, and Preservation of Maine's Highest Peak*. Boston, Massachusetts: Appalachian Mountain Club Books, 2006.

Neff, John W., and Howard R. Whitcomb. *Baxter State Park and Katahdin*. Charleston, South Carolina: Arcadia Publishing, 2012. (Images of America series).

North, James. *History of Augusta*. Augusta, Maine: Clapp and North, 1870. (Reprint: Somersworth, New Hampshire: New England History Press, 1981.)

Palmer, Kenneth T. *Maine Politics and Government*, second edition. Lincoln, Nebraska: University of Nebraska Press, 2009.

Parker, Gail Underwood. *It Happened in Maine*. Guilford, Connecticut: Globe Pequot Press, 2004.

Péladeau, Marius, and Roger G. Reed. *The Kennebec Arsenal: An Historical and Architectural Survey*. Augusta, Maine: Kennebec Historical Society, Augusta Historic Preservation Commission, and Maine Historic Preservation Commission, 1997.

Pesha, Ronald, editor. *The Great Gold Swindle of Lubec, Maine*. Charleston, South Carolina: The History Press, 2013.

Pfanz, Harry W. *Gettysburg: The Second Day*. Chapel Hill, North Carolina: University of North Carolina Press, 1987.

Pulsipher, Jenny Hale. *Subjects unto the Same King: Indians, English, and the Contest of Authority in Colonial New England*. Philadelphia: University of Pennsylvania Press, 2011.

Radforth, Ian Walter. *Royal Spectacle: The 1860 Visit by the Prince of Wales to Canada and the United States*. Toronto: The University of Toronto Press, 2004.

Reilly, Wayne E. *Hidden History of Bangor: Lumbering Days to the Progressive Era*. Mount Pleasant, South Carolina: Arcadia Publishing, 2013.

Richard, Mark Paul. *Loyal but French: The Negotiation of Identity by French-Canadian Descendants in the United States*. East Lansing, Michigan: Michigan State University Press, 2008.

Rickover, Adm. Hyman G. *How the Battleship Maine Was Destroyed.* Annapolis, Maryland: Naval Institute Press, 1974; 1995 edition.

Roberts, Kenneth. *I Wanted to Write.* Camden, Maine: Down East, 1949. 1977 reprint.

Roberts, Kenneth, compiler. *March to Quebec: Journals of the Members of Arnold's Expedition.* Garden City, New York: Doubleday & Co., Inc., 1947.

Robinson, David, and Elizabeth Tanefils, *The Saco River.* Charleston, South Carolina: Arcadia Publishing, 2010.

Rolde, Neil. *Continental Liar from the State of Maine: James G. Blaine.* Gardiner, Maine: Tilbury House, Publishers, 2006.

Rolde, Neil. *An Illustrated History of Maine.* Augusta, Maine: Friends of the Maine State Museum, 1995.

Rolde, Neil. *Maine: A Narrative History.* Gardiner, Maine: Tilbury House, Publishers, 1990.

Rolde, Neil. *Maine in the World: Stories of Some of Those from Here Who Went Away.* Gardiner, Maine: Tibury House, Publishers, 2009.

Russell, Isabel. *Katharine and E.B. White: An Affectionate Memoir.* New York: W.W. Norton & Co., 1988.

Savigneau, Josyane. *Marguerite Yourcenar: Inventing a Life.* Chicago and London: The University of Chicago Press, 1993

Scee, Trudy Irene. *City on the Penobscot: A Comprehensive History of Bangor, Maine.* Charleston, South Carolina: The History Press, 2010.

Scott, Geraldine Tidd. *Ties of Common Blood: A History of Maine's Northeast Boundary Dispute with Great Britain 1783-1842.* Bowie, Maryland: Heritage Books, 1992.

Shettleworth, Earle G., Jr. *The Blaine House.* Charleston, South Carolina: Arcadia Publishing, 2014.

Shettleworth, Earle G., Jr., *John Calvin Stevens on The Portland Peninsula, 1880 to 1940.* Portland, Maine: Greater Portland Landmarks Inc., 2003.

Silverthorne, Elizabeth. *Sarah Orne Jewett: A Writer's Life.* Woodstock, New York: The Overlook Press, 1993.

Smith, Earl H. *Mayflower Hill: A History of Colby College.* Lebanon, New Hampshire: University Press of New England, 2006.

Smith, Margaret Chase. *Declaration of Conscience*. New York: Doubleday & Company, Inc, 1972.

Smith, Mason Philip, *Confederates Downeast: Confederate Operations in and around Maine*. Portland, Maine: The Provincial Press, 1985.

Snow, Edward Rowe. *Storms and Shipwrecks of New England*. Carlisle, Massachusetts: Commonwealth Editions, 2003 (update of 1943 edition).

Snow, Ralph L. *Bath Iron Works: The First Hundred Years*. Bath, Maine: Maine Maritime Museum, 1987.

Souder, William. *On a Farther Shore: The Life and Legacy of Rachel Carson*. New York: Crown Publishers, 2012.

Souliere, Michelle Y. *Strange Maine: True Tales from the Pine Tree State*. Charleston, South Carolina: The History Press, 2010.

Spiller, Virginia. *350 Years as York: Focusing on the Twentieth Century*. York, Maine: Town of York 350th-Anniversary Committee, 2001

Stevens, John Calvin, II, and Earle G. Shettleworth Jr. *John Calvin Stevens: Domestic Architecture, 1890-1930*. Scarborough, Maine: Harp Publications, 1990.

Stover, Arthur Douglas. *Eminent Mainers: Succinct Biographies of Thousands of Amazing Mainers, Mostly Dead, and a Few People from Away Who Have Done Something Useful Within the State of Maine*. Gardiner, Maine: Tilbury House Publishers, 2006.

Sweet, Melissa. *Some Writer! The Story of E.B. White*. Boston: Houghton Mifflin Harcourt, 2016.

Thompson, Ellie. *History of Broadcasting in Maine: The First 50 Years*. Augusta, Maine: Maine Association of Broadcasters, 1990.

Trudeau, Noah Andre. *Gettysburg: A Test of Courage*. New York: HarperCollins Publishers Inc., 2002.

Trulock, Alice Rains. *In the Hands of Providence: Joshua L. Chamberlain and the American Civil War*. Chapel Hill, North Carolina: University of North Carolina Press, 1992.

Tucher, Andie. *Froth & Scum: Truth, Beauty, Goodness, and the Ax Murder in America's First Mass Medium*. Chapel Hill, North Carolina: University of North Carolina Press, 1994.

Ulrich, Laurel Thatcher. *A Midwife's Tale: The Life of Martha Ballard, Based on Her Diary, 1785-1812*. New York: Alfred A. Knopf, Inc., 1990.

Varney, George Jones. *A Gazetteer of the State of Maine with Numerous Illustrations*. Boston, Massachusetts: B.B. Russell, 1881.

Weems, John Edward. *Peary: The Explorer and the Man*. Boston: Houghton Mifflin Co., 1967.

Wheeler, George Augustus. *History of Castine, Penobscot, and Brooksville, Maine Including the Ancient Settlement of Pentagöet*. Bangor, Maine: Burr & Robinson, 1875.

Wheeler, George Augustus, and Henry Warren Wheeler. *History of Brunswick, Topsham, and Harpswell, Maine*. Boston: Alfred Mudge & Son, Printers, 1878 (1974 reprint).

Wilberg, James. *Sumner Sewall: Maine's First World War Fighter Ace*. Reno, Nevada: Aeronaut Books, 2019.

Williamson, Joseph. *History of the City of Belfast in the State of Maine*. Portland: Loring, Short & Harmon, 1877.

Williamson, William D. *The History of the State of Maine; from Discovery, A.D. 1602, to the Separation, A.D. 1820, Inclusive*. Hallowell, Maine: Glazier, Masters & Co., 1832 (two volumes).

Willis, William. *The History of Portland*. Somersworth, New Hampshire: New Hampshire Publishing Co., 1972. (Facsimile of 1865 second edition published by Bailey & Noyes.)

Wilson, Laurie. *Louise Nevelson: Light and Shadow*. New York: Thames & Hudson Inc., 2016.

Wittreich, Paul. *Forgotten First Flights*. Xlibris Corp., 2009.

Woodard, Colin. *Unsettled: Triumph and Tragedy in Maine's Indian Country*. Portland, Maine: MaineToday Media, 2014.

Young, Christine Ellen. *A Bitter Brew: Faith, Power, and Poison in a Small New England Town*. New York: Berkley Publishing Group, 2005.

## Other publications

Keating, Thomas J., M.D., M.S. "A Public Trust for the Common Good: Medical Professionalism and Medical Education in Nineteenth- and Twentieth-Century Maine." *Maine History*, winter 2016.